SHOESTRING SOLDIERS:
THE 1ST CANADIAN DIVISION AT WAR, 1914–1915

ANDREW IAROCCI

Shoestring Soldiers

The 1st Canadian Division at War, 1914–1915

UNIVERSITY OF TORONTO PRESS
Toronto Buffalo London

© University of Toronto Press Incorporated 2008
   Toronto Buffalo London
   www.utppublishing.com
   Printed in Canada

   ISBN 978-0-8020–9822-1

Printed on acid-free paper

Library and Archives Canada Cataloguing in Publication

Iarocci, Andrew, 1976–
   Shoestring soldiers: the 1st Canadian Division at war,
   1914–15/Andrew Iarocci.

   Includes bibliographical references and index.
   ISBN 978-0-8020-9822-1

   1. Canada. Canadian Army. Canadian Division, 1st – History.
   2. World War, 1914–1918 – Regimental histories – Canada.   3. World War,
   1914–18 – Personal narratives, Canadian.   I. Title.

   D547.C2I27 2008   940.4'1271   C2008-900020-X

University of Toronto Press acknowledges the financial assistance to its
publishing program of the Canada Council for the Arts and the Ontario
Arts Council.

University of Toronto Press acknowledges the financial support for its
publishing activities of the Government of Canada through the Book
Publishing Industry Development Program (BPIDP).

This book has been published with the help of a grant from the Canadian
Federation for the Humanities and Social Sciences, through the Aid to
Scholarly Publications Program, using funds provided by the Social
Sciences and Humanities Research Council of Canada.

Contents

Acknowledgments

It is a little unfair that the cover of this book bears only one name, when so many others have shaped it so profoundly. Without the support and encouragement of my parents, Marsha and Tony, my brother Paul, and my family, this project would have been impossible. Throughout long years of school, I have been generously blessed with more than a few exceptional teachers. I owe a debt to each one of them, especially Professor Terry Copp, of Wilfrid Laurier University, who supervised the dissertation from which this book emerged. I must also extend profound thanks to Professor Geoffrey Hayes, of the University of Waterloo, for his mentorship and friendship. Professors Pat Brennan, Cynthia Comacchio, Richard Fuke, Jack Hyatt, David Monod, Roger Sarty, and Suzanne Zeller have each shaped my approach to the study and writing of history.

While historians spend many of their working hours alone at the archives table or computer, history is anything but a solitary pursuit. Mentors, colleagues, students, and friends share experience, research, ideas and so much more. Nearly a decade ago, on Terry Copp's 1998 Canadian Battlefield Foundation Study Tour, Lieutenant-Colonel David Patterson and Dr Serge Durflinger showed me and a dozen other students around the Canadian battlefields in Europe – including the Ypres Salient – for the first time. Little did I know then how many times I was to return to this beautiful Flemish town. On later research trips to the Western Front, I was fortunate to stay at a welcoming bed and breakfast operated by Charlotte Cardoen-Descamps and her family on their Poelcapelle farm – a true home away from home, situated at the heart of the 1915 battlefields. Back in Canada, John and Tammy Maker never hesitated to open their Ottawa home to me as I carried out research at the Library and Archives a few blocks away. Tim Cook gave freely of his time and expertise, commenting in detail on the manuscript in its elementary stages. Jim Wood shared his innovative research on the pre-war Canadian Active Militia, while Mark Osborne Humphries shared insights from his work on shell shock. Bob Brown, Gordon McKinnon, Céline Garbay, and Tjarko Pot brought rare sources to my attention that I would have otherwise missed. Others patiently listened as I reflected on the project: Mike Bechthold, Tupper Cawsey, Sarah Cozzi, Michelle Fowler, Jeff Nilsson, Karen Priestman, Kevin Reeder, Ed Storey, and Lee Windsor. Len Husband, editor at the University of Toronto Press, was unceasingly kind and patient as we worked through the project together. The attention to detail provided by both the anonymous manuscript reviewers and the copy editors, Kate Baltais and Harold Otto, saved me from many mistakes, although any errors or omissions are mine alone.

While the Canadian Battlefields Foundation subsidized my first visit to the Canadian battlefields in Europe, the Laurier Centre for Military Strategic and Disarmament studies provided an office and other crucial support throughout my years as a graduate student and adjunct faculty member at Wilfrid Laurier University. I have also been fortunate throughout my graduate and postgraduate studies to receive generous funding from the Department of National Defence Security and Defence Forum, including an R.B. Byers Postdoctoral Research Fellowship during 2005–6. Finally, this book has been published with the help of a grant from the Canadian Federation of Humanities and Social Sciences, through the Aid to Scholarly Publications Program, using funds provided by the Social Sciences and Humanities Research Council of Canada.

SHOESTRING SOLDIERS:
THE 1ST CANADIAN DIVISION AT WAR, 1914–1915

Introduction

Individuals from all walks of life rushed to answer the call to arms across the Dominion of Canada as five powerful German armies invaded Belgium in August 1914. Many of Canada's first wave of volunteers had been born in some other part of the British Empire, while others crossed the border from the neutral United States to enlist when war was declared. Some had never spent a day in uniform, but more than a few had soldiered before, either with the Canadian Militia, the British army, or the military forces of some other nation. Frank Tidy, of Kildonan, Manitoba, was 28 years old when he joined up in September. He had put in eleven years with the Queen's Own Rifles in Toronto before the war. Thirty-nine-year-old Frederick Basford, English-born, had spent two years in the British army before emigrating to Canada; Basford was working as a shoe laster when he decided to sign up for overseas service. John Augusta was born in Bangor, Maine, in 1888. Earning a living as a clerk, he had seen no prior military service before joining the Canadian Expeditionary Force (CEF). Neither had Foster Lickers, a rubber worker from the Six Nations Indian Reservation near Brantford, Ontario; at 27 years of age, Lickers joined the 15th Battalion in 1914. Scores more of his Six Nations kinsmen volunteered to serve overseas by 1918, but Foster was to spend much of the war in captivity after falling into enemy hands at the Second Battle of Ypres. Clement Brereton was born in India; although just 19 years old when he joined the 10th Battalion in 1914, he had already served four years in the Royal Navy before the war. Each man had his own story, but in August and September of 1914, they gathered from far and wide to find a coveted place in Canada's first contingent. In the coming months and years they shared common destinies as soldiers of the Great War.

Within a few weeks of the declaration of war more than 30,000 men had been mobilized in Canada for overseas service. In October the contingent crossed the Atlantic in a hastily assembled armada of ships to join the Allies. These men – the Clement Breretons, John Augustas, and Frederick Basfords – supplied the raw material for what was soon to be known as the 1st Canadian Division. By late 1916, Canada's military commitment to the British imperial war effort had expanded to four overseas divisions. Throughout much of 1915, however, the 1st Division was the lone Canadian divisional formation in the British Expeditionary Force (BEF).

Upon the outbreak of war, the nucleus of the 1st Division was organized at Valcartier, Quebec, under the ever watchful eye of Sam Hughes, the eccentric minister of militia in Prime Minister Robert Borden's Conservative government. No camp actually existed at Valcartier when the first recruits arrived, but this mattered little, as most of the contingent's brief tenure there was occupied with organizational and administrative chores. Systematic training would have to wait until the Canadians reached England, where a long-serving British professional, Lieutenant-General Edwin Alderson, was appointed to command the new division. Under Alderson's tutelage, the Dominion soldiers spent the cold and damp winter of 1914–15 training within sight of Stonehenge in sprawling pre-war Territorial Army camps on Salisbury Plain. Four months later the Canadians landed at St Nazaire, ready to commence active service in France and Belgium. The 1st Division was set to begin what turned into forty-five months of fighting against a capable, well-equipped, and highly motivated enemy. This book explores the division's first year of war, from its arrival in England in October 1914 through to the closing months of 1915, when it settled down to garrison sodden breastworks and trenches for the war's second winter.

For Canadians, the 1914–15 narrative can be conveniently ordered in five phases. The first encompasses the four-month training period in England, lasting from October to February. That winter proved to be one of the wettest on record. Great endurance was demanded of the men as they trained through the rainy months. The second phase began more optimistically with the Canadians' initial deployment along the Franco-Belgian border, near the legendary town of Armentières. It was on the outskirts of Armentières that the 1st Division, with the help of two battle-tested BEF divisions, was gradually initiated into the rites of trench warfare. In mid-March the Canadians participated in the Neuve Chapelle offensive, the inaugural British set-piece operation of the war, and a harbinger of things to come in later and grander battles.

The third phase of the early Canadian war experience was possibly also the most dramatic. In April the 1st Division was transferred further north to Lieutenant-General Herbert Plumer's V Corps in the Ypres Salient, a sector of the Western Front already imbued with special meaning for tens of thousands of British Empire soldiers. German efforts to capture Ypres in the autumn of 1914 had ended in bloody failure and stalemate, but General-Oberst Herzog Albrecht von Württemberg's Fourth Army was about to make a second attempt to eliminate the salient, this time with the aid of chlorine gas, a horrific new weapon on the Western Front. The strength, courage, and skill of the Canadians were tested to extreme limits in the Second Battle of Ypres, as the Fourth Army offensive came to be known. By month's end approximately one-third of the men serving in the 1st Division had been killed, wounded, gassed, or captured – more than 6,000 casualties – but the Germans failed in their bid to wrest control of Ypres. The town remained in Allied hands for the duration of the conflict, serving as a physical and a moral bastion of resistance against German occupation of the last small corner of free Belgian territory. Costly early victories like the one at Ypres mattered especially at a time when the war's outcome was totally uncertain.

The beginning of the fourth phase in May witnessed the arrival of much-needed reinforcements and redeployment to General Douglas Haig's First Army on the La Bassée front. Although the Canadians had barely recovered from their ordeal at Ypres, they were soon committed to costly offensives near the villages of Festubert and Givenchy. These actions continued until mid-June, when the exhausted division was transferred to a quieter area near Ploegsteert (the troops simply called it 'Plugstreet'), not far from where the Canadians had first deployed in February. This marked the beginning of the fifth and final phase of the 1st Division's experience prior to the formation of the Canadian Corps. At Ploegsteert, the division was back under the command of the Second Army, serving with III and II Corps respectively. Defensive activities characterized the period, although the division played an almost forgotten supporting role in the Loos offensive that September just as the Canadian Corps came into being. The men finished off the year with aggressive raiding, but also fighting trench foot and bad weather as much as the Germans.

Canadian Historians and the First World War

Canadian historians have traditionally interpreted the war as a major step forward in their country's transformation from colony to nation. Military historians have applied this interpretation more specifically to the operational record of the Canadian Corps. During the interwar period, Canada's official military historian, A.F. Duguid, described a transition from an amateur colonial contingent in 1915 to a professional, homogeneous Canadian Corps, allegedly 'the most powerful self-contained striking force on any battle-front,' by mid-1917.[1] The crowning achievement, according to this interpretation, came with the breakthrough at the Battle of Amiens in August 1918 and the deep advances of the Hundred Days leading up to the Armistice of 11 November. Just as Canada had emerged from the war as a whole and independent nation, the story goes, so had the Canadian Corps progressively achieved its own distinct identity as the spearhead of the BEF. What better place to begin such a narrative than the twin venues of Salisbury Plain, where it seemed that little useful training had been accomplished, and Ypres, a desperate battle fought by an ostensibly ill-disciplined band of roughnecks who made it through thanks more to courage and grit rather than skill and good sense? Conforming ideally to the nation-building paradigm, such a portrait of 1914–15 continues to provide a desirable historiographic contrast with the image of a professionalized Canadian Corps in 1917–18.

Duguid's assessment of the Canadian war experience has been revised and reinforced by later generations of military historians emphasizing the importance of tactical, operational, and technological learning curves on the Western Front. Bill Rawling was among the first to articulate this paradigm, in his 1992 study *Surviving Trench Warfare: Technology and the Canadian Corps*. Rawling suggested that Canadians succeeded on the offensive at Vimy Ridge, Passchendaele, and Amiens because they had learned from the battles of 1915 and 1916 that 'fire-power was as important as courage in taking enemy positions and that soldiers had to be technicians, not just rifle carriers.'[2] Desmond Morton underscored Rawling's argument the following year with the publication of his landmark survey of the CEF, *When Your Number's Up*:

> The fifty months from August 1914 to November 1918 witnessed a remarkable transformation in almost everything that affected the soldiers ... the crude formations of semi-trained battalions in 1915 gave

way to the sophisticated teamwork of fire and movement that troops practiced in the winter of 1917. From [staff officers] would come the solution to the problem of trench warfare: how attackers could get through the thickening band of barbed wire, trenches, and trackless mire to the green fields beyond before the enemy could gather the forces to destroy them ... [the tactics] fitted Canadians like their well-worn tunics.[3]

Subsequent studies have taken the learning curve in different directions. In a 1994 article published in the *Journal of Military History*, Ian Brown contended that 'multiple learning curves' could be drawn for the various armies on the Western Front, but that the Canadian Corps' curve surpassed even the Germans' in the steepness of its slope.[4] A few years later Shane Schreiber argued, in *Shock Army of the British Empire*, that successful Canadian operations during the final three months of war resulted from a 'pragmatic, and at times innovative approach' predicated on deliberate all-arms cooperation.[5] Tim Cook's *No Place to Run*, focusing on the long-forgotten theme of gas warfare in the Canadian Corps, is broadly premised on a sense of progress and increasing sophistication.[6] The same is true of *We Lead, Others Follow*, Kenneth Radley's recent organizational history of the 1st Division.[7]

Each of these studies is based on compelling evidence. Like other armies, the Canadians reworked their tactics and technique over time. Just as importantly, the logistical infrastructure supporting operations drastically expanded throughout the conflict. Compared with 1917 and 1918, many of the basic necessities of trench warfare, such as reliable high-explosive ammunition and heavy guns, were in crucially short supply in 1915.[8] As one Canadian veteran later recalled, 'all through 1915 you were on a shoestring and a pretty frayed shoestring at that.'[9] Notwithstanding these material deficiencies, a close examination of 1914–15 uncovers evidence of sophistication and skill in the Canadian division that other narratives – preoccupied with the colony-to-nation transformation and the learning curve – have tended to pass over. Indeed, the capabilities of the 1st Division in 1915 stand in even sharper relief when we consider the 'shoestring' military resources available at that stage of the war. The generation of 1915 understood that firepower was just as important as courage. But, while courage abounded, firepower was in chronically short supply that year.

Canadian military historians have often underrated the significance of the early war experience. Perhaps the earliest published account of the Canadian fighting during 1914–15 appears in the first volume of

Sir Max Aitken's *Canada in Flanders* series. As Canada's self-styled official 'eyewitness' at the front, Aitken summoned his best journalistic voice to evoke gallant images of Second Ypres, Festubert, and Givenchy, but his appraisal of Canadian military training was less complimentary. The Canadian Division, he wrote in 1916, 'contained, no doubt, a sprinkling of South African veterans, but it consisted in the main of men who were admirable raw material, but who at the outbreak of war were neither disciplined nor trained, as men count discipline and training in these days of scientific warfare.'[10] With these words Aitken established an enduring stereotype of Canada's first contingent.

In contrast with Aitken, a more positive assessment of early Canadian training appears in *Canada in the Great World War*, a six-volume wartime collection published by a team of journalists. In the second volume, one of the authors admitted that the main parade grounds in the Salisbury camps were badly flooded, but reminded readers that a full range of basic training was carried out on higher, firmer ground despite poor weather.[11] *Guarding the Channel Ports*, the third volume in the series, offers intricately detailed narratives of the fighting at Ypres and near La Bassée. The heroic exploits of junior officers and men are celebrated while senior officers are chastised: 'Neuve Chapelle, Festubert, and Givenchy had all taught the same lesson – a lesson the British corps commander seemed slow to learn – that daylight raids without powerful and effective artillery preparation were suicidal.'[12] It was, in fact, a lesson that the 'British corps commander' knew all too well. Corps commanders, unfortunately, were not always able to fight at the time and location of their choosing.

Although published nearly seventy years ago, the first and only volume of A.F. Duguid's *Official History of the Canadian Forces in the Great War* remains the most comprehensive account of Canadian training and operations from late 1914 up to September 1915.[13] Despite the intricate detail of this massive tome, there are compelling reasons to revisit the period. Duguid, an engineer by profession, served with the 1st Canadian Division, living through the events he wrote about. True, the work of all historians is shaped by their own time and place. But as a participant in the war, Duguid can hardly be considered an impartial observer. The key players in Duguid's story were his own colleagues, friends, enemies, and former superiors. Many of these men were still living while Duguid worked on his volume, if not when it was finally published in 1938. Every word and phrase had to be carefully chosen and constructed: reputations were at stake. A case in point is the controversy between Duguid, as the official historian, and Richard Turner and Garnet Hughes, as players in the Second Battle of Ypres. Duguid – and other officers for that matter – felt that Turner and Hughes had performed poorly during the battle. Duguid avoided saying so outright in his draft chapters, but when Turner and Hughes reviewed them, both insisted that they had been treated unfairly, demanding more positive coverage in the final product.[14] Although Duguid spent two decades collecting, organizing, and distilling evidence with painstaking care, the Turner-Hughes controversy shows that he simply could not escape the strictures of writing contemporary history. Nor, obviously, does a reading of his work take into account everything that has since been written on the Canadian war effort. The time has come for a reappraisal of the first year of fighting in light of ninety years of historiography, memory, and mythology.

The early war period received necessarily less detailed treatment by G.W.L. Nicholson in *Canadian Expeditionary Force, 1914–1919*, the official Canadian survey of the war that finally appeared in 1962. Nicholson's brief assessment of early training is preoccupied with the poor weather in England.[15] Perhaps because *Canadian Expeditionary Force* covered the entire war, the account of Second Ypres served as a point of departure for the book's broader narrative. 'In their first major operation of the war,' Nicholson wrote, 'Canadian soldiers had acquired an indomitable confidence which was to carry them irresistibly forward in the battles which lay ahead.'[16] Following sections on Festubert and Givenchy are largely narrative, and lack the obvious frustration that characterizes Duguid's appraisal of the La Bassée attacks.[17]

For the next two decades historians had little to say on 1914–15, until three popular books were published on Second Ypres between 1985 and 1988. None of these explored training in great depth, but they tended to reinforce the view that the 1st Division was a well-meaning, albeit amateur and ill-prepared force when it entered combat at the beginning of the war. This was especially the case with Daniel Dancocks's book, *Welcome to Flanders Fields*, and George Cassar's volume, *Beyond Courage*.[18] Dancocks in particular was a master of narrative who knew how to reach ordinary readers with the experiences of ordinary soldiers.[19] Although his work was based on archival research, Dancocks made no attempt to move beyond conventional interpretations of the period.

While acknowledging that the Canadian war experience was characterized by growth and transformation, *Shoestring Soldiers* seeks to escape the broader nationalistic and learning curve paradigms. It places the early training and fighting squarely in the historical context of 1914–15, arguing that operational outcomes were determined by a broad spectrum of variables, including training, weather, leadership, technology, strategic considerations, logistics, morale, enemy capabilities, and sometimes blind luck. The book concludes that, despite a series of costly battles that resulted in frighteningly high casualties, throughout its first year of war the 1st Canadian Division was an effective combat organization, one that made a vital contribution to the Allied cause.

The opening chapters evaluate the impact of pre-war military service on the officers and men of the 1st Division before reassessing their training experiences in England and on the continent. Training was neither perfect nor complete, but the evidence suggests that the Canadians who landed in France in February 1915 were well prepared for battle by contemporary standards (not to mention that the content and scope of their training shared much in common with the practices of 1916–18).[20] The story turns next to Second Ypres, a battle steeped in the mythology of urine-soaked handkerchief gas masks and jammed Ross rifles, controversial Canadian weapons that suffered the additional curse of having been sanctioned by Sam Hughes before the war. While it appears that many Canadian soldiers encountered trouble with their rifles, it was the lack of artillery support that caused the greatest difficulties at Ypres. Notwithstanding these disadvantages, this study shows that on balance, the 1st Division performed effectively. Although they had plenty of it, courage alone was not what saved the Canadians from total annihilation at Second Ypres. It was skill and training, along with good morale and positive leadership that saw them through their trial by fire and gas.

The book turns next to the costly BEF offensives along the La Bassée Canal. The exigencies of coalition warfare dictated that a battered 1st Division be committed to these attacks with little time to recover from the gas battle at Ypres. Contrary to popular perceptions of Great War leadership, British commanders were not trying to kill as many of their soldiers as possible, but were instead reacting to French demands that the BEF take the offensive with whatever forces were available. Despite the 1st Division's hasty reconstruction after Second Ypres and a chronic shortage of artillery ammunition, the Canadians at least displayed effective cooperation between infantry and engineers, as well as capable leadership on the battlefield. Although officers and soldiers functioned within a rigidly hierarchical command structure, those at even the most junior levels found ways to exercise agency. When orders did not accord well enough with the situation on the ground, troop leaders and their men reacted intelligently, minimizing casualties. Leonard Smith, a historian of the French army, referred to this particular style of agency as proportionality. According to Smith's theory, soldiers of the Great War balanced risks to life and limb with the potential benefits that might result from a given course of action. When risks clearly outweighed benefits, combat was avoided or delayed.[21]

The book finishes with a survey of the 1st Division's experience of trench warfare on the 'quiet' Ploegsteert-Messines front during the summer and autumn of 1915, including participation in the ill-fated Loos offensive that September. Here we discover further evidence of a fully functional, aggressive division that was well integrated with its counterparts in the BEF. We leave the men of the 1st Canadian Division at the end of 1915, as they struggled to keep warm and dry in their soaked, freezing trenches and breastworks near the Franco-Belgian border.

There are some aspects of the 1914–15 experience that this study does not explore in great depth, either because they have already been exhaustively treated in the existing literature or because they are ultimately tangential to the central argument. The few chaotic weeks spent organizing the contingent at Valcartier during August and September are not revisited in detail. There was little time for training at Valcartier, and what really matters is that somehow, in excess of 30,000 men were assembled and put onboard ship in a matter of weeks. It is unlikely that a similar feat could be repeated today in as little time.

Much of the Valcartier controversy can be traced back to the erratic character of Sam Hughes, Prime Minister Robert Borden's minister of militia from 1911 through 1916. But if that minister were alive today, he would be disappointed to discover his exclusion from much of this story.[22] While Hughes's personality deeply influenced the Canadian war effort, he neither trained the 1st Division nor commanded it in battle. Once the Canadians crossed the Atlantic, their destiny was shaped by factors that escaped even Hughes's obsessive control.

Compared with earlier accounts of Second Ypres, readers will find discussion of Hughes's prized weapon, the Ross rifle, to be limited in this book. Veterans of 1915 often referred to the Ross and its alleged defects in their postwar recollections. Curiously, however, there is relatively little mention of weapon malfunction in the immediate post–Second Ypres official sources. This is true even for the battle reports of the most heavily engaged infantry battalions and companies.

Canadians would no doubt have been far better off with British rifles, but perhaps the impact of the Ross was less significant than postwar mythology implies.[23] Operational evidence from April 1915 suggests that Canadian soldiers at Second Ypres were as likely to run out of ammunition as they were to experience malfunction.

The following chapters are based on a broad range of official military documents, as well as private diaries, letters, postwar memoirs, and various published accounts. Most important among the official sources are the war diaries kept by units throughout the war. Some battalions maintained more detailed records than others, but in the aggregate, the war diaries provide the most comprehensive picture of a battalion or brigade's daily routine. In addition, there are seemingly endless files of battle reports, operation orders, field messages, instructional manuals, and training bulletins to consider.

Some of the more candid impressions of the war experience were recorded in the letters, diaries, and memoirs of men who were there. Historians have argued that soldiers censored the worst aspects of their experiences out of their letters to save loved ones from worry. While this was certainly true of some men, others seemed willing to share the more graphic details of combat service with family and friends.[24] Men were even less prone to censor their diaries, since these tended to be kept privately. Entries, however, were typically scribbled in a hurry by busy soldiers. As such, these sources often just scratch the surface of daily life at war. Postwar oral testimony from veterans must also be treated carefully, as years of reflection and Legion-hall storytelling invariably reshaped memories decades after the fact.

Invaluable among published secondary sources are A.F. Duguid's exhaustive 1938 official history and accompanying volume of appendices. There are also the excellent battalion and regimental histories, at least sixty of which were completed during the interwar years. As historian Tim Cook argued, the regimental histories filled an important gap left by Duguid's incomplete official history project.[25] It is true that these works were published with the regiments' reputations in mind, but the histories incorporated eyewitness accounts and other personal insights from survivors that would otherwise have been lost to posterity. Kenneth Radley's history of the 1st Division – the first monograph study of any of Canada's Great War divisions – has also proven a valuable reference, especially on matters relating to personnel and staff.[26]

Much of the operational analysis in this book is based on a primary source that cannot be found in any library, archives, or museum. This is the very ground on which the men of the 1st Canadian Division lived, fought, and died in 1915. Today the battlefields of Neuve Chapelle, Second Ypres, Festubert, Givenchy, and Ploegsteert appear much as they did more than ninety years ago. Trenches, dugouts, and bunkers have mostly disappeared, but the ridges, valleys, and roads that shaped operations have not greatly changed. Many of the men also remain, buried in the hundreds of Commonwealth War Graves Cemeteries that have transformed the Western Front from a battle zone into a place of commemoration. On several occasions I have visited the battlefields, armed with maps, compass, binoculars, and camera, in an effort to understand the terrain and assess its impact on tactics and decision making.[27] While it is impossible to fully recreate the ground on the written page, this monograph relies heavily on maps and illustrations to acquaint readers with the geographic character of the battlefields.

This book finishes with 1915. The Great War lasted for three more agonizing years, until imperial Germany was finally exhausted by relentless battlefield attrition and the slow starvation imposed by the Royal Navy's blockade. The Canadian Corps played key roles in a long list of battles and campaigns throughout the struggle. It is clear, however, that the first few generations of soldiers who passed through the 1st Canadian Division in 1915 knew how to make war and contributed to Allied survival throughout a very difficult year of fighting.

1 Soldiering and Canadian Soldiers: The State of the Art at the Outbreak of War

According to traditional narratives, the high summer of 1914 was as beautiful and peaceful as any then in recent memory. Across the European countryside farmers tended crops, while their urban counterparts strolled the thoroughfares of London, Paris, Berlin, Brussels, and Vienna. An industrialized Europe seemed to have reached a new pinnacle of confidence, stability, and prestige. Along with Great Britain, the continental powers were masters of extensive colonial empires spanning much of the globe. Since 1815 there had been no major protracted European conflict fought on such a scale as the Napoleonic Wars. For many living in a new mechanized age of progress, war seemed unthinkable.

Appearances, of course, were deceiving. Since the defeat of Napoleon, European conflicts had been relatively localized and short. But thanks to the introduction of ever more efficient and destructive small arms and artillery – products of the machine age – wars had been increasingly bloody since mid-century. Although far from Europe, the American Civil War was neither short nor localized. Sensitive observers could hardly ignore the destructive power of machine technology on the battlefields of the divided republic. Six years after the American fighting ended, similar technology was employed in the Franco-Prussian War of 1870–1. Bloody confrontations like the one at Gravelotte–St Privat in August 1870 heralded the suffering of a later generation of French and German soldiers. After winning an impressive victory against France in 1871, the newly proclaimed German Empire steadily developed into a major power of concern to all others in Europe. France vowed revenge for both lost territory and the high reparations exacted by a menacing neighbour.

By the turn of the century, most continental nations boasted sizeable conscript armies that could be mobilized at short notice and transported to the battlefront by rail. Shielded by the English Channel, Britain relied on the Royal Navy to protect its international interests, but its lead over the German High Seas Fleet narrowed after 1905 as the two nations engaged in an expensive maritime arms race. In the spring of 1914 Winston Churchill, First Lord of the Admiralty, remarked before the House of Commons that 'The causes which might lead to a general war have not been removed ... There has not been the slightest abatement of naval and military preparation. On the contrary, we are witnessing this year increases of expenditure by Continental powers beyond all previous expenditure. The world is arming as it was never armed before.'[1]

Although Europe was a well-equipped arsenal at the time of Churchill's speech, there is little reason to suppose that war was the inevitable outcome of the Sarajevo crisis that summer. On 28 June Archduke Franz Ferdinand, heir to the Austro-Hungarian throne, was assassinated, along with his wife, by a Bosnian Serb during an official visit to Sarajevo in the province of Bosnia-Herzegovina. An expansionist and bellicose Germany, under the rule of Kaiser Wilhelm II, supported an Austrian ultimatum that fundamentally challenged Serbian sovereignty in the aftermath of the assassination. In actuality the ultimatum was a thinly veiled pretext for war, but at first it seemed that the provocation might backfire, for the Serbian response proved more accommodating than German or Austro-Hungarian military commanders initially hoped. Yet not all of the Austrian demands were satisfied, an outcome prompting the Dual Monarchy to declare war on Serbia on 28 July. Two days later the Russians mobilized in support of their junior Balkan neighbour; on 1 August Germany declared war on Russia after the latter refused to stand down. According to the war plan of the late Chief of the General Staff, Alfred von Schlieffen, German commanders hoped to neutralize the French Army before Russia could fully mobilize. Within three days long columns of Germans invaded Belgium, en route to northwestern France. According to an 1839 treaty, Britain was to guarantee Belgian sovereignty in the event of war. Consequently, the German violation of Belgian neutrality drew the British into the conflict on 4 August. Treaty or no treaty, German control of the Belgian channel coast was unacceptable to an island power whose first line of defence was its navy.[2]

In August 1914 the Chief of the German General Staff, Helmuth von Moltke, was unenthusiastic about waging war against France and Russia simultaneously but felt that it was better to fight sooner rather than later: the Germans perceived both opponents to be growing stronger with each passing year. When Kaiser Wilhelm II hesitated to sign the German army mobilization order on 1 August, Moltke forcefully intervened, convincing his emperor that Germany must strike France through neutral Belgium at once, in part because exceedingly strong French fortifications had been built after 1871 along the Franco-German border. Most importantly, France must be incapacitated before Russian forces fully mobilized in the east. Much of Europe went to war that August in large part because Wilhelm's military leadership decided the time was right to expand Germany's continental influence. For their part, the French welcomed the opportunity to redress the disgrace of 1871.

Canada at War

As a British Dominion, Canada was automatically at war when Britain was at war on 4 August 1914. With few exceptions, English-speaking Canadians actively endorsed direct military involvement in the European fighting. This is not to suggest that they simply followed the imperial lead without any sort of considered analysis. Quite to the contrary, as historian Ian Miller has shown, Canadians paid close attention to continental affairs since the great naval crisis of 1909, when British Prime Minister H.H. Asquith announced that Germany was expanding its Dreadnought fleet. Between then and 1914 Canadian interest in imperial defence intensified through a series of crises that had been resolved short of war.[3] Diplomacy failed this time, yet whether or not they were legally bound to participate, Canadians believed that Germany must be stopped.

But what force would Canada send? Throughout their history inhabitants of Canada depended partly on sporadically trained citizen militiamen, but mostly upon British imperial garrison troops for defence. Despite periodic urging from the mother country, the young nation had never boasted a standing professional army of any size.[4] By 1914 Canada's Militia comprised two elements. The Permanent Active Militia (PAM) was a modest force of several thousand full-time professional soldiers. The Non-Permanent Active Militia (NPAM) was a considerably larger voluntary force of part-time soldiers organized into local regiments across the country. (As a matter of convention, this work will refer to the PAM as the Permanent Force and the NPAM as the Active Militia.[5]) Sam Hughes, the minister of militia and defence for Robert Borden's Conservative government from 1911 through 1916, was as much in favour of the Active Militia as he was antagonistic towards the Permanent Force. The outspoken minister, rarely afraid to cause offence, publicly dismissed professional soldiers as 'barroom loafers' during a visit to Halifax in 1913.[6] It was perhaps no coincidence that Hughes was also a temperance advocate.

Thanks in part to Hughes's intervention, the assembly of an overseas contingent at Valcartier in September 1914 was characterized by improvisation, urgency, and no small degree of melodrama. Somehow, despite the minister's controversial decision to scrap carefully orchestrated pre-war mobilization plans, more than 30,000 recruits arrived at Valcartier throughout the month.[7] Camp facilities were established at breakneck speed, and while some scattered training was accomplished, the pace was uneven. Much of the time in Canada was spent unloading trains, setting up tents, organizing units, and issuing kit and weapons. The expeditionary force soon moved to Quebec City and embarked in a less than orderly fashion on an armada of ships, reaching Plymouth eleven days later. For the next sixteen weeks the Canadians trained on the Salisbury Plain under their new British commander, Lieutenant-General Edwin Alderson.

Compared with later commanders of Canadian divisions and the Canadian Corps (formed September 1915), historians have written little on Alderson, in part because he did not leave behind extensive personal papers. Moreover, unlike Julian Byng or Arthur Currie, each of whom commanded the Corps later in the war, Alderson was not involved in any of the great offensive victories that Canadians love to remember. Nor did Alderson leave his job as corps commander on especially good terms with his Canadian counterparts. Because he was British, Alderson was easily expendable as a scapegoat after the 2nd Division's debacle at St Eloi in April 1916.[8] Politically, it was much too difficult to fire any Canadian divisional or brigade commanders whose performances were less than satisfactory, and it was equally problematic to direct blame higher up the chain of command where at least some of it belonged. For all of these reasons, Canadians have largely forgotten Alderson. This is unfortunate, because he was the right man for the job of commanding the Canadian division in 1914.

As a veteran of the British Empire's colonial wars in Africa, Alderson's military career dated back to 1878. Like many of his counterparts in the British Army, Alderson was an avid horseman, and for good reason; mounted troops played important roles throughout the late

nineteenth-century imperial campaigns. Alderson was also an intel-
lectual soldier of sorts. In 1899 he published an account of his service
with the mounted infantry of the Mashonaland Field Force.[9] Just
before setting out for service in South Africa in 1899, Alderson – then
a lieutenant-colonel – completed a second book, *Pink and Scarlet, Or
Hunting as a School for Soldiering.*[10] More than anything else, this curi-
ous volume is a guide to horsemanship and the fox hunt. Throughout
the text, however, Alderson draws basic parallels between hunting and
military field service. Promoted to the rank of brigadier-general during
the South African War, Alderson found himself in command of Canadian troops. In 1900 the Royal Canadian Dragoons and the 2nd Canadian Mounted Rifles served with Alderson's Mounted Infantry Column.
A positive relationship developed between Alderson and his Dominion
soldiers, one which facilitated his appointment to command the Canadian Division fourteen years later.[11]

Throughout much of 1915 Edwin Alderson was to lead the 1st Division through some of its toughest fights, until he was appointed to
command the Canadian Corps that September upon the arrival of the
2nd Canadian Division in France. In both capacities he overcame a
series of administrative and operational challenges with courage and
quiet determination. Alderson's approach is doubly commendable
because he was fighting a war on two fronts. In France and Belgium he
led his Canadians against a capable and well-equipped enemy. But as
the commander of Dominion troops, Alderson also had to think of his
reputation in Ottawa. When necessary, he was more than willing to
cross Sam Hughes. This was no mean feat. Before the division shipped
out to France in February 1915, Alderson arranged to supply as many
of his infantry battalions as possible with 1908 Pattern field equipment
that was far superior to the Canadian-designed Oliver leather gear.
This must have raised Hughes's nationalistic ire, for the minister had
always insisted upon equipping his boys with Canadian-manufactured
accoutrements, whether or not the goods were up to the job.[12] It may
seem like a trivial detail, but infantry equipment is heavy and uncomfortable even under ideal conditions, so it was important to kit out the
men with the best gear available. Throughout 1915 and early 1916 the
rift between Alderson and Hughes progressively fractured into an
almost unbridgeable gulf, in part over the former's criticism of the
Ross rifle, a weapon sanctioned by Hughes that seemed to malfunction
at the worst moments. In early 1916, when needed reinforcements
for the Canadian Corps were not forthcoming, Alderson bypassed

Hughes's disorganized administrators in England to voice his concerns directly to the Duke of Connaught, Canada's Governor-General.[13] The gloves had come off.

Alderson could never fully escape the strictures of Ottawa politics when dealing with Hughes, or even with his own senior Canadian subordinates, but when it came to the rank and file of the 1st Division, he was a plain speaker and a soldier's soldier. As he wrote to a friend in 1915, 'I am a very firm believer in telling men, as far as it is desirable, the why & the wherefore of the reason of asking them to do anything out of the ordinary ... as you know better than I do, these Canadians, with their high average of intelligence, appreciate being treated like this.'[14] It was this sort of attitude that had earned Alderson the respect of Canadian soldiers back in South Africa.[15] But just who were 'these Canadians' who arrived in England in 1914? What sort of men did Alderson have to work with there?

It is estimated that about two million Canadian men were of age (between 18 and 45 years) for military service upon the outbreak of hostilities. There is no record of how many recruits were rejected during the first weeks of the war, but the total number accepted for service with the first contingent approached 36,000, of whom 1,500 were officers.[16] At least two-thirds of the officers were Canadian-born, but more than 65 per cent of the other ranks had come to Canada from the British Isles at some point before the war. About another 5 per cent hailed from the United States or other countries. Despite their varied places of birth, most of the men who filled the division saw themselves as Canadians and loyal members of the British Empire at the same time. The two categories were by no means mutually exclusive for the generation of 1914.

The volunteers came to Valcartier through every province, with Ontario supplying the most men (13,957) and Prince Edward Island the fewest (134). The other provinces provided an average number of 3,100 men for the contingent. Although it is difficult to sketch a typical recruit, a few generalizations are possible. Virtually the entire force consisted of white males – there is no definite means of determining what proportion of the first wave of volunteers was francophone, as there was no language or ethnicity box to check off on the attestation forms. Aboriginal Canadians were officially refused until December 1915, but many already belonged to Active Militia units and managed to work around regulations at the discretion of local recruiting officers.[17] African Canadians were rejected outright. Later in the war only a small number, mainly from Nova Scotia, were allowed to serve overseas.[18] Beyond these broad ethnic fault lines, there was no typical recruit in 1914, possibly with the exception that many were familiar with military life before joining the CEF. A significant portion of the 1st Division's original batch of other ranks had worn military uniform prior to 1914 and virtually all of the officers possessed some form of military experience.[19]

Many early CEF men had served in the Active Militia as well as the British Army. Of these, a number had fought in the South African War of 1899–1902. After South Africa, the British and Canadian governments pursued various initiatives to encourage former British soldiers or sailors to emigrate to Canada, in part to bolster the capabilities of Canada's Permanent Force and Active Militia regiments. As a result of one such scheme, more than 600 ex-servicemen emigrated before 1914 with assistance from the Naval and Military Emigration League (NMEL).[20] Many other former soldiers found their way to the Dominion for different reasons, and not all came from Britain. While the United States remained neutral until 1917, eager Americans flocked to Canada for a chance at adventure upon the outbreak of war. Some of them had served in the army or navy, perhaps in the Spanish-American War.[21] Other foreign nationals of the first contingent, such as Raymond Brutinel or Daniel Tenaille, had soldiered in the French army before moving to Canada. These men were strangers neither to military training nor to the realities of active service.

It is possible, using the nominal rolls of 1914, to sketch a statistical portrait of pre-war service among the original members of the 1st Division. In the 7th Battalion's headquarters, 93 per cent (13/14) of the officers possessed some form of military experience. Of these, 75 per cent had soldiered with imperial units and 25 per cent with Canadian Militia units. Of the sixty-five other ranks attached to battalion headquarters, 82 per cent had served before the war, more than half of these with imperial regiments. A sampling of 200 officers and men from across the four companies in the 7th Battalion reveals that fifty-six had served in Canadian Militia units, fifty-nine with British units (including colonial police), eleven with Canadian and British units and one with the United States Army. In sum, 63.5 per cent of the men in this sample had some form of prior service in military or paramilitary units.

In an 8th Battalion sample of the same size, twenty-four men had served in the Militia, fifty in Imperial units and five in both Canadian and British formations. Although fewer than in 7th Battalion, two of every five men in the 8th Battalion sample knew the rigours of military life before arriving at Valcartier.[22]

Only a comprehensive statistical analysis of the 1st Division can determine if trends in these two battalions reflected the broader composition of the division in 1914. But even if the divisional averages were as high, or higher than those of 7th and 8th Battalions, the implications of such results would still be highly debatable, largely because the practical value of Active Militia training is so controversial.[23] Carman Miller, an authority on the pre-war period, suggested that as late as the turn of the century, the Active Militia was little more than a 'glorified police force,' a useful instrument for maintaining domestic order, but one quite unprepared for war and without modern logistical infrastructure.[24] Rural regiments generally lacked adequate facilities and equipment for proper training, while the city units put as much effort into elaborate social events as genuine military pursuits. A series of impressive armoury buildings was constructed around the country between 1890 and 1914, but these state-of-the-art facilities often had to be shared with the general public for miscellaneous functions to justify their expense. Even before a $20,000 armoury was fully completed in Brantford, Ontario, in 1893, it had already been loaned out to the Woman's Christian Temperance Union for a fundraising concert; Sam Hughes later encouraged such practices during his tenure as minister of militia.[25] As multipurpose facilities, armouries in Canada's larger cities were generously equipped with recreational facilities, including extravagantly furnished lounges, bowling alleys, skating rinks, banquet halls, and other public attractions of little immediate military relevance.[26]

The capabilities of Canada's pre-war Permanent Force are as debatable as the Active Militia's. Historian Stephen Harris, who has assessed the senior military leadership in Canada during the pre-war decades, concluded that the chief attributes of a professional army – defined as technical expertise, corporateness, and responsibility to the state – were by no means fully developed by 1914.[27] Canada's military was indeed heavily politicized, with entire regiments often identified as Liberal or Conservative bastions.[28] Officers with good connections progressed rapidly through the military hierarchy, with or without the right qualifications. Yet to dismiss the pre-war Militia as a band of opportunistic dilettantes would be grossly unfair. The example of Vancouver's 72nd Highlanders is instructive. In 1911 the regiment boasted a highly experienced cadre of commanders and staff. As a squadron commander in South Africa ten years earlier, R.G. Leckie – now in command of the 72nd Highlanders – was mentioned in dispatches after participating in the engagement at Hart's River. Major

William Francis Dugmore was Leckie's second-in-command in 1911. A veteran of the British Army and a holder of the Distinguished Service Order, Dugmore had served in at least seven imperial campaigns between 1895 and 1906. The adjutant, Captain Gilbert Godson, was twice wounded in South Africa, mentioned in dispatches, and decorated with the Distinguished Conduct Medal. Four of the eight company commanders with the 72nd Highlanders in 1911 had served extensively in South Africa. Two of the remaining four had served in the British army before coming to Canada.[29] It is safe to say that these Vancouver militiamen knew a great deal about the business of war.

Even if the militia boasted a leavening of experienced officers, it remains to be determined how much practical training actually occurred in peacetime. The dozens of regiments spread across the country during the two decades preceding the First World War make reliable or universal measurements of the value of training programs difficult, but some degree of generalization is possible from the evidence. As far back as the Crimean War, and especially since the Fenian scares of the 1860s and the withdrawal of British garrison troops from Canada in 1871, public enthusiasm for things military and investment in Canada's volunteer forces ebbed and flowed. Although there never seemed to be enough government funding to support the aspirations of every regiment, the situation improved under the leadership of Frederick Borden, Prime Minister Wilfrid Laurier's minister of militia from 1896 through 1911. Two and a half million dollars were put towards the militia in 1902–03. By 1912–13 this figure had risen to seven and a half million.[30] During the intervening period new camps were constructed for summer training exercises. Amid much political controversy, it was finally decided in 1904 that an artillery camp was to be located at Petawawa, Ontario, a remote location offering a safe venue to train with the latest quick-firing field guns.[31] Around the same time, Canada established its own engineer, signals, service, and ordnance corps. Beginning in 1903 elements of the new service corps provided valuable logistical services at summer training camps. A signalling school was set up that same year.[32] Proper support was now possible for the country's infantry, artillery and cavalry regiments. As new research by historian James Wood shows, a series of well-informed professional journals were published by and for militia officers across the country.[33] A new picture of Canada's pre-war military forces is now emerging – one showing that the enthusiastic Dominion soldiers were better prepared for war in 1914 than some of the earlier literature suggested.

The bulk of Canada's soldiers upon the outbreak of war in 1914 were among the 77,000 volunteers of the Active Militia who drilled periodically throughout the year at the local armoury and, ideally, spent a couple of weeks each summer working under Permanent Force soldiers at camp.[34] During the earlier part of the 1890s, infantry training in Canadian militia camps was often limited to the company level and below. By 1899, however, a new manual was published on battalion and brigade movements in the field, describing techniques for advancing over broken terrain against enemy forces of varying strength.[35] There is evidence, even before the hard lessons of the South African War and Frederick Borden's reforms, that at least some regiments engaged in realistic training activities. The Queen's Own Rifles regularly defended Toronto boroughs against 'enemy' forces drawn from other Active Militia regiments in Toronto or Hamilton. By one historical account written in 1960, 'a lot of genuine military endeavour went into these exercises. Scouts crawled forward to feel out the enemy's strength and positions; flanking parties maneuvered to prevent encirclement; shelter trenches were dug; cover was used to advantage: all very elementary perhaps, but just as fundamental now as then.'[36] Exercises of this sort continued across the country during the first decades of the twentieth century. In the summer of 1912 British Columbia served as the battleground. In a fictitious scenario Vancouver Island was designated as Redland, while the rest of the province became Blueland. After war was declared between the two countries, Blueland invaded Redland. The Blueland commanders were Major W. Hart McHarg and Lieutenant-Colonel R.G. Leckie; both men were destined to command infantry battalions in 1915. Meanwhile, a lieutenant-colonel of the garrison artillery by the name of Arthur Currie was entrusted with the defence of Redland. The *Canadian Military Gazette* lauded the weekend exercise as a great success, as 'all ranks were keenly interested; there was an absence of merely perfunctory work; outposts were real, and discipline excellent.'[37]

Despite these local initiatives, the annual appraisals submitted by successive General Officers Commanding the militia (GOCs) between 1890 and 1914 sometimes give a less than encouraging impression of militia equipment and training programs.[38] In 1892 Major-General Ivor Herbert warned that not enough Canadians were trained to command formations above the battalion, while too few had received any sort of formal instruction in staff work at any level.[39] Among the rank and file, a major handicap was the limited number of annual training hours completed by rural militiamen. It was often difficult for men in remote areas to reach local training facilities or camps, while farm duties understandably superceded military commitments. It was observed in 1911 that the 12th York Rangers, a rural regiment consisting mostly of town-dwellers from Aurora, Ontario, accomplished far more training at summer camp than was possible at an armoury during the year.[40] City soldiers, on the other hand, tended to spend too much time in the drill hall, with less opportunity to train in the field among larger formations.[41] A high turnover rate among the other ranks was a second overarching problem cited time and again by the militia GOCs. During one of the summer camps at Niagara, inspecting officers discovered that nearly 40 per cent of the sergeants had only just been awarded their stripes. 'Such a force,' warned the Major-General the earl of Dundonald, GOC at the time, 'certainly does not provide the trained framework needed to make a citizen army efficient in time of war.'[42]

Notwithstanding the recurring complaints voiced in the GOC reports, the expansion of the militia between the South African War and the outbreak of European hostilities in 1914 provided a comprehensive framework on which to flesh out an overseas contingent. If peacetime turnover among the infantry and cavalry units was a constant headache, at least the technical and support services had been formed and staffed with a cadre of experts, many of whom attended specialist courses in Britain. General Ian Hamilton, inspector-general of British Empire forces, was duly impressed when he visited the militia summer camps in 1913 on an exhaustive 14,000-mile cross-country rail tour. At the conclusion of the inspection, Hamilton prepared a largely positive forty-four-page report comprising eighteen broad recommendations. Some pertained to administration and organization, while others related more directly to training.[43] As might be expected, Hamilton found a long list of deficiencies, particularly in terms of arms and equipment. The militia was short several hundred field guns, howitzers, and machine guns; 150,000 shovels were needed if Canada was to go to war. The inspector-general called for accelerated expansion of Canada's forces, but admitted that a great deal had improved since Sir John French had inspected the militia in 1910. Hamilton was especially 'surprised' by the high standard of skill displayed by artillery batteries.[44] Much had been accomplished at Camp Petawawa since it opened eight years earlier.

The Canadian militia was not at all in bad shape in 1914. As the case of the 72nd Highlanders and the statistical evidence for the 7th and 8th Battalions have shown, many of the officers and men who served in the militia had also spent time in the British army, and some had already been to war in South Africa. If militia training was often limited to the company and battalion levels, so too would be much of the 1st Division's fighting during 1915. Whatever the extent of pre-war experience across the division, anecdotal evidence in later chapters shows that it was applied in direct and useful ways by the officers and men of the Canadian Division throughout their first year at war. This is ultimately what counted.

The Anatomy of the 1st Division, 1914–15

The 1st Division's organization developed gradually as it trained in England during the first winter overseas (Appendix A).[45] The three infantry brigades represented the greatest proportion of divisional manpower. With approximately 900 officers and men in each of four battalions, plus brigade headquarters staff, each brigade consisted of about 4,000 personnel at full strength. When the contingent was initially organized at Valcartier, existing Active Militia regiments were amalgamated to form composite infantry battalions, each of which received a simple numerical designation. This step was necessary in part because there were simply too many under-strength peacetime regiments for each to form its own overseas battalion with the first contingent. In some instances more than a dozen regiments of varying size were pooled together to create a full-sized battalion. The 2nd Infantry Battalion, for example, was based on the 9th Mississauga Horse, 14th Prince of Wales's Own Rifles, 15th Argyll Light Infantry, 16th Prince Edward Regiment, 34th Ontario Regiment, 42nd Lanark and Renfrew Regiment, 43rd Duke of Cornwall's Own Rifles, 49th Hastings Rifles, 57th Peterborough Rangers, 59th Stormont and Glengarry Regiment, and the Governor-General's Foot Guards. In contrast, just four pre-war regiments, including Toronto's 48th Highlanders, comprised the 15th Battalion.[46] Some militiamen who would rather have worn their own cap badges overseas criticized the numbered-battalion system, arguing that in composite units 'there is no team work among' the officers or companies. Such concerns turned out to be largely unfounded, as the overseas battalions soon developed unique and cohesive regimental identities, often based on shared regional backgrounds. In some instances, an informal sobriquet might even be adopted; the 4th Battalion, made up of central Ontario regiments, was soon dubbed the Mad Fourth; Winnipeg men in the 8th Battalion referred to themselves as the Little Black Devils. Pre-war regimental affiliations were adapted to the wartime system.[47]

Two of the division's three infantry brigadiers who served during the first year of the war are already well known. Arthur Currie, at the head of the 2nd Brigade and destined to command the Canadian Corps from June 1917 through to August 1919, has been the subject of three biographies and numerous shorter studies.[48] Although Currie hardly boasted a soldierly physique, he was among the most dedicated and skilled officers to rise to senior command in the British Empire forces during the Great War. Before 1914 Currie had served with an Active Militia artillery regiment, but otherwise lacked practical military experience.

Richard Turner, in command of the 3rd Brigade, was a merchant from Quebec City and a hero of the South African War. As a lieutenant in the Royal Canadian Dragoons, Turner was awarded the Distinguished Service Order (rarely given to such a junior officer) for a daring river crossing near Pretoria in 1900. Later that year he and two other men won the Victoria Cross at Lillefontein after saving two field guns from falling into Boer hands. Although Turner's First World War career has not been studied as closely as Currie's, his leadership at the brigade and divisional levels continues to draw heavy criticism from historians.[49] There is little doubt that Turner made mistakes on the battlefield, but his most controversial decisions at the Second Battle of Ypres in April 1915 must be viewed within the broader operational context of the moment if we are to understand his actions.

Malcolm Mercer, in command of the 1st Brigade, is one of Canada's forgotten generals. Perhaps because of Mercer's untimely death as commander of the 3rd Division at Mount Sorrel in June 1916, little has been written about his wartime career. Only recently has a brief biographical sketch been published, although not by a military historian.[50] Like Currie, Mercer was a pre-war militiaman, but the closest he had come to seeing 'action' was as the officer commanding a company of strike breakers at Sault Ste Marie back in 1903.[51] Of the three brigadiers, only Turner had been to war before 1914.

Each infantry battalion was commanded by a lieutenant-colonel and consisted of four companies. These in turn consisted of about 225 men subdivided into four platoons. Canadian battalions were initially organized temporarily into eight smaller companies, but reverted to the more practical four-company arrangement before crossing the English Channel. The transition was a lengthy, controversial process rooted in the experience of the South African War, but the four-company organization ultimately prevailed because it was impractical for a battalion commander to control eight companies once his forces were dispersed across a battlefield.[52] Beyond its four companies, each battalion incorporated machine-gun, transport, and signals sections; in February 1915 the battalion machine-gun sections were increased from two to four guns, giving the infantry a higher level of immediate fire support.[53]

The group of men appointed to command Canada's infantry battalions in 1914 and early 1915 comprised a mixture of part-time and professional soldiers. In the 1st Brigade, A.P. Birchall (4th Battalion) was a British regular who had served on the Canadian militia staff immediately before the war. F.W. Hill (1st Battalion) was a former mayor of Niagara Falls and an officer in the 44th Lincoln and Welland Regiment. David Watson (2nd Battalion) was a newspaperman from Quebec and Robert Rennie (3rd Battalion) a businessman from Toronto. Like Hill, both were Active Militia officers.[54]

The 2nd Brigade boasted a capable team of battalion commanders. The most experienced was Louis Lipsett (8th Battalion), an imperial officer who had helped standardize Canadian militia training before 1914.[55] Sadly, this highly respected officer was killed during the last days of the war while in command of a British division. The outspoken George Tuxford (5th Battalion) was a 44-year-old militiaman who had come to Canada from Wales.[56] William Hart-McHarg (7th Battalion) was an Irish-born lawyer with considerable militia experience, as well as service with the Royal Canadian Regiment in South Africa. Russell Boyle (10th Battalion), a rancher, was born in Port Colborne and put on his first military uniform at age 14. An avid militiaman, Boyle had served as a gunner in South Africa, where he was decorated several times for bravery.[57]

In the 3rd Brigade, R.G. Leckie (16th Battalion) was an engineer in civil life, but the Halifax-born militiaman had graduated from the Royal Military College and served in South Africa with the 2nd Canadian Mounted Rifles.[58] Frank Meighen (14th Battalion) ran a milling company before the war, but also commanded the 1st Regiment, Canadian Grenadier Guards.[59] F.W. Loomis (13th Battalion), from Quebec, had served in the Active Militia before the war, but lacked combat experience.[60] Difficult days lay ahead for Loomis, who was in command of the St Julien garrison when the Germans attacked Ypres in April 1915. In addition to a long militia career, J.A. Currie (15th Battalion), from Ontario, was also a Member of Parliament and close friend of Sam Hughes.[61] Even before the Canadians ventured overseas in

1914, Currie displayed a fairly realistic sense of the challenges they were to face. In August 1914 he wrote, 'Modern battles are fought over a front of twenty to fifty miles. The infantry advance slowly with the spade. Frontal attacks are almost impossible. The frontage is so great that it is impossible for the infantry to carry on a swift surprise flank attack.'[62] Currie appears to have started off on the right foot with his battalion in France, but he was later disgraced for allegedly quitting the battlefield in a drunken state at Second Ypres.

The Canadian cavalry regiments of the first contingent consisted primarily of Permanent Force elements, including the Royal Canadian Dragoons (formed in 1883), Lord Strathcona's Horse (formed in 1901) and A and B Batteries of the Royal Canadian Horse Artillery (formed in 1905). The 2nd King Edward's Horse, a British imperial unit of mixed composition, was seconded to the Canadians in February 1915. To the chagrin of Prime Minister Robert Borden, Lord Kitchener assigned a British officer and politician, Colonel J.E.B. Seely, to command the Cavalry Brigade. Borden wanted more Canadians in charge.[63] Seely, in contrast, was delighted with the opportunity for a field command.[64]

The 250-man divisional cyclist company was under command of Captain R.S. Robinson, a tough veteran of the South African War. When a division was on the move, the cyclists functioned as advanced reconnaissance parties. They were also useful as messengers in an age when wireless communication was in its infancy and telephone cables were cut frustratingly often by heavy troop traffic or artillery fire. Even as late as 1945 many armies still included bicycle units.

The primary function of the division's artillery brigades was to 'assist other arms in breaking down hostile opposition.'[65] As of late 1914 divisional artillery strength was organized into three 750-man brigades, each divided into four batteries. There were four 18-pounder field guns (with a maximum range of 6,500 yards) per battery, giving each brigade a strength of sixteen guns. The divisional artillery initially included a single heavy battery of four 60-pounder guns (with a maximum range of 10,000 yards) and a horse-drawn ammunition supply column. In France the heavy battery was exchanged for a pair of British howitzer batteries that supported the Canadians throughout 1915. As well, it was normal for the divisional guns to be supplemented by those of neighbouring outfits, and vice versa, as required by operational circumstances.

Up until the last decade of the nineteenth century a field gun's rate of fire and accuracy were limited by the absence of an integral recoil system. Without any means of absorbing recoil when fired, a gun rolled backwards several feet with each round and then needed to be relaid on target. This changed in 1896 when French Army officers developed a hydro-pneumatic cylinder capable of absorbing recoil, thereby eliminating the necessity to re-lay. The secret of the 'quick-firing' recoil mechanism was heavily guarded by France, but other armies copied it before long.[66] Canadian gunners were first equipped with 18-pounder quick-firing pieces about 1906.

In 1914 artillery fire fell under three general categories: direct, indirect, and predicted. Direct fire occurred when the gunner could see the target by his own line of vision, either with the naked eye or through an optical sight, usually at ranges less than 1,500 yards. Indirect fire was somewhat more complicated, because the gunner could not see his target. Instead, a third-party observer within sight of the target relayed the fall of shot back to the gunner by telephone or some other means of communication. A third technique coming into use by 1914 was predicted fire or map-shooting, whereby an invisible target was engaged based on map coordinates. If not always accurate, an advantage of map-shooting was its surprise effect. While ordinary indirect fire involved trial-and-error shots that heralded a pending attack, predicted fire could be unleashed without warning.[67]

At the outbreak of the Great War there were essentially two types of artillery ammunition available: shrapnel and high explosive. A shrapnel round consisted of a steel shell loaded with hundreds of marble-sized lead-alloy balls. At a particular point in the round's trajectory, the nose cone burst off the shell and a hail of spherical shrapnel was projected forward in a conical pattern against unprotected infantry and other soft targets. High-explosive shells, more powerful than shrapnel, were intended for use against fortifications and buildings.[68] Shrapnel was more plentiful than high explosive in British ammunition stocks during 1914–15, but reliable shells of all types were in short supply during the early Western Front battles.[69]

Brigadier-General H.E. Burstall was given command of the Canadian divisional artillery. An officer of considerable experience, Burstall was a graduate of the Royal Military College, but had also completed Staff College training in Britain. During the war in South Africa he served as a lieutenant, later joining the South African Constabulary.[70] Subordinate to Burstall, in command of the 1st Canadian Field Artillery (CFA) Brigade, was Lieutenant-Colonel E.W.B. Morrison. Although he stood just five feet, six inches tall, 'Dinky' Morrison was a respected veteran of the

South African War who had served on the militia staff.[71] He later rose to command the Canadian Corps artillery at the end of 1916. Lieutenant-Colonel J.J. Creelman commanded the 2nd CFA Brigade in 1914. An outspoken, sometimes temperamental officer, Creelman was a highly educated lawyer, industrialist, and militiaman who was to remain active in the veterans' community until his death in 1948.[72] Lieutenant-Colonel J.H. Mitchell, in command of the 3rd CFA Brigade, was a 49-year-old militiaman with experience in infantry and artillery regiments.[73] Later in the war he was to command the artillery of the 3rd Canadian Division.

The rapid rates of artillery and small-arms fire that were technically achievable in 1914 could not be sustained without timely resupply of ammunition. Lieutenant-Colonel J.J. Penhale's 1st Canadian Divisional Ammunition Column (DAC) was under immediate control of Burstall's divisional artillery headquarters. Ammunition columns were generally organized into four sections. Three of these carried small-arms and 18-pounder ammunition while the fourth delivered larger calibre ammunition for the division's heavy guns. In addition to the divisional ammunition column, each artillery brigade was equipped with its own column. The brigade ammunition columns received material from the divisional column and delivered it to their respective batteries. Each of the brigade ammunition columns also assumed responsibility for supplying small-arms ammunition to a particular infantry brigade in the division. As well, the personnel and horses of the ammunition columns might be called on to replace casualties in the artillery brigades at short notice.[74]

The engineering component of the 1st Canadian Division was organized into three field companies with a gross strength of about 600 officers and men. The duties of the field companies included the preparation of fortifications, construction or improvement of roads and bridges, demolitions work, and purification of drinking water. A selected number of troops in each field company was mounted on bicycles or horses to facilitate participation in reconnaissance activities. Most of the division's engineer officers were professional engineers. Lieutenant-Colonel C.J. Armstrong, in command of the engineer brigade, was trained as a civil engineer. Before the First World War he had served with the 5th Royal Highlanders in Montreal, and was among the volunteers who fought at the Battle of Paardeberg during the South African War.[75] Captain T.C. Irving, in command of the 2nd Field Company, was also a peacetime civil engineer and militiaman.[76]

Major F.A. Lister, a Permanent Force officer from Sarnia, Ontario, was given command of the divisional signallers in 1915.[77] The signal

company of an infantry division consisted of four sections and a headquarters. These elements comprised cable-laying detachments, telephone detachments, visual signallers, cyclists, and motorcycle dispatch
riders.[78] In the 1st Division, No. 1 Signal Section was attached to divisional headquarters while the three remaining sections were paired off
with infantry brigades. The signal company included telegraphists from
the engineers, while the Canadian Signal Corps supplied visual signallers and telephone experts.[79]

The general supply and maintenance of forces in the field was performed by three echelons of transport. First-line transport was controlled by the subunits of the division; each infantry brigade, for
example, was equipped with its own wagons and equipment for local
transport requirements. Second-line transport comprised the divisional
ammunition column (discussed above in conjunction with the artillery)
and the divisional train. These elements received material from corps
level and distributed it to the brigades.[80] The divisional train, equipped
with horse-drawn wagons and motor lorries, was also responsible for
transporting the division's baggage, stores, and supplies.[81] Third-line
transport included the motorized divisional supply column, which was
controlled at corps level and operated primarily in the rear area.

Lieutenant-Colonel W.A. Simson assumed command of the divisional train in 1914. Small in stature, the 42-year-old Haligonian set a
high standard for his soldiers and was not afraid to let them know it.
He was a transport specialist of the Army Service Corps, a young
branch of the Permanent Force at the outbreak of war; he had also
belonged to the 63rd Halifax Rifles and joined the 4th Canadian
Mounted Rifles for Service in South Africa.[82] Simson's experience and
tough approach paid dividends when the shooting started.

In the Salisbury camps all ranks of the 1st Canadian Division engaged in
individual and unit-level training between October 1914 and February
1915. By the second week of November, Alderson issued formal directives
for the training of infantry, mounted troops (cyclists and cavalry), artillery,
engineers, signallers, and support personnel. A sampling of the war diaries shows that most units spent an average of four to six hours training
each day, although this estimate can vary widely according to unit commander, weather conditions, and the availability of space. These hours
did not include time devoted to a range of other chores such as maintenance of horses and equipment, the movement of troop formations
around the sprawling training area, and work on camp infrastructure.

Divisional engineers in particular were occupied with road work and construction projects in the effort to accommodate large numbers of men and horses in a space that had hitherto served as a seasonal training camp for the British Territorial Army, a part-time force comparable to Canada's Active Militia.

Was Canadian training during the winter of 1914–15 productive? Before attempting to answer this question in the next chapter, it is instructive to sketch out the purpose and scope of military training at the time. As soldiers of the British Empire, Canadians trained for war according to an established body of standards and principles that had been codified before 1914 in a series of official War Office manuals. Among the most important were *Infantry Training*, *Field Service Regulations*, and *Training and Manoeuvre Regulations*. It was through these media and other supplemental printed material that collective experience was disseminated among the battalions of Canada's new division.

Textbooks of the Trade

Popular and scholarly historians alike have tended to dismiss the British army of 1914–18 as anti-intellectual and resistant to the transmission of innovative ideas, concepts, and lessons.[83] An exception is Paddy Griffith, who has argued that the army effectively disseminated knowledge through Printing and Stationery Depot publications. Part of a mobilization plan dating from 1912, the depot was activated in 1914 under the command of Captain S.G. Partridge, a seasoned military bureaucrat who was to fill the post throughout the war. In the beginning Partridge ran a relatively humble operation, but this changed dramatically with the expansion of the BEF and the arrival of Dominion forces in England. By 1915 the print runs for some publications reached six figures. Nearly everyone in British uniform could access a standard body of knowledge, either directly, or through instructors and superior officers.[84]

While the wartime scale of Partridge's operations was something new, the practice of codifying doctrine and procedures in War Office publications was long established. As a pre-war edition of *Training and Manoeuvre Regulations* stated, '[training] principles are laid down in the Training Manuals and it is the duty of all commanders to see that they are strictly observed.'[85] As such, the Canadian soldiers training on Salisbury Plain drew from existing literature already in general use by British forces. All manuals, however, were subject to change. Even as the contingent arrived in England the most recent battle experience of the BEF was already being integrated into updated editions. A good example is *Some Notes on the Minor Tactics of Trench Warfare*, a pamphlet promoting cooperation between infantry and engineers under the siegelike conditions of the Western Front.[86] Other manuals and pamphlets ranging in subject from how to shoot a revolver to the preparation of field latrines purveyed the latest practical lessons. Although some publications were in short supply during the early months of training, evidence suggests that commanding officers improvised with what was available.[87]

Soldiers of the First World War were conditioned to display exemplary personal courage and physical endurance in battle. According to *Training and Manoeuvre Regulations*, the basic purpose of training was to develop each soldier's 'mental, moral, and physical qualities as highly as possible.'[88] But if commanders saw combat as an individual adventure that placed a premium on bravery, few expected to win battles through courage alone. *Training and Manoeuvre Regulations* emphasized equally that soldiers' technical skill must be developed 'by theory and practice' such that 'various arms' could be employed 'in co-operation to the best advantage ... Advanced training is devoted to the study and practice of the principles of co-operation.' Battle was a collective endeavour demanding effective cooperation among each arm: infantry, artillery, engineers, mounted troops, and service support. Long before the first shots were fired in 1914, it was clear that victory would come to the forces best able to combine the power and capabilities of all branches of service.

The basics had to come first, however, especially in late 1914, by which time the old pre-war British army had suffered high attrition and needed to be reinforced with a much larger citizen army. With this task in mind, professional officers sat down to write a series of semi-official training supplements. Conforming more or less to army standards, these pocket manuals served as easily decipherable how-to guides for officers who found themselves charged with training and commanding a brand new platoon, company, or battalion.

Rapid Training of Company for War is the title of one such supplemental publication that first appeared in November 1914. Its author was Captain Arthur Percival Birchall, a career officer whose service in the 7th Royal Fusiliers dated back to the turn of the century. In 1913–14 Birchall partook in an exchange program with the Canadian militia, working on its instructional staff in western Canada. As a company officer with the Royal Fusiliers, Birchall had already gained much experience leading regular troops, but his work in Canada revolved around the citizen soldiers who served in the Active Militia, so he was well placed to comment on the intricacies of turning ordinary civilians into disciplined fighters. Birchall admitted that raising and training an effective citizen army under wartime conditions was an ambitious undertaking, but he remained optimistic, believing that the solution to the Empire's crisis lay in efficient training tempered with a good dose of common sense.[89] Birchall soon practised what he preached as commanding officer of the 4th Canadian Battalion on Salisbury Plain.

It is clear from the pages of *Rapid Training* that Birchall was no iconoclast. Steeped in the sacred pre-war rites of the British army, he warned young officers that 'trousers should never be worn on parade or on duty. They are frequently known as "slacks," which sufficiently indicates their sphere.' It was unacceptable to wear shoes instead of riding boots, and 'fancy socks' were nothing less than abominable. Under the category of mess etiquette, the Fusilier officer noted that 'bad language and risqué stories are taboo in a good mess' and 'the hall-mark of a bad one.'[90] But devotion to minor details of dress and deportment belie the progressive features of *Rapid Training*. Birchall tempered his writing with pragmatism and a keen sense of the latest developments on the Western Front, as well as earlier experiences in the South African War: 'A few years ago it was thought that a soldier was a machine, and should never be allowed to think for himself; the South African War altered all that, as far as our Army was concerned; the soldier is now taught to use his brains and to take advantage of ground and cover, with results which have been amply justified during the present war.'[91] Because soldiers were capable of making intelligent decisions, Birchall implored officers to foster initiative among junior ranks.

As a career soldier, Birchall knew all too well that citizen soldiers – even those who had eagerly served in the Active Militia – had a great deal to learn. Training and practice were essential, and *Rapid Training* urged readers to make the best use of limited time. During heavy rain, field activities could be replaced by indoor instruction.[92] It was advice that would come to resonate especially deeply for thousands of Canadian soldiers camped on the flooded Salisbury Plain. More generally, Birchall condensed the goals of basic company-level training into a series of topics, including physical fitness, marksmanship, small unit tactics, defensive work and fortifications, and night operations, as well as various specialized skills (scouting, machine guns, and signalling).[93] Such criteria, based upon pre-war doctrine as well as early wartime experience, are useful benchmarks against which to measure the formative training of the 1st Canadian Division in England (examined in Chapter 2). But first the stage is set with a survey of training subjects among the different branches of service.

Canadian Military Training, 1914–15

The daily routine for Canadian recruits on Salisbury Plain typically started with thirty minutes of fitness training. According to the 1908 *Manual of Physical Training*, 'a soldier should be well disciplined, a good marcher, intelligent, smart, active and quick, able to surmount obstacles in the field and capable of withstanding all the strains and hardships of active service.'[94] Daily exercise assumed various forms, but often consisted of bayonet practice, sports, and Swedish exercises, a system of gymnasticlike drills.[95] In addition to stationary exercises, route marches of two to three hours in duration appear regularly on training schedules. Although soldiers on the Western Front were sometimes transported by rail or motor vehicles from one sector to another, local movements from billeting areas into the front line were almost universally accomplished on foot. Marching across country with rifle, ammunition, water bottle, and pack helped to develop physical stamina. More importantly, route marching in company or battalion formations taught soldiers to move for miles at a time in large groups, in daylight or darkness, without falling into a disorderly rabble. The timely deployment of reinforcements about the battlefield could be decisive, particularly in defensive scenarios where reinforcing units might become intermixed with retiring troops. Physical training and route marching fostered the endurance, cooperation, and mobility demanded in *Training and Manoeuvre Regulations*.

Musketry was a fundamental component of training in 1914. Beyond marksmanship, the subject encompassed care of weapons and ammunition, the theory of fire, judging distance, range practice, and field practice.[96] In addition to rifle instruction, *Musketry Regulations* included lessons on hand grenades, machine guns, and bayonet fighting. Soldiers spent a finite number of hours on the rifle range, but much additional work was completed in classroom settings. A special Canadian manual of rifle and musketry exercises was printed in 1914 for the Ross rifle, which differed in design from the Short Magazine Lee Enfield (SMLE) rifle used by British forces.[97]

As it remains in the early twenty-first century, close order drill was an elementary skill learned by recruits in 1914. It consists of simple positions and movements for assembling groups of soldiers and moving them about from one point to another. During the eighteenth and early nineteenth centuries, commanders used close order drill to manage troops in combat. Before 1850 the ranges of weapons had been shorter and rates of fire slower. To maximize the effects of firepower, it was necessary to organize soldiers shoulder to shoulder in strictly controlled mass formations, a capability demanding constant close order drill. Once the infantryman or gunner learned the drill movements and voice commands, relatively little was demanded of his personal initiative.

Technological change had upset this equilibrium well before the first shots were fired in 1914. Beginning in the 1850s, infantrymen were widely equipped with rifled muzzle-loaders designed to fire the Minié-style bullet. The result of greater accuracy over longer ranges was horrifically evident in the high casualty rates of the American Civil War. After 1880 the development of breech-loading rifles and reliable water-cooled machine guns made the battlefield more dangerous again, as lethal ranges were extended, rates of fire increased, and accuracy improved even further. After 1896 the widespread employment of quick-firing artillery guns further threatened close order formations at longer ranges than ever before. By 1914 close order drill was simply an elementary tool for developing 'discipline, cohesion, and the habits of absolute and instant obedience to the orders of a superior,' and was usually practised (in squad, section, platoon, or company-sized formations) on the parade square. Wartime publications warned that close order drill should not be taken to extremes at the expense of more important lessons.[98] It no longer served any direct purpose on the battlefield. If the infantry were to avoid complete destruction in combat, new tactics were required.

Improved small arms and artillery weapons afforded great advantages to entrenched defenders. As such, pre-war military doctrine maintained that attack formations must remain somewhat concentrated if they were to overcome an increasingly powerful defence.[99] While subsequent experience on the Western Front proved this assumption largely correct, commanders also recognized that dense attack formations offered inviting targets to enemy gunners and infantrymen. Extended (or open) order drill – the offensive movement of large numbers of troops in loosely spaced formations – was the 'least worst' solution to the problem of negotiating a fire-swept battle zone during the First World War era. To account for the exigencies of terrain, extended order drill was practised on different types of ground in platoon, company, or battalion-sized formations. Under cover of friendly artillery fire, groups of soldiers crossed open areas in leaps and bounds; while one unit advanced, another would go to ground and provide fire support.[100]

While pre-war doctrine placed much emphasis on the offensive, soldiers were also trained in defensive techniques. *Infantry Training* described three types of defence: active, passive, and the delaying action. Active defence was intended to 'create and seize a favourable opportunity' for decisive offensive action, while passive defence was used to 'beat off' an attack without hoping to 'turn the tables' on the enemy by resuming offensive operations. Delaying actions required troops under attack to hold the line until friendly reinforcements arrived.[101]

All three styles of defence required leaders to effectively locate and prepare defensive positions. Although trench warfare was not yet under way on the Western Front when the 1914 edition of *Infantry Training* was published, the section discussing defensive positions prophetically suggested that only 'a few' sentries should remain in the front trenches while the bulk of the defensive force waited in deep, covered trenches behind the firing line. Front and rear would be connected by communication trenches. Even during the first weeks of the war, British training bulletins underscored the importance of 'digging in' below ground.[102] Basic entrenching lessons for recruits focused on the construction of fire trenches. Topics included siting and layout, concealment, construction specifications, use of tools, digging in frozen ground, overhead cover, loopholes, and working under fire.[103] Effective entrenching skills depended in turn on good physical fitness and reinforced the importance of daily physical training.

Night operations proved challenging throughout the war, but the benefits of operating in the dark were obvious from an early stage. Basic training in night work included identifying objects and sounds, practising silent advances, orientation and navigation by stars, reconnaissance, and entrenching.[104] Outpost training, also known as protection, was based on a set of procedures for sentries to provide early warning of enemy activity. The applications of all types of arms, including machine guns, were incorporated into outpost work.[105]

Each of the above training subjects was practised by all branches of service, but there were additional skills for specialists to master. Cavalrymen received lessons in equitation and the care of horses, the use of pistols and swords, and pursuit techniques. If sword practice seems misplaced in modern war, it is instructive to recall that Canadian cavalrymen, on horseback, lethally employed their swords against German soldiers as late as 1918, mostly notably at Moreuil Wood (in

March) and Le Cateau (in October).[106] The fundamentals of reconnaissance and scouting were also part of the basic course for mounted units. Some of the divisional cyclists were trained as motorcycle dispatch riders, an important communications function.[107]

Artillery was the most technically sophisticated military trade in 1914. As stated in the 1914 edition of *Field Artillery Training*, gunners were required to master the tactical and technological principles of shooting as well as the art of horse handling, since horses pulled most of the guns and ammunition. Divided into six periods of two weeks, the artillery syllabus included semaphore, gun drill, laying, fuze setting, reconnaissance, camouflage, and ammunition supply. Wagon and carriage drivers received additional training in harness fitting and stable management.[108] Above all else, *Field Artillery Training* emphasized the importance of cooperation between artillery formations and other branches of service. While effective artillery operations demanded teamwork and tight coordination, training also strove to develop initiative and self-reliance at all levels of responsibility, since the chaos of battle would often interrupt the established chain of command, undermining the best-laid plans.

The First World War belonged as much to the engineers as to the gunners and infantry. Basic engineering techniques and principles applied throughout the war, including the construction of trenches and earthworks, the defence of localities, field craft, and bridging were laid down in the 1911 *Manual of Field Engineering*. The sections on trenching and the defence of localities are of particular interest in this manual. A locality was defined as any distinctive point of immediate tactical significance, such as a hill, crossroads, village, or wood. Explicit instructions were provided for each situation, but variations in geography and the layout of built-up areas required flexibility on the part of commanders.[109] Although British approaches to field fortification have drawn some criticism from historians, illustrations dating from late 1914 depict fully developed trench lines complete with wire entanglements and obstacles.[110] As later chapters will show, the BEF modified its defensive approach later in 1915, with ever greater emphasis on permanent fortifications arranged in depth.

Canada may not have been fully prepared to fight the Great War in 1914, but neither was any other country among the world's military powers. The Dominion's Permanent Force was only a few thousand strong, while the much larger Active Militia was unevenly trained. Notwithstanding these obvious deficiencies, Canada's first overseas contingent boasted excellent human capital and a substantial proportion of experienced soldiers. The men who set out for England in 1914 came of age in a society and culture that valued military prowess and soldierly qualities. They were eager to test themselves where it counted.[111]

Training is a subjective term requiring a clear frame of reference, especially in a military context. British Empire forces, including the Canadians, went to war in 1914 with codified training objectives and specialized courses for the different branches of service. All troops received the same basic instruction – physical fitness, musketry, extended order drill – while the specialists were to follow their own courses. Meanwhile, new lessons from the front were distilled into pamphlets and bulletins to be distributed across the British forces.

Many Canadians cheered the outbreak of war in August 1914, but with the contingent's arrival in England it was time get down to the business of training. The first test of endurance for the new Canadian Division came not on the battlefield, but on the flooded pastureland of Salisbury Plain.

2 Training for War:
The Salisbury Plain Camps

Vessels carrying the men of the 1st Canadian Infantry Brigade sailed into Plymouth Sound on 14 October 1914, among the first elements of the Canadian Expeditionary Force to land in England.[1] The chaos that had reigned supreme when the ships were loaded at Quebec City resumed very shortly as hundreds of soldiers poured down the gangplanks. The western Ontario men of the 1st Battalion were fortunate, as they had to wait only four days before disembarking from the *Laurantie* at the Devonport Dockyard. The troops of the 2nd Battalion, arriving on the *Cassandra*, were not so lucky. They sat on board until 25 October before unloading.[2] The 4th Battalion's experience upon disembarkation is probably typical of what other Canadian units witnessed during their first days in England. After completing a three-hour march to Bustard Camp on Salisbury Plain, the men of the 4th became disorganized in the middle of a night rainstorm as company officers attempted to locate their assigned areas and get the troops under shelter. No liaison had been arranged with the camp authorities, and the men wandered around in the dark for a couple of hours before it was determined that the battalion was short thirty-five tents; angry 4th Battalion officers accused the 1st and 3rd Battalions of 'helping themselves' to as many tents as they pleased.[3] It was an inauspicious introduction to the Salisbury Plain, where the officers and men of the 1st Division spent the next three months training for war.

The initial disarray of the Canadian contingent, coupled with poor weather throughout the autumn and winter months, has convinced historians that the Canadian training experience of 1914–15 was of little practical value.[4] There is much evidence to support such an interpretation. Complaints about weather, mud, illness, and other miscellaneous hindrances appear often in soldiers' accounts. As an anonymous 16th Battalion man observed, 'the ground is awful ... the mud, inches deep, of soft watery stuff, is awful too, in and all around the camp.'[5] Incessant rain and muck interrupted training schedules, and there were certainly Canadians who set out for the front in February 1915 feeling less than adequately prepared for combat. W.F. Graham, of the 2nd Battalion, recalled years later that 'we were very poorly trained. All we had was a lot of drill and a little bayonet practice and things like that.'[6] Of his arrival near Armentières, Private Harold Peat later wrote, 'if ever a bunch of greenhorns landed in France, frankly, we of First Contingent were that same bunch.[7]

As if to underscore the testimony of Graham and Peat, some commanders tended to cancel daily training at the first sign of rain. Most, however, continued to work themselves and their troops with stoic disregard for poor weather conditions. An officer serving with divisional headquarters later wrote that the mud of Salisbury Plain 'was not allowed to interfere with our training; from early morning until sunset we were kept busy.'[8] The muck was worse in some areas than others. Heavily travelled pathways within the tented camps boasted the deepest soup, but as a veteran of the 16th Battalion observed, the adjacent training fields had not been 'chewed up' quite so badly.[9] When the weather was especially uncooperative, indoor teaching replaced outdoor training. Brigadier-General M.S. Mercer recounted in his private diary that a British officer of the Northumberland Fusiliers provided musketry instruction to the troops on particularly stormy days.[10] As well, the sheer numbers of men stationed on the plain meant that variations in training existed from unit to unit. Sometimes there was just not enough space to perform an assigned task on given day, but a broad survey of the division's training experience in England reveals that most units followed the prescribed syllabi as closely as circumstances permitted.

Beyond inclement weather and shortfalls in training, Canadian disciplinary transgressions in England have supported the argument that the 1st Division was not the sharpest instrument of war in 1915. It seems that alcohol was a universal factor in Canadian misdeeds, but in contrast with training and weather-related controversies, it was contemporary prohibitionists rather than latter-day historians who suggested that boisterous conduct undermined the 1st Division's moral fortitude and combat capability. Minister of Militia Sam Hughes, a vocal temperance advocate, initially banned wet canteens at Valcartier and Salisbury. The minister's approach backfired when his boys landed in England; pubs and taverns were the first stops for many thirsty soldiers after the uncomfortable transatlantic voyage. While waiting to disembark, 200 restless gunners of the 2nd CFA Brigade were granted a few hours of shore leave. According to Captain Harry Crerar, 'it was mighty enjoyable, the few hours on terra firma. A number of men found it too extraordinarily so and with the aid of a thirst acquired from weeks of abstinence, hit the can pretty severely ... however, there was no harm in them and outside of the hard work of a few of us superintending their embarkation up the ladder, I didn't grudge them their spree.'[11] The results of such forays were not always quite as harmless as Crerar suggested. As historian Tim Cook has illustrated, reckless Canadian drinking nourished a bad reputation among the local populace.[12] Complaints soon found their way to Alderson, who promptly restricted leave passes into civilian areas and ordered his officers to read the relevant passages of the Army Act to their men. A Canadian private recorded in his diary that the 'adjutant read military crimes and penalties [to us]. Also orders from General [Alderson] that all passes stopped on account of drunks, etc, which is giving Canadians [a] bad reputation.'[13] Alderson's response was the correct one, but he was a wise enough leader to realize that he could not indefinitely prevent the troops from enjoying their alcohol. Consequently, the divisional commander scrapped Hughes's ill-advised ban, setting up wet canteens in the Canadian camps where soldiers could legally purchase beer and relax in isolation from the locals; it was not to be the last time that Alderson overruled Hughes. Canadian temperance groups were outraged, but Alderson's decision was popular with most soldiers. As Captain Crerar observed at the time, 'I am very much in favour of a beer canteen ... and so called temperance people like our Minister of Militia cause a lot of harm in forcing their hard, fast doctrine on the military. The lack of canteen simply tends to crime and deceit, for tell a man he can't have what years have taught him to regard as his right ... and he proceeds to get it, somehow ... wet and cold weather tends to make the men search comfort in the bottles and the weather we've been having almost excuses the archangel for excesses of that nature.'[14] Indeed, it has been shown that the daily rum ration issued to British Empire troops throughout the First World War was essential to strong morale. In this respect, moderated consumption of alcohol may actually have increased rather than reduced combat effectiveness.[15] The argument that intemperate Canadian soldiers would make poor fighters says more about the moral preoccupations of early twentieth-century temperance advocates than about the actual capabilities of the the 1st Division in 1915.

This chapter revisits the controversy surrounding the formative training of the 1st Canadian Division in England. In contrast to existing historical narratives, it argues that Canadian troops were actually relatively well prepared for war by the time that they crossed over to France in early 1915. The first part of this chapter examines an introductory syllabus issued by divisional headquarters for the week of 6–14 November 1914, before turning to a comprehensive syllabus covering the division's remaining time in England, from mid-November 1914 through to February 1915.

Early November was full of headaches and distractions for the commander and staff of the 1st Canadian Division. Equipment was disorganized. More than 30,000 men and 7,600 horses were restless and out of shape after the two-week Atlantic crossing and protracted disembarkation.[16] Although the Salisbury camps were spread out over a large area, there was a dearth of training space, since artillery and rifle ranges had to be shared with British units.[17] Supplies were also overstretched with the sudden influx of troops. Training schedules were interrupted for any number of reasons. King George V and Queen Mary visited the Salisbury Plain camps to inspect Canadian troops in early November. On another occasion, Canadian detachments were sent to London to participate in the Lord Mayor's parade.[18] Later in the month a very busy General Alderson and other senior officers attended a memorial service for Field Marshal Earl Roberts, a distinguished veteran commander of the Victorian period and the honorary colonel of the Canadian contingent; gunners of the Royal Canadian Horse Artillery fired a salute in Roberts's honour.[19] The divisional war diary records rain showers for approximately ten days in November, mostly in the first two weeks. Training cancellations did occur as a consequence, although several weeks of the month were mostly dry during the daylight hours.[20]

The Syllabus of 6–14 November

On 6 November divisional headquarters issued a tentative syllabus of recruit training to be followed by all troops for the next eight days. Mainly comprising basic skills that helped recondition the troops after two weeks aboard ship, the syllabus specified particular items for each arm of service.[21] By most accounts the preliminary syllabus was carefully followed. As instructed, the divisional cyclists pedalled for miles around the countryside, bringing the men back into shape.[22] The gunners of Lieutenant-Colonel E.W.B. Morrison's 1st CFA Brigade had their hands full caring for their horses after long hours of daily gun drill. There were also the finer arts of signalling, gun-laying, and fuze setting to master.[23] The other two artillery brigades completed similar work, although Lieutenant-Colonel J.J. Creelman bragged that his 2nd Brigade gunners were 'doing well, doing everything and doing it first.'[24] Major Andrew McNaughton, a battery commander in Creelman's brigade, delivered a series of innovative talks on infantry-artillery cooperation. The lectures were passed around throughout the division. Six years later McNaughton delivered them once again, virtually unchanged, at the Staff College at Camberley.[25] Meanwhile, the 600 men of the divisional ammunition column (DAC) learned to care for their 600 horses. Half of the battle was sorting out all of the driving harness and related accoutrements.[26]

Lieutenant-Colonel C.J. Armstrong's 1st Canadian Engineer Brigade was in high demand for work on buildings and infrastructure in and around the Salisbury Plain camps. Tasks ranged from surveying ground for new construction projects to road work and repair of existing buildings. Separate training exercises were conducted for mounted and dismounted engineers, according to the syllabus, but the men also benefited from the practical tasks regularly assigned on short notice.[27] Working in camp on different types of construction projects against deadlines required improvisation and creativity. Conditions in France and Belgium were not to be radically different, and the road maintenance performed by the engineering companies in rainy weather under heavy traffic prepared them for the challenges of front-line service. The engineers' already hectic schedule explains why Alderson's staff assigned them fewer training tasks on the first syllabus.

Lieutenant-Colonel W.A. Simson's Divisional Train was put to work the moment it arrived in England. All of the division's stores and equipment needed to be transported from Plymouth to Salisbury and then delivered to the appropriate users. Simson's transport wagons had been shipped across the Atlantic disassembled, so the first task was to round up all of the individual components and get the wagons rolling. At full strength, the train was supposed to be equipped with about 140 wagons, but as of 11 November, only seventy were on hand, and just forty-five of these were fully serviceable. With a shortage of transport, the train was busy all the time. Simson remarked that his men were working too hard to complain about inclement weather.[28]

The situation was similar among the three infantry brigades. Brigadier-General M.S. Mercer's men in the 1st Brigade covered all of the basic skills with minor variations among the battalions.[29] In Brigadier-General Arthur Currie's 2nd Brigade, the daily diary entries for Lieutenant-Colonel G.S. Tuxford's 5th Infantry Battalion are particularly illuminating because they list activities on an hourly basis (Appendix B). Although the 5th Battalion men enjoyed several abbreviated days during 6–14 November, they still managed to log a total of forty-five training hours, exceeding Alderson's thirty-six-hour syllabus.[30] A report from the 8th Battalion mentioned practice attacks, rear guard actions, extended order drill, night tactics, and a cross-country run. Although battalion attacks and rear guard actions were not called for in the syllabus, Lieutenant-Colonel Lipsett secured permission from his brigadier for the variations.[31] In Brigadier-General R.E.W. Turner's 3rd Brigade the 13th Battalion at first trained the hardest (Appendix C), but the others soon fell in line.[32]

The November-February Syllabus

On 14 November divisional headquarters issued the twelve-week syllabus of training for all arms in the division (Appendices D through H). During the next two months the syllabus was amended on a couple of occasions. The pace was accelerated, with additional training hours per day, while various subjects were added, including first-aid training, sanitation, cable laying, and other practical front-line tasks.[33] There was indeed much to be done in a short time.

Captain R.S. Robinson, in command of the cyclists, had seen men die in action on the dusty veldts in South Africa, and he was determined to prepare his troops for every conceivable hardship that they could face on the Western Front.[34] In late November the cyclists participated in a tactical scheme along with divisional cavalry troops and the 8th Battalion. Two days later, when the GOC Southern Command visited the Canadian Division, the cyclists were involved in a divisional drill for his benefit. Route marches on bicycles continued despite poor road conditions, and in early December the company engaged in yet another tactical exercise with cavalry and infantry. The purpose was to practise rear-guard defence for a retreating body of infantry. As the main force withdrew, the cyclists delayed 'enemy' infantry with small-arms fire and then successfully 'demolished' a bridge in a bid to prevent the enemy from crossing a stream. Additional route marches, some lasting two days, introduced the men to the challenges of navigation and resupply under inclement weather conditions over poor terrain. In between route marches and field exercises the men continued with routine training.[35] The specialized aspects of cyclist work focused on mobility, scouting, and the transmission of messages in battle scenarios. This preparation was to serve Robinson's company well in the semi-fluid operations of April 1915.

In common with the division's cyclists, its three brigades of field gunners found themselves fully occupied around the Salisbury camps. The field artillery brigades had initially been organized into three batteries, each equipped with six 18-pounder guns, but during November and December a fourth battery was added to each brigade, while the number of guns per battery was reduced from six to four.[36] Three depot batteries (two guns per battery), were formed and equipped with the surplus guns.[37] By some historical accounts the sudden reorganization constituted a major interruption, but evidence suggests that this was not entirely true.[38] Lieutenant-Colonel Creelman observed that the four-gun battery arrangement was more manoeuvrable than the six-gun version. He also appreciated the opportunity to 'cull' some personnel who may not have been performing up to standard.[39] Captain Harry Crerar, of the 8th Battery, recorded in his diary that he 'didn't think [the reorganization] will affect us adversely.'[40]

While the gun crews rehearsed their drills, horse team drivers learned to manage their four-legged friends. Battery officers, meanwhile, received lessons in map shooting, and were briefed on the outcome of tactical exercises attended by more senior officers. When a British brigadier visited on 14 November, the 1st and 3rd Batteries demonstrated their ability to manoeuvre the guns into action in covered positions.[41] Later that month the brigades participated in a tactical scheme as part of a full divisional demonstration attended by the GOC Southern Command.[42] Along with other divisional elements, the guns deployed for offensive action and then assumed a defensive position on the Avon River.[43] December's poor weather was harder on horses than men, but training continued. Captain Crerar summed things up just before the Canadians' first Christmas overseas; 'the rain and wind are always with us ... even in our tents. However, the training can't be stopped on that account so we carry on just the same, and in spite of wet clothes and wet feet, the men are wonderfully cheery.'[44] According to the diarist of the 2nd CFA Brigade the hardships of training in the scattered camps of Salisbury Plain fostered a high degree of proficiency in the handling of horses and guns by day or night with minimal noise and maximum speed.[45] Yet there were still other frustrations to contend with. Lieutenant-Colonel Creelman lamented the presence of officers' wives in the vicinity of the training area: 'The wives here are interfering considerably with their husbands' work. If I order out the Brigade at night without previous notice, mounted orderlies have to round up husbands in neighbouring villages and gather them together. Our training is being handicapped and I am told that it is worse with the infantry. These women should never have been allowed to leave Canada and in time they will become an annoying problem.'[46]

Conjugal visits notwithstanding, the gunners pressed on with their program. In anticipation of battle casualties, sections of drivers from the ammunition columns joined the batteries for gun drill. Visiting British officers shared the hard lessons of combat directly with the Canadian batteries.[47] Finally, at the year's end, officers from all three brigades attended a shoot in conjunction with observation aircraft. Pilots used heliographs and wireless sets to communicate with the gunners on the ground.[48] Lieutenant Hugh Dunlop, an ammunition column officer, recorded that the exercise lasted all day.[49]

The gunners absolutely depended on efficient support from Dunlop and his fellows in the divisional and brigade ammunition columns. Although the concept of supplying ammunition to combat units seems simple enough in theory, it was a complex and dangerous task in practice. Horses, wagons, and harnesses required constant attention. Wagon drivers learned on the job how to move heavy loads under appalling road conditions, a skill that was to pay off in the coming months. But hauling ammunition was only the first challenge; getting the correct type of ammunition – be it 18-pounder, heavy calibre, or small arms – to infantrymen and gunners at the right moment was even more important. As such, the art of battlefield communication was a crucial aspect of ammunition column training. Anticipating the difficulty of transmitting messages in combat scenarios, the columns experimented with different means of signalling, including visual techniques and messengers on horseback.[50] Beyond its function as a supply unit, the divisional ammunition column served as a reinforcement pool for the artillery batteries, not only for manpower, but also for horses and transport wagons. While the DAC cross-trained with the gun crews, officers attempted to match DAC horse harnesses with field artillery equipment, since the gunners' horses might need to be replaced on short notice in combat.[51] When Colonel Victor Williams, the Canadian Adjutant-General, returned from a front-line tour, a crowd of officers flocked to hear him speak about transport, supply, aircraft, entrenching, and concealment of artillery. According to a man who was present, Colonel Williams was bombarded with questions; his talk was 'just what we wanted.'[52]

Like the troops of the DAC, the 1st Canadian Engineer Brigade had few moments to spare, as the field companies were fully occupied with camp infrastructure projects. These tasks curtailed the engineers' formal training syllabus, but also offered practical experience, especially with road maintenance. Infantry reinforcements joined the engineers for heavy road work. This early liaison formed the basis of working party arrangements that were to continue on the Western Front. Other assignments such as telegraph wiring and light railway construction were also directly applicable to front-line service.[53] By early January 1915 the engineer companies resumed an abbreviated training course according to the *Manual of Field Engineering*. During the week that followed, the sappers completed eight-mile route marches, physical training, musketry, company attacks, extended order drills, bayonet fighting, visual training, outposts, patrols, and night work. Later in the month the companies moved on to entrenching, field fortifications, wire obstacle construction, and demolitions techniques. There was time to work with British engineers on specialized tasks such as the laying of pontoon bridges and demolitions.[54] The engineer brigade did not come close to completing the training program laid down in the divisional syllabus, but the men did learn to work as a team on challenging projects at short notice.

The 1st Canadian Divisional Signal Company, with a strength of approximately 200 men and fifty horses, set to work immediately upon its arrival in camp. Like the engineers, the signallers trained on the job. In addition to Permanent Force and Active Militia personnel, recruits for the signal company included employees of civilian telephone and telegraph companies.[55] Charles Maitland Sprague, of Belleville, Ontario, a telegraph operator and militiaman before the war, was destined to serve with the signal company from 1914 through 1918. Early in the war he noted that 'the Divisional operators are mostly all CPR [Canadian Pacific Railway] men.'[56] The injection of qualified telegraphists was especially welcome, as the pre-war Canadian Signal Corps consisted of visual signallers and telephone operators, but no telegraph operators.[57] A typical training day for signallers attached to infantry battalions included thirty minutes of physical training in the morning, two or three hours of visual signalling practice with heliographs before lunch, and then a few hours of practical schemes during the afternoon. This field work might be followed by a short lecture on map reading or dispatch riding before dinner, and then some further instruction after dark on night operations and Begbie lamps (tripod-mounted lights used to transmit visual signals).[58]

Lieutenant-Colonel Simson's 1st Canadian Divisional Train worked without rest during the stay in England. In late November Simson ensured that divisional units were provided with appropriate wagons. The contingent had been equipped with at least six different versions, and he was concerned that each branch of service receive a model appropriate for its daily transport requirements.[59] Ultimately the division received standard British General Service (GS) wagons. But since even the sturdiest wagons were useless without healthy horses, Simson regularly toured the Salisbury camps to ensure that the division's animals were in good shape. British supply officers with experience on the Western Front occasionally visited the divisional train to lecture on the delivery of supplies in operational zones.[60]

An early infantry training scheme in Mercer's 1st Brigade called for an attack against a fictitious divisional formation.[61] Subsequent scenarios revolved around the concept of blocking a mobile enemy force. Seven days of brigade-level exercises provided an opportunity for the battalions to meet pending attacks or block advancing formations, precisely what was to be demanded near Ypres in April 1915. In early January, for example, the 3rd Battalion 'defended a position on Bushall Down against 1st, 2nd and 4th Battalions.'[62] Such schemes were not simply invented and executed by battalion officers without consulting higher headquarters. On the contrary, a divisional order dictated that copies of battalion and brigade exercises 'will be submitted to headquarters at least 48 hours before the time set for the commencement of schemes.'[63] During the course of tactical training, the men's physical stamina and soldierly attitude were growing stronger. With blatant disregard for punctuation, Private Frank Betts of the 4th Battalion described his trek back to camp upon returning from his 1914 Christmas leave in Nottingham: 'I got to Salisbury ½ past two am. And had to walk eighteen miles to camp slept by a haystack for an hour then proceeded on my way you say it is bad we have hardships don't let that worry you because it is a mere trifle. When I can go 40 hours without sleep and walk the distance of eighteen miles and nothing to eat you can see by that I am as tough as pig iron. I did not feel so bad afterwards.[64] After the war, a veteran of the 2nd Battalion recalled that the demanding training of the Salisbury camps 'weeded out' the weak, and 'the rest of us were tough as nails. Training was strict and hard, we never lost any time. Didn't matter what the weather was, you went out in it.'[65]

The 2nd Brigade's training regimen resembled that of the 1st Brigade's.[66] The meticulously detailed diary of G.S. Tuxford's 5th Battalion, which accounts for activities on an hourly basis, shows what sort of work was possible under the inhospitable weather of Salisbury Plain. Throughout the second half of November the battalion engaged in standard basic training. Practice attacks, probably at the company level, were conducted after the troops had been lectured in offensive techniques. At the end of November the battalion participated in full-scale divisional exercises.[67] Tuxford's troops, along with the other battalions, learned to attack under artillery and small-arms fire.[68] According to one scenario, the 8th Battalion launched a night attack against an 'enemy' force, but was repelled by unexpected reinforcements.[69] A few days later the troops were involved in battalion-level defence and retirement schemes. Similar offensive and defensive manoeuvres continued in early December, such as the following: '[2 December] Billeting scheme in, and defence of, Shrewton. Occupation of an outpost position by night and resistance of a night attack. Three companies [were] attacking the battalion. Weather showery, heavy rain and windstorm in the evening and at night. [3 December] Battalion training. Advance and attack on a position held by a skeleton enemy. In the afternoon company training in musketry. Weather fine.'[70]

A week later two companies from the 8th Battalion served as the enemy force in a defensive exercise staged for the division's mounted troops.[71] As in the 1st Brigade, bad weather did not always save the troops from exercises. According to Sergeant William Alldritt, a machine-gunner in the 8th Battalion, this 'morning we had company parade and fire control. I had No. 3 section for a while. During the afternoon the Sgt. Major had the Battalion and we spent a very profitable time. It rained a little and it rained a lot during the night.'[72] Alldritt spent much of January training with his machine-gun detachment, making 'the most of the 3 weeks at our disposal.'[73] Although the 5th Battalion was placed in quarantine after Christmas – probably because of a meningitis outbreak – strenuous activities continued, including eight-mile route marches. It appears that the quarantine was not quite obeyed according to the letter of the law. There was a war to fight after all.[74]

The training activities of Brigadier-General Turner's 3rd Brigade warrant special attention, given the controversial performances of Turner and some of his subordinates at Second Ypres in April 1915. Turner, unfortunately, was absent during a portion of the brigade's formative training period. While returning to brigade headquarters from a musketry course for senior officers in mid-December he broke his collarbone in a motor vehicle accident and did not resume command until 13 January.[75] The impact of Turner's convalescence on infantry training at the battalion level was probably negligible, but it would have been a setback at brigade headquarters, limiting chances for the brigadier to get acquainted with his staff. As for the battalions, it appears that their training more or less reflected what was achieved in the other two infantry brigades, although there is less evidence of brigade-level training.

Eyewitness accounts suggest that battalion officers in the 3rd Brigade conducted exercises in a serious manner, often supplementing long route marches with surprise tactical schemes at some unexpected moment along the way.[76] The 13th Battalion trained aggressively at the company and battalion levels, putting in ten-hour work days.[77] In comparison, the 14th Battalion fell short of expectations during the first weeks in England, but improved by early December, despite the temporary loss of its commander, Lieutenant-Colonel Frank Meighen, who was seconded to fill in for Turner during the brigadier's convalescence following the automobile crash.[78] Throughout January, a series of lectures delivered by visiting British officers complemented field training. The highly anticipated *Notes from the Front* were also regular features of indoor classes.[79]

Under the command of Lieutenant-Colonel J.A. Currie, the 15th Battalion was destined for the worst tragedy of any Canadian unit at Second Ypres. It seems that this was not a consequence of poor training, as there is every indication that the ill-fated battalion worked as hard as the others.[80] As for the poor weather, Lieutenant-Colonel Currie claimed that just as the English farmers on Salisbury Plain worked their fields with stoic disregard for the wet and cold, his soldiers trained in rain or sunshine.[81]

In his 1932 history of the 16th Battalion, H.M. Urquhart criticized the training habits of his former unit, but admitted that the tactical exercises 'must have been a great help to the 16th Battalion on the night of

22 April 1915' – the evening when the Germans attacked the Ypres Salient with chlorine gas.[82] Within the battalion there was a degree of friction between young citizen-volunteers and older professional soldiers. Just before Christmas a board of officers assembled at Lieutenant-Colonel Leckie's headquarters to investigate and report on the 'duties, qualification, and attitude of the Regimental Sergt. Major in regard to the efficiency of the Battalion.' The board determined that while the senior non-commissioned officer of the battalion was a very knowledgeable and capable instructor, he was failing to cultivate self-respect and personal pride among his subordinates, who very much required the guidance of an experienced regimental sergeant-major (RSM). The zealous RSM was encouraged to adopt a 'more sympathetic attitude' towards his men as they confronted the challenges of training.[83] Aside from this episode, there is relatively little evidence of discord within units, suggesting that positive cohesion was developing within the division. The infantry battalions' regional basis facilitated good relations. Many of the men were already acquainted from pre-war militia camps or other community circles.

In common with the gunners, signallers, engineers, and other troops attached to the division, specialist personnel received separate training in their particular trades. In addition to ordinary infantry skills, a week-long syllabus for the men of Lieutenant E.D. Bellew's 7th Battalion Machine-Gun Section included reconnaissance, semaphore, fields of fire, wagon drill, technical lectures, defence in close country, and other specialized activities.[84] Other battalion machine-gun sections followed similar training schemes during December. It was precisely these skills that would be put to use during the coming operations of 1915, earning Victoria Crosses for two Canadian machine gunners at Second Ypres.[85] Later in January machine-gun training was adjusted to reflect the changeover from two- to four-gun sections.[86]

Combat Leadership Training

Shortly after the November-February syllabus was prepared by General Alderson's staff, the War Office directed that officers and non-commissioned officers must participate in staff rides and tactical exercises without troops (TEWTs) as part of their training.[87] The objective was to give participants 'instruction and practice in carrying out the duties that might fall to them in war,' stressing the importance of being able to develop workable operational and administrative plans at short notice.[88] According to *Training and Manouevre Regulations*, the 'force' under command of TEWT participants must always be imagined as one component of a larger all-arms formation: 'the action of all arms, and of the administrative services, and the relation of the small force towards the larger force of which it forms a part, must be kept in view at all times throughout the course of the regimental exercise.'[89] In mid-November senior Canadian officers participated in an eight-hour tactical exercise in which they responded to an attack at the divisional level. A fictitious operation order included instructions for each branch of service. Infantry commanders were required to write up marching orders and schemes of defence, including 'details of trenches for firing line, supports, reserves and for connecting trenches, and latrines.' Similarly, artillery commanders were instructed to lay out their batteries, 'with details of trenches and pits' and provide marching orders and logistical arrangements.[90] Participants later shared the lessons of these exercises with junior ranks.[91]

Staff rides and tactical exercises were not limited to senior ranks. As stipulated in *Training and Manoeuvre Regulations*, leaders at all levels of command learned to solve problems while working in small syndicates on the ground or at the map table. On 3 December, for example, the headquarters staff and company officers of the 5th, 8th, and 10th Canadian Battalions participated in a staff ride with their Brigade Major, Lieutenant-Colonel H. Kemmis-Betty. The tactical scenario involved the deployment of the 5th Battalion as an advance guard in an attack against an enemy supply depot. Officers were asked on the spot how they would deploy the battalion and were later required to submit a map showing the battalion's dispositions. In December officers of the 2nd and 3rd Brigades worked through several staff rides and exercises.[92] Battalion war diaries indicate that officers from across the division were involved in a number of additional independent staff rides throughout the training period in England.[93]

Army Schools and Courses

While much of the individual soldier's training was carried out at the unit level during the early months of the First World War, courses and schools were already teaching specialized skills before the end of 1914.[94] The impact of training schools on combat performance is admittedly difficult to measure. Siegfried Sassoon dismissed the 'School' as a haven for 'blank-cartridge skirmishing in a land of field day make-believe,' suggesting that the whole affair was really only a holiday for officers and men who 'needed a rest' from active service.[95] The literary evidence cannot be dismissed, but neither should Sassoon be allowed the final word on army schools. As historian Paddy Griffith has argued, schools and courses did not serve merely as rest depots or convenient dumping grounds for unwanted personnel. Although the schools varied in quality, Griffith characterized them as 'universities of higher tactics,' where officers and soldiers could go to develop their technical and tactical skills.[96] Although other historians have argued that the British army was resistant to innovations in training, tactics, and technique, careful scrutiny of the first months of the war suggests otherwise.[97] Basic lessons were shared through pamphlets and *Notes from the Front*, while training schools offered formal settings for instruction in new skills.

The schools and courses of 1914–15 were perhaps not as plentiful or well organized as in the later war years, but officers and men of the 1st Canadian Division attended them on a regular basis, bringing new knowledge back to their parent formations. In December 1914, Major Raymond Brutinel's Motor Machine-Gun Brigade convened a course on the Colt machine gun. Divisional orders instructed each battalion commander to choose one officer and one non-commissioned officer to attend Brutinel's course; when the students returned they served as machine-gun instructors for their respective battalions.[98] A provisional school for qualifying lieutenants and captains was also held in December at 3rd Brigade headquarters to ensure that junior infantry officers were functioning at a common level of proficiency. While the junior officers were tested, the division's senior infantry officers attended a musketry course at Hayling Island.[99] In early January a representative sampling of junior officers and non-commissioned officers from across the division attended the same course. The objective was not to teach basic shooting to raw recruits, but rather to ensure that experienced instructors were distributed evenly throughout the division. The requirement is reflected in divisional orders, which dictated that no man below the rank of sergeant would attend the Hayling course, and all students were to have pre-war military experience.[100]

Within three months of the outbreak of war the Dominion of Canada mobilized, equipped, and transported a full divisional contingent to England. For the next three months the Canadians were shaped into an active infantry division. Circumstances in the Salisbury Plain camps were far from ideal. Heavy wind carried tents away, and the men worked, trained, and slept in perpetually soaked wool uniforms, although the chilling temperatures, rain, and flooding were not dissimilar to normal service conditions in France and Flanders.[101] There is no question that poor weather, fatigue duties, and other distractions interrupted formal schedules on Salisbury Plain, but training did not cease. Determined officers like G.S. Tuxfurd, R.S. Robinson, and J.J. Penhale worked their troops with studied disregard for mud and rain. Some of the divisional units, such as the engineers and signallers, simply learned on the job in good or bad weather. Leaders at all levels from platoon up to division participated in combined-arms exercises with and without troops, and the training syllabi issued by divisional headquarters were predicated on the most up-to-date literature available. This weight of evidence indicates that the Salisbury training cannot be written off as inconsequential. And the preparatory cycle was not yet complete. For the next several weeks the division was committed to introductory tours of duty on the front lines of northern France and Belgian Flanders. The German enemy was now to become yet another variable in the complex training equation.

3 Across the Channel: Apprenticing for War

The training of the 1st Canadian Division did not cease when the troops crossed the English Channel in February 1915. Having learned the basics on Salisbury Plain, the eager Canadians passed into the custody of two British regular divisions for a gradual introduction to combat service in the vicinity of Armentières, near the Franco-Belgian border (see fig. 3.1). Some Canadian troops first entered the firing lines on French soil while others found themselves on the Belgian side of the border, in Ploegsteert Wood. This sector was reputed to be relatively quiet, but as the troops soon learned, it was by no means an inactive front.

The division suffered its first dead near Armentières. Their graves can still be visited today in the dim shade of lonesome clearings under the dense canopy of Ploegsteert Wood. While the number of men killed or wounded during routine trench duties ('daily wastage') was limited, most units lost a few people. Casualty levels increased slightly in March when the Canadians assumed responsibility for their own portion of the front line around Fleurbaix, a few miles south of Armentières (fig. 3.2). Losses then peaked in the middle of the month as British forces on the Canadians' right flank pressed an attack towards Neuve Chapelle and Aubers Ridge. The Canadian infantry were not called upon to deliver any direct assaults of their own. Instead, they supported the attack from their trenches, while the divisional artillery fired on the German lines opposite the Canadian front to divert the enemy's attention from the principal British thrust. The division spent the rest of March on trench duty in the Fleurbaix sector before moving west to Estaires for additional training and reorganization.

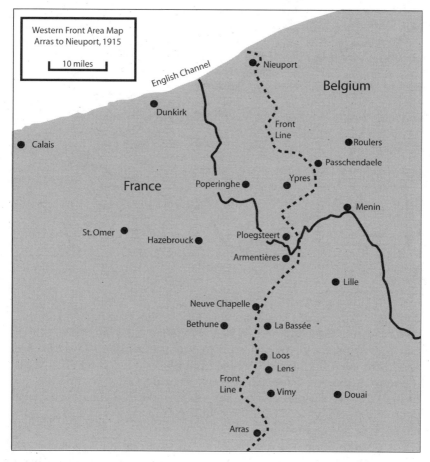

Figure 3.1

Orientation

Beginning in mid-February, the 1st Canadian Division was attached to the 4th and 6th British Divisions (III Corps, Second British Army) for trench orientation.[1] From 17 through 23 February (Period A), the 1st Canadian Infantry Brigade, 1st Canadian Field Artillery (CFA) Brigade, 1st Field Company, a section of signallers, and No. 2 Divisional Train Company were assigned to the 6th Division. From 21 through 28 February (Period B), the 2nd Canadian Infantry Brigade, 2nd CFA Brigade,

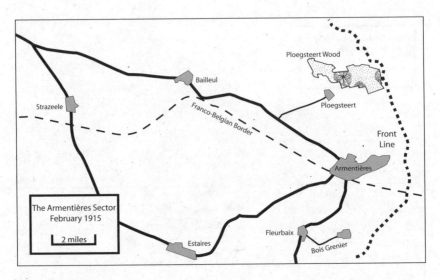

Figure 3.2

2nd Field Company, a signal section, No. 3 Divisional Train Company, battery staff of the 1st Canadian Heavy Battery, and a number of officers and men from the divisional cyclist company ventured into the front lines with the 4th Division. Finally, from 23 February through 2 March (Period C), the 3rd Canadian Infantry Brigade, 3rd CFA Brigade, 3rd Field Company, a signal section, a group from the divisional cyclist company, and possibly No. 4 Divisional Train Company were attached to the 6th Division for instruction.

Each of the three brigade groupings was paired with its respective British division according to a standard pattern. The Canadian brigade headquarters and signal unit were attached to a corresponding British infantry brigade. Likewise, each of the three infantry battalions in a Canadian brigade was dispersed throughout a British infantry brigade, while each Canadian Field Artillery brigade was attached to a Royal Field Artillery counterpart. The Canadian Engineer companies partook in the work of any number of the Royal Engineer field companies in the division to which they were attached. Additionally, a number of Canadian staff officers joined British divisional headquarters for periods of four to six days.[2]

As had been the practice in England, the various arms and units of the division were assigned particular training objectives during their tours in the lines with the British. Engineers, signallers, cyclists, and other specialists worked directly on actual field tasks. In the Canadian artillery brigades all commanding officers, adjutants, battery commanders, forward observation officers, and a proportion of non-commissioned officers took their turns with their British counterparts to observe 'exactly how things' were done. This included learning how gun emplacements should be prepared and concealed from air and ground observation.[3]

Instruction for infantrymen fell under two categories: practical work in the trenches and training behind the lines. While rotating through the trenches each Canadian soldier was paired individually with a 'well trained regular soldier who was to teach him everything he knew under the supervision of the platoon sergeant.'[4] Likewise, all Canadian section, platoon, and company commanders were matched with British counterparts. It was a far better arrangement than some later Canadian arrivals on the Western Front were to enjoy.

Once the initial orientation phase was complete, Canadian platoons rotated through the trenches under their own officers, who were in turn supervised by British captains. Canadian company commanders, meanwhile, observed how British officers managed the Canadian platoons. After the front-line rotations, Canadian infantrymen were instructed behind the lines in 'all subjects of trench warfare,' including trench and obstacle construction, sanitation, drainage, and field hygiene. Meanwhile, Canadian infantry battalion commanders worked closely with British battalion commanders to get familiar with the daily operational and administrative details of command in a combat zone.[5]

A survey of unit-level war diaries for Periods A, B, and C reveals a range of experiences dependent on local circumstance. The divisional cyclists, for instance, served as advance guards for other units moving towards the front, furnished fatigue parties, and provided immediate protection for headquarters units.[6] The signallers, meanwhile, went directly to work laying and repairing telephone lines.[7] While attached to British field and fortress engineer companies the Canadian engineers tackled obstacle construction and breastworks.[8] Transport companies of the divisional train carried out their regular logistical duties while attached to brigade groups in the trenches and rear areas.[9]

Retracing the activities of the division's three artillery brigades and their batteries for the later part of February is complicated by the piecemeal manner in which they were deployed with British artillery units. During rear-area stints, the batteries worked on fuze setting, entrenching, and concealment.[10] Canadians observed the guns in action, learning from experienced gunners on the job. The 1st CFA Brigade ventured into the front lines on 17 February and was attached to the 2nd, 12th, 24th, and 38th Royal Field Artillery Brigades. Under this arrangement Canadian forward observation officers assumed their posts in the firing trenches under British supervision. The importance of effectively camouflaged positions was reinforced when German aircraft bombed near an emplacement as Canadians visited.[11] A 2nd CFA Brigade war diary entry typifies the gunners' experience in the lines:

> A.M. Officers attached to different batteries were taken to Observing Stations to observe fire which however was not possible owing to fog. Other ranks were attached to the men doing the same duties and learning all possible from the experienced soldiers.
> P.M. Inspected Batteries and found their cover most excellent from view of aeroplanes. Learned many helpful hints.
> About noon howitzer opened fire on enemy's trenches firing 20 rounds.[12]

When the fog lifted, awestruck Canadians watched as heavy howitzers destroyed a recently discovered German gun position.[13]

Upon returning to rear areas, Canadian officers shared their experiences with the other ranks who, because of their larger numbers, were unable to reach the forward positions. It was an imperfect arrangement, but one that seemed to work well enough. After a lieutenant of the 3rd CFA Brigade lectured his gunners on concealment of emplacements, the men soon showed 'considerable adaptability' in disguising gun positions.[14] Gunners and drivers of the ammunition column were also incorporated into the orientation process. Besides keeping 'a sharp look out for spies,' the DAC men practised hitching and unhitching horses and loading wagons at a quick pace in preparation for operational scenarios. Officers of the column reported to the 4th British Division on 22 February for a week's worth of special courses on the supply of ammunition in the field.[15] The Canadians were keen to attend, since most of the British lecturers had already seen action on the Western Front.[16]

Every infantry soldier in the division had an opportunity to visit the front lines and work with a British 'buddy' before regrouping into his own platoon for a stint in the trenches. The companies of the 1st Canadian Battalion mixed with a selection of British regiments, including the 1st Leicesters, the 2nd York and Lancasters, and the 1st Buffs (East

Kent Regiment). Private George Bell recorded his first impressions of the front lines: 'We found many things unlike what we expected. Trenches were scarcely trenches at all, merely parapets made by piling sandbags of earth on top of each other, about six bags thick at the bottom and three at the top. But as we filled fresh bags we kept lowering the level of the trench floor and thus bettered our protection. Some built dugouts by putting bags of earth on corrugated iron, giving fairly good security against fragments of shrapnel.'[17] The troops needed all of the protection they could get; two companies of the 2nd Battalion found themselves digging in under enemy fire soon after arriving at the front for the first time.[18] Behind the trench lines an officer from the 16th Brigade provided grenade training while the 12th Field Company, Royal Engineers, demonstrated the latest defensive techniques.[19] According to the 1/16th London Regiment (15th Brigade/6th Division), the Canadian Ross rifle left much to be desired, but the men of the 1st Brigade were 'highly adaptable to the conditions of trench life' and displayed excellent discipline.[20]

Battalions of the 2nd Brigade recorded fewer details of their rotations through the lines during Period B. The records of the 5th Battalion mention only routine training in the line with British regiments. The 7th Battalion's diary is just as vague, although it lists casualties three days in a row in Ploegsteert Wood. A private of the 8th Battalion was wounded in an attempt to rescue an injured British soldier of the Somerset Light Infantry.[21] It was fortunate that additional losses were avoided. As one of the Canadian sergeants recorded in his personal diary, 'the Germans are watching our lines very closely and we have to keep down very low.'[22] The men of the 10th Battalion came under shellfire for the first time on 22 February while they were digging trenches in the front line. There were also plenty of opportunities to lob grenades over the parapet.[23] Reflecting on his initial experiences in the line during Period B, a private of the 2nd Brigade recalled that 'nothing could surpass the patience of' his British teachers 'or their brotherly kindness to us as comrades in arms.'[24]

In the 3rd Brigade, the 13th Battalion learned its first lesson even before reaching the front line area: marching long distances over rough cobblestone roads was hard on the ankles. The battalion reached the forward area on 24 February (Period C) with the 16th Brigade.[25] A Canadian non-commissioned officer recorded his impressions of the experience:

We went in first with the Leicesters. We had a good place to enter the line, most of the way being protected by breastworks. When we got in I stuck my head over to see the enemy's trenches and I certainly ducked again pretty quickly – they seemed right on top of us and were really only 60 yards away … that same night we went to other trenches, this time to those occupied by the York and Lancs. We had a harder time getting in, as the communication trench was filled with water and we had to keep in the open. There was a full moon shining and the Germans spotted us and gave us a regular hail of bullets.[26]

The 13th Battalion's regimental historian later wrote of what the men learned during the introductory tours: how to post sentries, screen cooking fires, dole out rations and rum, keep clean, and 'scores of other things that are vital when men gather in opposing ditches to do one another death.' Notwithstanding this new knowledge, at least one member of the battalion was under no illusions about the difficulty of what lay ahead on the Western Front, as he remarked in a letter home that 'both sides are very strongly entrenched and an attempt to make an unassisted infantry attack would be suicide.'[27]

Like their counterparts in the 13th Battalion, the men of the 14th Battalion cursed the pavé roads as they marched to Armentières. Once in the line several French-speaking soldiers of the battalion volunteered for a patrol into no man's land with troops of the Rifle Brigade. British officers praised the Canadians for their conduct. The 15th Battalion received its first taste of heavy artillery fire on the night of 24 February, and the soldiers of the 16th Battalion were treated to high-explosive shelling in their billets before they set out for the front lines.[28] The 3rd Brigade newcomers duly impressed their British instructors from the 16th Brigade. The war diarist for the 1/16th London Regiment recorded that the 15th Battalion officers had 'a good hold of their men and the discipline appeared good. The men quickly grasped the work and all ranks took a very keen interest and showed great anxiety to learn all they could.'[29]

Cold rain may have interrupted training activities in England, but the front lines in France needed to be manned, maintained, and supplied with brave disregard for the weather. Men had already been killed, injured, or incapacitated in England by training accidents and illness, but they had never been shot at or bombarded. At the front careless mistakes were immediately answered by the enemy, even in relatively 'quiet' areas. Death or injury could strike at any moment in the combat zone or behind the lines. The 1st Battalion lost its first casualty within hours of disembarking at St Nazaire when a private slipped under a train and died after having an arm and leg severed. While the divisional cyclist company was building up breastworks near Bac St Maur a private was wounded in the stomach by an enemy sniper. An engineer lieutenant from the 2nd Field Company was killed by a bullet through the forehead as his section constructed a listening post. Eleven Canadian soldiers were wounded, one of them fatally, as they reconnoitered a hill in Ploegsteert Wood in search of suitable positions for new gun emplacements. Private F. Ferland, a 15th Battalion soldier and veteran of the United States Navy, was killed on 27 February. The 7th Battalion lost two of its youngest members, Lieutenant B. Boggs and Private A.E. Clapp, during its initial orientation tours through the front line in Ploegsteert Wood. Although this was supposed to have been a calm sector, the battalion's historian wrote after the war that the loss of Boggs and Clapp reminded 'us that we were at war in earnest.'[30] These are just a few examples of the tragedies that struck randomly in each company, battery, battalion, and brigade during the second half of February 1915. As a Canadian battalion commander noted, 'death was sailing about in the air everywhere.'[31] News circulated quickly throughout the division, and by early March – well before the Canadians reached Ypres – it was probable that most soldiers had heard of someone who was injured or killed by enemy action. These most difficult of lessons reminded the men that they were playing for keeps in a deadly game. Despite such tragedies, Captain Harry Crerar was confident enough to note that 'we are ready any minute of any day, to get going and I'm sure the Canadian Division will do as well as the rest of them for they have the right spirit, the Canadians, and their training by this time is pretty well completed to the standard of Imperial troops.'[32]

Into the Line

As of early March all elements of the 1st Canadian Division had completed their introductory rotations through the trenches. The division assumed responsibility for defending 6,400 yards of frontage near Fleurbaix, about three miles southwest of Armentières. Another week passed before Canadian troops were involved in any major action, but the realities of trench warfare were immediate, as they had been near Armentières. Captain R.S. Robinson, in command of the divisional cyclists, noted in a letter to his wife that his men were not safe even while they rested behind the lines, as 'one platoon was shelled out of their barn, another section had a shell explode in the adjoining room in their billet, while another shell came through the kitchen roof.'[33] During the first week of March the cyclists patrolled the immediate rear area, conducting traffic control and protecting headquarters.[34] Rear security was a vital duty, particularly because local residents were permitted to move about behind the lines relatively freely. As an 8th Battalion soldier observed in a letter home, farmers were sowing crops within a mile of the front.[35] Local civilians, intentionally or not, were damaging Canadian telephone networks, although some officers suspected that wire cutting was the work of 'nefarious' German agents disguised as farmers.[36] Such rumours were almost universally unconfirmed, but frequent mention of possible espionage and undercover operatives underscored a general sense of insecurity experienced by the men in their new environment. As with all soldiers, rumours accompanied the Canadians throughout their wartime journey.[37]

One way to reduce the chance of death or injury was to strengthen fortifications. To this end the engineer companies went to work in the front lines around Fleurbaix at night in an effort to improve overhead cover, build dugouts, and join isolated firing positions with communication trenches.[38] On 9 March the engineers prepared pontoon bridging materials in anticipation of the Neuve Chapelle-Aubers Ridge offensive.

While the engineers built new defences, the signal company ensured that effective communication was possible within the division as well as with neighbouring formations. This required the regular inspection of telegraph and telephone lines and the installation of a more sophisticated switchboard. Major Lister monitored the communications procedures exercised by brigade signals personnel, implementing improvements as necessary.[39]

The 1st CFA Brigade set up headquarters just southeast of Fleurbaix. Three batteries registered targets in the enemy lines the next day, drawing counterbattery fire against forward observation posts in the process. The 3rd Battery responded to enemy snipers by shelling their hiding places. A few days later the brigade located enemy gun emplacements by observing muzzle flashes, and returned fire, silencing the German artillery. The 2nd CFA Brigade fired against similar targets, based on information received from forward observation officers. In circumstances where enemy artillery fire originated from an unknown location, the 2nd Brigade's guns responded with 'searching' fire.[40] The 3rd Brigade's forward observers located plenty of targets for the gunners. When the 11th Battery fired six rounds at a house where enemy soldiers were seen to be gathering, observers noted that the

Germans 'displaced at the double.' Meanwhile, the 10th Battery 'set fire to something in rear of [the] trenches' after dropping a dozen rounds on the German front line.[41]

As the 18-pounders of the field brigades banged away at the enemy, the 1st Heavy Battery's 60-pounders were set up in two positions, with hedges and screens providing all around cover and flash concealment. Up until the Neuve Chapelle–Aubers Ridge operation, the Heavy Battery concentrated its scarce ammunition against larger buildings and potential observation points, such as church towers.[42]

Gunners and soldiers watched the artillery duels with great anticipation, but much of the heavy lifting was left to the men in the ammunition columns who guided their horse teams and wagons through crowded roads behind the lines. The DAC distributed artillery shells, field gun spares, as well as .303 and .45 calibre small-arms ammunition (the latter being for officers' Colt pistols) to the respective artillery brigade ammunition columns, which in turn delivered material to their own organizations. Supplies were scarce. In early March, DAC counted 5,500 rounds of 18-pounder shrapnel rounds, but no high explosive; just eighty shells were on hand in the column's dump for the 60-pounders. No high-explosive shells were forthcoming, probably because all available stocks were reserved for the guns shooting in direct support of the British attack further south against Neuve Chapelle.[43] The Canadians would simply have to make do with this shoestring ammunition budget.

The 1st Canadian Divisional Train, like the DAC, was occupied with practical concerns as the division assumed responsibility for its own portion of the front line. Lieutenant-Colonel Simson ordered that wagons should be modified to roll as quietly as possible, since ration parties had frequently been shelled during the night when the sound of their vehicles reached the ears of German gunners. The challenges of transporting material efficiently along the heavily travelled but narrow roads of the Fleurbaix sector were immediately apparent. Undaunted, Simson modified the system by making necessary arrangements with superiors and subordinates, noting that the train's operations at refilling points were 'improving very much, but can improve more.' During the next few days Simson's companies engaged in an effort to reduce time spent at refilling areas, which tended to attract enemy gunfire.[44]

The battalions of the 1st Brigade began occupying trenches around Fleurbaix on 1 March. Lieutenant-Colonel F.W. Hill's 1st Battalion suffered casualties from German artillery prior to reaching the front, and more men were killed or injured by gunfire and sniping during the next few days. In his postwar memoir Private George Bell explained that sniping casualties resulted inevitably from the nature of the terrain and the orientation of the trench lines in this sector: 'This was considered to be a quiet sector, but quiet, we learned was a relative term. Fritz had some fine marksmen and he was always ready to break the monotony of trench life. Our trenches zig-zagged along, following the natural contour of the ground. In the parados in the rear of the trench, were small gaps through which men could pass to the tiny latrine immediately in the rear.'[45] Due to the curvature of the trenches, German snipers were able to shoot through the latrine exits from *behind* the Canadian lines at particular spots. After suffering two such casualties, a resourceful officer in the 1st Battalion blocked the gaps. Experiences were similar in the other battalions. The 3rd Battalion lost two men in a hurricane of shrapnel fire. Artillery forward observers were especially vulnerable to retaliation, as they often worked in buildings or steeples. Accidents happened too. A corporal was seriously wounded by a bayonet thrust when he attempted to cross from one company area into another without providing a password.[46] The margin for error was extremely narrow on the Western Front.

In the 2nd Brigade soldiers discovered that sniping was heavy during the twilight hours. Lieutenant-Colonel G.S. Tuxford's 5th Battalion men attempted to improve cover along the trenches, but were limited by a shortage of building materials; there was rarely enough to do a proper job. The sniper fire continued. In one unlucky instance, two 8th Battalion men were wounded in the legs by a single bullet.[47] A sergeant summed up the difficulties quite succinctly in a brief diary entry: 'Germans [are] 400 yards away and they are good shots.'[48] Duty in the rear areas did not guarantee safety. The 10th Battalion lost men to shellfire after returning to billets from the trenches.[49] The Canadians endured a good deal of harassment from their more experienced enemy, but they were not about to surrender the initiative. At night small patrols from the 2nd Brigade braved the hazards of no man's land, creeping towards the German lines in search of intelligence and perhaps a prisoner or two.

Prior to entering the trenches opposite Fromelles, the officers of the 3rd Brigade listened to an address by Lieutenant-General Henry Rawlinson, then in command of IV Corps. Rawlinson reminded the Dominion soldiers that they were about to face 'a cunning, cruel, and unscrupulous enemy. If you make a mistake, you will not get the chance to make a second one.'[50] The gravity of Rawlinson's caveat was reinforced the next day when a German sniper claimed the life of a 14th Battalion soldier not long after the unit arrived in the front line near the Rue Petillon. A few days later, Lieutenant-Colonel Meighen's battalion was relieved by Lieutenant-Colonel J.A. Currie's 15th Battalion. The relief took three hours – 'far too long' according to Meighen. Smooth reliefs were almost always challenging and dangerous affairs, since the simultaneous crowding of incoming and outgoing troops in the trenches during a change of garrison presented enemy artillery with an especially rich target. Prior to entering the line Lieutenant-Colonel Currie implored his men to take the greatest care while moving about the trenches or participating in working parties. The troops were warned not to display reckless 'bravado,' but instead to go silently about their work, maintaining the initiative by firing at enemy sniping and machine-gun positions. A few lives were spared by chance. Approximately half of all German shells impacting the battalion area failed to explode.[51]

The 15th Battalion war diary records a series of 'lessons' based on early trench rotations. Because the 15th was a highland battalion, the men wore colourful checked glengarry caps as part of their uniform. Tours in the front trenches revealed that this distinctive headgear attracted unwelcome attention from enemy snipers. As a consequence, Lieutenant-Colonel Currie ordered that only khaki tam o'shanters (another type of Scottish headdress) were to be worn in the line. A second lesson suggested that sentries should be posted in pairs during the night; the extra man would ensure that his partner was keeping an alert watch along the parapet. Currie also observed that working parties should operate only by night in order to minimize the risks posed by snipers; the men could rest during the day and remain out of sight at the same time. Finally, it was noted that cases of frostbitten or 'cobbled' feet could be prevented by removing boots, changing socks, and massaging the feet at least once each day.[52] Within a short time, soldiers of the 15th Battalion came to understand the essentials of front-line duty.

Perhaps no Canadian outfit suffered as much misfortune that March as did the 16th Battalion. A sergeant from B Company was wounded in the chest early one afternoon, but not evacuated until after dark, possibly because stretcher bearers could not safely reach him during daylight. In the days that followed several men were mortally wounded, but even death seemed to bring no peace. The burial service for one of the men was harassed by small-arms fire, despite its location behind the lines. While inexperience might account for these casualties, local geography was a more likely culprit; the Germans enjoyed good vantage points in the sector. The 13th Battalion war diary reported no casualties or sniping after relieving the 16th Battalion on the evening of 6 March, but a visit to the Rue Petillon Military Cemetery reveals the graves of 13th Battalion men who were killed on 7 March.[53]

The frequency of sniping casualties sustained by the 1st Canadian Division during its early March trench tours raises questions of Canadian competence and the value of training. Were the troops inadequately prepared to face these hazards, or were they victims of circumstance? The evidence points to the second explanation. Canadian soldiers had already sustained casualties during their orientation tours with the 4th and 6th British Divisions in late February. Many were also warned prior to entering the lines in early March that the Germans did not forgive mistakes or carelessness, as Rawlinson emphasized in his motivational talk with the 3rd Brigade. Part of the problem can be traced to the shallow water table in the Fleurbaix sector. This precluded the construction of deep trenches, and as a consequence, the front lines consisted of sandbagged and earthen breastworks built above ground.[54] Because engineering materials were in short supply it is likely that the breastworks were not universally as high or as thick as they should have been. A moment's carelessness drew fire from German marksmen. The relative elevation of the German and Allied positions exacerbated the situation; the Germans were firmly established atop Aubers Ridge, opposite Armentières, and from the high ground they enjoyed an extensive view of the Allied lines.[55] This combination explains the frequent sniping casualties sustained by Canadian units. Indeed, the war diaries of experienced British battalions serving in the same area show similar loss rates.[56] The trench rotations of February-March 1915 impressed the gravity of combat service upon all ranks of the 1st Division. The Canadians lost their innocence well before transferring to the Ypres Salient in April.

Neuve Chapelle and Aubers Ridge

From a tactical perspective, the village of Neuve Chapelle presented a suitable target for attack in March 1915. It formed a German salient in the British line, and the high ground behind the village, along the Aubers Ridge, overlooked much of the British frontage (fig. 3.3). Pushing the enemy out of the village and off of the ridge would improve the local

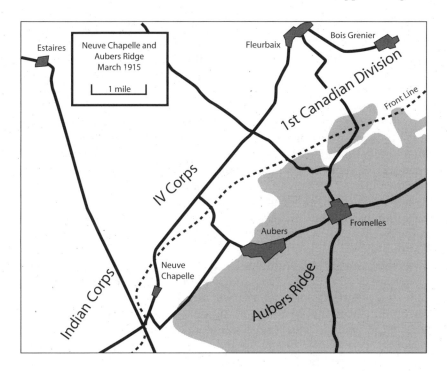

Figure 3.3

situation for Allied troops. While the British plan to capture Neuve Chapelle in March 1915 was carefully defined and rehearsed, the second phase of the operation, to be directed against Aubers Ridge, was less clearly outlined. The artillery fire plan for 10 March was especially effective; Neuve Chapelle fell in a matter of hours. But as British and Indian assault troops advanced beyond the village, their lines of communication grew tenuous and artillery support less accurate. Higher headquarters lost touch with events at the sharp end, and mistakenly continued to press attacks even after German reinforcements arrived on the scene. The operation broke down after three days because the set-piece character of the first day's success could not be maintained as British forces penetrated deeper into the enemy's defences.[57] It was feasible to break into and capture the enemy's front line, but holding it against counterattack from the second and third lines was another matter entirely. This 'capture-hold' conundrum often seemed insoluble over the next three years.

The Canadian artillery played a role in the British plan at Neuve Chapelle by firing on enemy positions opposite the Canadian lines. This shelling was designed to mislead the Germans into believing that an attack from the Canadian sector was imminent, thereby luring strength away from the British front where the actual attack was developing. It was also hoped that the Canadian shelling would draw retaliatory fire from hidden German batteries.[58] Should this occur, the Canadians were encouraged to 'freely expend' their scarce shells against the German guns. Accordingly, the batteries of the 1st Brigade shelled enemy emplacements on discovering their location on 10 March. Misty weather limited effective observation the next day, although in one instance the gunners engaged a German mortar that had been dropping bombs in the Canadian trenches.[59] The 2nd CFA Brigade was actively engaged with similar targets during the battle. According to Captain Crerar, of the 8th Battery, close cooperation with forward observers permitted accurate shooting: 'We had quite a lot of firing yesterday and made excellent practise. I believe we are really getting quite a reputation for ourselves. One target – a house – with an infantry officer observing for us – first shot, "to right," second, "just over," third, "got him," fourth, "knocked hell out of him," fifth, "through the same hole," sixth, "through the hole again," seventh, "That finished him. Thanks very much."'[60]

After most of the 1st Canadian Division moved into reserve at Estaires on 27 March, the CFA Brigades remained in the lines at Fleurbaix under the command of Major-General F. Davies's 8th Division, a conglomerate of pre-war regular units that had been formed and deployed to the Western Front in October 1914. The CFA brigades' daily routine of target registration and shelling German batteries, trenches, and buildings continued under British command until 1 April.[61] The 1st Heavy Battery, meanwhile, was successfully able to register longer range targets with the assistance of aircraft observers.[62]

Because the outcome of an artillery engagement depended very much on the quality of available intelligence, the Canadian gunners were eager to learn about enemy artillery dispositions and capabilities. Unexploded German shells, fuze caps, and shell fragments unearthed in the Canadian lines were carefully collected and studied for what they might reveal about ordnance developments and the broader state of German technology.[63] The Germans were also eager to discover what their enemies were up to, so the Canadian artillerymen went to great lengths to conceal their emplacements, hide muzzle flashes from view, and keep their locations secret, even from friendly forces. An officer from the 3rd CFA Brigade complained that too much information pertaining to the location and arrangement of Canadian gun positions was made available in the *Summaries of Information* that were regularly distributed throughout the division: 'The Summaries of Information which have been issued to all units, although very interesting to us, are no doubt more so to our enemy. The summaries give the information in too much detail ... they describe the position of our guns with map references [and] also make references to any damage to our material. It seems hardly fair to the batteries who do their best to conceal themselves to have their positions put in print where one and all may see.'[64] The sharing of information was useful, but it came with some risk.

The Canadian infantry battalions were not called upon to attack during the Neuve Chapelle–Aubers Ridge offensive, but they played an active support role, suffering about a hundred casualties in the process. The basic goal was to 'hold [the] enemy to their ground while 4th [Corps] attacked Neuve Chapelle on our right.'[65] The infantry complied by delivering sustained volleys of small-arms fire against the opposing lines. A private later recalled the experience: 'For three hours we fired as rapidly as we could force clips of ammunition into the magazine and for days my shoulder was sore from the recoil of the rifle. We took no particular aim, had no particular target, and it is doubtful if we killed any Germans, but it kept the enemy from making a counterattack and from sending reinforcements to the section of the line being attacked by the British.'[66]

On the first day of the offensive each battalion lost a few men killed or wounded. The troops continued to fire on the Germans the next day, and were rewarded with violent shelling that destroyed a nearby dressing station and supply depot. The Canadian ruse was apparently successful, as enemy troops opposite the 3rd Battalion behaved as if they were anticipating an attack; at night the Germans fired an unusually heavy volume of flares and illumination rounds.[67] Patrols from the 3rd Brigade discovered that the Germans were holding their forward positions in strength behind thick belts of barbed wire and deep water obstacles.[68] Although the Canadians were spared having to make a direct assault, even from the comparative safety of their own trenches they witnessed sights that they would not soon forget. A soldier's diary entry recorded the death of Lance-Corporal Duncan Patterson: 'While we were blazing away, Pat[t]erson was hit. The bullet struck his rifle, as he was firing, between the stock and barrel, and glanced off into his neck and body. We tried to staunch the blood but Mowat, the stretcher bearer, made signs of "no good" and whispered "jugular." He was dead in a few minutes. We could see him die, and as he was the first man killed, and we were covered with his blood, we got quite a turn.'[69]

Upon returning to the front shortly after Neuve Chapelle, the 15th Battalion displayed a predisposition towards active defence by aggressively patrolling no man's land in search of information regarding enemy dispositions. After receiving aerial reconnaissance map tracings of the German defences, Lieutenant-Colonel J.A. Currie's troops sited their weapons to better effect, dominating sniping activities for the next few days. While the battalion worked to improve its own positions, it also noted subtle changes in the German lines, such as an additional layer of sandbags. As always, casualties accompanied trench tours. In mid-March, Private G. Stanley was killed in the presence of his own son, who served in the same battalion.[70]

From Estaires to the Salient

After completing its instructional tours and serving for one month in the Fleurbaix sector, the 1st Canadian Division was withdrawn to Estaires for a few weeks where it regrouped, trained, and prepared to march north into Belgium. Early in the month divisional headquarters issued instructions for the establishment of brigade grenade companies. Each battalion was to contribute one platoon of grenadiers, although additional men were trained and then returned to their parent units to stand by as replacements.[71] In early April the divisional engineer brigade was assigned responsibility for the manufacture of field expedient grenades; each of the three engineering field companies was to supply grenades to its affiliated infantry brigade.[72] The most common type of grenade in use by British forces at this time was the jam-pot, a simple design in which a half-pound of explosive, five-second fuze, and detonator were packed into discarded jam tins along with bits of scrap iron.[73] Other substitute materials were also transformed into various types of bombs. As one infantryman later recalled, 'we used empty milk cans, filled with powder, and put on a time fuze. When we ran short of pellets we filled cans with broken glass, an even more deadly weapon than when filled with bullets. Anything that would kill or maim seemed to be an accepted rule of war.'[74]

A total of 2,000 grenades was to be on hand for each infantry brigade (800 in the support trenches, 400 in the fire trenches, and 800 with the brigade grenade company), but this may not always have been possible. The combined training of machine gunners and grenadiers was also proposed, although it is uncertain how far the scheme progressed before the German offensive against Ypres later in the month.[75]

After the front lines stabilized in November 1914, and no man's land grew increasingly dangerous to navigate, the opposing forces sought to undo each other's positions through mine shafts beneath the battlefield. The German Army scored an early mining success at Festubert in December when tunnellers destroyed the front-line positions of an Indian Brigade with ten underground explosions.[76] Mine defence had already been addressed by the infantry brigades while the 1st Canadian Division was deployed in the Fleurbaix sector, but orders were issued later in March for each brigade to form its own mining section. Under the command of a lieutenant, each section was to consist of two officers, four sergeants, six corporals, two batmen, and fifty-five sappers (engineers). It was hoped that recruits for the sections would have had some mining experience in civil life.[77]

The interlude at Estaires found the divisional cyclists, signallers, engineers and transport elements occupied with regular responsibilities and therefore less likely than the infantrymen to be training. The divisional signal company was forever busy keeping units in touch with one another, but there was time at Estaires for officers to attend classes on telegraphy.[78] Divisional engineers, on the other hand, enjoyed little relief from their regular chores as they were assigned to work on local defences. The engineers often became targets for long-range German shelling because they were operating in conjunction with large groups of infantry near to the front.[79] Meanwhile the transport troops of the divisional train were interminably scrutinized by their commanding officer, Lieutenant-Colonel Simson, regarding the state of wagons, harness, and horses. An enraged Simson excoriated No. 2 Company for improperly marked wagons, poorly fitting harness, and a generally sloppy appearance. After a few days of clean-up and reorganization the transport men received much better reviews.[80]

The divisional guns remained active in the lines for several days after the Canadian infantry left Fleurbaix for Estaires. There was less opportunity, consequently, for additional artillery training prior to the division's move north to Ypres, although exercise rides and stationary gun drill appear on daily schedules during the first two weeks of April. Under the command of the 8th British Division until late March, the Canadian gunners continued with the routine they had grown accustomed to during the previous few weeks.[81] The 1st and 2nd CFA Brigades were especially active: the 1st Brigade fired twenty-five retaliatory rounds on 30 March after German mortars and guns caused heavy infantry casualties nearby. The 2nd CFA Brigade drew considerable enemy fire and one of the 6th Battery's guns was damaged as a consequence. Undaunted, the Canadian gunners replied in kind, remaining alert to new targets.[82] The 1st Canadian Heavy Battery, meanwhile, successfully registered indirect targets in conjunction with aircraft observers: '28 March: Fair, cold and moderate wind. Registered targets by means of aeroplane, mostly cross-roads. Fired 23 rounds at eleven targets, registration by airplane, in the morning. Registered 21 targets with 3[?] rounds, 6 being registered with one round each. Aeroplane working very satisfactorily.'[83] While providing logistical support for the gunners, troops of the DAC received first-aid instruction three afternoons per week. The medical lessons were put to use almost immediately when a German aircraft bombed Estaires, causing light casualties.[84]

Canadian infantrymen engaged in a uniform program of training during late March and early April 1915, first at Estaires, and then further north in Belgium. A tired soldier from the 1st Battalion wrote home in a letter that 'we are supposed to be in a rest camp, but if this is a rest, give me the trenches. It should rather be called a training base. Each morning we go out for a twelve to fifteen kilo march over rotten roads with cobble stones, and in the afternoon practice advancing over rough ground and then digging ourselves in, getting over and through barbed wire, bomb and grenade throwing, etc.'[85] A letter written by a 13th Battalion officer confirmed that his troops spent six to eight hours each day at similar activities.[86] It was the same story in other units.[87] Most soldiers had probably already learned something of how to construct wire obstacles while serving on working parties in the Fleurbaix sector, but this skill warranted additional practice, not simply for defence of one's own line, but also for the timely consolidation of new positions that might be gained through offensive operations. Infantry assaults delivered from entrenched positions also demanded rehearsal, since confusion easily resulted if the troops did not depart their lines in a coordinated fashion. The recent experience at Neuve Chapelle sparked innovation. An infantry officer noted that 'we are diligently learning new methods of attack never before laid down in any book. It reminds me of the pictures one used to see of the storming of castles in the Middle Ages. Ladders are carried, bridging materials, explosives, etc.'[88] The 16th Battalion's records show that the men executed a mock night attack on 3 April. Although the sky was pitch black and the ground around Estaires extremely muddy, the exercise reportedly went well.[89] The importance of delivering a rapid assault was emphasized; the 4th Battalion practised attacks across recently ploughed fields to familiarize the troops with operations over uneven ground. Infantrymen and engineers experimented jointly in search of the best means to circumvent wire entanglements.[90] In the 2nd Brigade, officers attempted to bridge the wire with sheets of perforated metal.[91] Such experimentation was commonplace.

Digging was a soldier's most important survival skill. This might seem a redundant training activity, since the troops had already spent many hours carving out trenches at the front, but an important distinction must be made between fortification work and hasty digging-in. Ordinary picks and spades were issued to working parties from engineer stores for the purpose of excavating trenches and preparing static defensive positions. Once they were complete, the working party turned in its tools and carried on with other duties. All soldiers, however, were issued with small collapsible entrenching implements that they carried with them at all times; the steel pick head was contained in a flat pouch on the rear of the soldier's belt, while the short wooden handle was strapped next to the bayonet scabbard (fig. 3.4). These simple tools were intended for use in emergencies, if for example, a man was caught in the open and needed to dig a small scrape in which to protect himself from small-arms or artillery fire. This task was complicated not only by the compact size of the personal entrenching tool, but also by the requirement that it be performed in the prone position, so as to present the smallest possible target to the enemy. Lives were to be saved at Second Ypres because the troops were able to dig themselves in quickly after going to ground in open fields.

The 1st Canadian Division was young when it marched out of Estaires in early April 1915, but it was neither inexperienced nor untrained. The division had spent just over six weeks on the continent as it prepared to move north into Belgium, and during this period all ranks observed what was expected of them, seizing the opportunity to test themselves in the presence of a dangerous enemy. Through practice and by example the troops learned how to behave in the front lines during offensive and defensive periods. In between trench rotations there was time for additional training and theoretical instruction. Perhaps more importantly, infantrymen, gunners, engineers, signallers, and support troops discovered that life on the Western Front could be very short. Losses during February and March were not especially heavy compared with what the division was to suffer at Ypres in April, but enough men were killed or injured to demonstrate that war was serious business. Beginning in

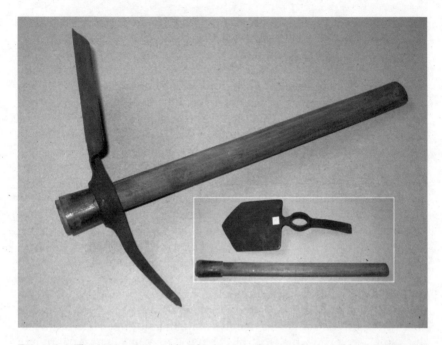

Figure 3.4. The 1908 pattern individual entrenching tool, carried by most British Empire troops throughout war (shown collapsed at inset). The head on this tool measured only about one foot in length. As such, it was best used for emergencies. More extensive digging required the larger general service spade. (Author's collection)

March, wooden crosses were officially issued by divisional headquarters for use as grave markers.[92]

Ordinary time was compressed on the Western Front. Men became veterans in days rather than months or years. As an officer of the 2nd Infantry Battalion wrote after the war, the men left Fleurbaix as initiated front-line veterans.[93] A *Toronto Star* correspondent attached to the 1st Canadian Division since its inception took a philosophical approach to the situation: 'Our six months' training, I think, has strengthened and trained our minds and spirits even more than our bodies. Certainly we're very different in our outlook and behaviour from the gang that we were at Valcartier ... Heaven is very near, and hell, too. But I think we're all quite tranquil. I know I may get killed the next minute, but I don't worry in the least about it. It's a great relief to be able to be like that.'[94]

4 Ypres: The Salient and the Armies

It is impossible for today's traveller to pass through Ypres and its environs without confronting ubiquitous vestiges of the Great War. Approaching the town by car – no matter the direction – large and small military cemeteries with unusual names appear ever more frequently in fields, farm yards, and village greens – Railway Dugouts Burial Ground, Essex Farm, Passchendaele New British Cemetery, and Bedford House, to name but a few. Entering town from the east brings one through the Menin Gate, an enormous archway bearing the inscribed names of 54,000 British Empire soldiers who were lost in the Ypres Salient between 1914 and 1917 but have no marked grave. At the same hour each evening authorities close the street under the gate as a crowd gathers to hear trumpeters from the local fire brigade play the 'Last Post.' The trumpets have sounded every day since 1928, with the exception of the 1940–4 occupation.[1] The cobblestone streets of Ypres are laid out just as they were in 1914. A short walk from the Menin Gate, the Grote Markt is dominated on the north side by the bell tower of the Cloth Hall, and behind it, St Martin's Cathedral. Both buildings were destroyed by artillery fire but have since been restored to their original splendour. The Cloth Hall now houses a modern museum examining the collective European experience of war. Small shops nearby on the market square sell fine chocolates cast in the shape of British helmets. The First World War will always be a part of Ypres.

Accelerated urbanization and industrialization have occurred on the immediate outskirts of town during the past few decades, but the cultivated fields on which the Second Battle of Ypres was waged appear very much as they did early in the war. It is still possible to retrace most of the engagements across the ground with a remarkable degree of certainty, although this will be become somewhat more difficult if the A-19 motorway is extended towards Ostend, effectively bisecting the fields where Canadian soldiers fought in April 1915. In anticipation of highway construction and further urban development, battlefield archaeologists regularly unearth fresh evidence of the Great War: human remains, bits of field equipment, trenches, and deep dugouts.[2] British military historian Lyn Macdonald suggested that only this enduring Great War legacy saved Ypres from falling into obscurity during the later part of the twentieth century.[3] It should be remembered, however, that the town was an important cultural and economic landmark long before 1914. Enthusiasts of art and architecture flocked to Ypres to take in the magnificent Cloth Hall and distinguished homes, the glad products of a lucrative textile industry. Religious devotees looked to Ypres with its churches, convents, and monasteries as an important centre of Flemish Catholicism. Even the ordinary soldiers who found themselves in Ypres during the early days of the war were struck by the beauty of the town and its treasures.

Ypres and the surrounding area served as a battleground on many occasions before the British, French, and Germans arrived in 1914. Circumscribed by ridges, the fortified town constituted a natural defensive bastion for centuries. Documentary evidence dating from the time of Julius Caesar mentions that the ridge lines 'divided two tribes.' Later, during the early Christian era, the ridges delineated an ecclesiastical border between two bishoprics. Several battles were waged there in the medieval period and beyond.[4] Blood was spilled again in 1914. After being turned back at the Marne in September, the German Army launched an offensive against Ypres in October; a successful penetration through Flanders to the channel coast could have unhinged the Allied left flank and interrupted cross-channel communication with the British Isles.[5] Stubborn British resistance and the arrival of French reinforcements narrowly prevented the Fourth and Sixth German armies from enveloping the town. After six weeks of fighting, combined British and Indian Army losses approached 80,000, while the Germans may have suffered more than 100,000 casualties.[6] While these figures are debatable, the fact remains that as early as the autumn of 1914, Ypres was already a powerful symbol of British sacrifice and determination. Over the next four years the town was to become a focal point of such significance that after the war Winston Churchill proposed that the ruins be maintained in perpetuity as a living monument to the British Empire war effort. Returning Belgian townsfolk naturally had other ideas. The Menin Gate was finally settled on as a compromise, while the rest of the town was largely restored to its pre-war layout.[7]

After the battles of 1914 the town remained in Allied hands, albeit situated in an uncomfortable salient, exposed to German fire from the northeast, east, and southeast. The Germans held high ground to the north, but several key ridges remained under Allied control; as in Caesar's day, the crests once again divided two tribes. Some critics of British strategy insist that abandoning the town completely would have eliminated the defensive difficulties intrinsic to all salients.[8] Was this a viable option in 1915? General Horace Smith-Dorrien may have thought so. Smith-Dorrien was to lose his job as commander of the Second Army in May 1915 after suggesting a limited tactical withdrawal to the General Headquarters (GHQ) line on 27 April, *after* the losses of 22–26 April rendered the northeastern extremity of the salient virtually indefensible: 'If the French are not going to make a big push, the only line we can hold permanently and have a fair chance of keeping supplied, would be the GHQ line passing just east of Wieltje and Potijze.'[9] Smith-Dorrien's proposal, however, was not at all the same as evacuating the town or the east bank of the Yser Canal, as some historians have suggested.[10] His successor, General Herbert Plumer, ultimately did withdraw Second Army troops to a shorter perimeter conforming to the GHQ line – without leaving the east bank in German hands. Anyone familiar with the topography must recognize that to evacuate the high ground on the outskirts of Ypres would only have caused further grief to Allied troops occupying a straight line along the west bank of the Yser (see fig. 4.1). It would also have signalled a major German victory to the rest of the world.[11]

There were other sound reasons to defend the Ypres Salient. In the first place, it was one of the few larger Belgian towns to escape what was proving to be a brutal German occupation.[12] The plight of the Belgians supplied a compelling moral justification for the British war effort, so it was difficult to consider surrendering the town even under dire circumstances. Having witnessed beleaguered columns of Belgian refugees for the first time, a Canadian soldier writing home from Ypres swore vengeance against the Germans for causing such suffering.[13] Arguably even more important, the town was a transportation conduit to the channel ports – key logistical arteries for the British Expeditionary Force. The ports had to be kept from the Germans in any event, since the presence of hostile naval bases on the channel coast was

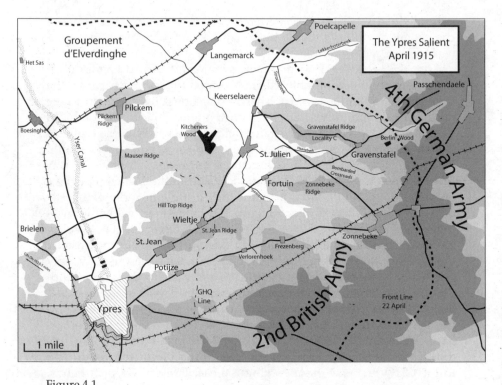

Figure 4.1

totally unacceptable to the British. After the war the strategic significance of the salient was embodied in the crest of the London-based
Ypres League. Depicting a lion guarding a portcullis gate, the crest represented 'the British Army defending the Salient, which was the gate to
the Channel Ports.'[14] Ypres had to be saved at all costs, and the British
Empire was to pay dearly. By the end of the Great War it was quite
likely the most sacred British battlefield in Belgium or France.

Few sectors on the Western Front could have been considered pleasant to serve in once the lines stabilized in late 1914, but Ypres soon
ranked among the most unpopular. Half of the battle was keeping water
out of the trenches.[15] The high water table and low elevation caused
perennial flooding, precluded construction of proper dugouts, and
made life generally miserable even during quiet moments. Because
Ypres was situated in a salient, the Germans surrounded the defenders
on three sides, affording their artillery observers clear observation of the

Allied lines. With constant traffic and stockpiles of war materiel in and around the town, there were plenty of targets for German shells. Allied commanders strictly emphasized the need for careful traffic control and concealment of transport. Canadian divisional orders forbade the movement of wagons or motor trucks except under the direct supervision of an officer. Vehicles were not to concentrate near headquarters, nor be parked in open areas. As much as possible wagons and other obvious targets were hidden alongside hedgerows, out of sight of German observers.[16]

In early 1915 the countryside around Ypres had not yet degenerated into the shell-cratered wasteland so often associated with the later war years. Although the opposing lines were clearly established, artistic renderings of the salient dating from this period reveal pleasant images of untouched green fields bearing little evidence of shellfire, barbed wire, or deep entrenchments (fig. 4.2). Indeed, as the ground dried up during that first spring of the war, British Expeditionary Force Routine Orders dictated that all personnel should assist local farmers to repair any damage caused to their fields by military occupation during the winter months. Where possible, mounted units were restricted from entering grazing lands, and special attention was called to the preservation of fruit trees and crops.[17] The regimental history of the 7th Battalion describes what Canadian soldiers saw when they first arrived in April 1915: 'Ypres in the early days of 1915 was still very much intact. Business flourished, the Cloth Hall was damaged, it is true, and so was the Cathedral Church, but commerce still carried on in the market square, the shops were well stocked and an enterprising photographer stationed himself inside the Cloth Hall itself to photograph those who wished to have the frescoes as a background, and the city, in spite of the dreadful first Battle of Ypres of the previous December, had not yet earned the sinister name which it still holds.'[18] The regimental historian for the 13th Battalion was less charitable when he wrote that Ypres 'even at that comparatively early date, possessed an evil and sinister reputation.'[19]

Allied Dispositions in April 1915

The terrain of Flanders Fields is generally imagined as flat and featureless, but this is not quite so. Although there are some expansive open areas with excellent fields of view, the ground north and east of Ypres is also dotted with small woods and tree lines. At some locations there

Figure 4.2. This detail from Arthur Nantel's *7 A.M., April 22nd, 1915* shows much of the countryside in the Ypres Salient untouched by shellfire in early 1915. Also illustrated are the relatively shallow trenches, with minimal parapets and rearward cover. (Canadian War Museum, AN 19710261–0501)

are relatively sharp rises and drops in elevation. While a commander standing at a given point might be able to see up to a maximum distance of 1,000 yards, intervening dead ground and winding stream beds easily rendered part of that field of view invisible. Langemarck and Poelcapelle, for instance, are both clearly visible from St Julien, but the three points are divided by low ground through which German troops might infiltrate unseen by a Canadian observer in St Julien.

In April 1915 French forces in the Ypres Salient were deployed along an east-west axis immediately east of the Yser Canal (fig. 4.3). On the right was General Quiquandon's 45th Algerian Division, consisting of two brigades of African-born Zouaves and Tirailleurs, plus two separate African battalions. To the left was General Roy's 87th Territorial Division, comprising reservists of the 173rd, 174th, and 186th Brigades. As of 17 April both French divisions, along with five Belgian companies, comprised

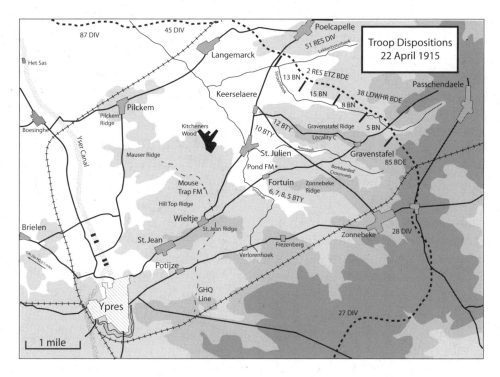

Figure 4.3

Groupement D'Elverdinghe, under the overall command of General Quiquandon. The principal artillery strength of the Groupement was organized in three components, one of which was equipped with 75 mm guns and the other two with a mixture of 75 mm and 90 mm guns. The French troops were also supported by two 120 mm batteries, and a few additional field guns.[20]

The BEF divisions deployed on a ten-mile front around the northeastern perimeter of the Ypres Salient belonged to Lieutenant-General Herbert Plumer's V Corps (Second Army), headquartered at Poperinghe. From north to south Plumer's corps comprised Alderson's 1st Canadian Division, Major-General E.S. Bulfin's 28th Division (83rd, 84th, and 85th Brigades), and Major-General T. D'Oyly Snow's 27th Division (80th, 81st, and 82nd Brigades).

A partially completed subsidiary line of detached redoubts and shelters existed atop Gravenstafel Ridge, approximately 1,000 yards behind

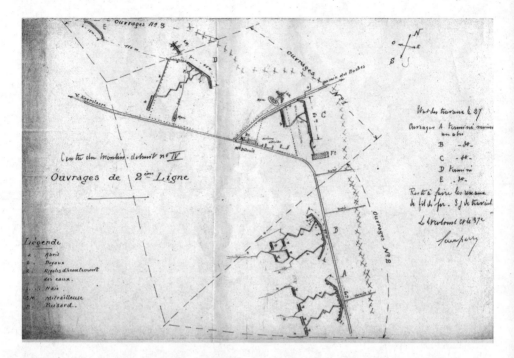

Figure 4.4. This French sketch, probably dating from February 1915, shows defensive redoubts of the subsidiary line (*2e ligne*) in what was later to become the Canadian sector. Locality C is visible at the top right, above the road to Keerselaere. (LAC, MG 30, E 8)

the Canadian front line. The most important redoubt on the ridge was Locality C, a position with commanding fields of view in every direction (fig. 4.4). Between one and three miles further to the rear of the V Corps frontage was the GHQ line, extending along a north-south axis from the Ypres-Menin road up to a point on the right boundary of Groupement D'Elverdinghe.[21] Consisting of a series of redoubts and wire-belts, the GHQ line offered excellent fields of view, particularly where it crossed St Jean Ridge at Wieltje.[22]

At the beginning of the Second Battle of Ypres the 4,500-yard Canadian front was divided into four sections between the Ypres–Poelcapelle and Ypres–Passchendaele roads (fig. 4.3). A report issued to divisional head-quarters by Captain T.C. Irving of the 2nd Field Company just before the battle described the conditions of Sections 1 and 2, on the right (southeast) end of the Canadian front. Section 1, on the far right, was approximately 1,650 yards wide and bisected by the Ypres–Gravenstafel road. Its three subsections consisted mostly of isolated lengths of breastworks constructed from 'heaped' mud about two feet thick at the bottom and only a few inches thick at the top edge. The area was heavily flooded and in some parts there was very little rearward cover or parados behind the breastworks. Several areas in Section 1 were vulnerable to enfilade fire from enemy snipers. Because the water table was only two feet below ground, it was generally not possible to build proper shell-proof dugouts. Consequently, troops of the 11th French Division who occupied this sector prior to the Canadians' arrival had constructed above-ground shelters directly up against the inside of the breastworks. The arrangement of the French shelters proved to be more a hindrance than an asset, since they limited the troops' ability to guard the trench at every point along its length. The only way to keep a proper lookout, besides removing the shelters altogether, was for unfortunate sentries to lie on top of them in relatively exposed positions. Canadian engineers of the 2nd Field Company attempted to improve the overall situation in Section 1 by constructing wire obstacles across the Ypres–Gravenstafel road and adding communication trenches, but these efforts were incomplete when the battle began on the afternoon of 22 April. The engineers did manage to strengthen some portions of former German trenches and build proper dugouts on isolated higher pieces of ground, but wherever they tried to dig, the Canadians discovered a grotesque stew of human excrement and decomposing corpses from the previous autumn's fighting. Officers requested large quantities of disinfectant to reduce the risk of disease.[23]

On the afternoon of 22 April troops of Lieutenant-Colonel Tuxford's 5th Battalion were holding Section 1. While A and B Companies manned the forward breastworks, C Company occupied an intermediate position 400 yards to the rear, and D Company was held in reserve at an intersection near Gravenstafel known as Bombarded Crossroads. Since assuming responsibility for the position three days earlier, the men of the 5th Battalion found themselves in a difficult situation; Section 1 was in poor repair, and the enemy made a constant nuisance of himself as Tuxford's men worked with the engineers of the 2nd Field Company to shore up the line. The battalion was shelled intermittently with high explosive and shrapnel; dismayed officers and soldiers cursed the enemy observer aircraft that seemed to cruise above the Canadian lines virtually unmolested by anti-aircraft fire. During the morning of 22 April Captain Edward Hilliam observed increased enemy air activity, and a heavy, albeit somewhat inaccurate, bombardment pounded the battalion's positions around noon. At this time D Company was detached from Tuxford's command and placed in brigade reserve. It did not return until 26 April.[24]

According to Captain Irving's report, Section 2 was little better than what the 5th Battalion confronted in Section 1. It was 1,250 yards wide and, like Section 1, was subdivided into three zones. Much of the sector lacked traverses and was enfiladed by the enemy. According to Irving, 'the ground where the men stand in the firing position is paved with rotting bodies and human excreta.' Sandbags were in such short supply that trenches had to be deepened despite the decaying corpses, in order to conserve bags along the parapet. Because of flooding, some parts of Section 2 were completely isolated. Engineers worked feverishly to drain the water.[25] Lieutenant-Colonel Lipsett's 8th Battalion moved into Section 2 during the evening of 19 April. Three companies – A, B, and D – were in the front trenches, with C Company in support on the reverse slope of Gravenstafel Ridge.[26]

To the left of Sections 1 and 2 were Sections 3 and 4, both defended by the 3rd Canadian Brigade on 22 April. As the 2nd Field Company helped to improve the defences in Sections 1 and 2, the 3rd Field Company carried out similar work in the other two sections. In most places the upper eighteen inches of the parapet were not bullet-proof, and the parados, where any existed, was too low to offer much protection. At one point there was a 200-yard gap separating a pair of disjointed positions. Most of the communication trenches spanning the fire bays were either flooded or under enemy observation. The engineers requisitioned additional supplies on learning of the poor state of the front-line defences north of Ypres, but this material had not arrived in any great quantity prior to the battle.[27]

On 22 April Section 3 was defended by Lieutenant-Colonel J.A. Currie's 15th Battalion, with three companies up front (D, C, and A). An advanced battalion headquarters under the command of Major William Marshall was situated midway between the forward companies and St Julien. Finally, Captain G.M. Alexander's B Company was held in reserve in St Julien near Lieutenant-Colonel Currie's battalion headquarters. Currie's troops had moved into the position just two days earlier, on 20 April. Their deployment was an inauspicious beginning to what was destined to be a devastating week. Prior to the battalion's departure for Section 3, Captain Trumbull Warren, an officer of D Company, was killed when a heavy-calibre German shell slammed into the

Grote Markt. As the troops arrived in the front trenches later that day they were dismayed by the poor state of the defences. In common with Sections 1 and 2, the shallow graves of French soldiers served as flooring for the fire bays. Because building materials and fresh sandbags were in short supply, it was only marginally possible to improve the defensive character of the position.[28]

On the far left of the Canadian front, Section 4 was manned by Lieutenant-Colonel F.O.W. Loomis's 13th Battalion. When Loomis's men arrived in Ypres aboard commandeered London motor buses on 16 April the weather was growing warm and pleasant for a change, but the troops had little opportunity to enjoy it as they were immediately billeted on strict alert at the village of St Jean. Five days later, on 21 April, the battalion moved into the front trenches on the left flank of the 3rd Brigade, next to General Quiquandon's 45th Algerian Division. In line from left to right were Major D.R. McCuaig's A Company, Captain R.H. Jamieson's B Company, and Captain W.H. Clark-Kennedy's D Company. Half of C Company under Major E.C. Norsworthy was placed in support positions 400 yards behind the firing line. The other half waited in reserve under Major V.C. Buchanan at battalion headquarters in St Julien. Loomis was in St Julien at battalion headquarters, where he also served as Town Commandant. The troops found the trenches in Section 4 to be in poor shape, but at least some barbed wire was strung in front of the forward trenches, and well-positioned machine-gun posts alleviated matters to a degree. As was the case in the other sections of the Canadian line, Section 4 was liberally covered with waste and rotting corpses. A 13th Battalion officer recorded in a letter that the 'parapet, parados and the trench bottom were just one mass of bodies covered over with a far too thin layer of earth, arms and legs sticking out whenever a rainstorm took a little earth away.'[29] There was not much to be done about these grisly reminders of earlier combat, but steps were taken to reduce the level of human excrement that polluted the front lines. Discarded biscuit tins henceforth served as portable latrines; at night the full tins were carried out of the trenches to rear areas and dumped into large pits with a mixture of chloride of lime.[30]

Beginning on 15 April elements of the Canadian divisional artillery gradually took over the emplacements hitherto occupied by gunners of the 11th French Division. Representatives from each of the Canadian artillery units were briefed directly by their French counterparts through interpreters. As a labour-saving measure, the French simply left their communications network in place and were compensated with fresh reels of telephone wire from Canadian stores. The Canadians were fortunate to have a pre-installed network, although the frequency with which lines were severed during the course of the battle limited the system's benefits.[31] As gunners of the 2nd CFA Brigade prepared for duty in the salient, their commanding officer, Lieutenant-Colonel J.J. Creelman, issued a special brigade order for the attention of all ranks:

> The Brigade is about to relieve a French Brigade in a portion of the front which is much more exposed than that recently occupied.
>
> By means of observation bal[l]oon the Enemy can see practically the whole area to be occupied by the Brigade.
>
> It is essential that all ranks should understand the extreme necessity of keeping under cover at all times.
>
> Groups must nowhere gather and games are not to be played in the open as such are likely to draw fire in the future, as they have in the past.
>
> Every effort is to be made to conceal not only gun positions, but also all horse and wagon vehicles are to be concealed as much as possible.
>
> Under no circumstances are horses or vehicles to be allowed to stand in the immediate proximity of Brigade Headquarters.
>
> It is probable that supplies can be brought up at night only, also that horses can be exercised under cover of darkness.
>
> No light or fires are to be shown at night.
>
> The foregoing is to be impressed on all ranks.[32]

Creelman's order underscored the vulnerability of the entire Canadian sector northeast of Ypres.

Most of the guns belonging to the 2nd and 3rd Brigades, plus two British 4.5-inch batteries from 118th Howitzer Brigade were deployed between Wieltje and St Julien. This amounted to a total strength of thirty-two field guns and eight howitzers under Canadian command on the east side of the canal at the beginning of Second Ypres. On 15 April the 1st Canadian Heavy Battery was transferred to No. 1 Group, Heavy Artillery Reserve (First British Army) at Lestrem, a few miles northeast of Neuve Chapelle. In return the Canadian Division received the 4.7-inch guns of the 2nd London Heavy Battery, to be deployed in Kitcheners Wood just west of St Julien, in the zone of Groupement D'Elverdinghe.[33] Typical of 1915, a strictly limited number of rounds was immediately available for each gun. On 22 April, for instance, the 2nd CFA Brigade had a stock of 2,800 rounds to feed its sixteen guns, providing a total of 175 rounds per gun. The brigade ammunition column, loaded and waiting at Wieltje, carried a reserve of 1,200 rounds (seventy-five rounds per gun). Thus, the immediate supply of ammunition on 22 April was very far below the figure of 2,000 rounds per gun prescribed by the Mowatt scale.[34] The guns of the 2nd CFA Brigade ultimately consumed 12,000 rounds during 23 and 24 April, translating to an average of 750 rounds per gun.[35] But if the number of available shells was inadequate, the logistical apparatus supplying the ammunition under chaotic traffic circumstances and heavy enemy fire was nothing short of impressive.

The St Julien front was supported most immediately by the 10th and 12th CFA Batteries, both of which belonged to Lieutenant-Colonel J.H. Mitchell's 3rd CFA Brigade. Major W.B. King's 10th Battery was located on the east side of the Poelcapelle road, approximately 1,200 yards southwest of the 13th Battalion's position, while Major E.W. Leonard's 12th Battery was a few hundred yards to the right of the 10th Battery. About 1,500 yards southwest of King and Leonard's batteries, to the rear of St Julien, were Major E.A. MacDougall's 9th Battery and Major H.G. Carscallen's 11th Battery. On the evening of 21 April half of the 8th Battery (the 2nd CFA Brigade) arrived to begin relieving the 11th Battery, but this was only partially complete by the next day. Consequently, some of the Canadian field batteries functioned as composite units throughout the battle.[36]

As of 16–18 April all four batteries of the 2nd CFA Brigade were deployed along a track running southeast from the Ypres–Gravenstafel road, approximately 3,000 yards to the rear of Sections 1 and 2. From left to right were Major H.G. McLeod's 6th Battery, Major Andrew McNaughton's 7th Battery, Major S.B. Anderson's 8th Battery, and Major E.G. Hanson's 5th Battery. In common with their infantry counterparts, the gunners were struck by the general untidiness of the billets and positions previously occupied by French forces.[37] After installing their guns, the batteries registered targets and remained in place until the evening of 21 April, when elements of the 1st CFA Brigade arrived to carry out a partial relief. Because the exchange of batteries was not yet complete when the Germans struck on 22 April, the 2nd CFA Brigade enjoyed a surplus of officers during the battle while the 1st CFA Brigade suffered a temporary deficit.[38] For the moment the remainder of the 1st CFA Brigade remained in reserve near Poperinghe.

As of 21 April the 1st Field Company assumed responsibility for all bridges crossing the Yser Canal in the Canadian sector, should they need to be demolished in a contingency. Once demolition parties were detailed for what must have seemed an unlikely eventuality, the company began constructing new huts for the division near Brielen, on the west side of the canal. The 2nd and 3rd Field Companies, meanwhile, were working with their respective infantry brigades in Sections 1 through 4 to improve front-line defences as much as shortages of building materials permitted.[39]

Canadian Divisional Headquarters were set up at Château des Trois Tours, a manor house that still stands a few hundred yards to the west of Brielen. The headquarters of Brigadier-General Arthur Currie's 2nd Brigade were situated near Fortuin at Pond Farm, along with the brigade's machine-gun and grenade troops. Brigadier-General Turner's 3rd Brigade was headquartered just north of Wieltje at Mouse Trap Farm. Useful observation of the battlefield area was impossible from Alderson's divisional headquarters, but expansive fields of view were available near Pond and Mouse Trap Farms.

Just prior to Second Ypres, elements of the 2nd and 3rd Infantry Brigades not deployed in the front-line trenches were assigned to various posts as part of brigade, division, or corps reserves. The 7th Battalion was in reserve for the 2nd Brigade behind Sections 1 and 2 at Fortuin, on the Ypres–Gravenstafel road, about midway between Gravenstafel and Wieltje. The 10th Battalion, meanwhile, had been sent back to Ypres on 19 April to form part of the Canadian divisional reserve. The troops were billeted along the Ypres–Gravenstafel road between Ypres and St Jean. After being relieved from duty in Section 4 by the 13th Battalion on 21 April, Lieutenant-Colonel Meighen's 14th Battalion, less B Company and the machine-gun section, was sent back towards Wieltje to form the 3rd Brigade's reserve. Major Hanson's B Company and Captain Williamson's machine gunners remained in St Julien under Lieutenant-Colonel Loomis's town garrison command, which included 13th Battalion soldiers plus one company each from the 14th and 15th Battalions. Finally, the 16th Battalion was billeted just north of Ypres along the Ypres–Boesinghe road, mostly on the west side of the Yser Canal, as part of Alderson's divisional reserve. On the evening of 21 April all of the 1st Canadian Brigade was held in II Corps reserve at Vlamertinghe, on the west side of the Yser Canal. The troops were on one-hour alert, not in anticipation of the pending German attack, but in case the brigade might be needed to support an assault further to the south by the 5th Division (II Corps), against Hill 60 near Zillebeke.[40]

German Strategy and Dispositions in April 1915

After German forces failed to secure decisive victory on the Western Front in 1914 it became apparent that the war would last longer than originally anticipated. In hindsight, the best course for Germany in early 1915 would have been to destroy the BEF before Lord Kitchener, the secretary of state for war, had an opportunity to mobilize the Empire's manpower and industrial resources. But the German command was not free to make decisions in a strategic vacuum. Chief of Staff Erich von Falkenhayn, under pressure from his Austro-Hungarian allies, elected to concentrate the German efforts against Russia.[41] In the context of early 1915 Falkenhayn felt reasonably secure with this decision, since his forces had managed to prevent a French breakthrough in the Champagne and had also weathered the British offensive at Neuve Chapelle in March.[42]

Germany's tentative defensive strategy in the west did not preclude limited offensive action against the French and British armies. Falkenhayn, after all, did not wish to create the impression that he was substantially thinning his forces on the Western Front. Moreover, after the British Army's surprising initial tactical success at Neuve Chapelle, the German commander realized that his forces must maintain pressure against the French and British. The Second Battle of Ypres was in part a demonstration to the Allies that the German Army remained capable of inflicting damage in Flanders. It also presented an opportunity to evaluate the impact of a new weapon – chlorine gas – on the stalemate that had developed in the west. After the war Falkenhayn claimed that he never imagined the attack would develop into a breakthrough operation. Consequently, local reserves were not available to fully exploit the sudden gap opened in the French lines north of Ypres on 22 April.[43]

The Hague treaties of 1899 and 1907 prohibited the use of projectiles that diffused asphyxiating gases, as well as 'poison or poisoned weapons' and 'weapons causing unnecessary suffering.'[44] Several countries, including Germany, conducted experiments with chemical weapons prior to the outbreak of war, but it seemed unlikely that gas would ever be employed in operations, since it endangered one's own troops and invited retaliation in kind. Ambivalent attitudes towards chemical weapons began to change after the front lines stabilized in late 1914; any possible solution to the deadlock, however unpalatable, had to be explored. In October German gunners fired tear-gas shells at French troops near Neuve Chapelle with little apparent effect. The Germans tried their 'T-shells' again on the Eastern Front in January 1915, but winter temperatures apparently prevented the liquid from vapourizing upon impact. The deficiencies of tear gas prompted German scientists to explore the use of chlorine clouds. Experiments suggested that chlorine, which was readily available in Germany, would incapacitate but not kill or permanently injure its victims. The possibility of using the gas to break through the enemy's lines without causing massive numbers of fatal casualties perhaps made the experimental weapon even more attractive, since its use could be justified on humanitarian grounds.[45]

Despite assurances to the contrary, German commanders remained sceptical about chlorine's potential, and at least slightly dismayed at the prospect of employing a 'dishonourable' weapon against worthy opponents.[46] The mode of delivery was also an issue. Shell shortages in early 1915 prevented immediate mass production of gas-filled projectiles.[47] Releasing the chlorine directly from cylinders presented a viable alternative, although the prospect of storing large numbers of gas cylinders in the front lines prior to the attack did not bode well for German infantrymen, given the possibility that enemy artillery might strike and rupture the containers. The weapon was also subject to the vicissitudes of weather. Gas could only be released when the wind was blowing in the correct direction. Unfortunately for the Germans, it usually blew the wrong way on the Ypres front. Notwithstanding all of the risks, the chlorine in fact proved very effective against French troops on 22 April, and almost equally so against the Canadians two days later. More broadly speaking, its use introduced a horrific new brand of 'frightfulness' to the Western Front, which until recently has not been carefully examined or well understood by historians.[48] Within months of chlorine's first appearance, both sides engaged in a chemical arms race that lasted until the end of the war.

Two German Reserve Corps (XXIII and XXVI) faced V British Corps and the Groupement D'Elverdinghe along the northeastern perimeter of the Ypres Salient (fig. 4.5). Both corps were under the command of General-Oberst Herzog Albrecht von Württemberg's Fourth Army, which also included XXVII and XV Corps, situated around the southeastern perimeter of the salient.[49] The primary territorial objective of the attack, according to German sources, was for XXIII Reserve Corps to capture a line from Steenstraat through to Pilckem while XXVI Reserve Corps secured the high ground along the road leading from Boesinghe through Pilckem and Langemarck, to Poelcapelle. The secondary objective was to secure control of the Yser Canal as far south as

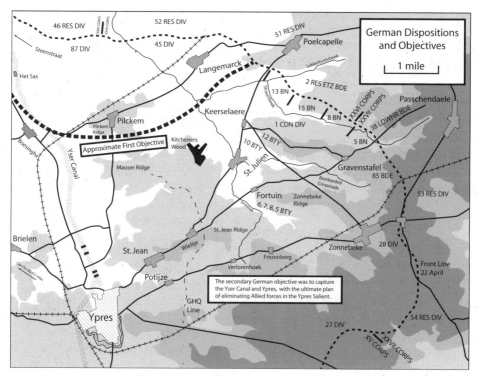

Figure 4.5

Ypres.[50] If this was achieved, Allied forces remaining in the salient would have to withdraw or risk encirclement and destruction.

The organizational structures of the four corps in the Fourth Army were not uniform. Some of the corps had two infantry divisions, each with two brigades, while others were strengthened with independent brigades. For example, General von Rathen's XXIII Corps comprised the 45th and 46th Reserve Divisions, but General von Hügel's XXVI Corps consisted of the 51st and 52nd Reserve Divisions, plus the 37th Landwehr Brigade and the 2nd Reserve Ersatz Brigade. In effect these two brigades gave von Hugel the infantry strength of an additional division.

Each German brigade in 1915 usually consisted of two regiments, with three battalions per regiment.[51] (Hence the total number of battalions in a German division was about the same as in a BEF division.) The German divisional engineers, mounted troops, cyclists, and transport personnel were also roughly equivalent to the British establishment. In early 1915 each German regiment had one machine-gun battalion with six gun crews.[52] This worked out to approximately twenty-four machine guns per German division, about the same as contemporary British establishments. The artillery strength of German divisions varied, but it was typical to have one field artillery regiment organized into three groups, each with three batteries. Two of the groups were equipped with field guns and the third with howitzers. The heavy artillery component assigned to XXIII, XXVI, and XXVII Corps included a single 42 centimetre (17-inch) 'Big Bertha' howitzer, twenty 20 centimetre (8-inch) howitzers and seventy-two 15 centimetre (5.9-inch) howitzers. The three corps were also equipped with sixteen 10 centimetre (4-inch) guns, and thirty-eight miscellaneous, obsolete, or captured guns.[53]

In peacetime the military forces of imperial Germany were organized into five categories. The Active Army consisted of troops whose age class had been called up for two years of compulsory service in the ranks. After completing their stint, able-bodied men passed into the Reserve for five years, then into the Landwehr for eleven years, and finally the Landsturm for seven years. The fifth category consisted of able-bodied males between the ages of 17 and 19 years who had not yet been called up for active service. These teenagers were categorized under a special branch of the Landsturm, liable for emergency combat service in wartime.[54] When it became apparent that the war would continue into 1915, increasing numbers of personnel from each category were called to the colours. Some men from the Landwehr or Landsturm were simply assigned to existing field formations as reinforcements. Others formed new units around cadres of professional officers.

By the end of October 1914 six new Army Corps had departed Germany for service at the front. The units comprising these corps were drawn from the first series of postmobilization 'New Formation Reserve' divisions. These divisions were designated numerically from 43 to 54, and their six parent corps from XXII to XXVII. Three of the four corps in Württemberg's Fourth Army (XXIII, XXVI, and XXVII) were composed entirely of New Formation Reserve divisions. Only the XV Corps included pre-war divisions, the 30th and 39th Infanterie, both of which had served in General von Heeringen's Seventh Army in Alsace-Lorraine during the 1914 campaign. In April 1915, however, XV Corps was concentrated against II British Corps in the southern portion of the Ypres Salient. Canadian troops serving under V British Corps fought primarily against the German XXIII and XXVI Corps.

The German soldiers serving in XXIII and XXVI Corps in 1915 originated mainly from three categories. Some were Landwehr men who had completed their active service between 1896 and 1906. The second group consisted of Ersatz Reservists; these men had never received training before the war. The same was probably true of the underaged Landsturm volunteers who comprised the third major category of personnel in Fourth Army. None of these teenagers had completed their active service prior to the outbreak of war because their classes had not yet been called up.[55] The average German soldier facing the 1st Canadian Division in the Ypres Salient was probably in his mid-twenties, and those with some prior training may have gone several years without engaging in any military activity before 1914–15.

Unlike their Canadian opponents, the divisions of XXIII and XXVI Reserve Corps did see combat in late 1914. The 45th Reserve Division, whose troops came from Pomerania, trained at the Jüterbog Camp, south of Berlin, between August and October 1914. Only days after arriving in Belgium the division entered the firing line at the Battle of the Yser on 21 October. Casualty rates soared; between mid-October and mid-November the 212th Regiment lost fifty-two officers and more than 1,600 men.[56] Subsequent to this costly fight the division remained in the line near Bixschoote before participating in the gas attack of 22 April.

The 46th Reserve Division, recruited from the Hanseatic Cities and the Grand Duchies of Mecklenburg, was formed at the same time as the 45th Reserve Division and trained at Lockstedt. Like the 45th Division, the 46th suffered heavy losses during the Yser battles of October and November. By 21 November, for example, only one original officer remained in the 3rd Battalion of the 214th Regiment. The 11th Company of the 214th retained only ninety of 253 original members.

The pattern is similar for the two divisions of XXVI Corps. The 51st Reserve Division, from Hesse and Thuringia, fought north of Ypres during October and November with frightening losses. By 1915 some of its junior officers were young Kriegsfreiwillige (war volunteers) whose commissions were only a few days old when Second Ypres began.[57] The 52nd Reserve Division, from the Rhineland, suffered particularly high casualties during the First Battle of Ypres; the 240th Reserve Regiment lost twenty-eight officers and 1,360 men over a ten-day period in October 1914. The regiment was destined to lose twenty-five officers and 1,268 men at Second Ypres. Attrition was hard at work in the first months of the Great War.

It is instructive to consider that the German New Formation Reserve divisions were established and began to train about the same time that the 1st Canadian Division assembled at Valcartier. The Germans' combat experience, moreover, must be weighed against their divisions' relatively short two-month training periods and the substantial proportion of fresh replacements arriving to replenish the casualties of First Ypres. In some respects the officers and men of the 1st Canadian Division may have been better prepared for battle in April 1915 than their counterparts in the German XXIII and XXVI Reserve Corps. The Canadians benefited from a substantial leavening of pre-war soldiers with active service under their belts, a four-month training period, and two months of experience in the front lines – without the acute organizational disruption or decline in morale and unit cohesion that can accompany high casualty rates like those sustained by the Germans at First Ypres. The Second Battle of Ypres was to challenge the Canadians beyond all possible imagination, but by the standards of 1915 the men of the 1st Canadian Division were not poorly prepared for action.

Like most salients, the one surrounding Ypres in 1915 was not an enviable defensive position, yet strategic and moral imperatives dictated that the town be defended against further German aggression. Much of the salient was guarded by trenches and static fortifications prior to Second Ypres, but as Captain Irving's engineer reports demonstrate, these defences remained in a primitive state as the battle began. On top of this, artillery ammunition was in short supply. The coming German offensive was to be an uphill struggle for the Second Army.

At Second Ypres General-Oberst Herzog von Württemberg's Fourth German Army enjoyed the advantages of plentiful artillery support and a secret weapon, but there is little reason to conclude that the troops of the Reserve Corps were better prepared for battle than their Canadian counterparts. All of the reserve regiments and brigades in the Fourth Army had been assembled after the outbreak of war, and its ranks were full of inexperienced volunteers who had recently arrived as replacements. In contrast, the men in Alderson's division had lived, worked, and trained together for an extended period. During the months leading up to April 1915, the Canadian troops had prepared for mobile as well as static operations. They were to apply both types of skills in the coming battle.

5 22 April 1915: Green Clouds

Two decades after the guns of April 1915 had fallen silent, A.F. Duguid wrote that Second Ypres was 'probably the most complicated battle ever fought by British troops.'[1] Writing coherent narratives of combat operations is always daunting, but Duguid was quite right. The Second Battle of Ypres is especially vexing. It was an unplanned, ad hoc defensive engagement for the Canadians and their allies. Beginning on the late afternoon of 22 April, British, Canadian, and French soldiers reacted to situations demanding decisive action, sometimes without any immediate guidance from higher headquarters. In many instances the reasons for a particular decision were literally buried with the decision maker. Oral orders were issued and executed without leaving any official trace or explanation, and historians are left to pick up the pieces.

Another complicating factor is the high number of Allied casualties, especially among officers.[2] By the morning of 25 April, the 2nd Brigade reported the effective strength of each of its four battalions: 5th Battalion = ten officers, 500 men; 7th Battalion = one officer, 150 men; 8th Battalion = six officers, 200 men; 10th Battalion = unknown number of officers, small party of men. Because so many officers and NCOs were killed, wounded, captured, or otherwise unaccounted for, it was not always possible to record precisely what had transpired in a given sector. While most surviving commanders prepared after-action reports at the end of April or early the following month, these range in quality from intricate to perfunctory. Consequently, the historian must seek out other types of evidence, such as personal correspondence and memoirs. Letters and diaries can be helpful, but they are circumscribed by an individual's personal physical radius of battle experience, and in some cases, by the legibility of handwriting; General Alderson surely wins the prize for the worst penmanship in the entire division! The ordinary soldier's limited knowledge of his whereabouts and role within the grand scheme of things is especially problematic in the context of Second Ypres because the Canadians were newcomers to the area. After hours of marching and countermarching, disoriented men often had no idea where they were by the time they reached the firing line. Of his company's journey to the front on the evening of 22 April, Private George Bell remarked, 'we march away in the darkness, stumbling through fields and across small streams. At night all ground looks alike and we have no sense of direction.'[3] In addition to war diaries and personal accounts like Bell's, the Canadian and German regimental histories published during the three decades after the Great War have proven useful. These narratives were based on official sources, as well as personal recollections, letters, and private papers of veterans – all of which were available to the historian through the regimental associations that thrived during the postwar years. Finally, Second Ypres was a fast-paced operation encompassing many simultaneous engagements waged across several miles of frontage by soldiers of at least four different nationalities. Alderson underscored this complexity in the introduction to his battle report: 'I fear that, at first sight, this report may appear somewhat long, but the period embraced is a considerable one. Two Cavalry Brigades and 47 Infantry Battalions were engaged, and the troops were unavoidably considerably mixed up together at different times. It is, therefore, not easy to make the account of the operations a clear one, except by writing at considerable length.'[4] With full knowledge of all these limitations, the next four chapters reconstruct and re-evaluate the operations of the 1st Canadian Division and affiliated formations between 22 and 26 April 1915. It was during these crucial four days that Canadian troops were most actively engaged in combat at Second Ypres.

The two weeks leading up to the German gas attack on 22 April witnessed a lot of activity in the Ypres Salient. It was very much a three-dimensional battlefield. Because the BEF lacked anti-aircraft batteries in the sector, enemy aircraft buzzed through the skies with near impunity. Field commanders hoped to fool the airborne observers with decoy artillery emplacements, while motor machine-gun troops tried their aim at German planes. Underground, both sides engaged in mining operations to the southwest of Ypres. Amid the trenches and breastworks, sniping was only one of many constant dangers. Keeping under cover might save a soldier from a sharpshooter's bullet, but it was more difficult to escape the plunging fire of an unseen Minenwer-fer (trench mortar). These weapons struck from concealed positions at close range with considerable accuracy; it was not unusual for a single mortar round to kill or injure more than a dozen men. A limited quan-tity of small-calibre mortars was supplied to British troops, but these initially proved unreliable, inaccurate, and not quite powerful enough to reach the German positions. Canadians had been subjected to mor-tar fire during their introductory tours in the Fleurbaix area. Thus, by the time they arrived in the Ypres Salient, Alderson's soldiers were able to determine the locations of the enemy mortar pits with reason-able certainty.[5] In some instances this intelligence provided little relief. German mortar teams were firing from such close proximity that it was difficult for Allied field artillery to respond without putting friendly troops at risk.

Excluding the 1st Canadian Division, which did not arrive on the corps front until 12 April, V Corps suffered 615 casualties (128 of whom were killed) between 7 and 13 April, amounting to the approximate combat strength of one battalion.[6] In the week that followed, the centre of Ypres was heavily shelled, possibly in retaliation for an attack that the 5th British Division mounted against Hill 60 south of the V Corps zone. Most of the men billeted in the centre of town were moved into outlying bivouac areas to escape the shelling, while troops in the front lines worked to improve the strength of defensive positions recently taken over from the French.

On 15 April a Second Army intelligence summary warned that the enemy might attack that evening, but the Germans did not comply. Aerial reconnaissance revealed no unusual activity behind the lines for the next three days, discrediting rumours of a pending attack. For the moment, British attention was focused on II Corps operations at Hill 60. Elements of V Corps (including the 1st Canadian Brigade) were warned to stand ready on that front.[7] Total V Corps casualties for the period 14–20 April nearly doubled to 1,115, of whom 240 were killed. Included in these fig-ures were seventeen dead and sixty-seven wounded Canadians.[8]

Working from hindsight, the historiography of Second Ypres makes much of unheeded warning signs of the gas attack.[9] On 13 April a German soldier of the 51st Reserve Division captured by French troops reported that an attack was planned against the Groupement D'Elverdinghe. Among other preparations, the German prisoner indicated that four batteries each consisting of twenty 'bottles' of asphyxiating gas had been placed in the forward trenches. As if to confirm his story, the prisoner produced a wad of chemically treated cotton that was to be used as protection from the fumes.[10] The French duly passed the information to the 28th Division, and in turn it reached Plumer's corps headquarters at Poperinghe. Two days later a German deserter from the 52nd Reserve Division stated that he saw no evidence of gas cylinders in the front lines. When asked to explain the cotton mask found in his kit, he reported that it had been issued as a protective measure against the possible use of chemical grenades by Allied forces.[11] Faced with such conflicting evidence, it was difficult for British or French commanders to accurately forecast the enemy's plans. But if the Allies were not prepared to face chlorine gas, neither were they blind to the risks of chemical toxins. Reports from V Corps indicate that on two occasions prior to 20 April the Germans used high-explosive shells 'which emitted fumes of an asphyxiating nature.'[12] These may have been lachrymatory shells (tear gas), since the effects do not appear to have been lethal. In any event, some British troops received simple protective masks at least three weeks before the chlorine gas attack. According to a report in the *Illustrated London News* on 3 April, 'bursting shells charged with high explosive are dangerous to life not only by reason of the shocks they cause and the fragments that fly from them, but from the poisonous nature of the fumes they give out ... As a protection, a special respirator has been adopted. At the top of it is a small valve which opens as the wearer exhales and shuts automatically as he inhales.'[13] The masks shown in accompanying photographs very much resemble those issued in much larger numbers after the gas attack later in April.

The days leading up to the attack were not free of incident on the Canadian front, but this was not unusual for the Ypres Salient. Even before his own brigade reached the line, a soldier of the 2nd Battalion noted that casualties were on the rise.[14] During a four-day trench tour just prior to the battle, the 10th Battalion lost nine men wounded and two killed as the troops repaired local defences. On 16 April the battalion war diary prophetically observed that much work remained to be done on its frontage, since 'we did not see how it could possibly be held if a determined effort was made to take it by a strong force.' The experience of the 10th Battalion was not unique; between 16 and 21 April the 14th Battalion had seven soldiers wounded and five killed. Lieutenant-Colonel Leckie, of the 16th Battalion, recorded that since arriving in the firing line two days earlier his troops suffered eight casualties. Three more men were hit before the battalion was relieved on 20 April. The 7th Battalion was very heavily shelled on 15–16 April, losing four men killed and ten more wounded. A storm was coming, but it was hardly preceded by the proverbial calm.[15]

Late in the afternoon of 22 April Lieutenant-General Alderson and Brigadier-General Burstall were inspecting artillery emplacements between St Julien and Gravenstafel Ridge when the Germans finally unleashed their secret weapon. Alderson later wrote that around 17:00 he 'suddenly' heard heavy small-arms fire coming from the right end of the French line. He then observed two clouds of 'yellowish-green smoke,' each of which expanded until they blended into a single body. As the officers rushed back to their horses at Wieltje they could hear the rifle fire moving closer as Germans advanced in the wake of French troops driven back by the gas clouds. As he crossed over the Yser on his way back to headquarters, the divisional commander feared with good reason that a significant part of the 45th Division had already retreated south of Wieltje.[16] After the battle, Alderson wrote that he 'never saw or even read of a worse tactical position' than the Canadian division found itself in that evening.[17]

Chaos immediately ensued in the centre of Ypres. From the 16th Battalion headquarters on Rue Dixmude, Lieutenant-Colonel Leckie watched in horror as large-calibre shells slammed into the streets and buildings: 'At about 4 p.m. that afternoon one of the enemy's huge shells exploded near our quarters shattering every window in the house. This was the prelude to a very heavy shelling of our section of the town. Panic stricken the inhabitants sought safety in flight. It was an appalling sight to see huge buildings crumbling to a heap of ruins, and it was equally demoralizing to see women and children in a state of collapse from fear, being led and supported through the streets of the town to the outskirts.'[18] Leckie gathered his men from their billets and deployed them in hasty entrenchments on the west side of the canal. Judging by the numbers of French troops fleeing through the neighbourhood, it appeared that the Allies were suffering a major reverse. The battalion commander steeled the men for whatever might follow.

On the west side of the canal, near the divisional transport lines, Lieutenant-Colonel Simson recorded a 'heavy cannonade' during the afternoon of 22 April, followed by 'greenish fumes' blowing on the east side of the Yser. As incoming artillery shells crashed 'unpleasantly near' the transport billets, Simson learned that his wagon companies were inundated with retreating French soldiers. When Simson returned to his

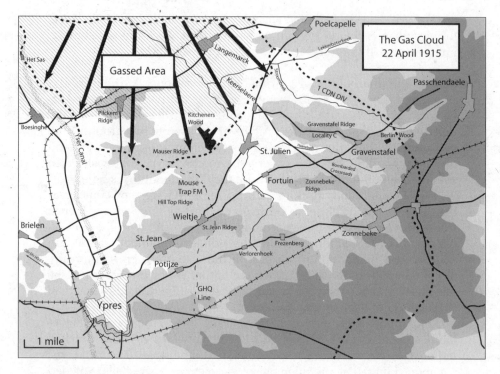

Figure 5.1

headquarters to carry out withdrawal orders, he found that a mild panic had ensued; the wagons were in a traffic jam, with much materiel left behind. Simson intercepted the drivers, organized the wagons, and insisted that all abandoned materiel be recovered at once. Having restored a semblance of order, Simson arranged to move the divisional train companies to safer locations.[19]

Near the village of Elverdinghe, Captain Robinson and his divisional cyclists watched as the heavy bombardment engulfed Quiquandon's troops under a 'cloud of greenish smoke.'[20] The cyclists were then summoned to divisional headquarters to act as emergency dispatch riders. A platoon-sized reconnaissance patrol ventured across the canal just after 22:00 under the command of Lieutenant F. Chadwick to gather intelligence for divisional headquarters.

Brigadier-General Arthur Currie was at Fortuin, near his Pond Farm headquarters, when he first encountered fleeing French troops, sometime between 17:00 and 19:00. Currie immediately ordered the 7th Battalion, in brigade reserve at Fortuin, to stand to.[21] Lieutenant-Colonel Hart-McHarg regrouped his men, keeping two companies at his headquarters, but sending A and D Companies up the Wieltje-Gravenstafel road to the Bombarded Crossroads.[22] Private Lesley Scott distinctly recalled this episode after the war: 'We got called to stand to, put our equipment on, and we went off in shrapnel formation, that was in scattered groups, five men in each group, so the shrapnel wouldn't cause too many casualties ... gas was rolling in, so we [went] straight for it and everybody was told to hold their breath ... We went into shrapnel formation right across ... the rear of the 2nd Brigade of artillery.'[23] Scott's description of the 7th Battalion's initial deployment on 22 April shows how extended order drill – what he refers to as 'shrapnel formation' – saved lives on the battlefield, clear evidence of the impact of training on combat operations.

About 19:30 Currie received orders from divisional headquarters instructing the 2nd Brigade to hold its positions and keep watch over its left flank. Meanwhile Currie apprised the 85th Brigade, on his right flank, of the situation in the Canadian sector. Having received word from Brigadier-General Turner, at Mouse Trap Farm, that the enemy had bypassed the left flank of the 13th Battalion and reached a point just west of St Julien, Currie ordered the 10th Battalion into the fray to assist the 3rd Brigade.[24]

After releasing the 10th Battalion, Currie dispatched his own brigade reserve force, the 7th Battalion, to Locality C with instructions to 'get in touch' with the 3rd Brigade's right flank and 2nd Brigade's left flank.[25] By the time that Lieutenant-Colonel Hart-McHarg received the order to proceed to Locality C, his men were already spread out between Wieltje and Bombarded Crossroads. Captain J.W. Warden, in command of A Company, later reported that his own troops advanced in extended order to a point about halfway between Wieltje and St Julien before receiving word sometime around 20:30 to report to Locality C.[26] Although the distances involved were relatively short, the roads were overcrowded with refugees and retreating French soldiers. Gas in the lungs certainly did not help matters; according to Major Victor Odlum, the men struggled to breathe and their eyes burned as they marched to Locality C.[27] Not surprisingly, it was after 21:00 before the 7th Battalion companies reached their destination. Had it not been for strict march discipline and excellent physical conditioning, the manoeuvre probably would have taken considerably longer.

While divisional and brigade headquarters attempted to bring matters under control on both banks of the Yser, the situation deteriorated in the 13th Battalion's area. During the Germans' preliminary bombardment earlier that day the three forward companies of the battalion were relatively untouched, but the two platoons of C Company holding the support lines with Major Norsworthy suffered heavy shelling (fig. 5.2). Norsworthy telephoned Major McCuaig in the front lines, informing him that he was about to withdraw the support troops a short distance in order to escape the worst of the gunfire. The telephone cable was promptly cut, leaving an isolated McCuaig in command of the front trenches. German infantry had not yet attacked McCuaig's trenches from the north, but they were approaching Norsworthy's support lines from the direction of Kitcheners Wood. The Canadian left flank was now in great danger of encirclement.

Following the gas attack and French withdrawal, McCuaig's gang linked up with a company of Algerian troops along the west side of the Ypres–Poelcapelle road, at right angles to the front line. A salvo of artillery rounds from the southwest struck the Canadian and Algerian position as early as 18:00, causing at least a dozen casualties. Had German troops fired the rounds from captured guns? Whether the shelling was the work of German or Allied gunners is impossible to confirm, but McCuaig had reason to believe that he was being outflanked at a relatively early hour that evening. This was indeed the case. At some time after 18:00 Germans, who had bypassed McCuaig's flank, continued to advance in a southeasterly direction, slamming into Norsworthy's battered platoons.[28] Norsworthy was wounded, but continued to direct the troops until he was killed along with 27-year-old Lieutenant Guy Drummond. Both men had been pre-war members of Montreal's prestigious 5th Royal Highlanders.[29] A few survivors reached McCuaig to report that the support platoons had ceased to exist.[30]

After Norsworthy's force was overrun, German infantry maintained pressure against Canadian and Algerian troops holding the Ypres–Poelcapelle road. Although McCuaig had bolstered the defenders with a pair of Colt machine guns under the command of Lieutenant J.G. Ross, the force was gradually driven back. Meanwhile, the 13th Battalion soldiers in the original front line were handicapped by the low parados behind their breastworks. According to one of the men, 'when the French ran the Huns came on in thousands ... we were between two fires, in this way – our front was high sandbags but rear of our trenches was so low they began shooting us in the back.'[31] The battalion was now clearly in serious trouble. At least one man who survived the next forty-eight hours claimed that he had fully expected to be overrun and killed.[32]

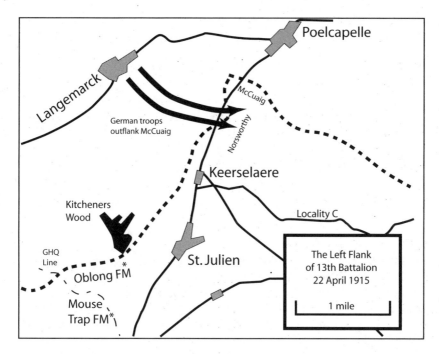

Figure 5.2

The annihilation of Norsworthy's support lines left a dangerous gap between Lieutenant-Colonel Loomis's St Julien garrison and the 13th Battalion's front line. The troops of the 14th and 15th Battalions under Loomis's command could temporarily protect the village, but there were not enough men to close the gap. Fearing the worst, and possibly unaware that the 7th Battalion was on the way, Loomis sent the following message to Turner's headquarters at 18:30:

> E.M. 276   22 April
> No doubt about heavy retirement going on on our left.
> Last report from our firing line by runner they were holding the line.
> St Julien command in position.
> Left must be supported quickly.[33]

Shortly after receiving E.M. 276 from Loomis, Turner's brigade-major, Lieutenant-Colonel Garnet Hughes (Sam Hughes's son), dispatched the following message to divisional headquarters:

B.M. 741   22 April
Your wire to us is down. Our left driven back and apparently whole line forced back towards St Julien. Two and a half reserve companies have been brought up and are occupying G.H.Q. line. Have no more troops available.
6:45 p.m.[34]

A few minutes earlier, *before* E.M. 276 was received from Loomis, Hughes had sent the following message to Currie's brigade headquarters:

S.C. 502   22 April 1915
The left of our left section is retiring having been driven in.
Will you be ready to support us?
6:32 p.m.[35]

Both B.M. 741 and S.C. 502 have drawn heavy criticism from historians. In *Beyond Courage*, George Cassar argued that the 3rd Brigade head-quarters 'conveyed an entirely wrong impression of the condition of the Canadian flank' through these messages.[36] Likewise, Daniel Dancocks argued, in *Welcome to Flanders Fields*, that Turner and Hughes 'dis-played their incompetence' by exaggerating the difficulties faced by the 3rd Brigade during the first hours of battle and overreacting to the threat. Dancocks asserted further that the 3rd Brigade's position, between the hours of 18:00 and 19:00, was 'not only intact but it had not even been attacked yet.'[37]

A careful reading of S.C. 502, B.M. 741, and E.M. 276 challenges Cassar's and Dancocks's criticisms. Although the positions of the 2nd and 3rd Brigades in Sections 1 through 4 had not yet been frontally assaulted at the time that these messages were transmitted, the left flank of Section 4 was directly threatened from the moment that the French troops fled the gas cloud. Loomis was in a good position to observe the dangerous gap separating the 13th Battalion's rear area from St Julien. The presence of German troops along the Ypres–Poelcapelle road was also obvious. Furthermore, the information provided by Loomis in E.M. 276 shows that Hughes was not at all far off-base in B.M. 741. As the message states, the Allied line was in fact driven back on St Julien along the Ypres–Poelcapelle road. And while the awkwardly worded S.C. 502 was sent to Brigadier-General Currie before Turner or Hughes had received word from Loomis, the information it contains was funda-mentally correct, since the troops on 'the left of the Canadian left' had been 'driven in' by the Germans.

When the full implications of the gas attack became apparent during the evening of 22 April, Major Marshall, at the 15th Battalion's advanced headquarters on Gravenstafel Ridge, and Captain Alexander, in command of the 15th Battalion reserve troops at St Julien, turned their men westward to shore up the damaged left flank, along with the 7th Battalion men then arriving at Locality C. The 14th Battalion's B Company, under Major P.R. Hanson, was on hand at St Julien as part of the town garrison. After learning that the Germans had broken through the 45th Algerian Division, Loomis ordered Hanson to prepare a defensive position on the northwestern edge of town. The Germans fired on B Company as it moved into position, wounding Hanson, and killing his second-in-command, Captain Steacie. Captain W.C. Brotherhood, a 28-year-old electrical engineer and militiaman from Stratford, Ontario, assumed command of the company, with orders from Loomis to hold the line at all costs.[38] At 20:00 Loomis pressed all surplus personnel, including headquarters staff and clerks, into the fire trenches before he dispatched a patrol to ascertain the enemy's whereabouts west of St Julien.[39]

After arriving at Locality C, Lieutenant-Colonel Hart-McHarg discovered that the boundary between the 2nd and 3rd Brigades remained intact. The condition of the 13th Battalion was less clear, with reports indicating that its left flank had been 'crumpled' up. At 22:30 Hart-McHarg sent his second-in-command, Major Victor Odlum, to reconnoitre Section 4 with instructions to report back to him as well as Brigadier-General Currie. Odlum encountered several stragglers from the 13th Battalion near Keerselaere (also known as Vancouver Corner, the postwar site of the *Brooding Soldier* monument), but he was unable to gather any coherent information from them. He observed, however, that the 13th Battalion's line was open next to the Ypres–Poelcapelle road, while German troops were advancing towards Keerselaere, just as Hughes and Turner had feared. Odlum prudently headed south in search of Loomis at St Julien. Arriving safely in the village against all odds, the 7th Battalion officer learned that German soldiers had reached Kitcheners Wood, just west of the town. Loomis explained that he was out of touch with the 13th Battalion's left flank, but had attempted to reinforce it earlier in the evening. Odlum then sent the following message to his battalion commander at 24:30 before heading to Currie's Pond Farm headquarters:

Left [of] Highland Bde [3rd Brigade] line, which originally rested on St. Julien Poelcappelle road in V.25.a has been [??] back, French on their left having been driven in. Major Norsworthy of 13th Batt and Capt. Drummond have been killed. Left of 13th Batt line has been reinforced lightly, but more reinforcements urgently needed.

Right of Highland [3rd] Bde line has not shifted.

Enemy are west of road named and are holding trenches across road.[40]

Odlum finally returned to his own battalion near Locality C early on the morning of 23 April, finding the situation there unchanged.[41]

Brigadier-General Currie, meanwhile, had dispatched one company of Tuxford's 5th Battalion to support Loomis at St Julien, although the nature of the situation there remained uncertain. Throughout the evening Currie had pressed Turner for information as to the disposition of his troops between the left flank of the 13th Battalion and the north end of the GHQ line. Just after 23:00 he received a message from Turner's headquarters that the 3rd Brigade held a continuous line from the left flank of the 2nd Brigade (8th Battalion) to the left flank of the 13th Battalion, and then due southwest, along the west side of the Ypres–Poelcapelle road to the GHQ line. Turner added that a counterattack was planned for 23:30.[42] The situation was in fact less stable than the message indicated, particularly in the area where the 13th Battalion's left flank butted against the Ypres–Poelcapelle road. Currie received a more accurate picture about two hours later when Odlum stopped at the 2nd Brigade headquarters to report what he had learned from Lieutenant-Colonel Loomis.

Within an hour of the initial attack against the 45th Algerian Division, Colonel C.F. Romer, a divisional staff officer, ordered the Canadian artillery to 'help by bringing arty fire to bear.' Although Romer's orders likely did not filter down to the brigade or battery levels until after 18:30, the guns of the 2nd and 3rd CFA Brigades went into action directly as their commanders witnessed the gas attack firsthand.[43] Within minutes, Major W.B. King's gunners of the 10th Battery (the 3rd CFA Brigade) were rubbing their eyes and coughing, as traces of chlorine hovered across the gun emplacements. Before long the artillerymen were swamped with Zouaves of the 45th Division, withdrawing en masse down the Ypres–Poelcappelle road. The battery fired for two hours, but the growing number of distressed French troops worried King, and he was probably not a man who worried easily. The 37-year-old from Port Colborne, Ontario, joined the Active Militia when he was just fourteen. In addition to long years as a gunner in the Canadian Artillery, he also spent five years with the South African Constabulary.[44] But what mattered now were the German soldiers within earshot of the 10th Battery emplacements. About 19:00 that evening King dispatched a patrol to the west and learned that large numbers of German troops were close by. Responding to this threat, he turned two of his four guns to the left and opened fire at a range of 200 yards on German infantrymen as they in turn poured small-arms fire into the gun emplacements. A Canadian soldier later recalled that 'the Germans … were no more than 300 yards away at the time. The guns opened fire on them at that distance point blank, and mowed the Germans down like flies. The lucky ones who were left ran for their lives.'[45] According to King, the enemy fire diminished after the first few Canadian shells found their easy marks over open sights. A second patrol confirmed that the Germans had withdrawn from the immediate vicinity of the battery. Nevertheless, the hard-pressed commander had little choice but to divide his firepower between battery defence and front-line infantry support.[46] The close brush with enemy troops prompted King to request a party of infantrymen to protect the 18-pounders from attack. Men from the St Julien garrison soon arrived.[47]

Later that evening King finally received orders to withdraw his battery to safer ground, only to discover that horse teams could not reach the emplacements. To make matters worse, some of the ammunition horses had been killed on the Ypres–Poelcappelle road, endangering the supply of shells. Nearby infantry of the 15th Battalion rushed over to the broken wagons to gather up the ammunition and carry it forward to the guns.[48] Two hours later, with no horse teams in sight, King commandeered enough animals from the brigade ammunition column to evacuate half the battery; tedious hours of practice switching horses from wagon-pulling to gun-pulling on Salisbury Plain now paid dividends. The remaining guns and limbers were hauled to safety by hand. Lacking further orders, and probably fearing encirclement, an exasperated King took the battery over to the west bank of the Yser and reported to Brigadier-General Burstall's artillery headquarters.[49] Lance-Corporal Frederick Fisher, a 13th Battalion machine gunner, was posthumously awarded the Victoria Cross in part for his role supporting King's withdrawal.

The 9th and 12th Batteries experienced similar difficulties that evening. At the first sign of trouble, Major Leonard, in command of the 12th Battery, opened fire against registered targets. The battery sustained heavy punishment from German artillery, with the loss of one 18-pounder. As enemy small-arms fire grew louder and closer during the evening, Leonard turned one of his guns to face the left flank, but hesitated to open fire because no clear targets were visible in the darkness. Thanks to the prompt arrival of horse teams, Leonard was able to evacuate his surviving guns without sustaining further damage. Major E.A. MacDougall, in command of the 9th Battery, was up front with one of his forward observers when he noticed the 'green coloured smoke' coming from the north. MacDougall got on the phone, ordering the battery to fire on registered targets plus what he observed to be the source of the mysterious smoke. Later, with fresh orders, MacDougall shifted all of his gunfire over to the German line opposite Sections 3 and 4. A broken phone cable and heavy enemy small-arms fire forced MacDougall back to the battery emplacements, where he discovered that the situation was no less desperate. He was probably glad to receive a telephone message ordering the battery to retire as soon as possible.[50] By midnight, both batteries were in action northwest of Wieltje, supporting what was to be the Canadians' first counterattack of the war.[51]

Captain William McKee was one of the handful of Prince Edward Islanders to serve with the 1st Canadian Division in 1915. The 33-year-old bachelor had sixteen years with the Active Militia under his belt, plus another year in South Africa with the 2nd Canadian Mounted Rifles.[52] Now he was in charge of the 3rd Brigade's ammunition column. His wagons were moving along the Ypres–Wieltje road when the Germans unleashed the gas. Sensing an emergency, McKee immediately dispatched 200,000 rounds of small-arms ammunition to Lieutenant-Colonel Loomis at St Julien. After learning that the 10th Battery had lost some of its supply horses and wagons, McKee sent an empty wagon to salvage the spilled 18-pounder ammunition. The next morning he was ordered off the Ypres–Poelcappelle road because of heavy shelling, but throughout the battle his wagons continually shuttled ammunition from the divisional refilling point at Vlamertinghe to wherever the brigade gun batteries happened to be located. This translated into return trips of five to ten miles through a crowded, shell-torn road network. The effort cost McKee's column fourteen drivers, twelve horses, and two wagons.[53]

Upon receiving an SOS signal from the infantry that afternoon, the 2nd CFA Brigade fired for two hours until ordered to withdraw to Wieltje. Major Hanson, in command of the 5th Battery, felt that his new position was untenable, and was in the process of staking out another location when a second divisional order arrived instructing the brigade to return to its original area.[54] By daybreak on 23 April the batteries were back in touch with the infantry battalions that they had supported the previous evening. Although the brigade's moves and countermoves wasted valuable time, the rationale behind the confused orders is clear. Burstall feared that the 8th and 5th Battalions might be forced to withdraw from Sections 1 and 2, and decided accordingly, that the guns must be moved to safety. After learning later in the evening that Sections 1 and 2 remained intact, he rushed the guns forward once again to resume fire support.[55] Despite the time spent in transit, the brigade fired nearly 645 rounds between 18:00 on 22 April and 06:00 on 23 April, approximately fifty-four rounds per hour – not much by standards of the later war years, but enough to make a difference. Much of this firing was in response to SOS messages from Sections 2 and 3. German sources suggest that the impact of the shrapnel was greater than Canadian troops may have realized. Oberstabsarzt Werner, a medical officer with the 234th Reserve Regiment, later reported that many of the casualties in his first-aid station were caused by shrapnel fire coming from hostile batteries from the direction of St Jean and Wieltje. From Werner's perspective, the Canadian shells seemed to be falling everywhere in the regimental area with deadly results. The German officer blamed artillery and machine-gun fire for temporarily halting his comrades at Keerselaere on 22–23 April.[56]

The fate of British batteries operating under Canadian divisional command amply justified Burstall's fears of encirclement. All four guns of the 2nd London Heavy Battery were lost when the enemy overran Kitcheners Wood earlier in the evening; a German officer had hoped to use them against the retreating French, but was disappointed to discover that the breechblocks had been removed.[57] The 458th and 459th Batteries of the 118th Howitzer Brigade, in action southeast of St Julien, narrowly escaped a similar fate. At 18:30 German infantry 'rushed' the supply wagons of the 459th Battery, shooting twenty-five men and seventy-seven horses, and destroying several limbers and wagons.[58] Despite this shock, the howitzers of both batteries remained in action until later that night, when they were withdrawn to the GHQ line, and subsequently to the west side of the canal.[59]

In an effort to protect Mouse Trap Farm and put more troops in the gap between the 3rd Brigade headquarters and St Julien, Brigadier-General Turner dispatched the 3rd Field Company, the brigade grenadiers, and the 16th Battalion to a position east of the farm.[60] Between 17:00 and 18:00, elements of the 14th Battalion, hitherto in brigade reserve, moved forward to dig in near the 3rd Brigade headquarters, on the GHQ line north of Wieltje. Heavy southbound traffic on the road between St Julien and St Jean made for slow progress. A 14th Battalion soldier later wrote:

> A steady tide of humanity – the most mixed and miserable lot of people I had ever seen moved by us in the direction of Ypres, leaving us barely room to squeeze through in the direction of the enemy. Most pitiful were the civilian population – mostly women and children – all utterly demoralized and passing seemingly in endless procession ... And of course, there were the wounded – hundreds of them – and the main body of French colonial troops in retreat, some of whom had been gassed with yellow faces and gasping for breath.[61]

Only well-conditioned and disciplined troops could have pressed on under such uninspiring circumstances. After digging in, the three companies held their positions overnight. Although the battalion was several thousand yards from the Canadian front line, it was no less precarious a position. Two patrols set out to investigate the enemy's whereabouts. The first reported troop concentrations as near as 500 yards and the second patrol fell into enemy hands. An ensuing skirmish near the main battalion position proved just how near the Germans had come.[62]

Earlier that evening, at about 19:30, Alderson received word from the 3rd Brigade that hostile small-arms fire had diminished while the enemy paused to consolidate his gains north of Ypres. Alderson dispatched a pair of staff officers to the east side of the Yser, one each to Currie's and Turner's brigade headquarters, to gain a better view of developments. Within the hour Alderson received operational control of the 2nd and 3rd Canadian Battalions, both of which had been held in the V Corps reserve along with the rest of Brigadier-General Mercer's 1st Brigade. Now that two extra battalions were available, the divisional commander ordered the 3rd Brigade to counterattack Kitcheners Wood as the Germans paused to catch their breath.

As Lieutenant-Colonel David Watson's 2nd Battalion formed up on the outskirts of Vlamertinghe, panicked refugees and suffocating Algerian troops flooded the area. French artillery batteries situated nearby were heavily engaged in an ear-splitting duel. It must have been obvious to Watson's men that something was terribly wrong on the east side of the Yser. The battalion marched away from Vlamertinghe at about 22:00 along the road to Brielen, where it turned southeast and headed for one of the pontoon bridges over the canal. From there the men marched almost directly east towards Turner's headquarters at

Mouse Trap Farm. Although the distance was only about five or six miles, progress was slow because of the congestion on the roads. Particularly on the west side of the canal, the 2nd Battalion troops were constantly running into ammunition wagons and civilian traffic. It took them more than three hours to reach Turner.[63]

By the time that Watson's battalion arrived at the 3rd Brigade headquarters, the battle for Kitcheners Wood had already been raging for several hours. The order for the counterattack, signed by Garnet Hughes at 22:47 on 22 April, stated that the '10th and 16th Bns. in that order will counter attack at 11-30 p.m. Bns. will assemble at C.23.a [between Wieltje and St Julien] north of G.H.Q. line. Clear wood C.10.d. Direction N.W. to U.27. Attack on frontage of two Companies. Remaining 6 Companies in close support at 30 yards distance on same frontage. Artillery shell C.5.c. and N.W. of that square.'[64]

In common with other military orders written at short notice, there is no mention of why the attack needed to be made, but this was probably clear enough to the men on the ground. The principles of active defence dictated that lost ground must be recaptured as soon as possible. Speed was essential in order to deny the enemy an opportunity to consolidate gains. More specifically, Kitcheners Wood presented a worthy objective because it was situated on a slight elevation immediately west of St Julien. Although the two points seem distinctly separate on a map, they are in fact quite close together; at a quick pace the southern edge of the wood can be reached from the centre of St Julien in minutes. As long as German forces controlled the wood, they could look down on Allied positions while using the tree cover to stage an attack that would threaten the village garrison as well as the 2nd, 3rd, and 85th Brigades. The Germans paused tentatively during the evening, but Alderson and his men on the ground safely assumed that the enemy was planning further offensive action; early counterattacks offered some means of throwing the Germans' advanced troops off balance, thereby gaining time for a better organized defensive posture.[65]

Because the commanding officer of the 10th Battalion, Lieutenant-Colonel Russell Boyle, and his second-in-command, Major J. MacLaren, were both wounded during the counterattack, the battalion's after-action report was written by the adjutant, Major D.M. Ormond, a Manitoba lawyer with a decade of Active Militia experience.[66] According to Ormond, some of the battalion officers suggested to Boyle prior to the attack that 'at least one platoon' should secure Oblong Farm, situated just southwest of the wood on the left flank of the attack

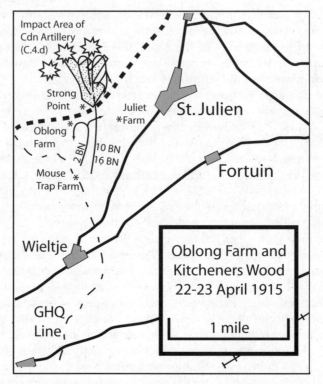

Figure 5.3

frontage, before launching the main assault (fig. 5.3). All of the officers apparently agreed that the buildings at Oblong Farm likely concealed German machine guns, but on second thought Boyle decided to bypass it, since Hughes's order did not explicitly state that either the 10th or 16th Battalion was responsible for masking the position.[67] Such minor assumptions were to cost many lives in this war. Hughes should have delineated specific boundaries in the operation order. Boyle, who as a combat veteran must have known better, was wrong not to take precautions against an obvious danger.

The troops formed up in the darkness with little trouble just before midnight, approximately 500 yards from the near edge of the wood, advancing steadily and quietly until running into a hedge obstacle. As the men struggled through the bushes they alerted the unsuspecting Germans to their presence, eliciting a fusillade of small-arms fire. In an instant the highly energized Canadians clashed with German troops in a trench on the edge of the tree line. According to the battalion war diary, 'brisk work with bayonet and [rifle] butt cleared the trench in less than a minute.'[68] Leutnant Grotrian, adjutant of the 2nd Battalion of the 234th Reserve Regiment (of the 51st Reserve Division), confirmed the ferocity of the attack in his official report:

> The advanced guard ran back to us and exclaimed, 'the English are coming!' But by this time the Canadians were already on top of our position. Bunnemann ordered the troops to open fire, and their fire slowed the enemy's advance, but the attack was too strong, and despite high losses, they entered our trenches. Hand-to-hand combat ensued. Our men resisted the superior force, and bayoneted some of the Canadians, but eventually we were overrun. Bunnemann and many others were killed in this valiant struggle. Some of our wounded were captured while others fled into the woods.[69]

Within fifteen minutes, the 10th Battalion soldiers had invested the southern portion of the wood. Shortly after midnight the supporting troops of Lieutenant-Colonel Leckie's 16th Battalion also entered the trees and became intermingled with the 10th Battalion.

Many of the tired German troops occupying Kitcheners Wood that night were taken completely by surprise and attempted to surrender to their marauding attackers. Canadian officers had cautioned their men not to treat prisoners harshly, but in the heat of battle, some of the Germans who raised their hands were bayoneted, shot, or clubbed, along with others who resisted. Leckie estimated that a hundred Germans were killed, 250 wounded, and a further thirty actually taken prisoner, but the accuracy of these numbers is impossible to confirm.[70]

As the Canadian troops pressed further into the trees, they tended to veer to the northeast, leaving pockets of Germans on the western edge of the wood.[71] About 24:15 Major Ormond returned to southwestern edge of the wood to investigate what lay beyond the left flank.[72] He discovered a mixed lot of between thirty and forty men from the 10th and 16th Battalions exchanging fire with a German strongpoint about fifteen yards away. Attempts to outflank the position in conjunction with a 16th Battalion machine-gun crew were unsuccessful because of the heavy German small-arms fire coming from the west and southwest, some of it apparently from the buildings at Oblong Farm. Having lost heavily, Ormond regrouped the men at his disposal about an hour later, gathered up the enemy's discarded shovels and began digging in for protection from the flanking fire.[73]

While the small party in the southwest corner of the wood attempted to reduce the German strongpoint, the forward troops of both battalions advanced straight through to the northern edge of the wood where they met renewed enemy resistance. Lieutenant-Colonel Leckie, the senior officer on the spot, reorganized the survivors of both units. Between three and four hundred able-bodied men were immediately available, discounting those engaged in other parts of the wood.[74] Having placed the line in the best order possible, Leckie returned to the rear in search of additional reinforcements. Captain Rae, of the 16th Battalion, was left in command of the forward troops.

Upon reaching the original German trench on the southern edge of the wood, Leckie witnessed firsthand the grief that the German strongpoint was causing in the southwestern corner. He discovered that Watson's 2nd Battalion had taken up positions across the southeastern edge and asked Lieutenant-Colonel C.H. Rogers, Watson's second-in-command, to help eliminate the strongpoint. Watson, in fact, had already received similar instructions from Turner.[75] The precise order of events at this juncture is confused, but it appears that C Company finally occupied Oblong Farm fairly soon after the 2nd Battalion arrived in the area.[76] At around the same time, Watson ordered Major G.W. Bennett's A Company to make an attack against the German strongpoint between Oblong Farm and Kitcheners Wood while the cover of darkness remained.

Major Bennett was no stranger to his job. A superintendent of public works from Ontario, Bennett joined the Militia when he was just 17 years old.[77] Now, in a darkened Belgian field, a mere 250 yards and a gentle slope separated Bennett from his destiny. The tall 51-year-old formed up his company for what was to be his first and last fight in the war that he trained for all his life (fig. 5.3). Prior to crossing the rise separating the company from the strongpoint, Bennett dispatched his second-in-command, Captain Leslie Gordon, to complete a hasty reconnaissance of the enemy position. When Gordon failed to return in due time, Bennett and one other man moved up to see for themselves what was going on. In Bennett's absence, an agitated Watson arrived on the scene, urging that the attack be launched before sunrise. At the last instant Bennett returned and ordered the platoons to advance. As they crossed the peak of the slope, the sky grew lighter, and the troops were annihilated by a storm of small-arms fire. Bennett and two of his platoon commanders were killed almost instantly. The remaining platoon leaders were wounded, and few soldiers from A Company were able to get anywhere near the strongpoint.[78] No more than about fifteen of Bennett's men were able to reach the comparative safety of the original German trench running along the southern edge of Kitcheners Wood.[79]

As Major Bennett's force was destroyed south of the wood, Captain Rae's position at the north edge grew untenable. Since Lieutenant-Colonel Boyle had been wounded and incapacitated, it was up to Leckie to decide what to do. Although the advanced troops dug feverishly in an effort to consolidate their lines, the fact remained that they were situated in a dangerous salient, with enemy troops on both flanks. Fearing encirclement, Leckie withdrew the survivors to the original German trench at the southern end of the wood.[80] Anticipating a counterattack at any moment, the men snatched up discarded German shovels and set about reversing the parapet.[81] Later that morning, survivors of the 10th and 16th Battalions counted themselves. In the 10th Battalion there were five officers and 188 men; the 16th Battalion numbered five officers and 260 men.[82]

Almost none of the evidence from the 2nd, 10th, or 16th Battalions mentions friendly artillery support in conjunction with the Kitcheners Wood attack. The exception is a statement from the 10th Battalion that 'our two supporting field guns ceased fire' shortly before midnight.[83] Yet the war diary of the 9th Battery states that its guns 'kept up a rapid rate of fire during the whole night on the northern portion of the wood.'[84] The 3rd CFA Brigade diary confirms that MacDougall's 18-pounders continued shooting until morning, when counterbattery fire forced them to relocate to Potijze. All the while 12th Battery was firing into grid square C.4.d., a zone on the northern boundary of Kitcheners Wood.[85] Unlike the 9th Battery, the 12th Battery emplacements remained undetected by enemy gunners. Evidence shows that Major Carscallen's 11th Battery fired at German positions around Kitcheners Wood from somewhere in the vicinity of Potijze. Although the Canadian infantry did receive artillery support throughout the night, it made little apparent difference to troops fighting near the German strongpoint, since this small target could not be engaged with gunfire without risking friendly casualties. It was likely, however, that the 12th Battery's sustained shooting against C.4.d. – an area clearly in German hands – dissuaded the enemy from counterattacking the tenuous Canadian position along the northern edge of the wood (fig. 5.3).[86] The guns prevented additional German reinforcements from reaching the area, but could achieve little against defenders ensconced among friendly troops and well supplied with ammunition. It was a dilemma that was to frustrate many attacks throughout the First World War.

Although the Ypres Salient was already an active combat zone on the morning of 22 April 1915, the situation changed dramatically when the German Fourth Army launched its chlorine gas attack against Groupement D'Elverdinghe. The Canadian front line was in a precarious state of defence prior to the attack, but the sudden withdrawal of French forces on the left flank of the 1st Division placed all remaining troops east of the Yser Canal in extreme danger. The Canadians, with just two months' experience on the Western Front, had only arrived in the salient a few days before the attack. Their response to the new threat was impressive throughout the first seven to ten hours of battle. Courage and sheer tenacity certainly had roles to play, yet soldiers throughout the division displayed the skill and cohesion that evolved from strong leadership, effective training in England, and formative experience in the front lines. When the call for reinforcements reached Canadian battalions in brigade and divisional reserve, the troops succeeded in reaching their unfamiliar destinations despite heavy traffic in the opposite direction and traces of chlorine gas in the air. This would not have been possible in the absence of rigorous physical conditioning and strict march discipline. Hours of drill helped the gunners to keep their pieces in action, even as the enemy infantry were within pistol range. When forced to relocate, the batteries moved swiftly about the battlefield, despite horse casualties and wrecked transport. Much of the evidence suggests that Canadian troops stuck together, rarely hesitating to lend a hand to strangers in neighbouring units, often under the command of unfamiliar officers. This speaks volumes about the high level of discipline and generally positive character of officer-man relations in the division.[87]

At the battalion, brigade, and divisional levels of command, leaders made decisions based on the best available information, and officers frequently dispatched reconnaissance patrols to gain a more accurate situational picture. While the information reported was not always completely accurate, the assertion that Turner and his staff overreacted during the first hours of battle is unfair. Alderson acknowledged in his battle report that Sections 3 and 4 were threatened early in the evening of 22 April as a result of the enemy's rapid progress.[88] The accounts of officers who were present in the area between the 13th Battalion and the 3rd Brigade headquarters confirm the precarious state of affairs between 17:30 and 19:00. Those who witnessed the action firsthand, such as Major King, knew without doubt that the Germans were well abreast of St Julien by 19:00. While Turner and Hughes were obviously under great stress, their messages reflected the reality of the situation more faithfully than historians have hitherto allowed.

With distant and comfortable hindsight the counterattack against Kitcheners Wood may seem reckless or sophomoric, but the decision was quite rational under the immediate circumstances, reflecting the principles of active defence. The wood immediately threatened St Julien, and by extension, the main Canadian line in front of Gravenstafel Ridge. It represented a logical point against which to apply pressure with reserves. Although very costly, the attack initially succeeded in driving German forces from the woods, delaying further German offensive action west of St Julien. In the words of Lieutenant-Colonel Leckie, 'we gave them an ungodly scare, and checked their advance.'[89] Casualties were heavy, but there was still much fighting to be done.

There was no rest for the 13th Battalion during the night of 22–23 April. As the regimental history reports, 'all night the defence was maintained under a veritable storm of rifle fire,' from front, flank, and rear.[1] Only two platoons, from C Company, had not yet been committed to battle. A desperate Major McCuaig hoped that these humble reserves would be released to him. For the moment, they remained at St Julien under the command of Major V.C. Buchanan, a Montreal stockbroker and militiaman.[2]

In the meantime McCuaig ordered his officers to withdraw the line running along the Ypres–Poelcapelle road, a distance of 300 yards, to a new position offering a broader field of fire. Lieutenant Ross's machine-gun emplacement provided much needed cover for the withdrawal, but just as Ross himself was about to pull back, Buchanan's men arrived from St Julien, along with a single company of the 2nd Battalion of the East Kent Regiment (the Buffs) under the command of a Captain Tomlinson.[3] Although McCuaig's earlier decision to withdraw was sound, Buchanan decided to reoccupy the original position along the Ypres–Poelcapelle road, perhaps because additional manpower was now available. The revision turned out to be a tactical error. Within a matter of hours the troops were once again compelled to withdraw, this time back into the battalion's front-line trenches. Time and space were running out.

Captain Tomlinson's company of Buffs was part of an emergency force dispatched from the 27th and 28th British divisions to operational control of the 1st Canadian Division. These troops helped fill the vacuum between the canal line and 3rd Brigade's left flank. The relief force, known as Geddes's Detachment, was named after its British commanding officer, Colonel Augustus Geddes. Alderson chose

Geddes over Turner and Currie because both brigadiers were already responsible for sizeable forces spread over broad areas. The same was not true of Brigadier-General Mercer, who had recently passed control of the 2nd and 3rd Battalions over to the 3rd Brigade, and was left with only two battalions to direct. After the war Duguid questioned Alderson's decision in the official history, stating that Mercer should have been the 'obvious' choice for command of the reinforcements.[4] Historian Daniel Dancocks pursued the controversy one step further, suggesting that Alderson's choice of a British officer rather than the momentarily underemployed Mercer 'can only be construed as a vote of nonconfidence in Mercer personally and perhaps in Canadian officers generally.'[5] Duguid was right to ask the question in the first place, but the basis for Dancocks's later speculation is weak. By the time that Alderson made his decision, Mercer was already on the move with the 1st and 4th Battalions to the east side of the canal. It is not clear, furthermore, how the Canadian brigadier could reasonably have assumed responsibility for three or four unfamiliar battalions from a different division several thousand yards from his existing headquarters. Geddes, on the other hand, was running a headquarters at St Jean – precisely where reinforcements were needed – as of 20:30 on the evening of 22 April.[6] At that particular moment he was in a much better position to command the force than was Mercer. Two decades after the war Lieutenant-Colonel F.W. Hill, who commanded the 1st Battalion in April 1915 and was Mercer's subordinate, wrote that Alderson's decision was 'not necessarily a reflection upon the professional ability of available Canadian officers'; as far as Hill was concerned, Geddes was the logical choice for emergency command in the circumstances.[7]

In addition to the combined force of the Buffs and the 13th Battalion soldiers under Major Buchanan, three 7th Battalion companies reached Keerselaere from Locality C before sunrise and dug in facing west along the Ypres–Poelcapelle road. Lieutenant-Colonel Hart-McHarg observed that German troops opposite his position were also digging in and requested support from Brigadier-General Arthur Currie to launch an immediate assault, before the German line grew stronger. The brigadier naturally refused, since there were barely enough troops available to hold the line between St Julien and what remained of Section 4. At 10:30 Currie learned from Hart-McHarg that a number of Germans had actually crossed to the east side of the Ypres–Poelcapelle road, taking possession of houses behind the 13th Battalion's position.

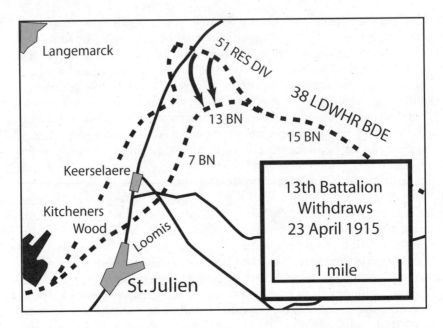

Figure 6.1

Shortly after noon Brigadier-General Turner informed Brigadier-General Currie that it was time to withdraw the 13th Battalion troops from the dangerous salient that was developing in the apex formed by Section 4 and the Ypres–Poelcapelle road.[8] Alderson agreed, suggesting that a new line be constituted from the western flank of the 15th Battalion's position towards the Keerselaere crossroads, where elements of the 7th and 14th Battalions were already in position.[9] This prudent decision shortened the front and economized on troop strength, but it also left the 15th Battalion's forward companies relatively vulnerable (fig. 6.1).[10] This was to become all too apparent the following morning – by which time it was too late to save what remained of the 3rd Brigade's positions.

Although acting under orders, Lieutenant-Colonel Loomis agonized over the withdrawal of his battalion. His battle report emphasized the absolute necessity of the manoeuvre:

To appreciate the merit of this movement it must be borne in mind that the enemy were entrenched and that the forward line of [our] trenches were practically blown to pieces and that a great many of the officers and men had time and again dug themselves out of the ground where they had been buried by the artillery shells. The enemy were keeping up a continual fire with machine guns during the night and with artillery, rifle and machine gun fire during the day. One of our machine guns was blown to pieces and the entire crew killed during the first part of the attack near Poelcapelle Road. The two other machine guns were completely buried and most of the crew killed. These latter two guns however, were dug out and all were taken back to that new position in the new line of entrenchment. The men were all night entrenching.[11]

After some of the most seriously wounded men were evacuated via the comparative, albeit temporary safety of the 15th Battalion's lines, the able-bodied men of the 13th Battalion began to pull out at about 22:00, under cover of darkness. The Germans followed in close pursuit, running headlong into a rearguard led by Lieutenants C.B. Pitblado and Melville Greenshields, with support from Lieutenant Ross's ubiquitous gun crew.[12] Despite Ross's suppressive fire, German grenadiers played havoc among the Canadians, whose own grenade supply was exhausted. A member of Pitblado's group, Philip Jensen, described the action in a letter written a few days later:

Just as we had the wounded ready we heard the hand grenades exploding, and the Germans came on in the thousands. We had to retire and leave the wounded, packs and everything, except rifles and ammunition (I had a dandy English rifle, firing ten rounds without reloading). Now we were open to machine gun fire, and they have lights [flares] which make it just like day.

Then my Officer [probably Pitblado] was told to form rear guard, so about twenty-five of us held them while the rest retreated. We would fire five rounds, reload, retire forty yards down and give it to them again. I saw fellows die that night in the same position as when alive.[13]

While Jensen's estimate of enemy troop strength is hyperbolic, the letter otherwise corroborates what is reported in the 13th Battalion's regimental history.

As the 13th Battalion prepared to evacuate, there was much activity further south about Keerselaere. An engineer officer, Lieutenant Peter Matheson, reported to Hart-McHarg with building materials and orders to fortify the area. Matheson was a jack of all trades. In civil life he worked as a draftsman, but he had also spent three years in the imperial infantry.[14] It was just as well, because at Second Ypres the engineers performed an eclectic range of tasks at all points in the battle zone, from rear areas up to the firing line, including bridge security, demolitions, transport, construction, and even service in the breast-works as riflemen. One of Matheson's fellow officers underscored the varied nature of his trade in a letter to his wife soon after the battle: 'I began to get jumpy from the constant strain on my nerves & want of sleep but everybody was the same. I have worked in all quarters of this battlefield from the firing line to the Batteries & I found after being subject to [enemy] shells for two days [that] to be under rifle fire only is easy; the zing of a bullet is positively soothing compared with the nerve racking jar of the shells.'[15]

Matheson and Hart-McHarg agreed that the 7th Battalion's existing position on a slight rise at the crossroads was probably the best avail-able, but before proceeding with additional work, the infantry com-mander decided to reconnoitre some ruined buildings on lower ground about 300 yards forward of the line.[16] The officers headed down the slope and entered the houses. One of the men by chance glanced out a window and noticed German troops behind some hedges less than a hundred yards away. As the officers hastened to reach safety under a hail of small-arms fire, Hart-McHarg was seriously wounded in the stomach. Major Odlum stepped forward to command the battalion. A newspaperman in peacetime, Odlum was as good a man as any to take over in the middle of a battle. Having served in South Africa as a private with the Royal Canadian Regiment, and later as a lieutenant with the 3rd Canadian Mounted Rifles, Odlum knew something about war.[17] Before the end of this one he would rise to command a brigade, but for the moment his first priority was to reinforce the defences at the Keerselaere crossroads. This he did, with assistance from engineers of the 2nd Field Company.[18]

Lieutenant-Colonel Hart-McHarg died of his wounds the next day. He was only one among hundreds of mostly anonymous men to be seriously injured or killed on 23 April. The 3rd Field Ambulance reported that the wounded were steadily 'pouring in' from an advanced dressing station at Turner's headquarters. Ambulances completed countless round trips between the station and field ambulance headquarters at Vlamertinghe. By noon, however, medical officers reported that they would be unable to evacuate all of the wounded before dusk 'as it is simply hell here.'[19] The situation soon changed from bad to worse as German gunfire obliterated the 3rd Brigade dressing station.[20] Pressure against Mouse Trap Farm was so heavy that engineers of the 3rd Field Company, whose own quarters has been destroyed by shellfire early in the battle, were pressed into service as brigade security elements and reconnaissance troops, tangling with German advanced parties less than 1,000 yards away.[21]

Much of the gun support in the eastern part of the salient came from Lieutenant-Colonel Creelman's 2nd CFA Brigade. The first few hours of daylight were strangely quiet for the gunners. Soon enough, however, the 6th and 7th Batteries were ordered to shoot at a German troop concentration, while the 5th and 8th Batteries fired in response to various requests passed on from the infantry.[22] During the day the brigade also supplied counterbattery fire and silenced at least one trench mortar based on information provided by forward observation officers. The following situation report, issued to divisional headquarters shortly before 14:00 indicates the quantities of ammunition devoted to particular targets:

> At request of infantry, 6th and 7th Batteries each fired 30 rounds at road running S.W. from Poelcapelle. This road was reported as being full of Germans. In retaliation for heavy fire 5th and 8th batteries each fired 20 rounds at enemy high command trenches. Again at request of IIIrd Inf Bde, 7th Battery fired on an old trench occupied by Germans V.24.d.4.0 to V.25.a.4.7. At 11:20 am 5th Battery fired on a battery whose flashes could be seen and silenced it. At 12:00 pm enemy shelled our left trenches ... this [we] replied to at 1:12 pm; battery was located in cover – woods C.10.b.5.0. 6th Battery ordered open fire thereon.[23]

Although Canadian artillery fire was carefully directed against German infantry along the Ypres–Poelcapelle road, there was never enough of it. In total, the 2nd CFA Brigade fired 500 rounds between 06:00 and 18:00 on 23 April.[24]

Near Kitcheners Wood the survivors of the 10th and 16th Battalions worked feverishly to strengthen their positions against possible counterattacks. The 10th Battalion was especially desperate for support, begging its neighbours and brigade headquarters for machine guns and engineering materials. That afternoon, Major Ormond called for 'tools, wire, stakes, and most important pistols and flares. We shall require all available stretcher bearers and ambulance[s].'[25] Weapons oil was needed too, as many Ross rifles were jamming.

Ormond estimated that the battalion had suffered 60 per cent casualties among the ranks, with only five officers left standing. The wooded strongpoint, against which 2nd Battalion had launched an abortive attack the previous evening, proved to be a continued source of grief for the 10th Battalion. Generously equipped with grenades and machine-gun ammunition, its German defenders punished the Canadian troops all day. The rate of attrition in the 10th Battalion's ranks, coupled with equipment shortages, prompted Ormond to warn brigade headquarters that his troops could not hold the next German attack.[26] Fortunately the enemy did not attempt any further advance in the battalion's area that day. This was at least in part the result of Allied counterattacks on other parts of the front.

Mauser Ridge

In the small hours of the morning of 23 April, Colonel Geddes ordered two companies of the 3rd Battalion of the Middlesex Regiment (3rd Middlesex) to enter the area south of Pilckem in search of French troops and the Anglo-Canadian left flank. They found neither, but did discover a force of Canadian infantry.[27] The Middlesex had stumbled upon the 1st and 4th Battalions, under the command of Lieutenant-Colonels F.W. Hill and A.P. Birchall respectively. These were the last Canadian infantry units to cross from the west side of the Yser into the battle zone on the east side. As was true of the 2nd Battalion several hours earlier, sound march discipline saved Hill and Birchall's troops from becoming hopelessly entangled with retreating French soldiers and various other traffic heading one way or the other. But what were the Canadians doing in this vacuum?

After a midnight conference, Generals Plumer and Alderson had agreed that the 1st Brigade troops should participate in a counterattack against new German positions along Mauser Ridge.[28] Shortly after crossing the canal, Birchall and Hill were briefed by Brigadier-General Mercer, whose staff was in the process of setting up an advanced headquarters on the east bank.[29] The battalion commanders learned that two French battalions on their left flank, between the Ypres–Pilckem road and the canal line, were to launch a counterattack towards Pilckem at 05:00. On the immediate right of the Ypres–Pilckem road, the 4th Battalion was to attack alongside the French, with the 1st Battalion in support. The Canadians' objective was the German line atop Mauser Ridge, about 1,500 yards distant (fig. 6.2). The intervening space was largely open ground, with a single line of hedges and willow trees bisecting the area about halfway between the Canadian and German positions.[30] As a Canadian private noted at the time, the battlefield was 'as level as a billiard table.'[31] The Germans were to enjoy all advantages of terrain.

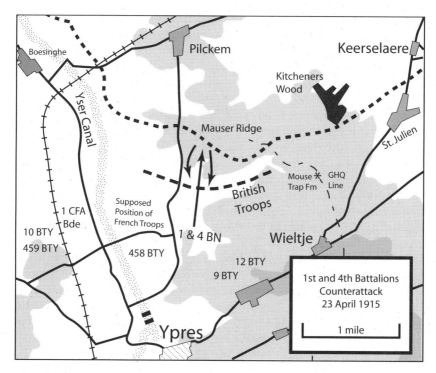

Figure 6.2

Upon crossing the canal, Lieutenant-Colonel Birchall and Brigadier-General Mercer attempted to secure their flanks before launching the assault. Birchall summoned Lieutenant John Bennett, a platoon commander in the 4th Battalion, sending him to Mercer's headquarters. The staff officer who received Bennett ordered him to travel by bicycle to Geddes's command post. Bennett did so, informing Geddes of the strength and dispositions of the two Canadian battalions. The subaltern was served coffee and provided with corresponding information regarding the location of Geddes's troops. Bennett returned directly to his own battalion headquarters before reporting back to Mercer, who dispatched him to the nearest French headquarters with a similar liaison mission. Thanks to the bicycle, Bennett was able to complete the round trip and reach his platoon in time for that morning's attack.[32] Although the lieutenant's testimony does not reveal what he learned of French intentions, it proves that Birchall and Mercer took steps to guarantee flank support prior to launching the counterattack.

As of 05:00 neither the French nor the Canadian battalions had begun to move. The reason for the French delay is unknown, but the 4th Battalion was momentarily blocked by Middlesex troops as they inadvertently marched across the Canadians' axis of advance – Bennett's announcement of the 1st Brigade's arrival had not yet reached the British officers in the field. Believing that the French were prepared to attack on his left, probably based on information received from Bennett's liaison trip, Birchall launched his assault sometime between 05:50 and 06:30 (Figure 6.2).[33] Half an hour later, Lieutenant-Colonel Hill informed Mercer that the 4th Battalion was not in touch with the French battalions that were supposed to be advancing on the Canadian left. The Canadians' right flank was in better shape, with one Middlesex company in touch.[34] Birchall's troops had managed to cover roughly half of the distance towards the German trenches on top of the ridge, giving Hill enough confidence to report that 'all goes well so far.'[35] This early optimism turned out to be sadly unfounded. Shortly after Mercer received Hill's message, Birchall reported that progress was slow and enemy rifle fire heavy.[36] After Hill indicated to Mercer that Birchall needed reinforcements, the 1st Battalion joined the advance.[37] In the meantime, Mercer informed Alderson that the 4th Battalion was stalled, had not established contact with the French, and needed more artillery support.[38]

British forces were no better off on the right flank. By 09:00 the troops of 3rd Middlesex took advantage of what little cover was available, entrenching themselves midway between the start line and objective, 'since a further advance without support was considered impossible.'[39] In the absence of French reinforcements, Alderson ordered Mercer to have his troops dig in next to 3rd Middlesex and extend the Canadian line all the way to the canal on the left, an additional distance of nearly a mile. As a result of heavy fighting since daybreak, Birchall's and Hill's troops were not strong enough to comply.[40] Birchall dispatched the following message to Mercer: 'As all my companies are up in line and I cannot well move them to a flank in daylight. I cannot extend our [line] towards Canal unless absolutely necessary. I am trying to find out situation between road and canal. Have sent a message to O.C. 1st Bn. giving your message and requesting him to extend his line to the left of the road.'[41] With only a hundred men to spare, Hill wisely installed his few reserve troops on an elevated piece of ground. From there they could remotely cover some of the gap and protect the Canadians' exposed flank.[42] Meanwhile, Birchall ordered his men to dig in wherever they were.

The problem of the open flank was apparently solved just after 11:00 when brigade informed the Canadian battalions that the French 'now have five battalions between you and the canal.'[43] It seems, however, that the French were well to the rear of Canadian firing line, since Birchall was unable to join up with them.[44] Accordingly, Alderson contacted French headquarters, requesting that the French troops advance to link up with the Canadian flank.[45] By 12:15 Birchall finally established contact with the French. Despite earlier reports of five French battalions being available, only a mere fifty men were present to fill the gap between the Pilckem road and the Yser.[46] Then, for reasons that are unclear, French headquarters informed the 1st Canadian Division that the Germans were 'apparently running short of ammunition.'[47] It was agreed that the Canadians, French, and 3rd Middlesex would resume their attack at the soonest possible opportunity, although it is difficult to explain why the Canadian or French commanders believed that the Germans were low on ammunition, since most reports indicate that the Allied troops were heavily shelled, machine gunned, and possibly even tear gassed throughout the day; according to Private Betts of the 4th Battalion, 'the Germans used gas shells but they couldn't make our boys retire.'[48] If the German fire died down, it was probably because the attackers had entrenched and were presenting fewer targets than they had during the initial advance. In any case, the attack did not resume immediately, as the Canadians waited for a cue from the French that did not materialize before mid-afternoon.

Birchall and Hill remounted their attack in conjunction with Allied troops during the afternoon. Elements of Geddes's Detachment arrived at 15:45, while units of the 13th Brigade also participated, along with a limited number of French troops.[49] The 13th Brigade advanced between the Ypres–Pilckem road and the Yser as Geddes's men passed through the 1st and 4th Battalions. Lieutenant-Colonel Birchall, the long-serving professional, took personal charge of C Company after its commander had been wounded. The second attack ultimately captured an additional 200 yards before disintegrating under 'withering' fire. Initial reports for the 4th Battalion show that eighteen officers and 487 other ranks were killed, wounded, or listed as missing that day.[50] Likewise for 3rd Middlesex, the second attack ended in 'very heavy casualties 300 yards from the enemy's position from concentrated fire of at least 8 machine guns and heavy frontal rifle fire.'[51] Lieutenant-Colonel Birchall was among the dead men who carpeted the gently sloping field.

The total volume of Allied artillery supporting the counterattack is difficult to measure. According to 1st Brigade sources, just a single battery of Lieutenant-Colonel Morrison's 1st CFA Brigade was firing on behalf of the vulnerable infantry. Although Brigadier-General Mercer confirms the statement in his private diary, it oversimplifies the gunners' collective contribution.[52] In a report to Brigadier-General Burstall, the Canadian artillery commander, Morrison explained that he was in the process of bringing two gun sections to the east bank of the Yser Canal early in the morning of 23 April when he received the order to support Mercer's troops. Accordingly, Morrison set up the guns on the west bank of the Yser, only about 1,000 yards from where the attack was to occur. The 18-pounders immediately registered the enemy trenches on Mauser Ridge. Much later in the day, at about 14:30, the two sections were joined by the 1st and 4th Batteries, plus one section each from the 2nd and 3rd CFA Brigades. These guns were ready in time to support the second phase of the counterattack, and the extra volume of fire was noted by eyewitnesses in the infantry.[53] According to Morrison, the guns fired all along the ridge line until the Canadian and Allied infantry approached the objective. They then switched targets, 'searching the reverse slope of the ridge until the conclusion of the attack.'[54] As at Kitcheners Wood the night before, the last phase of artillery fire may have prevented German reinforcements from moving forward to launch a counterattack, but it was of little direct assistance to Canadian infantry attempting to secure the ridge. Morrison, however, could do no more under the circumstances without risking friendly casualties.

If Morrison's guns were insufficient for the task, there is also compelling evidence that additional artillery units were firing in conjunction with the 1st CFA Brigade. Brigadier-General Burstall's artillery disposition maps show Major King's 10th Battery in position on the west side of the canal, just north of Morrison's guns that morning.[55] According to King, his battery reached this position with specific instructions to support the pending counterattack.[56] Also in action near King's battery were the 4.5 inch howitzers of the 459th Battery RFA. The 458th Battery RFA supported the attack from directly south of the start line.[57] Thus, in addition to the 1st CFA Brigade, the infantry were supported by four additional 18-pounders and eight 4.5 inch howitzers.

It is probable that the shrapnel fire of the Canadian field guns did not prevent the well dug-in enemy troops from manning their parapets. High-explosive ammunition might have proven more effective, but at least the gunners were not handicapped by a lack of target information. The battalion commanders requested gunfire through their brigade headquarters.[58] Intelligence was passed to the 10th Battery directly from Burstall's divisional artillery headquarters.[59] Burstall's private diary confirms that the guns received updated information throughout the day from divisional headquarters as well as from forward observers with the infantry battalions.[60]

Further east, with the 3rd CFA Brigade, Major MacDougall's 9th Battery suffered a relentless bombardment near St Jean. MacDougall was permitted to withdraw during the morning, but decided not to move before dusk, since pulling his guns out in broad daylight would only have caused additional casualties.[61] Major Leonard's 12th Battery, spared the heavy punishment endured by the 9th Battery, supported British troops at Mauser Ridge, using high explosive to destroy a house sheltering German machine guns.[62]

Under the circumstances, there was little that the officers and men of the 1st and 4th Battalions or their British counterparts could have done differently to ensure success, at least in terms of ground captured. According to Duguid's official history, the dawn advance was 'carried out in the most perfect order,' as the respective companies 'leap-frogged' towards their objectives and battalion machine gunners provided suppressive fire with their Colt guns.[63] Eyewitness accounts confirm the 'leap-frogging' described by Duguid; according to Private Albert Adams, of the 4th Battalion, he and his fellows would advance about twenty-five yards at a time, taking cover intermittently.[64] The battalion's assault conformed with the tactical guidelines outlined in training manuals and rehearsed on the drill field.[65]

Uncertain of French intentions, Birchall could only delay the counterattack for so long, as precious minutes of darkness were running short with the approach of dawn on the morning of 23 April. When the sky grew lighter he faced a conundrum experienced by countless other leaders throughout the First World War: go, wait, or stay put? With time running out, clear orders from above, and Ypres within reach of German troops, Birchall decided to advance. Contrary to the enduring popular stereotype of First World War commanders thoughtlessly ordering their troops forward to meet certain death, Birchall led the second attack personally, assuming responsibility for C Company when its commander was incapacitated. As Private Betts wrote home, 'I suppose you saw in the papers about the 4th [Battalion]. Our Col. Birchall was killed. He sure was a brave man. He went up the field just as if there was not a war on, and the bullets, shrapnel, Johnsons and war shells were as thick as hail.'[66] Birchall's men believed in him. As it did for so many of his soldiers, the battalion commander's choice cost him his life. It is difficult to criticize his decisions within the broader operational context as it existed at 05:30 on 23 April 1915.

Officers at brigade and divisional headquarters did their best to adapt plans to the fluid circumstances that day. When Alderson learned of the 1st Brigade's high losses, he issued orders to dig in and await further reinforcement. The issue of interallied liaison was somewhat more problematic. With Canadian, British, and French units operating side by side in a relatively confined space, the coordination of effort posed a special challenge. Cooperation between Canadian and British formations was facilitated by placing Geddes's Detachment under Alderson's operational control. Effective coordination with the French was much more difficult to achieve. The dispatch of Lieutenant Bennett to the French and the British headquarters shows that the 1st Brigade attempted to secure its flanks before advancing against the ridge. Language barriers may have complicated this liaison effort, but there was little more that Birchall or Mercer could have done to guarantee French cooperation.

Should Plumer and Alderson have ordered a counterattack under such circumstances? To have remained in defensive positions below the ridge would only have given the Germans more time to bring supplies forward, consolidate their gains, and more importantly, the opportunity to renew their advance. Although the Fourth Army's original objective was limited to a line running along the Yser Canal, the initial success against Groupement D'Elverdinghe on 22 April prompted General-Oberst von Württemberg to order a canal crossing directed towards the more distant target of Poperinghe, the location of the V Corps headquarters. An assault at Het Sas lock on 22 April resulted in a limited German bridgehead on the west bank of the canal that the 87th French Division was unable to turn back. Yet the counterattacks at Kitcheners Wood and Mauser Ridge finally prompted Falkenhayn to order the Poperinghe initiative abandoned. As such, Württemberg refocused his efforts on eliminating the salient, east of the Yser. This development was most unwelcome for Allied troops in the northeastern part of the salient, who had to repel subsequent German attacks, but at least pressure had been relieved against the west bank of the canal.[67]

At a more local Canadian level, Lieutenant-Colonel Loomis depended on the counterattack to relieve pressure against St Julien and the left flank of the 13th Battalion. At 09:48 that morning Loomis sent a message to Turner's headquarters urging that the attack be 'pressed otherwise our line will be cut off.'[68] Taking all variables into account, the Mauser Ridge operation made sense. While costly in terms of casualties, the Canadian and Anglo-French attacks of 23 April influenced German command decisions in the Allies' favour.

Although it was not in vain, the sacrifice of Birchall's and Hill's troops was a high price to pay. Dozens of soldiers lay dead or dying on the open battlefield during and after the counterattack. Evacuation under fire was impossible for many, but others managed to escape in unexpected ways. Canadian soldiers who participated in the actions of 22–23 April later recounted stories of French North Africans fleeing the battlefield in panic. While it is clear from the evidence that organized French resistance on the east side of the canal was minimal on 23 April, at least one Canadian soldier probably owed his life to a courageous Zouave of the 45th Algerian Division. After being incapacitated by an exploding shell, Private Sidney Radford, of the 1st Battalion, lay bleeding among a group of wounded men in a shallow pocket of ground. An Algerian came along, hoisted Radford onto his shoulders, and carried him to shelter, all the while waving his revolver defiantly at the enemy. Radford found himself in the cellar of a nearby farmhouse, where he remained under German shelling for some time before being evacuated to hospital. Others were not so lucky; as stretcher bearers finally carried Radford away, the house was completely pulverized by German gunfire.[69]

It is too easy to assume that poor training and leadership account for costly attacks like those mounted by the 1st Brigade on 23 April 1915, but careful analysis reveals that such factors as time, terrain, liaison, and logistics conspired against the Canadian soldiers. Conversely, the training that Lieutenant-Colonels Birchall's and Hill's men had received in England and France saved them from complete destruction on Mauser Ridge. Leadership at the battalion level also mattered. When Hill was ordered to fill the gap between the Canadians' left flank and the canal line, he demurred, instead using his limited reserves to control the area by machine-gun and rifle fire. It is doubtful that any other two units could have achieved much more than the 1st and 4th Battalions; even the experienced British regiments of the 13th Brigade were unable to recapture Mauser Ridge later that day. We find further evidence of tactical skill in the 13th Battalion's withdrawal. Few manoeuvres are more difficult to execute than a withdrawal under direct fire.

There was a dearth of Allied artillery in the Ypres Salient, but the gunners who supported the 1st Canadian Division worked diligently and capably with the resources available to them. Despite contradictory orders, heavy German gunfire, and the general fluidity of the battle zone, the Canadian artillery brigades and ammunition columns moved swiftly about the area, bringing the guns into action where they were needed. In common with their infantry colleagues, artillery officers modified orders to accommodate immediate needs, such as when Major MacDougall delayed the 9th Battery's withdrawal until the cover of darkness was available. Likewise, the adaptive engineers carried out a range of tasks across the battlefield, often under enemy observation. All of the Canadian troops must have neared exhaustion by the end of the day. They were to enjoy little respite. The worst of the Second Battle of Ypres still lay ahead.

7 24 April 1915: The Breaking Point

The thirty hours of battle following the gas attack of 22 April severely tested the training, endurance, cohesion, and morale of Canadian soldiers. Thanks in part to prompt counterattacks and reinforcement, there was some evidence of diminished German initiative throughout the afternoon and evening of 23 April, but the danger of a further breakthrough remained very real. A number of factors exacerbated the desperate defensive situation. Many officers and men had been awake and active for between thirty-six and forty-eight hours by the break of dawn on 24 April 1915. Coupled with the effects of exposure to chlorine gas on 22 April, lack of sleep impeded judgment under already stressful conditions. Hunger and thirst further aggravated the general level of fatigue. And by dawn on 24 April, three Canadian battalions (the 4th, 7th, and 10th) had lost their commanders. Leadership increasingly devolved upon lower ranks, as majors were substituted for lieutenant-colonels, lieutenants for captains, and so on.

During 22 and 23 April, Alderson was able to influence the battle to a surprising extent. It appears that communication between divisional and brigade headquarters was especially effective during the 1st Brigade's counterattack against Mauser Ridge. In that instance Alderson's job was undoubtedly facilitated by the relative proximity of Mercer's command post to divisional headquarters at the Chateau des Trois Tours. But the command hierarchy was about to get much more complex with the arrival of reserves throughout the northeastern portion of the salient. Although these fresh troops were most welcome, the sudden influx of manpower in a confined operational area invariably complicated command arrangements and planning. This was particularly so in the Canadian sector, where two Canadian brigade headquarters and a British divisional headquarters were already situated in close proximity. Many of the incoming reinforcements were temporarily assigned to Alderson, whose responsibilities increased considerably with each new brigade assigned to his command. Yet situated physically much nearer to the Canadian brigadiers than Alderson was Major-General Thomas D'Oyly Snow, in command of the 27th British Division. By many accounts Snow was a peculiar man, perhaps of questionable stability, and not likely the most effective general officer in the British Expeditionary Force. A grouch under the best of circumstances, Snow's ill-humour in early 1915 was probably aggravated by a serious accident that had resulted in a fractured pelvis.[1] Now, in a moment of supreme crisis, V Corps appointed Snow to command all reserve troops in the Ypres Salient, in addition to the 27th Division. Confusion inevitably resulted when the officers in the field were uncertain whether to follow the orders of their own divisional chain of command, the closest superior officer, or Snow. Alderson's voice was now but one among several issuing orders to the same brigades.

Terrain and limited space for manoeuvre posed additional challenges beyond Canadian control. Much of the ground northeast of Ypres was now under German observation, making movement by day very difficult. The main roads radiating out of town towards Poelcapelle, St Julien, Keerselaere, and Gravenstafel were easy targets for pre-registered artillery, as was Ypres itself. Traffic moving from the west bank of the Yser into the battle zone was forced to run the gauntlet of crowded, narrow, and heavily shelled streets through the town. Finding the safest route became something of a gruesome sport. As one Canadian officer later recalled, the road passing around the north end of Ypres was under direct small-arms fire, while artillery might fall just about anywhere else: 'Dante lacked imagination when he wrote *Inferno*. He ought to have ridden with me through Ypres twice during the middle of the night at a mad gallop over slippery cobble stones with the whole town on fire and stranded vehicles and bodies of dead men and horses blocking all the roads. I shall never forget it.'[2]

Beyond the danger posed by shot and shell, travellers also had to contend with nearly constant traffic jams on the road network as battalions, brigades, and parts thereof sought out their destinations. It is little wonder that transport wagons experienced difficulty moving ammunition and supplies to the gun emplacements and breastworks as the survival of the entire Canadian front was threatened. Just when it seemed that things could not get any worse, the Germans released a fresh dose of chlorine against the Canadian lines on the morning of 24 April. For Alderson's men it was to be the most difficult day of the Second Battle of Ypres, and also the most controversial.

Throughout 22–23 April the front-line companies of the 15th, 8th, and 5th Battalions were subjected to punishing artillery fire, but they had otherwise experienced relatively little direct contact with the enemy.[3] On the morning of 24 April, however, elements of the 51st Reserve Division and mixed units of General von Carlowitz's XXVII Reserve Corps launched a renewed attack between Kitcheners Wood and the middle of the 8th Battalion's frontage (fig. 7.1). On the Germans' left flank the attack was preceded by a chlorine gas cloud – what a contemporary journalist referred to as a 'murderous miasma' – spanning approximately one mile of the Canadian line.[4] Troops of the 2nd Reserve Ersatz Brigade followed behind the cloud with strong reinforcement provided by 'Brigade Schmieden,' a group comprising mixed battalions from the XXVII Corps.[5] The gas saturated the area where the 15th Battalion joined the 8th Battalion, poisoning a good number of men from both units.

Before the gas was released Lieutenant-Colonel Lipsett had good reason to expect trouble, having received reports that the 'enemy were busy in the ditch in front of his trench' which seemed 'to indicate an early attack.'[6] The veteran officer called for artillery fire against the points where German troops seemed to be forming up, but this evidently did no damage to the gas cylinders. As precautionary measures, the 8th Battalion also arranged and rehearsed an SOS signal with its supporting artillery batteries, laying additional telephone wires to improve the odds of maintaining contact. Early that morning Lipsett observed the ominous green cloud from his battalion headquarters and activated the SOS. After fifteen minutes of preliminary shell and mortar fire, German troops attacked Lipsett's trenches, only to be shredded by 18-pounder shrapnel and the small-arms fire of 8th Battalion soldiers.[7]

The situation was much worse in the 15th Battalion's trenches. Within minutes of the initial bombardment both the adjutant and battalion signal officer were wounded.[8] At the eye of the storm, several officers of A Company were incapacitated almost immediately. Troops who were not overcome by the sickly greenish vapours attempted escape to the rear.[9] Some reached the battalion's support trenches, where Major William Marshall was in command. At least the troops were in good hands there. The 40-year-old Marshall, from Hamilton, Ontario, had spent twenty-one

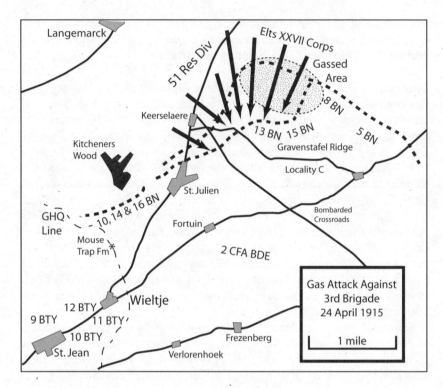

Figure 7.1

years with the Active Militia before the war, including two years in South Africa as a lieutenant with the Royal Canadian Regiment.[10]

Major McLaren, in command of C Company, later reported that the effect of the chlorine on the troops was almost immediate. The gas floated over the front trenches just as the men were 'standing-to' as per ordinary dawn routine. In McLaren's immediate vicinity, at the centre of the battalion's frontage, wet handkerchiefs were of no use. Even those who had managed to retire to the reserve trenches were 'so weak they could not hold a rifle and others died in the trench from suffocation.'[11]

Historians have noted that the 3rd CFA Brigade was out of range and unable to support the 13th and 15th Battalions on the morning of 24 April 1915.[12] The reality was that most of the brigade's guns had been assigned other tasks and simply could not be in two places at once. During the afternoon of 23 April, the 10th Battery had established contact with a French forward observation post near the Yser Canal. From its position west of the canal, the battery was able to deliver effective fire into the German flank on Mauser Ridge, which explains why King's guns did not return to the 3rd Brigade area until the afternoon of 24 April.[13] On direct orders from Brigadier-General Burstall's headquarters, Major Carscallen's 11th Battery joined King's guns early on the morning of 24 April to take fuller advantage of German targets east of the Yser. Word of Burstall's order did not reach Lieutenant-Colonel Mitchell at the 3rd CFA Brigade headquarters until after the move was completed, but Carscallen assumed mistakenly that his commanding officer was aware of the redeployment.[14] As a consequence, Mitchell was left even more short-gunned than he had originally believed when SOS calls began to arrive from the gas-drenched apex later that morning.

Major MacDougall's 9th Battery was in position near St Jean on 24 April, but it had not been tasked to support the apex. After registering on enemy positions first thing that morning, MacDougall was called up to cover the 10th and 16th Battalions' withdrawal from Kitcheners Wood. That afternoon he moved his guns to a new position, just north of Potijze, from which they supported a British counterattack against St Julien.[15]

While MacDougall's battery remained in action throughout the day, Major Leonard's 12th Battery attracted counterbattery fire near St Jean at about 10:00 that morning. Leonard sent immediately for the horse teams, but only one gun was hitched up before the shelling reached an intensity that precluded further movement. Eventually the remaining guns were relocated a short distance. From their new position a steady fire was maintained against Keerselaere until midnight.[16]

If the 15th Battalion lacked gun support, Lipsett did his best to provide additional manpower, dispatching two of his 8th Battalion reserve platoons from their dugouts to the junction of Sections 2 and 3.[17] Captain Horley's platoon took up a position at the extreme left flank of the 8th Battalion's line, while Lieutenant McLeod's platoon moved into the trench on the 15th Battalion's right flank. McLeod found no signs of life, but he did not specify if the bodies of any 15th Battalion soldiers remained. The Germans soon approached this trench from the northwest in order to avoid the heavy small-arms fire issuing from Section 2. They attacked McLeod's men from front and rear, finally forcing the platoon to withdraw at 13:00.[18]

Given the damage sustained by Lieutenant-Colonel Currie's forward companies, it would be easy to dismiss the 15th Battalion from the narrative at this juncture, but troops of Major Osborne's D Company continued to resist for at least four or five hours after the gas attack. Although Osborne was to be captured later in the morning, his carefully detailed battle report, which finally reached the 15th Battalion in June 1918, argues that C and D Companies fought as best they could under the choking conditions. As a result of sustained shelling throughout 23 April, the troops had been occupied with reconstruction work all night before the gas attack. Sleep was not an option. Meanwhile, Osborne deployed two machine guns on his left flank to help cover the position of Captain Tomlinson's Buffs. As a precautionary measure Lieutenant C.V. Fessenden had constructed additional traverses on the left flank, providing excellent protection against enfilade fire after the 13th Battalion shortened its line on 23 April.

Immediately after the morning gas attack, Osborne's troops and survivors from C Company found themselves firing point-blank at German troops on both flanks. It was an unfair match, as German forces directly in front poured additional fire on the distracted Canadians. As the choking survivors struggled to keep the Germans at bay, ammunition began to run out. Osborne sent runners to St Julien in search of fresh cartridges and support troops, but these men never returned before he was captured. It is unlikely that they ever reached St Julien through the masses of enemy troops. There is nothing in Osborne's report to indicate weapon malfunction; his soldiers simply ran out of ammunition and were overrun.[19]

The dissolution of the 15th Battalion exacerbated an already dangerous situation for the 13th Battalion and Captain Tomlinson's Buffs. After the previous evening's tactical withdrawal, the Canadian battalion and the British company were situated on the apex of a small salient, subjected to harassment from several directions (fig. 7.2). During the night of 23–24 April, three companies of the 14th Battalion helped the 13th to consolidate its left flank. The two battalions escaped the worst of the gas on the morning of 24 April, but were 'literally blown out of their trenches.'[20] One of the 14th Battalion companies lost all of its officers. Although the troops had spent the last few hours of darkness digging, the shelling obliterated most of the trenches and breastworks. Under the incessant gunfire, two of the 13th Battalion's machine guns were buried and could not be recovered. By these criteria the position was no longer defensible, and the penetration on the 15th Battalion's front compelled the 13th Battalion to pull back once again, this time under orders from Major Buchanan. According to Lieutenant-Colonel Loomis, the survivors executed a fighting withdrawal, with 'every inch of the ground contested' by 'selected' men.[21]

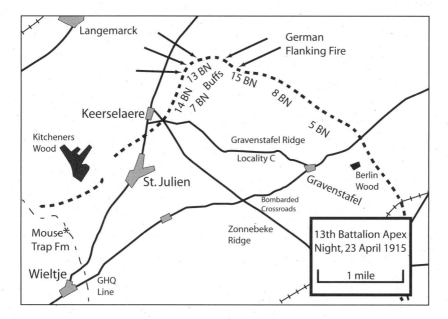

Langemarck

German
Flanking Fire

13 BN
Buffs
14 BN
7 BN
15 BN
8 BN
5 BN

Keerselaere

Kitcheners
Wood

Gravenstafel Ridge

Locality C

St. Julien

Gravenstafel

Berlin
Wood

Bombarded
Crossroads

Mouse
Trap Fm

Zonnebeke
Ridge

13th Battalion Apex
Night, 23 April 1915

Wieltje

GHQ
Line

1 mile

Figure 7.2

Unfortunately, neither A Company, nor Captain Tomlinson's men received the withdrawal order soon enough to coordinate their actions with the other companies. As a result, many men from A Company were captured or killed, as were most of the British troops. Lieutenant Pitblado, who had led the 13th Battalion rearguard during the previous night's withdrawal, was shot through the knee as he conferred with another officer, who was also hit at the same time. A few moments later, bullets again struck both men in the legs just before they fell into enemy hands.[22] The severity of their injuries testifies to the heavy small-arms fire that sliced the air.

On the extreme right of the Canadian line, in Section 1, Lieutenant-Colonel G.S. Tuxford and his 5th Battalion were surprisingly isolated from the key developments of 22–23 April. As a result of the heavy traffic congestion and artillery fire, it was difficult for service wagons to maintain contact with the battalion. Tuxford had heard rumours that poisonous gas had been used against the French divisions, but when his adjutant called him outside early that day to witness the 'greeny, yellow smoke' blowing over the trenches of the 8th and 15th Battalions, he was still uncertain if that was actually what the gas looked like. The presence of chlorine was confirmed when Tuxford telephoned Lieutenant-Colonel Lipsett at the 8th Battalion headquarters, 'and he replied personally, choking and gasping in such a manner that I thought he was done for.'[23] Later in the morning Lipsett requested support from Tuxford as the 8th Battalion's front was attacked. Tuxford dispatched three platoons from C Company, leaving one platoon in place on the higher ground behind his lines. Soon after issuing his first request, Lipsett asked for more troops and received the fourth platoon from C Company, leaving Tuxford with just two companies (A and B) to defend Section 1.[24] At some point during the day a company-sized party of Germans broke through on the 8th Battalion's left flank and set up machine guns in a cottage several hundred yards to the rear of Tuxford's position.[25] The men from A and B Companies could stand hunger and fatigue, but now their position was growing increasingly precarious from a tactical standpoint.

The troops of Tuxford's C Company were welcome reinforcements on Lipsett's left flank. At least two or three officers from both battalions were killed while getting the men into position, but Lipsett later claimed that this infusion of support saved his trenches from annihilation. As it was, the gas-choked men were torn apart by trench mortar, artillery, and small-arms fire.[26] Somewhat better rearward cover in the centre of Lipsett's trenches rendered the troops there less vulnerable to enfilade fire, but the nature of the terrain in this zone permitted German troops to form up unobserved in front of their own trenches, while a tall mustard crop afforded some cover as they advanced towards the 8th Battalion's parapet. The Germans launched at least five frontal attacks against this point during the day and night of 24 April. Each was beaten back, although some Germans managed to reach the Canadian wire before being shot down at point-blank range.[27] Sergeant Bill Alldritt painted a desperate picture in his final diary entry: 'Robertson and Roberts were killed … Main casualties in our trench – Lieut. Reynolds for one. Germans massing. Frith, dead. Eccles dead. Robertson and Roberts and Burns of my [machine] gun teams killed and Hamilton, Flower wounded.'[28] According to some sources Alldritt 'died at this post' on 24 April.[29] In fact, the machine gunner was captured and survived the war. A thoughtful German soldier found his discarded diary on the battlefield in May 1915 and somehow mailed it back to Alldritt's hometown of Winnipeg. The original diary survives, with traces of Flanders' mud staining its pages, in the Library and Archives of Canada. Alldritt died in 1933 at 52 years of age.

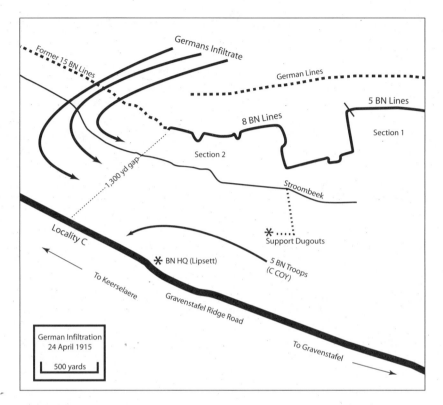

Former 15 BN Lines

Germans Infiltrate

German Lines

5 BN Lines

8 BN Lines

Section 1

Section 2

1,300 yd gap

Stroombeek

Locality C

Support Dugouts

* BN HQ (Lipsett)

* 5 BN Troops
(C COY)

To Keerselaere

Gravenstafel Ridge Road

To Gravenstafel

German Infiltration
24 April 1915

500 yards

Figure 7.3

The situation at Lipsett's command post was no less desperate than in the forward trenches. With the dispersal of the 13th and the 15th Battalions, a number of German troops had infiltrated the zone between Locality C and the 8th Battalion headquarters. Although only about 800 yards separated the two positions, much of the intervening ground was dead or covered by tall crops, leaving the Germans to move about with near impunity (fig. 7.3). In response to German incursions, Lipsett deployed a small number of 5th Battalion reinforcements to occupy an intermediate position between Locality C and his own headquarters, but there were no spare troops available to fill the 1,300-yard gap between the left flank of Section 2 and Locality C to the southwest.[30]

Meanwhile, the single company of the 7th Battalion remaining at Locality C under 44-year-old Captain John Warden had been under heavy pressure since the Germans struck on the morning of 24 April.[31] From his vantage point atop Gravenstafel Ridge, Warden observed the kilted highland soldiers of the 3rd Brigade falling back shortly after 05:00 under the greenish cloud, which passed over Locality C and killed at least two of his men (fig. 7.4). Although under direct artillery fire, Warden minimized casualties by spreading his single company of men at intervals along trenches that had been built to accommodate an entire battalion. According to Warden, the 3rd Brigade troops 'suffered most severely while falling back,' but he did not specify whether it was gas, artillery, or small-arms fire that exacted the greatest toll. The stalwart company commander made clear, however, that the 3rd Brigade troops may have retired too soon and without complete justification: 'They were gassed, but from the rapidity of their retirement I am of the opinion that they were not worse gassed than the 8th Battalion, who I observed were still holding on. This would be about 5 a.m.'[32] Brigadier-General Arthur Currie shared Warden's negative appraisal of the 15th Battalion's performance: 'The 8th Battalion were subjected to exactly the same bombardment as the 15th Battalion but never left their trenches ... The retirement of highlanders exposed [the] left of 8th Battalion and right of 7th Battalion [at Keerselaere].'[33] While it may have been true that both the 8th and 15th Battalions were gassed to the same extent, Warden and Currie were probably unaware that Lipsett's troops received primitive respirators prior to the attack.[34] There is no evidence that the troops of the 15th Battalion were similarly equipped, nor were they afforded the same degree of artillery support as provided for Lipsett's men by Creelman's guns. In contrast to Warden and Currie, Sergeant Alldritt, who was present in the 8th Battalion's trenches, recorded that 'nearly all the 3rd brigade [was] wiped out' during the 'argument' with the Germans that morning.[35] It is unlikely that any other troops would have behaved differently than those of the 15th Battalion under the same conditions.

Warden gathered in his men to make room for the oncoming Canadians as an unidentified major from the 3rd Brigade assumed command of the trench. Within a few minutes a large number of enemy troops advanced through the 1,300-yard gap between Locality C and the 8th Battalion's lines. Warden's men opened fire, possibly in conjunction with the 8th Battalion's troops, inflicting especially heavy losses on the Germans, many of whom were trapped in the Canadian crossfire (fig. 7.5). There had not been enough soldiers to fill the gap, but Warden's response showed that well-directed small-arms fire could at

Figure 7.4. The northward view of the battlefield from Locality C is as impressive today as it was in 1915. From this vantage point, Captain Warden observed the destruction of the 3rd Brigade on the morning of 24 April. The church steeple at Poelcapelle is just visible in the distant middle horizon. (Author's photograph)

least temporarily prevent the enemy from passing through. After the Germans redirected their efforts against Locality C, they were again driven back by small-arms fire, thanks in part to the position's excellent field of view. Within the hour a second attack was launched behind a group of men wearing British or Canadian uniforms. Warden suspected that it was a ruse, but the major from the 3rd Brigade refused to issue a firing order, believing the men to be bona fide Canadian prisoners. Warden grew anxious, estimating that his soldiers were outnumbered by ten to one, and ordered them to fire when the enemy was within fifty yards. The major immediately countermanded the order, but Warden again ordered his men to fire. A second time the major called on the troops to cease firing, yet Warden prevailed and the attack was driven back. Whether the men were prisoners or not, there was little choice but to fire or be overrun. An embittered Warden later claimed that the 3rd Brigade troops abandoned the trench soon after, leaving the attenuated 7th Battalion company on its own.[36]

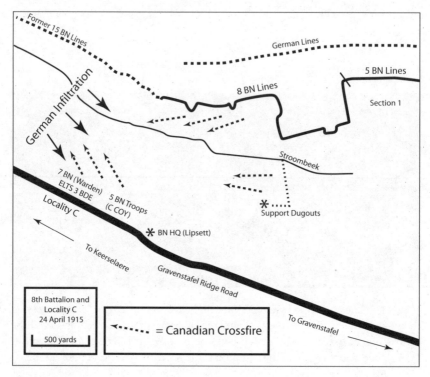

Figure 7.5

When Brigadier-General Turner learned of the desperate circumstances confronting the 2nd and 3rd Brigades in and around Sections 2
and 3 he ordered the remnants of the 10th and 16th Battalions to withdraw from their positions south of Kitcheners Wood. Command of the
10th Battalion reverted to the 2nd Brigade, while the 16th Battalion was
sent to 'support the troops retiring on St Julien.'[37] Historian Daniel
Dancocks criticized Turner's decision to redeploy the 16th Battalion,
on the ground that he did so for the wrong reason.[38] Dancocks predicated his verdict on a message that Garnet Hughes sent to divisional
headquarters at 04:55, stating in part that 'Left of Second Bde section
trenches has been driven in' and that, consequently, reinforcements
would be sent from Kitcheners Wood.[39] The message makes no mention of the fate of the 13th or 15th Battalions, and it is unclear if Turner
appreciated the gravity of the situation on the 3rd Brigade's front at

this early hour. Nevertheless, his belief that the 2nd Brigade's left flank was in trouble was far from mistaken. Turner's timely decision to send reinforcements from a less-threatened area demonstrated a degree of forethought that is difficult to condemn, unless one insists on taking unfair advantage of hindsight.

After the 10th Battalion's ordeal of 22–23 April, just three officers and 171 other ranks were available to complete the march to the 2nd Brigade's area. Currie directed Major Ormond's survivors to Locality C, placing them under Lipsett's immediate command. Lipsett in turn ordered Ormond to 'secure Locality C,' impressing on him 'the necessity of our not allowing the Germans in to Locality C.'[40] Ormond carried out a hasty reconnaissance and then moved his men – many of them badly affected by gas – into position. There they discovered the remnants of Captain Warden's company, plus a mixture of troops from other unspecified units.[41] According to Warden, the 10th Battalion men arrived before 09:00, but precisely what transpired between that hour and noon is conjectural.[42] Ormond's otherwise detailed report is difficult to follow at this point, but it indicates that the mixed group of Canadians fired intermittently at a distant mass of enemy troops while under heavy artillery and machine-gun fire. Casualties accumulated quickly in the Canadian trenches, as the explosions and automatic-weapons fire along the parapet threw heaps of sand and debris onto the troops that 'fearfully' jammed their weapons.[43] Warden was compelled to withdraw from the left portion of his trenches, which was soon after occupied by Germans. The fighting was hand to hand in places as the Canadians exchanged fire with the Germans across an improvised barrier. Warden could see that the 8th Battalion was holding on to its positions, but he could observe no friendly troops west of Locality C. After none of the three patrols he sent toward St Julien returned, Warden concluded that his left flank was completely surrounded.

The situation in the void between Locality C and St Julien deteriorated rapidly during the morning. The collapse of the 15th and 13th Battalions left a wide gap through which the Germans could threaten Sections 1 and 2 on the east side and St Julien in the west. Lieutenant-Colonel Loomis was fully aware by 08:00 that the 3rd Brigade was falling back steadily on his right. At 08:45 Loomis received a message from Turner's headquarters instructing him to counterattack. He already suspected this to be out of the question. When he saw firsthand the isolated groups of battered Canadians in the front trenches, his assumption was proven correct. Loomis proceeded directly to Turner's headquarters, explaining the gravity of the situation in person. The 3rd Brigade was almost totally exhausted by the middle of the morning of 24 April; the grenade officer estimated that the entire brigade had been reduced to the effective strength of just one battalion. It was certainly no longer a homogeneous formation, but one in which all sorts of troops had 'mingled' together in the struggle to survive.[44]

In addition to the 3rd Brigade's remaining elements, three companies of the 7th Battalion were dug in north of St Julien at Keerselaere. Despite the loss of Lieutenant-Colonel Hart-McHarg, it appears that Major Odlum had the battalion well in hand. The men had worked through the night of 23–24 April to reinforce their position in conjunction with engineers, but starting at 03:30 many of Odlum's troops were torn apart by German shellfire. Although the 7th Battalion men were spared the worst effects of the gas cloud, at as early as 05:00 their positions were engulfed with both wounded and unwounded 3rd Brigade men attempting to escape the chlorine. Odlum gathered up an unspecified number and added them to the strength of his reserve company. At about the same hour he sent a message to Brigadier-General Currie asking for instructions. Currie replied that the 7th Battalion was transferred to the operational control of the 3rd Brigade. Odlum, however, was unable to get in touch with Turner's headquarters either by telephone or runner. In the meantime fresh patrols informed Odlum that confusion reigned between his right flank and the left flank of the 2nd Brigade.[45] Enemy troops were seen to be firing less than 300 yards from the rear of the battalion's position; B and D Companies were attacked frontally by massed formations. According to the company commanders, Captain T.V. Scudamore and Major P. Byng-Hall, the German infantrymen, marching shoulder to shoulder, were shot down in satisfying numbers. Sergeant H.A. Peerless, of B Company, inflicted especially heavy damage with his Colt machine-gun.[46] The Germans nevertheless subjected Odlum's men to relentless machine-gun and artillery fire, both of which impeded the supply of fresh ammunition along the Keerselaere-Zonnebeke road. Victor Odlum lost his own brother that day. Twenty-seven-year-old Joseph Odlum, a corporal in the 7th Battalion, was obliterated by shellfire while hauling ammunition up the line.[47]

The 7th Battalion's position grew increasingly untenable by midmorning. Lieutenant John Thorn and a party of B Company men managed to drive the enemy away from a house on the left flank, but were soon pushed back to their own lines.[48] Renewed attacks from the rear forced Odlum to relocate his headquarters, only to be shelled and machine gunned at the new location. In desperation he sent two platoons from C Company into the gap between his rear and the left flank of Locality C. An hour later he learned that the Germans had overwhelmed the other half of C Company, on the right of his line. The battalion was now surrounded on three sides as the combat reached a fever pitch. A man from D Company never forgot the severe wounds suffered that morning by a French-Canadian buddy: 'the bullet had hit his ammunition pouches and the bunch of them had exploded and ... all his insides were hanging out between his fingers like rolls of sausage. He comes sneaking back and says "what'll I do?" We knew he couldn't last long, so I says "crawl up by the bush over there and lie down, a stretcher will be along ..." I knew that was the end of him. There wasn't a bit of blood at all, just the insides were hanging out over his fingers.'[49] Dead and wounded men dropped to the ground in ever increasing numbers as the Germans closed in.

Still unable to get in touch with Turner, Odlum located Lieutenant-Colonel J.A. Currie, who was then attempting to rally the survivors of the 14th and 15th Battalions. The two officers decided to form a new line extending from St Julien in a northeasterly direction towards Locality C. The survivors of the 7th Battalion withdrew to this position at intervals, with one element covering another as it disengaged. Upon gaining touch with Warden's company at Locality C, Odlum was dismayed to discover that all of its officers were wounded. When it became apparent that the new position was too dangerously exposed to enemy fire, Odlum withdrew about 1,500 yards south to some trenches near Fortuin. He attempted once again to contact the 3rd Brigade headquarters without success, but reported to Brigadier-General Currie that he was available nearby with 200 men.[50] German sources confirm that their 101st and 102nd Reserve Infantry Brigades seized control of the 7th Battalion's original position near Keerselaere about midday on 24 April.[51]

Lieutenant Edward Bellew, the 7th Battalion machine-gun officer, a graduate of Sandhurst and a veteran of the 18th Royal Irish Regiment, attempted to cover the withdrawal of a 7th Battalion rearguard from Keerselaere to St Julien. Surrounded by Germans, Bellew continued to operate a Colt until it was out of ammunition, then resisted with rifle butt and clenched fists until overwhelmed.[52] It comes as little surprise that a battle report prepared by the officer in command of the 234th Infantry Regiment, one of the German units operating in the 7th Battalion's sector,

listed 'uninterrupted' machine-gun fire as a chief obstacle in its attacks.[53]
Notwithstanding Bellew's obstinacy, the main rearguard, under the command of Major Byng-Hall, had already been cut off from escape to Odlum
and Currie's new position. Amid the confusion a number of 7th Battalion
men were taken prisoner, including Byng-Hall himself.[54] Private George
Drillie Scott later recalled his last moments of combat that day:

> In the midst of my pain and confusion of that bad moment, I heard
> [stretcher bearer] Hunt's voice, 'Has anyone any iodine,' I was asked to
> throw him my bottle and as he raised it to pour out some for the
> wounded man he was attending his finger and thumb and the bottle were
> shot away. The next thing I heard was Captain Scudamore saying 'Everybody stand up' and a bandage was used as a white flag. I saw two scared
> looking Germans advancing to take us. There was not much left to take.
> Of the men we were sent to relieve only ten were left alive, and of my
> company only four were taken alive ... the two advancing Germans had
> hundreds behind them.[55]

Writing to Odlum from captivity at Kriegsgefangenenlager Bischofswerda,
Byng-Hall explained that the bulk of his troops were taken prisoner as they
attempted to break out towards St Julien. Although the Canadians
were engaged in constant small-arms fighting throughout the morning,
nowhere does Byng-Hall indicate any difficulties with Ross rifles.[56] According to Lieutenant Thorn, who was captured about 13:00 that afternoon, he
and his outnumbered troops simply ran out of ammunition. Although
exhausted, bloodied, and beaten, the prisoners' ordeal was only just beginning. Long years of agonizing captivity lay ahead.[57]

At 11:30 Turner informed Brigadier-General Currie that he was holding the GHQ line with about 700 troops.[58] Although Turner still controlled organized troops south of Kitcheners Wood (the 2nd and 3rd
Battalions) and a mixed bag of 3rd Brigade soldiers in St Julien, the village was under severe pressure. Fearing for the security of the 2nd Brigade's left flank, at about 11:00 Currie warned the 85th Brigade
headquarters, situated on his right flank, that he might have to withdraw from Sections 1 and 2, but not for 'some time yet.'[59] Less than an
hour later, however, Currie ordered Lipsett and Tuxford to pull back to
Gravenstafel Ridge – before Turner issued his own withdrawal order.[60]
Lipsett was acutely aware that his left flank was exposed, yet confident
in his troops' ability to withstand further attack, so long 'as Germans
were prevented working round my rear.'[61] It is not clear how this could

have been achieved, but he elected to ignore the order in any event: 'I got the order to fall back; but in a short time I got word that 3rd Brigade were preparing to make a counter attack to recapture their trenches. I could not get in touch with the Brigade nor Divisional Headquarters but I decided that this information created a new situation and that under the circumstances I would be carrying out the wishes of the GOC Div [Alderson] and Brigadier [Currie] if I held my position ... Colonel Tuxford in the next Section received my decision to remain with much delight.'[62]

Whether or not Lipsett was truly out of contact with brigade headquarters is open to question. He had received several messages by telephone during the preceding hour, so it is unclear why he simply could not have called back to Currie requesting permission to hold his position. More importantly, Lipsett knew for certain that Currie was already aware of the counterattack plans fifteen minutes before issuing the order to retire; it was the brigadier, in fact, who had informed Lipsett by telephone that the '3rd brigade will counter attack with two battalions through C.18.a on D.7.c. Also 2 bns of York and Durham bde will be employed to restore situation on left of 2nd Inf Bde.'[63] Complicating the picture further, Currie made no explicit mention of the 11:45 retirement orders in his operational narrative, perhaps because they seemed unfounded, on further consideration, after the heat of battle had passed. He did admit, however, that at 12:30 he had instructed the 8th Battalion to 'hang on' pending the arrival of two British battalions from the 150th (York and Durham) Brigade which had been detailed to launch a counterattack and restore the 3rd Brigade's right flank.[64] It is not obvious what made Currie change his mind regarding the retirement of the 5th and 8th Battalions, but it is possible that he reversed his instructions simply because he trusted and respected Lipsett's judgment on the spot; Lipsett, after all, had been Currie's instructor on a militia course before the war. (Lipsett had been a major at the time; Currie was a lieutenant-colonel.)

About the same time that the 5th and 8th Battalions received abortive orders to retire, Major Ormond, of the 10th Battalion, could already observe for himself that miscellaneous troops, belonging neither to the 7th nor the 10th Battalions, were heading to the southwest on their own initiative. Shortly afterward, Ormond moved his troops back to an unspecified road below Locality C. There he ran into Lieutenant-Colonel J.A. Currie and an officer from the 14th Battalion, neither of whom was interested in returning to the crest of Gravenstafel Ridge with what troops were available. Ormond was wounded and evacuated soon after.[65]

Hope shared by (Brigadier) Currie, Lipsett, Tuxford, and the 85th Brigade for a counterattack in Turner's area was ultimately dashed. At 13:00 Turner received a telephone message from divisional headquarters instructing him not to proceed with the attack, 'As Germans seen massing in C.6 [north of St Julien] you must not counter attack but utilise the Bns of York and Durham to strengthen your line and hold on.'[66] A subsequent telephone conversation confirmed the cancellation, but somehow Turner construed the message as an order to withdraw *all* of his troops – in including the new British arrivals – back to the General Headquarters line.

Accordingly, at 13:40 Turner's headquarters ordered all units under command of the 3rd Brigade to retire to the GHQ positions, thereby exposing the 2nd Brigade's entire left flank to the enemy.[67] Five minutes later, the 2nd Brigade headquarters learned that the counterattack had been cancelled, but Currie was not present when the message arrived.[68] Sometime after 12:30 Currie had set out for the GHQ line to personally direct the British counterattacking force. According to Currie's battle narrative, neither of the battalions from the 150th Brigade would move without orders from its own chain of command. At that time Currie learned from a 3rd Brigade staff officer that the counterattack had been cancelled.[69]

Turner's withdrawal order reached Loomis at 14:10, thirty minutes after it was issued, by which time St Julien had been reduced to a mass of rubble.[70] Loomis immediately sent word through runners to the troops under his command ordering them to fall back.[71] The messages reached their destinations unpredictably during the next couple of hours. According to a captain from the 14th Battalion, the remnants of his unit and the 13th Battalion had been fighting a series of improvised rearguard actions after being forced out of the trenches they originally occupied that morning. He reported after the battle that this composite battalion group did not receive the order to retire to the GHQ line until about 16:30, more than two hours after Loomis had sent word.[72]

Only a portion of Lieutenant-Colonel Watson's hungry and thirsty 2nd Battalion troops received provisions before dawn on 24 April, but all ranks were busy keeping the enemy at bay, digging trenches, salvaging ammunition, and burying the dead. Using a captured flare pistol, one of the company officers was able to catch German troops in the open on several occasions. Early in the morning, the 2nd and 3rd Battalions were called to relieve the 10th and 16th Battalions after Turner had ordered the latter two to move further east in support of the 2nd and

3rd Brigades. The operation proved especially challenging because in some places the opposing lines of infantry were separated by just twenty-five yards. To avoid losses, the incoming troops were compelled to relieve the outgoing troops one man at a time, but the 16th Battalion men managed to get away with relatively few casualties, thanks to cover provided by the 2nd Battalion grenadiers.[73] In the morning Watson's men observed Germans moving against St Julien and Keerselaere: 'The assembly and the assaults of German infantry against the Canadian line towards St Julien could be clearly observed. As on the previous day, the enemy utilized motor vehicles to convey their troops into the battle zone, and those crowded the roads. The German infantry advanced in close formation, suffering marked losses from the fire directed against them.'[74]

Enemy losses notwithstanding, at 12:00 Watson received word from the 3rd Battalion that the Germans were entrenched in the village. Soon afterward the 2nd Battalion came under attack, but masses of German soldiers were cut down by machine-gun fire. Just before 14:00 Watson received orders to withdraw to the GHQ line in conjunction with elements of the 14th Battalion. The two battalions pulled out at intervals, suffering heavily in the process.[75] Likewise, two companies of the 3rd Battalion were 'practically wiped out' when they withdrew to the GHQ line that afternoon.[76]

Just after 14:00 on 24 April, having learned that the counterattack by the 150th Brigade had been cancelled and that the 3rd Brigade was engaged in a general withdrawal, Brigadier-General Currie was confronted with an open left flank of several thousand yards between the left edge of the 8th Battalion and the GHQ line. The only Canadian troops present in that gap, as far as he knew at the time, were the survivors of Captain Warden's force, a handful of 10th Battalion men, and the remnants of Odlum's 7th Battalion somewhere south of St Julien. According to Currie's personal narrative, he went at this time to the headquarters of Major-General Snow's 27th British Division, near Potijze, in order to send a message to Alderson's headquarters.[77] Lieutenant Edison Lynn, of the 2nd Field Company, happened to be present throughout Currie's visit. According to Lynn, Currie remained in the dugout for approximately fifteen minutes. During this time the brigadier wrote out a message, but the visit mostly consisted of Snow heaping incoherent verbal abuse on the Canadian brigadier. Currie was aware that British reinforcements were arriving in the area, as he suggested to Snow where they would be most helpful. Snow's reply, according to Lynn, was not favourable: 'Snow appeared to me to lack concentration. He seemed to be listening to General Currie with one ear, and with the other, to the whine of the shells passing overhead ... when Currie suggested the diversion of [Snow's] troops to weak points in the line, General Snow fairly exploded. He shouted to General Currie 'Have you come to teach me my profession and dictate to me how I shall handle my Division?' He [Snow] shouted remarks which I could not readily catch or follow ... General Currie remained silent.'[78] Brigadier-General Currie left the dugout without making further progress or receiving any assurance of the 27th Division reinforcements.

Currie was not the first officer to suffer Snow's abrasive treatment that day. Just prior to the brigadier's arrival, Lynn watched as Snow lost his temper with Captain Paul Villiers, an officer from Turner's staff. When Villiers proved unable to provide the precise locations of the 3rd Brigade troops, probably because Snow would not stop shouting, the Canadian was ordered away to find 'definite information.'[79] By this hour, the survivors of the 3rd Brigade were spread all over the map, and it was impossible to pinpoint their exact locations.

What is most significant about Lynn's testimony concerns neither Currie nor the unfortunate Villiers, but rather, the conduct of some of the battalion officers and men of all three Canadian brigades. Before visiting Snow's dugout, Lynn had been directing a working party from the 2nd Field Company. While the engineers completed their work, Lynn noticed that significant numbers of men 'from each Brigade' were heading towards the GHQ line; in some cases there were two or three uninjured soldiers escorting individual wounded men to the rear.[80] In other instances, small groups of men without officers were simply heading south, as had been observed earlier by Major Ormond. With his work complete, Lynn deployed his engineers at intervals to intercept all men who appeared not to be suffering any injury. By 12:00, well before Turner issued the order to withdraw to the GHQ line, Lynn's men had allegedly gathered 800 soldiers, one regimental sergeant-major, and five officers. His report indicates that approximately 145 of the men came from the 1st Brigade, at least 190 from the 2nd Brigade, and 460 from the 3rd Brigade. Unsure what to do, Lynn put the troops to work improving the defences his men had completed earlier. Within a short while, Brigadier-General Currie appeared and collected the men from the 2nd Brigade. Lynn's account of what happened next reads like a biblical passage: 'He sized up the lot, then said – "Come you men of the 2nd Bde. Fall in here, I have a job of work for you to do." The Regimental Sergeant-Major came forward. He formed up the men in fours and they marched away with General Currie at their head. Just before reaching the crest of the ridge they halted and then, group by group, in extended order, they passed out of sight. General Currie went over the ridge with the first group.'[81] Lynn subsequently consulted with the commanding officer of the neighbouring King's Scottish Light Infantry and received orders to distribute the remaining troops from the 1st and 3rd Brigades in nearby GHQ trenches. The KSLI officer also provided rations and 17,000 rounds of ammunition for the Canadian troops; Lynn salvaged an additional 4,000 precious rounds from a nearby dump. The troops were then reorganized into their own battalions under whichever officers or non-commissioned officers happened to be present, but Lynn exercised overall command of the position under the authority of the KSLI officer. Throughout the night of 24–25 April, one man in seven stayed awake on sentry duty. All ranks, according to Lynn, were hungry and exhausted, and many were 'apparently affected by gas.'[82]

Brigadier-General Currie later challenged Lynn's counting of the 2nd Brigade troops, suggesting that not more than a hundred men were from the 5th, 7th, 8th, or 10th Battalions.[83] However, a subaltern eyewitness from the 7th Battalion estimated that Lynn collected at least 200 2nd Brigade troops. Lieutenant Walter Curry, of the 3rd Battalion, confirmed Lynn's estimates for the 1st Brigade troops, while two officers from the 3rd Brigade reported that the engineers collected in excess of 450 men from that brigade.[84] It appears, then, that Lynn's count was accurate.

No one seems to have recorded the stragglers' battalion affiliations, but approximate estimates are possible. A substantial number probably came from the 13th and 15th Battalions, since both units had more or less disintegrated during the morning. Most of the 1st Brigade troops must have come from the 2nd and 3rd Battalions, but it is also possible that a few men from the 1st and 4th Battalions drifted into the area after the previous day's counterattack against Mauser Ridge. The 5th and 8th Battalions were both relatively intact on 24 April, so it is probable that most of the 2nd Brigade troops were from the 7th or 10th Battalions.

The total number of men collected by Lynn is startling on first consideration, but under the circumstances it is easy to imagine how such disorder came about. During the evening of 22 April, several battalions had been portioned out as needed in company-sized lots some distance from their own headquarters. The sustained combat of 23–24 April left isolated pockets of men to fend for themselves, as the better part of at least three battalions (the 7th, 13th, and 15th) were encircled in the wake of the second gas attack. It is hardly surprising that disorganized groups of men should be found retiring in such conditions, particularly when many were suffering from chlorine poisoning.

Despite Snow's apparent refusal to support Currie's troops, he had already made arrangements for five battalions from the 82nd, 84th, and 150th Brigades to advance into the gap between the left flank of Section 2 and the north-south axis running between St Julien and Fortuin. Although these brigades were drawn from three different British divisions (the 27th, 28th, and 50th), Snow had recently been authorized to command all reserve troops in the salient, and he was therefore able to direct the battalions to wherever he thought they were needed. Into the eastern end of the gap, towards Locality C, marched the the 1st Suffolk and the 1/12th London Regiments, both from the 84th Brigade. These British troops arrived at approximately 15:15, before Currie returned from his meeting with Snow. They were guided forward by Currie's brigade major, Lieutenant-Colonel Herbert Kemmis-Betty, and Major Kirkaldy, the 8th Battalion adjutant, who was wounded shortly afterward.[85] The commanding officer of the 1st Suffolks, Lieutenant-Colonel W.B. Wallace, explained to Kemmis-Betty that the two battalions had orders to move northeast and 'clear out any of the enemy met with.'[86] The Suffolks advanced towards Locality C with the 1/12th London in support.[87] According to Kemmis-Betty, the British troops were showered with heavy shrapnel fire, but they continued to press forward, taking care to avoid small-arms fire from St Julien. Although it was impossible to drive the Germans off the crest of Locality C, the attack did alleviate some of the pressure against Lipsett's position.[88]

A short time after the 84th Brigade launched its counterattack, a combined force drawn from the 82nd and 150th Brigades advanced towards St Julien. The 1st Royal Irish Regiment took the lead with two companies forward and two in support. About 300 yards beyond the GHQ line the Irish came under heavy machine-gun fire, but managed to prevent an enemy force from outflanking their left. The 1/4th East Yorkshires and 1/4th Yorkshires, both of the 150th Brigade, advanced in open order formation to the left of the Irish. By coincidence the three battalions collided head-on with a German attack originating in St Julien. A violent close-quarters struggle ensued, with two batteries of the 2nd CFA Brigade receiving fresh wagons of ammunition in time to shell German reinforcements who attempted to join the fray.[89]

Major Hanson's 5th Battery was heavily engaged in this action: 'About this time [17:00] a line of infantry came out of the woods to our left. The left [gun] section was taken out of position, switched about 120° L, and commenced firing with open sights. The two sections were firing at about 2,000 yds range at the enemy in the open and apparently inflicting heavy casualties. Seven or eight lines of infantry were seen to come out of the wood, each line being met by a heavy shrapnel fire.'[90]

The display of strength and fire-power rudely surprised the Germans, who elected to retire just north of St Julien until the next morning.[91] It is not clear if the British or Canadians were aware of the German withdrawal, but it made little difference, since Brigadier-General Turner ultimately ordered the British battalions to fall back on the GHQ line at the end of the day.[92] Notwithstanding Turner's orders, it was doubtful that the imperials could have achieved much more with the support that was available. The Germans may have evacuated the village, but they had moved to defensible positions on elevated ground from which St Julien could be dominated by fire. As it was, the 150th Brigade was subjected to heavy artillery from the direction of St Julien throughout the counter-attack, with high casualties. The commanding officer of 1/4th Yorkshires was mortally wounded, and his battalion lost twelve men killed, sixty-six wounded, and seventeen missing.[93]

Although the British counterattacks of 24 April relieved pressure against the 2nd Brigade, Tuxford and Lipsett called on the 3rd Royal Fusiliers (85th Brigade) in search of additional support. The Fusiliers could spare no men, but Tuxford scrounged up an ad hoc reserve force of about 1,000 troops from several imperial battalions, including the 2nd Cheshires, 8th Durham Light Infantry, 2nd Northumberland Fusiliers, and 1st Suffolks. He used some of the British men, including about a hundred Northumberlanders, to strengthen the 8th Battalion's left flank while others cooperated with the 5th Battalion.[94] Once again, Lipsett reported that the arrival of fresh troops prevented the enemy from overwhelming his own 'semi-asphyxiated' soldiers.

The impact of Canadian artillery fire on 24 April was limited by a shortage of guns and ammunition, as well as slow communications. There was no dearth of worthy targets, but information was often obsolete by the time it reached the overtaxed batteries. At 15:00 that afternoon Brigadier-General Burstall's headquarters dispatched a message to the 2nd CFA Brigade, then located south of Wieltje, indicating the presence of enemy troops on the Ypres–Poelcapelle road.[95] By the time the message arrived, at 17:00, the target was lost. During the morning gas attack, the 2nd CFA Battery engaged in counterbattery work, but the guns were falling critically short of ammunition; by early afternoon the 7th and 8th Batteries had just a hundred rounds left between them. With no word on reinforcements or ammunition, Creelman ordered the two batteries to turn their remaining shells over to the 5th and 6th Batteries and head for the rear. Fortunately, an unexpected fresh supply of ammunition arrived shortly afterward, allowing the remaining two batteries to support the 1st Royal Irish counterattack with good effect.[96]

Only through monumental effort were transport units able to get ammunition forward to the frantic gunners. Although the main roads assigned to the 1st Canadian Division for logistical purposes were regularly under fire, somehow the wagon drivers managed to steer their horses through the deluge.[97] From noon on 22 April to noon on 23 April the divisional ammunition column issued 6,800 rounds of 18-pounder shrapnel, 200 rounds of 4.5-inch high explosive, 140 rounds of 4.5-inch shrapnel, and more than a million rounds of .303 calibre small-arms ammunition from its refilling point south of the town of Brielen. But once German offensive activities resumed, the absolute number of shells delivered fell by nearly 50 per cent during the following twenty-four-hour period. From noon on 23 April until noon the next day, the DAC issued just 3,100 rounds of 18-pounder shrapnel, a hundred rounds of 4.5-inch high explosive, and 845,000 rounds of .303 calibre. The numbers might have dropped even more dramatically had transport officers not devised a better delivery system. Up until 24 April the wagons had been dumping their cargo at the divisional refilling point, where it was then retrieved by brigade transport. This changed, by temporary arrangement, when all incoming ammunition was delivered to the divisional refilling point by truck. The infusion of mechanical transport freed up the divisional ammunition wagons for deliveries to brigade dumps, or in some instances, directly to the gun batteries.[98] Additional supplies arrived through 28th Division's channels. Virtually all of this work was completed under enemy observation in the midst of heavy troop traffic.[99]

True to their corps motto, *ubique* (which they shared with the artillery), the Canadian divisional engineers were everywhere on 24 April, from the Yser bridges right up to the front line.[100] For much of the day the sappers were involved in the preparation of GHQ fall-back positions; engineer officers plotted precise estimates of the number of trenches to be dug, how much wire would be required, the location of dugouts and the size of working parties needed. Altogether the engineers asked for 3,400 infantrymen, although it is unlikely that anything approaching this number was available for fatigue parties on 24 April.[101] Lieutenant Lynn performed an invaluable service by gathering 800 stragglers, while Lieutenant Hertzberg, also of the 2nd Field Company, led a section of sappers in a last-ditch defence at Gravenstafel Ridge.[102] The men of the 3rd Field Company found themselves in the fire trenches after Turner's withdrawal to the GHQ line. The sappers quickly excavated new defensive positions, settling down for the next onslaught.[103] Flexibility was the key to survival.

Leadership and Decision Making on 24 April 1915

For Canadians the most controversial aspects of the Second Battle of Ypres involve the command decisions of 24 April, including Brigadier-General Arthur Currie's abortive morning withdrawal orders (and the failure of Tuxford and Lipsett to execute them) and Brigadier-General Turner's handling of his own troops and British reinforcements later that day.[104] Ex post facto analysis often shapes the historical reputations of military commanders.[105] This phenomenon may also apply to Currie and Turner. Currie's subsequent displays of excellence as a divisional and corps commander, not to mention his postwar deification as a national icon, have largely overshadowed his less spectacular work as a brigadier in April 1915. Similarly, Turner's controversial leadership at St Eloi in April 1916 has tended to reinforce the conclusion that he was out of his depth at Ypres, although his complete wartime experience has yet to be studied anywhere near as closely as Currie's has been.[106] If, for a moment, we discount their subsequent wartime careers, the apparent performance gap between Currie and Turner at Second Ypres narrows considerably.

It is perhaps not surprising that Currie elected to omit his 11:45 retirement orders from his battle narrative. Had this order been carried out, Currie might well have found himself as heavily criticized as Turner later would be for withdrawing the 3rd Brigade that afternoon. In the event, Lipsett's and Tuxford's refusal to retire to the crest of Gravenstafel Ridge saved Currie from potential embarrassment after the fact.

Currie's decision to leave his command post in search of reinforcements posed a much greater challenge to his own reputation. Frequent suggestions in battalion message records that Currie was 'missing' during the day imply that he should have remained at his headquarters to receive information and make decisions.[107] Much of the area traversed on foot by Currie was under enemy observation. His decision to venture out was incredibly risky. In retrospect it might have been wiser to dispatch an assertive staff officer, such as Lieutenant-Colonel Kemmis-Betty, who probably would have commanded at least as much respect as Currie in the dugout of an irate British divisional commander. Currie's influence as a Dominion brigadier-general was ultimately of little consequence during his impromptu meeting with the ill-humoured Major-General Snow.[108]

A fresh appraisal of Turner's conduct is equally warranted. As early as 14:00 on 24 April, Snow had ordered Turner to 'use every man' to drive the enemy away from Fortuin.[109] Turner refused, but it is not difficult to understand his reluctance to obey the commander of another division, especially since the 1st Canadian Division had just issued what Turner understood to be clear orders to retire.

In a subsequent message, Alderson implored Turner to 'maintain your line,' but by the time it arrived Turner was already pulling troops back to the GHQ positions.[110] Another order from Alderson instructed Turner to use British troops to 'make head against the Germans,' yet by this hour the counterattack of the 150th Brigade and the 1st Royal Irish Regiment was already under way. The message made no specific mention of what role the 3rd Brigade ought to play.[111]

It is possible that Turner ordered his troops to withdraw through a series of misunderstandings, but this is not fully convincing. He may also have decided that his battalions were too badly damaged to recapture their positions or participate in further counterattacks. This was not an unreasonable conclusion in the circumstances, and might explain his refusal to reverse the order. In hindsight, Turner's withdrawal was disastrous, but disaster had already destroyed or dispersed nearly three-quarters of his brigade before the order was even issued. As Lynn's testimony reveals, individual survivors decided for themselves when it was time to pull out. Even the best-disciplined soldiers and officers could not withstand chlorine poisoning and relentless enemy attacks. According to the mythology of Second Ypres, the Canadians were impossibly brave. In reality, courage had its limits.

The 3rd Brigade's withdrawal unquestionably placed the 2nd Brigade in great jeopardy. Yet a careful survey of the terrain along the GHQ line raises important questions relating to Turner's decision. Because most of the GHQ defences faced eastward, they were not especially helpful to those tasked with defending the area between the

Figure 7.6. This composite photograph shows the expansive view today from the GHQ line from the eastern edge of Wieltje, atop St Jean Ridge. One can see from Poelcapelle across to Passchendaele on the horizon; views to the east and southeast are just as excellent. (Author's photograph)

Yser Canal and St Julien. Notwithstanding its vulnerability to flanking fire from the north and northwest, the GHQ line was a useful bastion against attacks from the east and northeast. Particularly where it crossed the St Jean Ridge east of Wieltje, the GHQ line offered an excellent field of view (fig. 7.6). It also blocked three roads leading into Ypres from northeasterly directions (from Poelcapelle, Passchendaele, and Zonnebeke). Finally, a number of prepared positions already existed in the GHQ line.[112] It is revealing to consider that the British line ultimately came to rest just forward of the GHQ defences at the end of the battle in late May.[113]

The controversies of 24 April reached down to the battalion level. This was especially true for Lieutenant-Colonel J.A. Currie, who appears to have lost his grip on the 15th Battalion during the morning gas attack. According to an officer who served briefly under Currie in 1914 before transferring to another battalion, the commander, who was also a Member of Parliament, was much more a 'politician than an officer,' but 'had under him the very best material possible in such officers as Marshall, Warren.'[114] Shortly after noon on 24 April, a reportedly drunken Currie stumbled into the 2nd CFA Brigade headquarters, behaved erratically, and had to be 'manhandled out.'[115] By some accounts Currie quit the battlefield soon after for the safety of Boulogne, but other officers claim to have seen him at work south of Locality C at around the same time that he is alleged to have fled.[116]

Currie defended his actions in the House of Commons after returning to Canada and offered no apologies in his 1916 memoir.[117] A series of reports and notes drafted by Currie at the end of the Second Battle of Ypres suggest that he was profoundly shaken, but he maintained that his 15th Battalion was not to blame for the loss of the apex: 'In the face of the terrible losses of officers and men in the Can[adian] Division, such petty matters as a few pounds or shillings do not count. I have lost 661 out of 881 available rifles. My loss was not due to errors on our part, but to carry out orders and holding our redoubts and trenches to the last.'[118]

The evidence supports Currie's version of events, to a degree. One of his companies, after all, was part of the St Julien garrison, and therefore under the command of Lieutenant-Colonel Loomis. And it was hardly Currie's fault that his remaining companies were targeted by gas. Yet Captain Warden's testimony indicated that the 15th Battalion did not weather the attack as well as the 8th Battalion did, even though the two were situated side by side. In the end Currie was the only battalion commander to lose his job after the battle; actually he was promoted to the rank of colonel and returned to Canada. Had Alderson's authority not been circumscribed by Canadian political considerations, he might well have subjected Currie to a court-martial.[119] Although Alderson's frustration was justified, it is ironic that Lieutenant-Colonel Creelman, one of Currie's more outspoken detractors, also suffered a breakdown, ultimately forfeiting command of the 2nd CFA Brigade as the result of a lengthy convalescence in England. J.A. Currie was not the only officer to lose his nerve in combat at the Second Battle of Ypres.

Canadian conduct and command decisions on 24 April 1915 must be appreciated within the broader context of crushing German attacks and broken flanks. Sheer exhaustion, shortages of ammunition, and uncertain communications compounded the effects of heavy enemy pressure and gas poisoning. After the battle, senior commanders, political figures, and newspaper reports extolled the courage of the Canadian Division. The men had indeed displayed courage, but this was no proof against gas or shellfire. Hundreds of Canadians reached their breaking point that day.

If not every Canadian resisted to the last bullet on 24 April 1915, does this mean that the men were poorly trained and led? It does not, for if they had been, it is likely that Gravenstafel Ridge would have fallen much sooner. In fact, there were countless examples of skill and effective leadership that day. At the battalion level, Tuxford, Lipsett, and Odlum each displayed great adaptability. Left to their own devices, junior officers like Edison Lynn and John Warden were not found wanting. The individual actions of countless infantrymen, gunners, engineers, and drivers are lost to history, but there is enough evidence to suggest a respectable level of skill throughout the division. Machine gunners like H.A. Peerless stood out in particular, probably because they were so few in number relative to ordinary riflemen. They were not finished yet. For another full day, the exhausted infantry survivors who had not been wounded or too severely poisoned continued to fight until withdrawn from the front lines. The gunners and other support troops were to carry on even longer. There was little more anyone could ask of them.

8 25–26 April 1915:
The Canadian Denouement

After three days of sustained fighting in the salient, men on both sides of the firing line verged on numb exhaustion. The beleaguered state of Alderson's division was already painfully obvious by dusk on 24 April. But the German divisions of the XXIII and XXVI Reserve Corps were also growing weak by the fourth day of fighting. Just as the Allies sacrificed heavily in the defence of Ypres, the Germans' rapid progress against the northern part of the salient was achieved at near-prohibitive cost. The Canadians and the British had repeatedly cut bloody swathes in the massed ranks of field grey. Realizing that ambitions needed to be moderated, the German Fourth Army headquarters discouraged further offensive activity against the Yser Canal, insisting that the two corps annihilate the remaining Allied pocket on the northeastern side of Ypres.[1] This translated into additional hammer blows against the Canadians, as well as against the 28th British Division. By 26 April 1915 much of what was left of Alderson's 1st Division was withdrawn from direct action.

The complexity of tactical developments along the Anglo-Canadian front during 25–26 April compounds the controversies regarding the previous days. Unfortunately for the historian, the quality and precision of primary evidence begin to decline at this stage of the Second Battle of Ypres. Many of the operational reports generated between the company and brigade levels come to an abrupt end on 24 April, often because their authors had been wounded and evacuated by that stage of the battle. After three days of action with little if any sleep, fatigue peaked among the surviving officers. Reports that do cover 25–26 April are relatively vague, with fewer explicit references to timings and locations. It is difficult to interpret the significance of such passages as 'the company then retired,' without knowing precisely how far the company retired or at what hour the retirement was completed.

The withdrawal of the 3rd Brigade on 24 April resulted in what must have been an uncomfortable meeting between Brigadier-General Turner and Lieutenant-General Alderson that evening. After repeated urging from Major-General Snow to move the 3rd Brigade and associated troops out of the GHQ line and back towards the front trenches, an exasperated Turner ventured to Canadian divisional headquarters on a motorcycle. According to Duguid and Nicholson's official accounts, the ensuing interview between Turner and Alderson convinced each commander 'that the other did not understand what was happening.'[2] The fact remained that the 3rd Brigade and the forces attached to it were largely exhausted by the morning of 25 April and played little active part in that day's operations. Brigadier-General Mercer's 1st Brigade was not much better off. The 2nd and 3rd Battalions had been heavily engaged under Turner's command since the night of 22–23 April, while the 1st and 4th Battalions had suffered crippling losses at Mauser Ridge. Among the Canadians, much of the fighting on 25 April was left to the 2nd Brigade and its supporting elements.

By the evening of 24 April Lieutenant-General Alderson hoped to use incoming British reinforcements to relieve tired battalions that had been fighting for forty-eight hours. His plans were shelved when V Corps issued instructions to counterattack St Julien. Although the attack was to go in at 03:30 the next morning, it was not until 20:00 on the evening of 24 April that Alderson's headquarters relayed the orders to subordinate units scattered all about the battle area.[3] There was precious little time to prepare.

The objective was simple but daunting: to force the enemy back north of St Julien and secure the left flank of the 28th Division. Brigadier-General Charles Hull, a professional soldier commanding the 10th Infantry Brigade (4th Division) was responsible for planning and leading the operation. Falling under his direct command, according to the plan at least, were the 10th and 150th Brigades, the King's Own Yorkshire Light Infantry and Queen Victoria Rifles (both of the 13th Brigade), 1st Suffolk and 1/12th London Regiments (both of the 84th Brigade), 4th Canadian Battalion, and one battalion of the 27th Division. Two brigades from the 50th Division were held in reserve at Potijze. Brigadier-General Burstall was tasked to coordinate artillery support from his own division, as well as from the 27th and 28th Divisions. An orders group was planned for 21:00 at Hull's headquarters on the northern outskirts of Ypres.[4]

The plan was clear enough on paper, but implementing it on schedule was another matter. In the first place, it was impossible for several of the participating officers to reach Hull's headquarters in time for the orders group. The attack, consequently, was delayed by two hours until 05:30,

Figure 8.1. Looking south into the killing fields from the edge of St Julien, where Hull's 10th Brigade counterattack was halted on 25 April. Although the brigade's losses were higher than any Canadian brigade suffered in a single action, the German defenders of the village also reported significant casualties among their own ranks. (Author's photograph)

with full daylight quickly approaching. Surprise was compromised when artillery batteries fired according to plan for the 03:30 attack; the gunners had not received word of the postponement. Because time was so short, only Hull's 10th Brigade participated in the main assault.[5]

Hull's attack frontage extended between St Julien and Kitcheners Wood, where the Germans enjoyed excellent fields of fire (figs 8.1 and 8.2). The British regulars of the 10th Brigade were practically annihilated; seventy-three officers and 2,346 soldiers fell dead or wounded – far more casualties than any Canadian formation had yet suffered in a single action.[6] No one who witnessed the attack could forget the sight of so many British troops being shot to pieces in the open. Men were amazed at the sheer audacity of the whole display. For a 14th Battalion officer, the 10th Brigade operation was the most striking aspect of a remarkable day: 'the feature of the 4th day was the brilliant charge of the Dublins and the Royal Irish in an attempt to dislodge the Germans from the outskirts of St Julien, which they were now holding, entirely.'[7]

Brilliant charges notwithstanding, the 10th Brigade's abortive counterattack demonstrated that professional status did not guarantee tactical

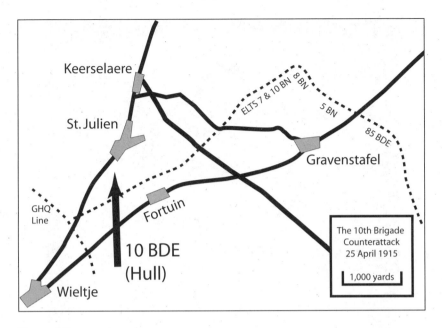

Figure 8.2

success on the battlefields of 1915. But there is more than one way to measure success. Historian John Dixon's recent appraisal of Hull's counterattack is highly critical of V Corps, the Second Army, and GHQ for encouraging such hasty action. Yet Dixon admits that the attack, however costly, effectively derailed the Germans' offensive ambitions for 25 April.[8] The principal German effort that day was supposed to be channelled directly south through St Julien. The sacrifice of Hull's brigade redirected the enemy thrust towards the vulnerable Canadian apex on Gravenstafel Ridge, buying more time for the defenders of Ypres. According to the German official history, the morning counterattack also 'greatly weakened the striking power' of German troops in the area.[9] Like the earlier counterattacks at Kitcheners Wood and Mauser Ridge, Hull's was a bloody tactical failure that paradoxically influenced broader operational circumstances in favour of the Allies.

During the night of 24–25 April, Alderson ordered what remained of the 1st Brigade to fill the void on the 2nd Brigade's left flank.[10] Brigadier-General Arthur Currie, meanwhile, deployed 300 exhausted survivors from the 7th and 10th Battalions along a 1,000-yard line next to the 8th Battalion. The troops immediately attracted rifle fire from

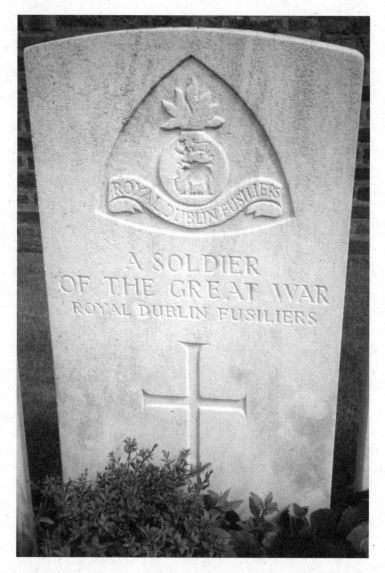

Figure 8.3. The grave of a Royal Dublin Fusilier, probably one of the men who was killed in Hull's St Julien counterattack. Casualties in the 10th Brigade were so heavy on 25 April that some of the graves survived three years of fighting, later to be concentrated in Seaforth Cemetery (Cheddar Villa), on the Wieltje–St Julien road. (Author's photograph)

ranges of less than 200 yards. By morning Currie began to wonder how much more his men could endure. His concern redoubled when he learned after lunch that Brigadier-General Hull's attack had fallen far short of expectations. To make matters worse, the expected troops from the 1st Brigade were nowhere in sight. With the 7th Battalion taking fire from the rear, it was clear that the 2nd Brigade's left flank was in the air. Currie hoped for a fresh counterattack to relieve some of the pressure, but Hull's unfortunate experience suggested that this probably would have accomplished very little of immediate tactical benefit. According to Currie's operational report, he issued orders to his battalion commanders sometime after 17:15 that all units would retire at dusk to a more secure position behind Gravenstafel Ridge. After the fact he cited the following reasons for his decision:

1 A number of British troops from the 8th Durham Light Infantry (151st Brigade) who relieved part of the 8th Battalion elected to abandon their posts, and remaining elements of the 8th Battalion had been surrounded and neutralized.
2 The British officer in charge reported that he could not hold out very much longer.
3 Major Odlum reported that his 7th Battalion troops were no longer able to function.
4 It appeared that the 10th Brigade would not renew its attack towards St Julien.
5 The 1st Brigade was not where it was supposed to be.
6 Canadian divisional headquarters reported that long columns of Germans were advancing from the north directly towards the apex.
7 The remaining fresh troops of the 151st Brigade were being held along the Ypres–Passchendeale road, well behind Currie's position. From this Currie deduced that his situation was deemed hopeless by divisional headquarters, otherwise the 151st Brigade would have been deployed directly in support of the 2nd Brigade.[11]

A review of the day's events suggests that Currie's decision was well considered, if also regrettable for leaving the flank of the 85th Brigade unprotected.

At about 03:00 that morning the 8th Durham Light Infantry arrived in the 8th Battalion area to relieve Lieutenant-Colonel Lipsett's troops. Thirty-four-year-old Lester Stevens was among the 8th Battalion men to be withdrawn that day. As he marched out of the shell-battered trenches, the militiaman and four-year veteran of the British army encountered youthful Durhams, just recently over from England. Stevens was dismayed to learn that this was their first visit to the front lines. The experienced soldier feared that these 'youngsters' – lacking fundamental trench training – would be unable to endure heavy pressure from the enemy.[12] His concerns were soon proved to be well founded.

The sky was beginning to lighten as the Durhams moved into position, so Lipsett elected to leave the troops of his right subsection (D Company) in place, as Stevens and the other men from the centre and left sections were relieved. While protecting the right-hand troops from unnecessary daylight exposure to enemy fire, the arrangement also improved the chances that positive contact could be maintained with the left flank of the 5th Battalion.

Later in the morning the remaining 8th Battalion troops could see that the enemy was digging new trenches on the exposed Anglo-Canadian left flank, perpendicular to the trenches formerly occupied by the 15th Battalion (fig. 8.4). Anticipating this encroachment, Lipsett's men had already excavated a sap towards Locality C during the night, in approximately the same direction as the German trench. This helped to secure the flank somewhat, but German enfilade fire was strong and could be felt as far east as D Company's position in the right subsection.[13] The small-arms fire passed directly through the position of the 8th Durham Light Infantry. According to Canadian accounts, a number of the untested British troops broke for the rear. Seventeen British officers and 234 men were killed or wounded, while two officers and 340 men went missing that day. As Lester Stevens feared, something had gone terribly wrong.[14]

Early in the morning Brigadier-General Currie visited the 5th Battalion, establishing a forward brigade headquarters at Tuxford's battalion headquarters. Currie was chagrined to discover enemy troops well to the rear of the 5th Battalion; about a hundred Germans, including an 'obnoxious' machine-gun crew, had ensconced themselves behind the battalion's headquarters.[15] At some point after Currie's visit, Tuxford intercepted a number of fleeing Durhams. After gathering up the anxious soldiers and adding them to his own line, Tuxford, in signature fashion, ordered his signal officer to shoot anyone attempting flight.[16] Aside from this incident, the morning was relatively uneventful on the 5th Battalion front, possibly because the Germans were distracted by the counterattack by Hull's 10th Brigade.

According to Tuxford's operational report, he received orders from Currie for an immediate withdrawal as early at 14:00 that afternoon.[17]

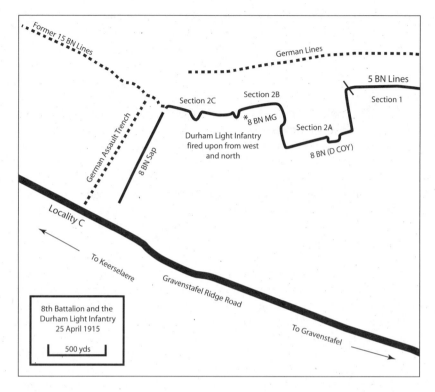

Figure 8.4

Tuxford later claimed to have been unenthusiastic about the daylight withdrawal, especially because enemy troops had infiltrated into his rear zone, but he did not contest the order. Telephone communication between the 5th Battalion headquarters and the two forward companies had been severed, so Tuxford wrote out the orders in duplicate, dispatching them separately with two officers, both of whom were seriously wounded on their way to the firing line.[18]

Meanwhile, the 8th Battalion soldiers who remained in the front line were fighting a close-quarters battle on all sides. After noon the Germans broke into subsection 2C, but were temporarily delayed by a team of battalion machine gunners firing from the left end of 2B (fig. 8.4). When the gun was put out of action, a platoon of Canadians set up a blocking position in 2B, fending off the enemy with hand grenades before being surrounded and captured. Not until 17:00 did the commander of D Company, Captain G.W. Northwood, a 38-year-old architect and militiaman from Ottawa, order some of the survivors to withdraw, while elements of two platoons delayed the enemy. Throughout the action D Company sustained heavy casualties; all of its officers and 139 other ranks were killed, wounded, or captured. It appears that the entire rearguard was destroyed.[19]

After the battle Lieutenant-Colonel Tuxford maintained that his two forward companies remained in position well after neighbouring Canadian units had withdrawn. German artillery fire was sweeping the reverse slope of Gravenstafel Ridge at this time, so it is possible that he had been simply unable to observe the epic struggle playing out in the 8th Battalion's trenches. In any event, Tuxford sent his staff to the rear, and then during the evening gathered up a mixed group of stragglers from the 7th, 8th, and 10th Battalions, leading them forward to cover the withdrawal of his forward men (fig. 8.5). German machine gunners menaced this operation from a cluster of cottages, but the Canadians discovered that it was possible to move at short intervals while the Germans refreshed the ammunition belts in their guns. RSM Alexander Mackie of the 5th Battalion, formerly of the Royal Horse Artillery, relayed the map coordinates of the German machine gunners to a British battery in the vicinity. Within a short time the cottages were shelled to oblivion. In conjunction with British troops on the right flank, Tuxford's mixed unit fired from the crest into masses of Germans who were pursuing the 5th Battalion withdrawal up the forward slope of Gravenstafel Ridge.[20] A composite group of 2nd Brigade troops remained in position near the Bombarded Crossroads on the Ypres–Passchendaele road – behind the ridge – until the early morning hours of 26 April.[21]

Upon arrival in the firing line, the 2nd Brigade 'reinforcements' from the 7th and 10th Battalions that Currie had rounded up during the night of 24–25 April found themselves in very close proximity to German forces. A sharp fight ensued before the opposing lines settled down to digging in. During the pause, Major Odlum liaised with Lieutenant-Colonel Turnbull, commanding officer of the ill-fated Durhams, suggesting that he use his reserve companies and other nearby miscellaneous British troops of whom 'no one seemed to be in command' to make a local counterattack. Turnbull was unsure whose orders he should follow, but he quite naturally rejected the suggestion of a subordinate officer from another division. In desperation Odlum called on Currie, urging the brigadier to press Turnbull into action, with hopes that this might relieve German pressure emanating from St Julien.

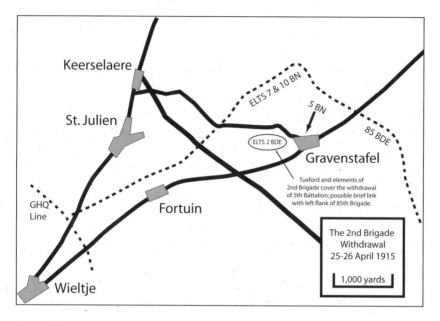

Keerselaere

St. Julien

ELTS 7 & 10 BN

5 BN

85 BDE

ELTS 2 BDE

Gravenstafel

Tuxford and elements of
2nd Brigade cover the withdrawal
of 5th Battalion; possible brief link
with left flank of 85th Brigade.

GHQ
Line

Fortuin

The 2nd Brigade
Withdrawal
25-26 April 1915

1,000 yards

Wieltje

Figure 8.5

Around 15:00, however, Odlum learned that Turnbull's forward troops had abandoned their positions, and by 15:30, 'troops of all units were pouring up over the crest, and retiring down the [reverse] slope of Gravenstafel Ridge.' Odlum and an officer from the 8th Battalion managed to gather up some of the soldiers and put them in position back on the ridge. One of these men may have been Aubrey Fisher, of the 8th Battalion, who was heading rearward in a bid to escape capture. He later recounted the incident: 'I hooked up with a bunch of other stragglers and there was an officer there, whose name I couldn't say … but whoever he was he should have got his decoration for what he did. There had been a parapet thrown up there and he connected every one of us, we still had our rifles … and then Fritzie … came forward … But we held them up to dark. They couldn't get forward anymore.'[22] Whether the unidentified man was Odlum or someone else, Fisher's recollection underscores the initiative displayed by Canadian and British junior officers during the retreat.

Odlum subsequently ventured to the 2nd Brigade's advanced headquarters, receiving orders to withdraw south of Bombarded Crossroads, which he in turn transmitted to forward remnants of the 7th and 10th Battalions. The orders never reached their destination. Most of Odlum's surviving troops, as well as those of the 10th Battalion, remained in position until early the next morning, by which time they were almost completely surrounded. By some miracle the forward officers managed to get the troops to safety through the morning mist without alerting the enemy.[23]

Quite understandably, Currie's withdrawal of the 2nd Brigade did not sit well with the 85th Brigade.[24] He now faced the same dilemma and criticism that Turner had confronted the day before. According to the British brigade war diary, Currie's men had completely abandoned their forward positions by 20:30 on the evening of 25 April, leaving the British left flank 'entirely exposed ... There were now only scattered detachments holding isolated positions between the left [of 85th Brigade] and the British troops at Fortuin and into this gap the Germans appeared to be advancing. The situation was most serious but did not appear to be realised by the G.O.C. 2nd Canadian Bde. who called at 85th [Brigade] H.Q. and explained he had ordered a retirement and apparently assumed that the battalions on his right would conform to his movements.'[25]

The 85th Brigade was understandably dissatisfied with Currie's decision, but perhaps the British did not appreciate the degree of pressure exerted on his left flank. With the western end of the Gravenstafel Ridge in German hands, the terrain dictated that the front-line positions of the 5th and 8th Battalions were untenable, since they lay in front of the forward slope of the ridge and could be handily enfiladed by enemy fire originating from Locality C. This heavy crossfire explains why troops of the 8th Durham Light Infantry were reluctant to hold their positions next to the 8th Battalion. Currie appears to have issued his retirement orders without official sanction, but it would not be the last time in 1915 that an officer made a rational decision based on exigencies that may not have been immediately apparent to higher or neighbouring headquarters.

Elements of the 11th Brigade arrived after dark to fill the gap left by the 2nd Brigade, but the incoming British troops were prudently deployed along the northern edge of the Fortuin–Passchendaele road, in front of Zonnebeke Ridge. This position was superior to that previously occupied by the 2nd Brigade, since Zonnebeke Ridge ran parallel to Gravenstafel Ridge, denying the Germans an opportunity to strike with enfilading fire. The redeployment also placed the Haanebeek Valley between the opposing lines. If the Germans were going to advance beyond Gravenstafel Ridge, they would have to pass through vulnerable low ground before confronting the British troops.

The whereabouts and activities of the 1st Brigade throughout the 2nd Brigade's ordeal warrant explanation. Not long after midnight on the morning of 25 April, Alderson issued a written order to Mercer instructing the 1st Brigade to deploy on the left flank of the 2nd Brigade.[26] At this time the 2nd and 3rd Battalions were still under Turner's control. Mercer, consequently, was left with the depleted 1st and 4th Battalions. The two battalions proceeded as ordered by 02:30, but were halted outside of Wieltje by Brigadier-General Hull (fig. 8.6). The 10th Brigade commander, in the process of organizing his morning attack, refused to allow additional troop traffic into an already congested area. In any event, the 4th Battalion was originally slated to participate in Hull's attack, so it is understandable that he set the Canadians aside for potential use as reserves. After standing by to support Hull's attack for over an hour, the two battalions were able to advance only a short distance up the Wieltje–Fortuin road before daylight rendered further movement inadvisable.[27] Unfortunately for the 2nd Brigade, Mercer's troops were about 2,000 yards off the mark, and could offer no direct support to Currie's left flank. When all four battalions of the 1st Brigade were finally reunited on the west bank of the Yser, Mercer was horrified to learn that 400 men from the 3rd Battalion were missing.[28]

At 09:30 on 25 April, Lieutenant-Colonel Loomis received orders from Turner to reorganize the remnants of the 3rd Brigade at St Jean. Loomis complied, and that evening Lieutenant-Colonel J.A. Currie arrived to relieve him. The force was subsequently ordered to the west bank of the Yser, where it remained until the next day.[29] The war diaries and regimental histories of the three battalions reveal little additional detail regarding their activities on 25 April. Survivors of the 13th Battalion spent most of the day in reserve near Potijze. That night they marched back to the west side of the canal for a short rest at Brielen, near divisional headquarters. For the next few days the battalion shuttled around the battlefield in support of various attacks, but it did not participate directly in any further offensive action.[30] The same was true of the 14th Battalion. During the combat and withdrawals of 24 April the battalion's survivors were intermingled with elements of other units, and by 25 April it was scarcely possible to assemble more than a handful of 14th Battalion troops at any given point. About a hundred men were finally marshalled at Wieltje during the night. The battalion

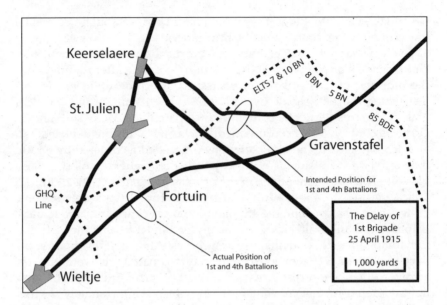

Figure 8.6

continued to sustain casualties in the support trenches; fifteen men were lost to shellfire on 27 April.[31] The handful of survivors from the 15th Battalion spent most of 25 April asleep in the GHQ line.[32] That evening Brigadier-General Turner and his staff were literally shelled out of their headquarters at Mouse Trap Farm by howitzer fire.[33]

The infantry were glad for the chance to shut their eyes to the violence for a few minutes, but there was little rest for the divisional engineers. Elements of the 1st Field Company went to work on the GHQ defences near Wieltje, where the sappers built loop-holed firing positions and gun emplacements in a series of defensive localities. Enemy fire and a shortage of labour prevented completion of all that was planned.[34] Other parts of the company, meanwhile, were assigned to guard and maintain the Yser Canal crossings. Any damage was to be repaired immediately with building materials supplied by V Corps. The company was also charged with general maintenance of the Ypres–Brielen road.[35] For the rest of the month and during the first days of May the 1st Field Company continued to work around the canal; construction of a new bridge began on 30 April.[36] The sappers of Captain Irving's 2nd Field Company were allowed a few hours of sleep near the canal during the early part of 25 April before resuming work on the GHQ fortifications.[37] The 3rd Field Company, meanwhile, worked under orders of Brigadier-General Hull, constructing barriers across the Ypres–Poelcapelle road and helping the survivors of the 10th Brigade to prepare defensive positions. The engineers were also responsible for keeping the roads passable to friendly traffic. When fallen trees at the Bombarded Crossroads hindered the evacuation of casualties, sappers arrived, probably from the 3rd Field Company, to clear the way.[38]

In the meantime Captain Robinson's small band of divisional cyclists covered lots of ground on the battlefield. After completing patrols and reporting on enemy dispositions in the French zone near Steenstraat and Het Sas on 24 April, the cyclists were ordered to Fortuin to reinforce Brigadier-General Hull's 10th Brigade. When Robinson and his men arrived they were told to report to the 3rd Brigade, where any spare hands were urgently needed. For the rest of that day the cyclists acted as dispatch riders between divisional headquarters and those of the infantry and artillery. Lieutenant Dennistoun completed a patrol under fire in the valley of the Haanebeek, while Lieutenant Chadwick took his section to guard the canal bridges. Several cyclists were wounded throughout the day.[39]

The 2nd and 3rd CFA Brigades, along with the howitzers of the 458th Battery RFA, supported the ill-fated 10th Brigade attack against St Julien and Kitcheners Wood on 25 April. According to the original fire plan, Creelman's guns were to open up in conjunction with the infantry assault. They would continue to fire on designated beaten zones until the forward observers reported that the infantry had reached their objectives.[40] These reports never came, of course, because the attack was delayed by two hours. New orders were issued at 05:15, and the guns again opened fire, but the war diary cryptically reports that the forward observers were unable to 'observe correctly,' possibly indicating that they had gone to ground and could not see what was happening as the British infantry were badly shot up by the waiting enemy. Soon enough, however, the Germans obligingly provided targets for the gunners when they launched a hasty counterattack from Kitcheners Wood later in the afternoon. Although the attack failed with bloody results, the enemy made a second attempt within an hour, but was again targeted by the 2nd Brigade's guns.[41] The 2nd and 3rd CFA Brigades also engaged other targets of opportunity as indicated by forward observers during the afternoon and evening, while the 1st

CFA Brigade and the 459th Howitzer Battery RFA cooperated with the French further west near the canal.[42]

Battery-level reports from the 3rd CFA Brigade offer a clear picture of the myriad challenges confronting the gunners at Second Ypres. With little respite, the 9th Battery fired throughout the day and night of 25–26 April. In the days that followed, its guns remained in action in conjunction with British, Indian, and French forces. Fire was sometimes pre-registered, typically adjusted with information received from multiple forward observers.[43] The circumstances were similar for the 10th Battery; after limbering up and moving back to the east side of the canal to rejoin their brigade, the battery's tired gunners fired all day.[44]

The records of the 12th Battery emphasize the occupational hazards of forward observation and signalling work. The battery posted a forward observer at Turner's headquarters for a forty-eight-hour stretch. Each time that the telephone line running back to the guns was broken by shelling or troop traffic, the observer ventured out to repair the damage under direct fire. Signallers encountered such risks on a routine basis: 'The telephonists who helped keep this communication up shared the danger. Gunner James, one of them, displayed exceptional courage and presence of mind and continued his work on the line after being wounded. A few days later he went out to repair the wire and did not return so has been officially reported as missing.'[45]

Although the 12th Battery relied on 'laddered' parallel telephone lines, no hour passed without some damage. There were often more than a dozen breaks to repair at any given moment. The strain of battle also began to show on the battery's guns. Two were put out of action by hostile fire, but quickly repaired while the remaining pieces were overhauled. The battery had fired 'a good many thousand rounds since the middle of April and both guns and equipment were considerably worse for wear.'[46] Wear and tear notwithstanding, the Canadian artillery remained in action around Ypres into early May.

Lines of communication shortened as the Allied positions constricted in the northeastern part of the Ypres Salient, but the delivery of ammunition did not get easier under the observation of enemy gunners and aircraft. Lieutenant Hugh Dunlop, a DAC officer, recorded the perils of travelling through the salient. Enemy fire presented an obvious danger to the ammunition wagons, but they were also threatened by such road hazards as shell craters, dead horses, and other detritus of war.[47] As the horse teams belonging to various units under

Figure 8.7. The grave of Gunner Percy Rivers (1st CFA Brigade) in Potijze Chateau Wood Cemetery, near the site of 27th Division headquarters, reminds the visitor that Canadian gunners continued to serve alongside British and French forces for several days after the Canadian infantry were exhausted. Rivers, a machinist and pre-war militia gunner from Victoria, was 21 years old when he was killed on 27 April 1915. Other Canadian gunners from the 1st and 2nd CFA Brigades buried nearby died on 28, 29, and 30 April. (Author's photograph)

Canadian command were exhausted or killed, the DAC assumed an increased transport burden, sometimes bypassing brigade transport to deliver materiel directly to the infantry and gunners. By noon on 25 April the DAC had issued close to 5,000 18-pounder rounds (92 per cent shrapnel), more than 800 4.5-inch howitzer rounds, and in excess of two million rounds of .303 small-arms ammunition. Only the highest degree of care permitted the overtaxed horses to remain in constant service under such harrowing conditions from 22 through 25 April.[48]

Battle Casualties

In his book *Surviving Trench Warfare*, Bill Rawling noted that Second Ypres was the worst battle of the war for the 1st Canadian Division. Approximately one-third of the division's 18,000 men were killed, wounded, or missing. Of the missing, 1,000 were later confirmed dead.[49] Detailed casualty analysis for the Second Battle of Ypres is complicated by the dearth of evidence to indicate proportionally which weapons caused which casualties. At the very least, however, the gross divisional casualty figures can be subdivided by unit and assessed with each battalion's experience in mind. Appendix I presents casualty types for each battalion, brigade, field company, and other relevant subunit in the division.[50]

Each of the three infantry brigades lost approximately 1,700 soldiers. The highest figure in the 1st Brigade belongs to the 2nd Battalion, with 541 killed, wounded, or missing. A substantial proportion of these losses involved A Company, which was badly hurt during the second phase of the counterattack against Kitcheners Wood. Conversely, the 3rd Battalion likely suffered most of its losses later in the battle, during the fighting around St Julien and the withdrawal of 24 April. The 1st and 4th Battalions undoubtedly sustained the worst of their losses in the counterattack against Mauser Ridge on 23 April. The 1st Brigade, consequently, incurred the greatest proportion of its casualties on the offensive rather than the defensive.

In the 2nd Brigade the highest number of casualties belongs to the 7th Battalion (580) by a significant margin –average casualities per battalion for the 2nd Brigade were 421. Although the battalion was not involved in a major counterattack, its troops played a highly mobile role, defending key zones at Keerselaere, Locality C, and the apex of the salient. In conjunction with the 10th Battalion, the survivors of the 7th Battalion remained in action until the morning of 26 April, longer than most others in the division. Statistics found in Victor Odlum's papers provide additional details for his battalion beyond the gross figures listed in sources for the 1st Division. According to Odlum's tally, virtually all of the 7th Battalion's casualties were sustained on 24 April, although this was obviously not the case. Neither Odlum nor any of the battalion officers had time to record the exact hour at which each man was killed or wounded, so it is probable that he simply estimated the date in many instances. A total of 574 names are listed under 24 April, each of them categorized as killed, wounded, sick or gassed, prisoner, wounded prisoner, or died of wounds. A location is also given, but this is invariably St Julien or Keereselaere; Odlum made no separate distinction for Locality C. Of the 574 listed on 24 April, 238 were killed in action (42 per cent), 161 were wounded (28 per cent), eight were evacuated as sick or gassed (1 per cent), 140 were captured (24 per cent), and twenty-seven were captured after being wounded (5 per cent). Sixty of the wounded men later died of their injuries.[51] Sadly, Odlum's numbers show that many of the men originally listed in 1st Division sources as missing were in fact dead. As well, it may be assumed that some of the men listed as killed, wounded, or captured may also have been gassed to varying degrees, so the figures must be treated with caution. Notwithstanding errors, inconsistencies, and extrapolations, the high ratio of killed to wounded (1.5 to 1) testifies to the extreme severity of combat experienced by the 7th Battalion.

The 10th Battalion's tally of 455 is not difficult to reconcile, since its troops participated directly in the counterattack at Kitcheners Wood. Of particular interest in the 2nd Brigade, however, is the contrast between the 5th Battalion (231) and the 8th Battalion (416). Because the two battalions served side by side throughout the battle, one would expect similar casualty rates, but it was also true that the 8th Battalion suffered more directly from the gas attack of 24 April, as well as from German enfilade fire coming from the western flank of the apex. Although Lipsett relieved three of his companies prior to Tuxford's withdrawal of 25–26 April, the final 8th Battalion company remaining in front of Gravenstafel Ridge was virtually annihilated in a rearguard battle. Tuxford's battalion, ironically, suffered fewer casualties than any other in the division, despite the fact that the two companies remained in their original positions until 25 April.[52]

Casualties vary most widely across battalions in the 3rd Brigade. The 13th Battalion falls into the normal range for the division (467), although given the battalion's position in Section 4 and around St Julien, an even higher figure might have been expected. The same is true of the 16th Battalion (344); its casualty rate is relatively low considering the battalion's involvement in the counterattack of 22–23 April. The 14th Battalion suffered fewer casualties (265) because it was not committed to any counterattacks as a complete battalion. Some of its troops spent much of the battle in reserve positions. The 15th Battalion, conversely, sustained more losses (675) than any other in the division. It is reasonably certain that most of these men were killed, wounded, or captured during the gas attack of 24 April. The initial casualty figure breakdown shown in Appendix I lists the bulk of the 15th Battalion's losses (626 of 675) under the category of 'other ranks, missing.' Other sources, however, indicate that a significant proportion of the 626 men listed as missing were in fact killed or wounded. According to Lieutenant-Colonel J.A. Currie, the battalion lost a total of seventeen officers and 674 men killed, wounded, or missing. Of these, Currie reports that seven officers and 157 men were captured after being gassed or wounded, but that 'the rest had paid the price for the Empire.'[53] By this it is not clear whether Currie meant that the remaining ten officers and 517 enlisted casualties were all killed, and therefore 'paid the price,' or that some paid with their lives while others paid with injuries. In his book, *Silent Battle: Canadian Prisoners of War in Germany*, Desmond Morton reported that the 15th Battalion lost four officers and 216 other ranks killed, and ten officers and 247 other ranks captured.[54] A tally discovered in 15th Battalion documents lists 207 prisoners from that unit.[55] At best, the figures listed in Appendix I represent an approximation of casualties for a battalion that was effectively destroyed.

The number of Canadian soldiers who were killed or incapacitated by gas at the Second Battle of Ypres will never be known. It is probable, however, that the chlorine gas was either directly or indirectly responsible for a significant proportion of the dead and wounded.[56] The German 234th Reserve Infantry Regiment reported after the battle that the number of Allied soldiers who were indisputably neutralized by gas or died of gas poisoning varied according to local circumstances. There were, however, notably high occurrences of gunshot wounds to the head in localities where gas concentrations are known to have been heavy.[57] Such injuries can probably be explained by the tendency of gassed soldiers to seek higher ground or quit their positions in search of fresh air. The moment a man abandoned his parapet, he was almost certain to be cut down by rifle fire.

Shell Shock

Concealed within the divisional casualty figures – or possibly discounted from them – are the officers and soldiers who suffered from 'shell shock' or nervous breakdowns. While some medical officers believed shell shock to be the consequence of nervous injury caused by explosions, others interpreted it as the psychological result of combat stress. To further confuse matters, medical officers and soldiers alike seem to have used the term interchangeably with fatigue, sickness, or simply 'being all in' for a few days after having 'been game' throughout the battle.[58] Direct references to shock and breakdown during and after Second Ypres are few, but enough anecdotal evidence survives to suggest that a range of individuals across the 1st Canadian Division suffered psychological or nervous symptoms. A newspaper column dating from June 1915 listed details of the thirty-five officer casualties in the 7th Battalion up to that point in the Great War: eight had been killed, fifteen wounded, five wounded and captured, three captured without wounds, one injured in a horse accident, and three 'nervously broken down.' These last three men, all lieutenants, represented 8.5 per cent of the battalion's total officer casualties up to that point in the war. There is additional evidence that a fourth officer from the 7th Battalion, Major Clive Cooper, also suffered from 'shattered' nerves, but it is not clear whether this occurred at Second Ypres or later, on the La Bassée front.[59] This significant proportion of cases in the 7th Battalion indicates that shell shock and nervous breakdown were common phenomena throughout the division.

Personal correspondence and diary entries offer candid snapshots of individual shell-shock cases in other units. On 28 April 1915 Lieutenant Ian Sinclair described the situation in the 13th Battalion:

Major Norsworthy, Guy Drummond, Gerald Lees, Ward Whitehead were killed. Major McCuaig wounded and missing, Eric McCuaig wounded and Horsey with a nervous breakdown were our losses in officers. I thought my nerves might give if I ever ran into an affair of that sort [the battle], but something seemed to change in me and I saw without any particular sensation things happen, which in my previous state of mind would have driven me mad. One of my men actually did go crazy this morning after we got out. Every battalion in the division suffered about as much and the whole is pretty badly wrecked.[60]

Sinclair's reference to one of his soldiers going 'crazy' on the morning of 28 April shows that stress symptoms might not reveal themselves until hours or days after the immediate danger of combat had passed. While Sinclair avoided a breakdown, 24-year-old Lieutenant Clifton Horsey was not so lucky. Horsey was evacuated with shock on 2 May, but returned to duty four days later. The unfortunate officer suffered two or three additional wounds on separate occasions before he was finally killed in action in June 1916.[61]

The trauma of combat was not limited to infantrymen. Lieutenant-Colonel Creelman recorded that his adjutant, Captain Charlie Hanson, experienced 'a nervous breakdown and had gone to a sanitarium.'[62] Hanson's medical board diagnosed him with traumatic neurasthenia, recommending that he return to Canada for home service. In September 1917 Hanson was discharged with a diagnosis of cardiac hypertrophy, believed to be an adaptive response to increased stress.[63] Creelman himself also suffered a breakdown. Sometime about 29 April the 35-year-old artillery commander was evacuated by ambulance with a high fever. After being treated at a dressing station, he was driven twenty miles to a clearing hospital before being transferred to a general hospital in England.[64] Creelman later explained his condition: 'I am practically recovered physically but do not feel quite equal to going back yet and resuming command of the Brigade. After a week or so in England I shall look forward to returning. I am ticketed as an "influenza" patient, technically it is called "shock". A Board sat on me at Rouen and decided that a rest would be beneficial.'[65]

Medical records confirm Creelman's statement, and a handwritten case sheet provides additional detail. Dated 1 May 1915, it reports that he suffered from gas poisoning and insomnia: 'once affected by gas [the patient] was all right as long as in responsible command. Then when relieved [he] lost control of himself. Ordered to go into hospital for influenza trouble. Had been reading temperature [of] 101, 102 & and on admission 100° ... has been deaf ... he thinks due to guns only ... cough, painful.'[66]

The same report suggests that the officer also experienced nightmares immediately after the battle.[67] In common with Sinclair's soldier who went 'crazy' after leaving the battle lines, Creelman does not appear to have manifested any symptoms until the worst moments of crisis had passed. His records also reveal how terms such as fever, influenza, and shock were used interchangeably.

There are few explicit references to other shell-shock casualties in the official battalion statistics for April 1915. Only three battalions, in fact, showed any 'sick' cases at all under their monthly tallies. The

13th Battalion listed two soldiers as sick, while the 5th and 8th Battalions each listed a single soldier as 'sick with gas fumes.'[68] Other shell-shock cases, more than likely, are concealed within the broader categories of killed, wounded, and missing men from across the division. As well, there is the possibility that men suffering from shell shock chose out of shame not to report themselves to medical authorities and simply carried on with their duties. It is certain, in any event, that more than four men fell sick during the battle, and a substantial number of troops must also have suffered from chlorine gas poisoning without being categorized as such. If so, the low reporting of gas casualties strengthens the assumption that shell-shock cases may have been evacuated without special distinction alongside the hundreds of other soldiers who suffered conventional gunshot and shrapnel wounds.

Morale and Cohesion

If the evidence points to frequent unreported cases of shell shock or nervous breakdown, it remains to be explained which forces held the 1st Canadian Division together over four days of intense close-quarters battle. John Baynes asked the same question forty years ago in his study of morale and courage among the 2nd Scottish Rifles at the Battle of Neuve Chapelle. One of Baynes's salient observations was that morale is very much a function of time, place, and circumstance. Individuals and groups may boast high morale on a particular day, but after suffering heavy losses and turnover in personnel, everything can change. A battalion badly damaged in action will never be quite the same again. Because morale fluctuates so readily, it is difficult to measure.[69] The Canadian experience at Ypres seems to confirm Baynes's observations of the Scottish Rifles.

As it existed on the afternoon of 22 April, the 1st Canadian Division was an organization high in morale. Most of the battalions and other units within the division were organized more or less along local or regional lines. Many of the officers and men who served together in war were already familiar with one another during peacetime as fellow militiamen, co-workers, school pals, or even neighbours. By April 1915 they had lived and trained together, serving side by side in the front lines. The hardships of the first winter in England had forged a common bond of identity. So had the initial experience of war leading up to Second Ypres. The average Canadian soldier believed in his training. Each of these factors contributed to overall cohesion at the Second Battle of Ypres.

Like glue at high temperatures, cohesion was imperfect under the exigencies of battle. The Canadian battalions rarely fought as complete units at Ypres. Most were split up into companies and dispatched where needed. As such, it was probably the smaller groups of chums within the infantry platoons that counted most. In situations where the Germans applied massive concentrated pressure, as against French forces on 22 April, or against the 3rd Canadian Brigade two days later, unit cohesion ultimately disintegrated as men fought to the death in small groups or withdrew to safety. This does not mean that training, leadership, or unit cohesion were lacking. Sometimes the German attacks were just too strong to repel.

Leadership also mattered. In his study of officer-man relations in the British army of the 1914–18 period, Gary Sheffield has suggested that most soldiers respected their commanders, who reciprocated by looking out for their men in a patriarchal fashion. There were always a few officers who were especially well loved or actively despised, but those fitting into either extreme represented a minority across the British Expeditionary Force on the whole. So long as an officer played fair and put the welfare of his men first, soldiers were willing to tolerate discipline, accepting that the commissioned ranks were entitled to special privileges.[70] The majority of Canadian soldiers in early 1915 had good reason to trust their superiors, men who already had been to war in South Africa, or perhaps had served for years in the British army. This study does not pretend to offer a comprehensive analysis of officer-man relations in the 1st Canadian Division, but anecdotal evidence suggests that relationships were generally positive. Recall that, back in England, Captain Crerar did not mind looking the other way when his gunners overindulged themselves with alcohol while on shore leave. Indeed, he ungrudgingly helped them stumble back up the gangway when they returned to ship. On the battlefield itself, officers shared the same dangers as their men did. It is instructive to recall that three of the twelve battalion commanders died in action at Second Ypres. Lieutenant-Colonel Birchall was especially revered for his selfless display of bravery at Mauser Ridge on 23 April. Further up the chain of command, Brigadier-General Turner was shelled out of his headquarters, while Currie and Mercer were both in harm's way throughout the fighting. The crucible of battle strengthened the reputations of leaders who stood the test. Most did, and when reinforcements arrived to fill the depleted ranks, they could look up to veterans who had already seen it all.

A capable leader must be able to interpret orders sensibly within a given operational circumstance. As the situation worsened between 22 and 25 April, junior officers, non-commissioned officers, and even ordinary soldiers exercised leadership and initiative in countless individual cases.[71] Louis Lipsett, Edison Lynn, John Warden, Alexander Mackie, and a great number of other ranks whose names are not recorded showed that personal initiative counted for a lot on the battlefield during the early part of 1915. This common sense approach was to become even more important during the fighting of May and June, when orders from above did not always accord very well with conditions on the ground. When possible and practical, subordinates modified instructions to suit immediate realities.

Rebuilding the Division

The dead and wounded soldiers of the 1st Canadian Division were replaced at a steady rate. At least forty officers and 2,091 other ranks joined the division on or about 5 May 1915, but battalion records indicate that additional reinforcements had arrived in smaller groups prior to that date.[72] By 28 April the 13th Battalion received 276 soldiers and four subalterns.[73] At other battalions the replacements arrived more gradually. In the 5th Battalion, fresh troops turned up each day during the first week of May in groups of a dozen.[74] An infantry officer in the 13th Battalion commented on the new arrivals in a letter home: 'We are well back from the firing line now and having a delightful "bum" and incidentally getting our drafts into shape and practically equipping the whole regiment again … A lot of lads have come over from England with the drafts but don't make up for the ones who are gone. I've certainly lost an awful lot of my friends, I won't go into details as to casualties as you will have seen the lists.'[75]

With the arrival of fresh troops from the reserve battalions in England, training recommenced almost immediately within the division. The 4th Battalion, which had received a draft of fifteen officers and 523 men on 29 April, completed an exceedingly difficult march with the rest of the division from Vlamertinghe to Bailleul, where it spent the next two weeks. Route marches, extended order drill, and musketry filled the days.[76] The picture for other battalions was similar. In the 7th Battalion the men cleaned themselves up, engaged in daily training, and attended a brigade memorial service for those who had not survived the battle.[77] After marching to Bailleul, the men of the 14th Battalion organized sporting events and received an additional 275 reinforcements 'of good quality.'[78] The veterans of the battalion were disappointed to learn, however, that many of the new arrivals came from Toronto rather than Montreal, while a group of Montrealers had been sent to Ontario-based battalions in the 1st and 3rd Brigades. The situation was remedied with some hasty personnel exchanges, which probably helped the replacements adjust more easily to their new surroundings.[79] As of mid-May most of the battalions in the division once again approached full strength.[80]

While the most tragic consequence of the Second Battle of Ypres was the high rate of dead, wounded, or missing men, it was also necessary to replace or repair kit, weapons, and equipment, a good deal of which had been jettisoned or destroyed during the fighting. Machine-gun crews constituted the backbone of Canadian rearguards at Second Ypres, so it comes as little surprise that nearly half of the division's forty-eight automatic weapons were destroyed or lost between 22 and 26 April. As of 1 May the 3rd Battalion required two complete guns and one spare barrel; and the 5th battalion required one complete gun and tripod, three barrels, eighty bolts, four pairs of asbestos gloves (for changing hot barrels), four transit cases, two spare parts kits, thirty-seven ammunition boxes, and two belt loaders. The 7th and 8th Battalions each called for four complete guns, while the 10th Battalion called for one gun and tripod. The 3rd Brigade losses were much higher; just one of its machine guns survived the battle.[81]

Some of the new kit issued in the wake of the battle had never been seen before. Within days of the first gas cloud, improvised respirators arrived, along with instructions explaining their correct use. These simple two-piece masks consisted of a pad, large enough to cover the lower part of the face, and a wad of cotton.[82] In the event of a gas attack, the respirators and cotton wads were to be immediately impregnated in a solution of sodium thiosulphate, two bottles of which were to be carried in each section at all times.[83] The wad was then held directly between the soldier's teeth, while the pad was placed over the mouth and nose and fastened with string. The masks required plenty of practice to use effectively, but ordinary soldiers appreciated having some form of protection. After the war Private George Bell remembered the early masks: 'A few days after [the battle] we were issued our first gas masks. Britain and France lost no time in trying to cope with this new instrument of war ... Crude as our first gas masks were, they gave us a certain feeling of security as we realized that the best scientific brains of the allies were working to give us the protection that we sorely needed. What chemical was used [in the cotton pad] I do not know, but it would remain effective about a week and then we would be given a replacement.'[84] Less cumbersome hood-type masks were developed later in the year, culminating with the introduction of the more efficient small-box respirator in 1916.[85]

There was precious little time available for more thorough integration of reinforcements and breaking in of new equipment. Less than three weeks after the worst of the fighting at Ypres, the 1st Canadian Division was to partake in an offensive near the La Bassée Canal. Hardened by the experience of Second Ypres, the veterans somehow managed to guide the new arrivals through some extremely difficult offensive actions.

'Glorious Gallantry'

As early as 26 April 1915, Sir George Perley, Canada's High Commissioner in Britain, wrote to General Alderson from London that the Canadians 'saved the situation' at Ypres.[86] On 6 May, as the battle still raged between British and German forces, Lieutenant-General Smith-Dorrien dispatched his own conciliatory message to Alderson, stating that had it not been for Canadian gallantry, the initial German break-through of 22 April 'might well have been converted into a serious defeat of our troops.'[87] A few days later Smith-Dorrien paid visits to various Canadian headquarters, remarking along the way that Canadian troops had 'undoubtedly saved the situation.'[88] The accolades from senior commanders did not cease with the end of the fighting around Ypres that spring; on the first anniversary of the battle, Field Marshal Sir John French issued a congratulatory statement extolling the 'glorious gallantry' of Canadian troops. For the past year he had 'watched with greatest interest the rapid growth of the Canadian contingent in the field,' and it was impossible in his opinion, 'to overestimate the value of the support thus given to our armies.'[89]

Of course, such public remarks from high-ranking officials and officers followed virtually all of the battles on the Western Front. Yet the brave talk after Second Ypres was not limited to brass hats and higher ups. The very soldiers who struggled for their lives in the smashed breastworks and gas-drenched farm fields celebrated the battle in their own way, often expressing themselves through poetry, as was fashionable at the time. Corporal Jocko Vinson, an Australian-born member of the 7th Battalion, penned 'The Canadians' Stand at Ypres.' The final two stanzas are especially rousing:

A hard struggle at hand, and every man they could find,
When the cry of a general soon passed through the lines,
'For God's sake hang on, men, it's the key to the West!'
And the boys from dear Canada sure did their best.

Although it proved costly the situation was saved,
And those that have fallen are ranked with the brave;
They have now left a name that will stand good and true,
For they died whilst defending the Red, White, and Blue.[90]

Private Archie Cronie, of the 4th Infantry Battalion, was no less modest in 'The Answered Call,' a ninety-line piece. According to Cronie, it was 'fifteen thousand and four Canadians ... Who blocked the way that led to Calais the outlet to England's shore.'[91] A carbon copy of Cronie's hastily scrawled poem is preserved in a collection of letters sent home by Private Frank Betts, a fellow infantryman in the 4th Battalion. And the fighting was no less important to those at home than among the soldiers who lived through it. The third anniversary of the battle, in 1918, coincided with massive German counterattacks across the Western Front. The channel ports were once again threatened as the enemy advanced towards Ypres, prompting Field Marshal Douglas Haig to issue his famous 'backs to the wall' order on 11 April. Victory appeared almost within the Germans' grasp, but in far-off Toronto the crisis did not overshadow the distant events of April 1915. On 23 April 1918 the *Globe* reported that 'life is too full and too busy now for anyone to stop and reflect on the greatness of the sorrow and the greatness of the joy that surround us on every side, but many an incident yesterday [22 April] compelled the busiest to pause in the rush and let the emotions sweep to the surface and, for a moment, have their way. "St Julien Day – Lest We Forget" – met the eye at every turn pinned to the shabby coat of the workingman, to the fur coat of the girl of wealth.'[92] The article refers to violet-coloured pennants sold by volunteers on Toronto city streets in honour of St Julien Day, the anniversary of the Second Battle of Ypres. By the end of St Julien Day in 1918 nearly $20,000 had been collected through pennant sales in Toronto. The value in 2006 currency is about $250,000 – a considerable sum for one day of fundraising.

Today most ordinary Canadians know of Vimy Ridge, but few can name any other battles from the First World War, perhaps with the exception of Passchendaele. Second Ypres is at best remembered as the

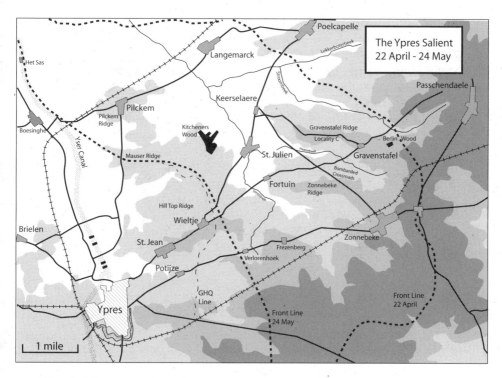

Figure 8.8

war's first gas battle. During the First World War and throughout the earlier postwar decades, it was a very different story. St Julien Day was celebrated in communities across the country at least until the 1960s. For those who lived through it, the Second Battle of Ypres was not merely a gas battle nor a stepping stone in Canada's journey to nationhood or military excellence. For the Archie Cronies and Jocko Vinsons it was an important experience in its own right, a moment when Canadian troops helped prevent a strategic disaster from befalling the Allies.

After the Canadians departed, the Second Battle of Ypres continued until 24–25 May, when the Germans launched their final offensive action against the 4th and 28th British Divisions along the eastern face of the salient. The Germans attacked six British brigades with elements of a total of five divisions under a five-mile-wide gas cloud. The results of the attack were mixed; in some places the Germans were able to break into the British lines where the defenders were badly affected by the gas, but in others, the line held against superior forces. By this stage of the battle, British artillery batteries were seriously short of ammunition and the infantry were exhausted. But after four weeks of fighting, German forces were also badly attenuated and the Fourth Army discontinued further operations against Ypres as of 25 May.

The use of chlorine gas achieved notable tactical success, particularly on 22 and 24 April, but ultimately the weapon proved indecisive, even against relatively inexperienced troops who lacked any protective gear. Although the Germans managed to capture a substantial parcel of ground north and east of Ypres (fig. 8.8), they had been unable to eliminate the salient, and it was to remain in Allied hands for the duration of the war. For its part, the 1st Canadian Division was battered, but not broken. It lived to fight another day, one that came all too soon.

9 On the Offensive:
The La Bassée Front, May–June 1915

The Second Battle of Ypres tested the 1st Canadian Division beyond all limits. The battered survivors of the gas clouds, close-quarters fighting, and counterattacks emerged from the salient as veterans. For many, the distinction was to be short-lived. Just two weeks after withdrawing from the furnace of the Ypres Salient, the old originals, along with new-comers who had since filled the gaps in the ranks, found themselves on the offensive in one of Canada's most difficult battles of the First World War. On the La Bassée Front, near the otherwise unremarkable rural villages of Festubert and Givenchy, Lieutenant-General Alderson's men were going to have ample opportunity to bring the fight back to the Germans.

The division had changed considerably since 22 April. Hardened by combat, the survivors of Second Ypres had gained much practical experience. Some of the lessons reinforced skills first developed in training, but actual combat was the only true teacher of much of what was learned at Ypres. The helpless feeling of lying exposed under shelling, or advancing into small-arms fire with traces of gas in one's lungs, could hardly be simulated in a training camp. At the same time, several thousand men in the 1st Division of May 1915 had arrived as reinforcements after the worst of the fighting at Ypres was over and therefore lacked combat experience. One can only estimate how many of these soldiers shared the same level of basic training as their veteran counterparts. Current scholarship suggests that about three-quarters of the reinforcements had been in uniform since 1914, but had remained behind with depot battalions in England until needed in late April or early May.[1] The remaining quarter had arrived in England with new battalions in late 1914 or early 1915. Describing soldiers from the latter category, Private George Bell, of the 1st Battalion, later wrote that 'we were reinforced with men from the second contingent. We were now veterans and these youngsters fresh from Canada had yet to see a battle. They would learn from us.'[2] Whether they came directly from the 2nd Division units, or had marked time with the depot battalions in England, the new men enjoyed only a brief opportunity to glean lessons from the old originals prior to going into action at Festubert.[3]

Writing as both the official historian and a veteran of 1915, A.F. Duguid remembered Festubert as 'the most unsatisfactory engagement of the 1st Canadian Division in the war.'[4] In late May and mid-June, Canadians assaulted heavily fortified German positions on featureless terrain devoid of cover. Results varied from one attack to the next, but in any instance where an assault was pressed fully home, the cost was always high. It would be a mistake, however, to dismiss these early offensives as nothing more than disastrous blunders committed by poorly trained troops and orchestrated by stubborn or inflexible commanders. Contrary to stereotypical views of 1915 operations, the Canadian attacks on the La Bassée Front did not consist of unimaginative linear waves of automatons marching relentlessly into machine-gun fire. On the contrary, each operation was something akin to a hastily improvised set-piece, comprising infantry, artillery, engineer, and support elements. Artillery ammunition was limited, and the attacks small and often ineffectual by the standards of 1916–18, but many of the ingredients of integrated arms operations were evident on the 1915 battlefield. If breakthrough was impossible, the Canadians were quite capable of achieving local tactical success when granted enough time to make a plan.

The operational evidence from May and June 1915 says a great deal about combat leadership in the 1st Division. Although there is no conclusive proof, it seems clear that in several situations officers at the battalion and company levels either modified or ignored orders when exigencies at the sharp end of the fight did not accord with strategically based directives that were filtering down through army, corps, and divisional headquarters. In common with what historian Leonard Smith has observed of the 5th French Infantry Division, Canadian officers exercised 'proportionality' by limiting the efforts of their troops when it appeared that the price of an attack was too high for what might be achieved. This is not to suggest that every leader simply chose to do as he saw fit, yet the concept of proportionality reminds us that officers and soldiers of the First World War were capable of assessing a situation and making intelligent decisions.[5]

The cost of some decisions in 1915 is all too evident in the fields and meadows of the La Bassée countryside. A short distance northeast of Festubert, on the site of a pre-war communal cemetery along Rue de Bois, one comes upon Le Touret Memorial and Military Cemetery (fig. 9.1). This striking classical monument commemorates missing British Empire soldiers from the half-forgotten battles fought in this region throughout 1914-15. The adjacent cemetery is the resting place of more than 900 men. Lying among them are three officers of Canada's 5th Battalion, all killed on 24-25 May 1915. Thirty-five-year-old Major Daniel Tenaille was a Parisian who joined the Canadian Expedionary Force in September 1914 after emigrating to Canada. Tenaille returned to France wearing a foreign uniform and died in battle on his native soil. Lieutenant James Maxwell Currie, who was born in India, was relatively old for a subaltern when he was killed in May at 46 years of age. Captain James Randall Innes-Hopkins, also killed in action, was an English-born veteran of the South African War. Why did these three officers, each hailing from a different corner of the world, die together near an obscure French farming village in the spring of 1915 along so with many other 1st Division soldiers? Why were the Canadians committed to such deadly battle only weeks after suffering through the carnage of Second Ypres?

On first consideration it is not at all easy to understand the First British Army's pursuit of offensive activities north of the La Bassée Canal while the Second Army remained locked in combat in the Ypres Salient throughout much of May. The answers lie chiefly with the intractable difficulties of coalition warfare. The commander-in-chief of the French forces, General Joseph Joffre, was understandably determined that the Germans be driven from his country in 1915. Joffre's basic strategic approach was to strike the large German salient on French soil on each of its flanks, in Artois and the Champagne, respectively. The mustachioed commander imagined that his powerful French forces would deliver the decisive effort, while the much smaller British Expeditionary Force supported the left flank by drawing German reserves away from the principal attacks. Falkenhayn's April gas offensive against Ypres interrupted Joffre's operations, but a measure of stability had been restored in Belgium by early May. The French commander was now eager to carry on with his plans.

British generals felt differently. Indeed, their subordinate strategic role on the Western Front had been a source of friction between the two allies since the outbreak of war. Field Marshal John French, the

Figure 9.1. The Le Touret Memorial, northwest of Festubert, commemorates more than 13,000 British soldiers who died in this region from 1914 up to late September 1915 but have no known grave. (Canadian and Indian soldiers with no known grave are commemorated on the Vimy and Neuve Chapelle monuments respectively.) The cemetery surrounding the memorial at Le Touret, with more than 900 burials, is the final resting place for several men of the 1st Division killed at Festubert in May 1915, including Major Daniel Tenaille, a native of France who served with Alderson's division. (Photograph by Andrew McLaughlin)

commander-in-chief of the BEF from August 1914 through December 1915, had originally hoped to deploy British forces on the Belgian coast, where his country's primary strategic interests lay.[6] But when the Germans invaded Belgium and France in 1914 there was little opportunity for British commanders to debate the question with their continental counterparts. Joffre wanted the BEF – then a modest force of six divisions – on his immediate left flank. The British complied with French wishes, just as they were to do throughout the winter of 1914–15. By early May, after the lacklustre performance of French troops at Second Ypres, French grew increasingly impatient with the demands of Joffre and his key subordinate, General Ferdinand Foch, then in command of the French Northern Armies.[7] Field Marshal French, however, had little to bargain with so long as his allies remained numerically superior to the BEF. Consequently, British commanders were compelled to persist with offensive action throughout May and June, even after it became painfully evident that the German fortifications north of the La Bassée Canal were far too solid to breach with the shoestring resources then available. As a former British staff officer wrote after the war, it would have been prudent to postpone such offensives until the British Expeditionary Force grew stronger in men, guns, and reliable high-explosive ammunition, but in coalition warfare one sometimes had to follow the 'least worst' practical course of action rather than the ideal course.[8]

Beginning on 9 May the French Tenth Army, with twenty-two divisions in its order of battle, struck the German lines between Roclincourt and Noulette, in an effort to drive the enemy off the high ground at Notre Dame de Lorette and the Vimy Ridge. Additional French forces attacked German positions further south, in the Champagne region. British General Douglas Haig, in command of the First Army, cooperated by launching a series of attacks against Aubers Ridge on the old Neuve Chapelle battlefield between Bois Grenier and Festubert, but these were largely unsuccessful and resulted in heavy losses. As early as 11 May, Haig concluded that, 'the [German] defences in our front are so carefully and so strongly made, and mutual support with machine-guns is so complete, that in order to demolish them a *long methodical bombardment* will be necessary by artillery [guns and howitzers] before Infantry are sent forward to attack.[9] British forces did not possess enough artillery or ammunition of sufficient quality to do the job in May 1915.[10] Yet Haig had little choice but to continue offensive operations, this time against Festubert. Although some important ground was captured, neither the French nor the British were destined to make war-winning gains during May and June. These two months of operations cost tens of thousands of Allied casualties.

As the fighting on the La Bassée Front drew to a belated close, British strategy on the Western Front was bitterly challenged by some people who felt that the war could be more effectively waged elsewhere, at least until the BEF grew powerful enough to pursue its own strategic objectives on the Continent. First Lord of the Admiralty Winston Churchill demanded more resources for the faltering Gallipoli expedition, arguing that 'the British have gained, in face of La Bassée, less than half the ground they have lost around Ypres.'[11] Churchill's criticisms were understandable, but not especially sensitive to the realities of coalition warfare in 1915. Not only did the diversion of resources to the Mediterranean Expeditionary Force come at the expense of the

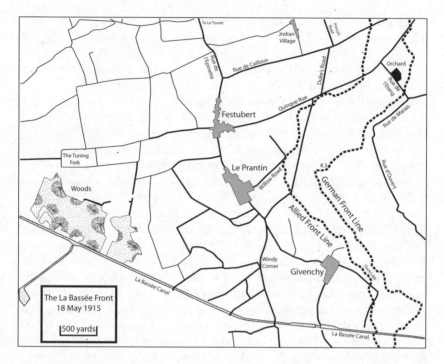

Figure 9.2

BEF, but the reallocation of British manpower to the Turkish front led
the French to accuse their ally of pursuing imperial goals instead of
fighting the Germans where it really mattered.

There was no simple solution to the Allied strategic dilemma: German forces occupied more than 19,000 square miles of French and Belgian territory. It was, and still is, difficult to criticize Joffre for wanting
them out at the first opportunity. With British land forces still too weak
to pursue an independent strategy on the Continent, Field Marshal
French and his BEF army commanders accommodated their French
counterparts, lest the delicate alliance fall to pieces.[12] These exigencies
ultimately dictated that the 1st Canadian Division, which had been so
badly damaged at the Second Battle of Ypres, participate in the La Bassée offensives. The BEF had few troops to spare.

Anyone who tours the old battlefields north of the La Bassée Canal will
immediately appreciate the difficulties encountered by British, Indian,

and Canadian troops as they advanced eastward from Festubert and Givenchy towards the town of La Bassée more than ninety years ago. In contrast with the concentric ridge lines of the Ypres Salient, the ground around Festubert is completely flat, with very broad fields of view in every direction. Like Ypres, the water table on the La Bassée Front is quite shallow, and the farm fields are cross-cut with deep drainage ditches and streams. These natural obstacles complicated any attack, as did the shell craters that multiplied in number as the fighting continued into May and June. Fortunately for the historian, the landscape around Festubert and Givenchy has changed very little since 1915. Even some of the wartime street names are still in use today (fig. 9.2).

The La Bassée Canal itself is the most obvious landmark in the area. During the war years countless tired and muddy soldiers refreshed themselves with a swim in this watercourse.[13] North of the canal, the famed 'Orchard' attacked by Canadian troops no longer exists, but its approximate boundaries can be readily located on the eastern side of Rue de l'Etang. Just west of Givenchy is an intersection known as 'Windy Corner' in 1915 (fig. 9.3). Today it is marked with a Commonwealth War Graves signpost directing visitors to the nearby Windy Corner Guards Cemetery. Like so many others from the First World War years, this large burial ground began as an improvised plot next to a battalion headquarters in January 1915. Many soldiers of the 4th Guards Brigade were buried there that spring; one year later the cemetery had expanded to nearly 700 graves. After the war hundreds of others were relocated to Windy Corner from smaller burial sites. The cemetery is now the resting place of more than 3,400 soldiers, including Canadians killed in the fighting around Festubert and Givenchy. The 'Tuning Fork,' a distinctive u-shaped bend in the road just east of Gorre still exists, as do the woods separating it from the banks of the La Bassée Canal. Visitors equipped with a compass and 1915 trench map can locate the positions of the British artillery batteries situated in and around the woods. Further north, the location of 'Indian Village' can be approximated along Rue de Cailloux (now posted as Rue Seche). In Festubert itself, the forlorn church is one of many on the Western Front rebuilt after the war in the modern style with drab reddish-brown bricks instead of the traditional stone. Such buildings serve as permanent reminders that countless villages and their rural environs were completely destroyed during the Great War (fig. 9.4). Edmund Blunden described what was left of this particular locality after months of fighting, in his poem, 'Festubert, 1916':

Figure 9.3. 'Those ruined houses seared themselves into me ... ' With its southward perspective, this 1919 photograph reveals the extensive damage in Festubert. The intersection in the foreground is Windy Corner. The building standing at centre was a brewery; the La Bassée Canal line is visible in the background. (LAC, PA-004462)

> But now what was once mine is mine no more,
> I look for such friends here and I find none.
> With such strong gentleness and tireless will
> Those ruined houses seared themselves into me,
> Passionate I look for their dumb story still,
> And the charred stump outspeaks the living tree.[14]

A Canadian recorded his impressions more prosaically: 'I don't think there is even one whole brick. In the cemetery the graves were blown up and the church was level with the ground.'[15] The devastation of Festubert and neighbouring villages was a sad harbinger of what was to befall Canadian troops in the pending attacks.

Notwithstanding the difficult terrain and shortages of artillery ammunition, the initial Festubert operations, beginning on 15 May 1915, showed some promise. More than 400 guns and howitzers pummelled German fortifications for sixty hours.[16] Assaults by the 2nd and the

Figure 9.4. The village church in Festubert as it appears today. Artillery fire flattened the original building during the war. As with so many French and Belgian villages on the Western Front, Festubert's postwar church was rebuilt with stark red brick in a more modern style than its pre-war predecessor. (Author's photograph)

Meerut Divisions achieved useful results against the veteran German 14th Infantry Division. The 8th Westphalian Infantry regimental war diary described the swiftness of the British and Indian assault troops:

> On the night of 15-16 May the right wing of the 3rd Battalion, which was posted in front of the so-called apple orchard was overrun. Here the opponent suddenly broke in at one o'clock in the morning by overrunning the listening posts, their pioneers cutting the wire obstacles, into the crippled position of Lieutenant Goetz's 11th Company. The company resisted desperately as long as the hand grenades and ammunition lasted. Since the enemy had advanced into the shelter trench, the company was also forced to retreat with heavy losses to the east side of the apple orchard.[17]

The stealthy night operation against Goetz's troops sounds much like an episode one would expect to encounter during the so-called stormtroop attacks of 1917-18. It shows, however, that Allied soldiers in 1915 were capable of adapting their tactical approach to realities on the ground.

The British attacks of 15-16 May compelled the 14th Infantry Division to withdraw from its forward positions north of the La Bassée Canal. Encouraged by the results, Haig ordered a follow-up attack for the afternoon of 18 May. This was to include the 14th and 16th Battalions of Brigadier-General Turner's 3rd Infantry Brigade, to be deployed under the command of the 7th Division until the rest of the 1st Canadian Division arrived in the sector. Turner's brigade was detailed to capture Quinque Rue, the North Breastwork, and the entire Orchard (fig. 9.5). In the meantime another veteran German division, the 2nd Guards Reserve – considered by Allied intelligence officers to be a first-class outfit – reinforced the attenuated 14th Division.[18] Now there was no time to lose. The British and Indian forces that opened the Festubert offensive had several days to organize and coordinate their attacks. In contrast, the Canadians found themselves repeatedly committed to battle with only hours to plan.[19]

The men of the 14th Battalion spent 17 May in the forward breastworks – little more than wicker screens heaped up with earth. The following morning, after a night of fitful rest, they assembled near Indian Village under the command of Lieutenant-Colonel William Burland, a twenty-year pre-war militia veteran. The 16th Battalion formed up on Burland's right flank. After a short delay, a pair of companies from each battalion launched an attack that afternoon. According to the

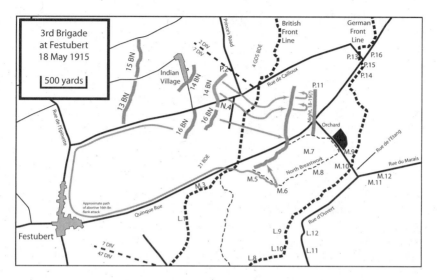

Figure 9.5

plan, two 14th Battalion companies and one 16th Battalion company
headed directly for the Orchard, while a second 16th Battalion company
executed a wide flanking manoeuvre towards the North Breastwork.
German artillery fire was heavy from the outset. The infantry, consequently, advanced in extended order, with fifty-yard gaps separating
each wave and five-pace intervals between each soldier.

An after-action report by Captain Andrew Holt, one of Burland's
subordinates, explains that the 14th Battalion companies achieved
steady progress until the way was partially blocked by troops of the
4th Guards Brigade, who had been held up on the left flank. The 14th
Battalion changed direction, bringing it into the path of the 16th Battalion. Amid the deafening chaos, Burland ordered his men to dig in, and
after some hasty reconnaissance, the 14th Battalion troops advanced a
few hundred yards further to settle down under shelling that continued until at least 02:00 the next morning. At daybreak Burland's
men pulled back once again, allegedly to achieve closer touch with the
16th Battalion. So far the operation had cost sixty-seven casualties,
including two officers.

The 16th Battalion sources tell the story differently than Holt does.
According to the war diary, the flank attack was aborted 'owing to [the]
non-arrival' of Burland's covering detachments; the 16th Battalion

troops, furthermore, reached their 'assigned line,' while the 14th Battalion men 'did not.'[20] Someone from the 16th Battalion reportedly got in touch with Lieutenant-Colonel Burland by telephone, asking him to bring his troops forward to close the gap between the Canadians and the 4th Guards Brigade. Burland initially complied, but then 'took [the] 14th away before daylight and left [a] gap of about 200 yards between [the 16th Battalion] and Guards.' The opening was covered with a machine gun, before two additional 16th Battalion companies arrived early on 19 May to offer relief. The 16th Battalion frontal assault company lost four men killed and sixty wounded.

Captain Holt's 14th Battalion report makes no mention of a telephone call to Burland, while the 16th Battalion diary narrative is problematic in that it concentrates on what Burland did not do and says relatively less about what the 16th Battalion troops actually accomplished. Fetherstonhaugh's history of the 14th Battalion speaks of difficult terrain, heavy German resistance, and the courage of individual men, but omits further specifics, while Urquhart's volume on the 16th Battalion claims that the flank manoeuvre against the North Breastwork was aborted only when officers learned from Burland just how poorly the frontal attack had fared.[21] The whole truth probably lies somewhere in between, yet it seems apparent that Burland exercised initiative by evacuating his troops from dangerously exposed positions in front of the Orchard. Had the attack been pressed further, it is probable that both battalions would only have suffered additional needless casualties.

As the 3rd Brigade carried out its abortive operation on 18 May, the whole of the 1st Division prepared to move into the La Bassée sector. The next day First Army issued an order establishing Alderson's Force, an ad hoc corps formation comprising the 1st Canadian Division and the 51st Highland Division, as well as artillery components from the British 2nd and 7th Divisions.[22] Alderson was given command of the temporary corps, but without a separate staff to manage such an extensive responsibility. As had been the case during Second Ypres, the divisional commander was once again in charge of more forces than he could reasonably have controlled. This unfortunate circumstance must be taken into account if his leadership record is to be fairly assessed. To his credit, Alderson was reluctant to throw his soldiers into the Festubert attacks without first taking stock of the situation. Haig, who had spent the past four or five days pressing his other divisional commanders to keep up offensive pressure, tolerated no delays from Alderson. Shortly after the Canadians arrived, the army commander recorded in his diary that 'Alderson seemed scarcely to realise that we were engaged in an *offensive* battle, and seemed anxious to delay until his troops had consolidated their trenches.' Impatient for action, Haig visited Alderson personally, leaving him with little choice but to commit the 1st Division and other elements of Alderson's Force to battle.[23]

During the evening of 19 May the 2nd Canadian Brigade proceeded into the front lines to replace the 21st Infantry Brigade and elements of the 47th Division in the recently captured breastworks. The relief passed without incident, but the morning brought heavy German shelling against the 8th and 10th Battalions; one of the 8th Battalion's companies suffered more than twenty casualties, including a mortally wounded officer. Additional losses were spared only because the troops had excavated hasty dugouts under the parapets of the trenches, underscoring the value of entrenching practice and basic instruction in field fortifications.[24]

Shortly before noon on the morning of 20 May the senior officers of the 2nd and 3rd Brigades convened at Burstall's artillery headquarters to receive orders for a new attack. The 3rd Brigade was to strike M.9 and M.10, two points situated immediately south of the Orchard (fig. 9.6).[25] The plan called for a high-explosive bombardment lasting up to 20:00 that evening, followed by a one-hour shrapnel bombardment. The assault by a combined force of infantry, grenadiers, and engineers was to begin just as the second bombardment ended, while elements of the 2nd Division attacked a cluster of houses on the left flank.[26] The next morning the 2nd Brigade was to follow up with an attack against K.5, a heavily fortified redoubt surrounded by deep, flooded ditches, belts of wire, and broad fields of fire. According to the plan, a group of grenadiers and a company-sized bayonet party were to approach the strongpoint via a communication trench originating near M.3. The assault on K.5 was to be preceded by only a short bombardment; trench mortar fire was supposed to smash through any German blocking parties encountered along the way.[27] This modest level of support was a far cry from the sixty-hour bombardment that had prepared the way for the attacks of 15 May.

The original operation order left only nine hours for the 3rd Brigade to prepare, while the 2nd Brigade would have had about twenty-two hours to get ready. Plans changed, however, before orders could be carried out.[28] A new directive was issued at about 15:00 that afternoon, just six hours before the 3rd Brigade's assault was supposed to commence. Both brigades were now instructed to advance in unison at

19:45 that evening, leaving fewer than five hours to prepare. British heavy artillery and Canadian 18-pounders would fire a three-hour preliminary bombardment, after which the 3rd Brigade was to secure L.12 and L.11, the Orchard, and two strongpoints at M.9 and M.12. Meanwhile, the 2nd Brigade was to capture K.5, with a fire plan similar to the 3rd Brigade's. Once the fortress was secured, the plan was for grenadiers to 'bomb' to the north and south as far as possible along the German trenches.[29]

On the 2nd Brigade's front the 10th Battalion attacked the K.5 fortress on schedule under the command of Major Percy Guthrie, a New Brunswick lawyer whose Active Militia service dated back to 1903.[30] Three key pieces of evidence describe the 10th Battalion's action at K.5: the battalion war diary, an after-action report by Guthrie (as acting battalion commander), and a short book on Festubert that Guthrie published in May 1916. Although at least two of the three sources originated directly with Guthrie, there is considerable variation among them. It is quite clear, however, that the attack, whatever form it may have assumed, failed to secure K.5. According to the war diary, the action was unsuccessful because 'no previous reconnaissance had been made [and] the bombardment preparing for this attack had been quite ineffectual and had not actually touched K.5.'[31] On their way to the objective the troops passed through a communication trench that was vulnerable to enemy small-arms fire, apparently with some casualties. As a consequence Guthrie called off the attack before any additional losses were incurred. In terms of explicit casualties, the diary indicates only that Captain C.T. Costigan had been wounded by a shell. A lieutenant was also killed in the same way.[32]

In contrast with the war diary passage, Guthrie's after-action report states that troops advanced a hundred yards towards an intermediate fortification (K.4), where the 'the enemy [was] driven out and a barricade built.' There is no explicit mention of K.5 or heavy casualties.[33] And in Guthrie's 1916 book – where we find the most detailed description of his battalion's actions on 20 May – he mentions, contrary to what was reported in the war diary, that he and a few other officers did in fact complete a reconnaissance patrol 'chiefly' in front of K.5 during the night of 19–20 May. According to Guthrie, the main object of the patrol 'was to find out where the wire entanglements and ditches were. Personally I got so close as to hear the Germans talking in a conversational tone and to see the heads of sentries along the parapet.' Guthrie recounted that he 'went over the trench line again' with a periscope the

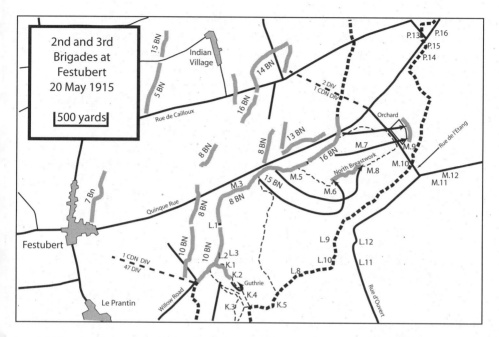

2nd and 3rd
Brigades at
Festubert
20 May 1915

|500 yards|

15 BN
Indian
Village
14 BN
5 BN
P.13
P.16
P.15
P.14
2 DIV
1 CDN DIV
Rue de Caïlloux
16 BN
Orchard
Rue de l'Etang
8 BN
8 BN
13 BN
16 BN
M.7
M.9
7 Bn
15 BN
M.5
North Breastwork
M.8
M.10
M.12
M.11
M.3
8 BN
M.6
Quinque Rue
8 BN
8 BN
L.1
L.9
L.12
Festubert
10 BN
10 BN
1 CDN DIV
47 DIV
L.2 L.3
K.1
L.10
L.11
L.8
K.2
Guthrie
Willow Road
K.4
Le Prantin
K.3
K.5
Rue d'Ouvert

Figure 9.6

following morning so as to 'check up' his observations of the previous
night's patrol. He then suggested to Brigadier-General Arthur Currie
that the men follow the communication trench running between Canadian lines and K.5 rather than attack in the open. At 20:30, according to
Guthrie's account, the two companies of the 10th Battalion advanced
about a hundred yards, but then 'had to stop' in the face of heavy
machine-gun fire. The alleged gains were held through the night, but
in common with the other two sources, Guthrie provided no information regarding the final tally of dead and wounded.[34]

Coupled with the lack of detailed casualty figures, the discrepancies
between Guthrie's two accounts and the 10th Battalion's war diary suggest that there is more to the story. Evidence from other 2nd Brigade units
reinforces such a theory. A party of grenadiers from Lieutenant-Colonel
Tuxford's 5th Battalion was attached to the 10th Battalion for the K.5
attack. Tuxford's after-action report reveals that the officer in charge of
the party, Lieutenant Mackay, was killed, but offers no further clues as to
the extent of the grenadiers' participation.[35] Even the precise details of

Mackay's death are less than clear. Tuxford recorded the date of death as 20 May, indicating that 5th Battalion troops played a definite role in the K.5 attack alongside the 10th Battalion. The 5th Battalion war diary, however, lists Mackay as a casualty on 21 May (with no casualties listed for 20 May), while the Commonwealth War Graves Commission records Mackay's death on 22 May.[36] Again, a series of minor discrepancies brings into question the true nature of the attack, for it is difficult to imagine that the 5th Battalion grenadiers could have participated without incurring a single casualty. Likewise, the 7th and 8th Battalion sources say little about the 10th Battalion attack, despite the fact that the 7th Battalion was supposed to have provided a working party.[37]

To borrow terminology from historian Leonard Smith's study of the 5th French Division, it appears that proportionality influenced Guthrie's leadership. Consequently, the 'hidden transcript' of the K.5 attack varied from what was written in the 'official' accounts.[38] Major Guthrie had witnessed terrible bloodshed at Second Ypres, so it is possible that the strong defences that he observed around K.5 during preliminary reconnaissance dissuaded him from aggressively pursuing what appeared to be a suicide attack order on 20 May, an opinion shared by Brigadier-General Currie.[39] This would explain the paucity of casualties among the 5th Battalion grenadiers, and the reluctance of the 10th Battalion's headquarters to report precise casualty statistics for 20 May. If Guthrie did limit the scope of his attack, he probably also downplayed the low casualty figures, since these would have raised suspicion that the troops did not press forward with due vigour.[40] It is also possible that the troops decided for themselves to go to ground in what was an impossible tactical situation, with Guthrie simply camouflaging this fact in his battle narratives. In either case, the K.5 incident is probably an example of leaders and troops on the ground exercising common sense when orders did not accord well with tactical realities. As Smith's study of the French army shows, this was by no means a uniquely Canadian trait. There is evidence, moreover, that British officers took similar steps at Festubert prior to the arrival of the 1st Canadian Division in the area. Captain Robert Ross, of the 51st Highland Division, dreaded the thought of an impending attack across the deadly fields: 'In imagination we saw the enemy squinting along the sights of his machine guns ready to sweep down in broad daylight all living things that dared to cross that intervening strip of hell. But the attack which would have been a madman's act, did not materialise. At the last moment it was cancelled.'[41] At the last moment indeed. Someone senior to Captain Ross had perhaps decided that the cost of attacking was not worth what might be gained. Not every story ended so gladly, but proportionality was a decision-making factor on the Western Front – albeit an implicit one – that needs to be considered.

The objectives assigned to the 3rd Brigade for 20 May were no less ambitious than the K.5 fortress (fig. 9.6). The 15th Battalion, under the command of Lieutenant-Colonel Marshall, was tasked to pass through the front lines of the 8th Battalion and complete a 1,500-yard dash against two strongpoints marked on the maps as L.11 and L.12. The responsibility fell on Captain R.S. Smith's B Company and Captain W.P. Musgrove's D Company. Along the way the troops had to pass near or through at least five other strongpoints. That afternoon a hasty reconnaissance patrol revealed just how open the ground was, so no one doubted the difficulty of what lay ahead.[42] Indeed, the first casualties fell to artillery fire along the Quinque Rue as the 15th Battalion moved into the 8th Battalion's lines.[43] The shelling intensified as the assault troops formed up in the front breastwork; 8th Battalion sources reveal that several men from both battalions were hit.[44] The assault troops advanced in leaps and bounds according to their tactical training, but the broken ground and flooded shell holes made it difficult to keep direction. Some of the men found temporary shelter in an abandoned trench until smoke provided cover from machine-gun fire. The battalion got moving again, but lost its way, drifting in a northeasterly direction towards the North Breastwork, which extended between M.6 and M.8. The Canadians were able to capture these two strongpoints, but the attack could go no further. Combined casualties for both companies reached 150, including 26-year-old Lieutenant Arthur Muir, of Winnipeg, who was wounded in the charge against M.8 and later killed when he was separated from his platoon; Muir's body was never recovered.[45] The survivors were able to hang on to their gains, roughly halfway between the Canadian and German lines.

Meanwhile, on the left flank of the 3rd Brigade, the 16th Battalion launched an assault against the Orchard and neighboring localities marked as M.9 and M.12 (fig. 9.6). Two reconnaissance patrols had explored the ground under cover of darkness during the previous evening. One of the patrols suffered six casualties and the other was nearly cut off, but they did manage to locate an unoccupied house near the intersection of Quinque Rue and the Rue de l'Etang, immediately northwest of the Orchard. A pair of machine guns was moved up to the house to offer covering fire for the next day's operations.

The Germans were also prepared, and 20 May brought heavy shelling and sniping down on the heads of the 16th Battalion soldiers. According to the war diary, 'bombardment by Germans beginning at 12:30. Fierce until 1:50. Our guns replied but did not appear to be nearly as strong – but I probably was mistaken in the great din.'[46] The diarist may well have intended a sarcastic tone regarding the Canadian counterbattery work, but his comment reinforces evidence from Second Ypres that soldiers tended to dismiss the importance of their own artillery fire because its effect was not always immediately apparent.

Lieutenant-Colonel Leckie protested the daylight zero hour of 19:45 to no avail. Strangely, Leckie left the battalion for a '96-hour leave' only hours before the operation was to begin, perhaps the consequence of his disapproval of the plan. In Leckie's absence, 44-year-old Major Cyrus Peck's A Company was to advance on the right flank and capture a house at M.10 before linking up with Lieutenant-Colonel Marshall's 15th Battalion troops.[47] While Peck launched his attack, Captain Frank Morison's C Company headed for the Orchard on the battalion's left flank.

Morison, a Toronto lawyer and militiaman, fared exceptionally well with his company.[48] With grenadiers in the lead, the C Company men negotiated a broad ditch and hedge on the western side of the Orchard, successfully crossing the killing ground under cover of their own artillery barrage.[49] Support troops followed up quickly with a machine gun, putting a nearby German crew out of action. After the war, a veteran of C Company proudly recalled that he and his fellows advanced under the barrage and 'got the better of [the Germans] before they realized that we had the orchard. So it payed [sic] to follow [the barrage] close[ly] there. That became known as the Canadian Orchard for the rest of the war.'[50]

Peck, who had served with several Active Militia regiments before joining the CEF in November 1914, ran into difficulty with German machine guns on the way to M.10.[51] Unfortunately, the Colt guns that had been installed in the empty house the evening before were knocked out and unable to help. With the way to M.10 barred, Peck's company changed direction and headed for the Orchard, by then in Canadian hands.

The next day, 21 May, witnessed a second attempt to capture K.5 (fig. 9.7). The 10th Battalion was once again ordered to make the assault, along with a company of grenadiers from the 1st Brigade, plus support elements from the 5th and 7th Battalions. Original orders called for a

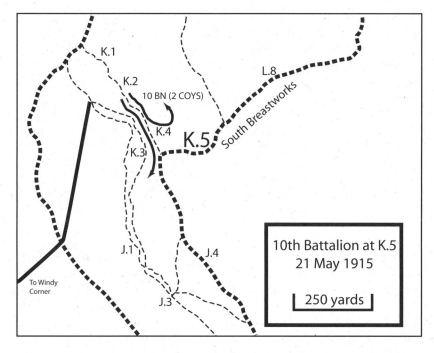

Figure 9.7

dawn attack, but operations were postponed pending the provision of additional artillery support. The firing was to commence at 17:30 and continue until the troops advanced towards K.5 three hours later. As had been true of previous attacks, there was little time to plan, but Major Guthrie was convinced that 'everything was ready in good time and each man knew just what he had to do. I felt sure the plan I thought of was the best one and the officers taking part thought so too.'[52]

According to the 10th Battalion diary – and Guthrie's plan – the two companies advanced along the communication trench leading towards K.5 with little difficulty. Just short of the objective the assault force divided in two groups, one infiltrating to the right and the other to the left in an attempt to encircle the objective. The troops on the left, more directly exposed to K.5, were halted by machine-gun fire, but those on the right managed to work around and establish themselves behind a barricade. Support troops and engineering parties immediately rushed forward to consolidate the gains.[53] When Tuxford's 5th Battalion men reached the scene, they engaged in a violent grenade duel with the Germans.[54] According to Major Guthrie, 'the bombers, under Captain Stewart and Sergeant Stevenson, did good work, as was evidenced by the torn and mutilated Germans here and there.'[55] The prompt consolidation of the bridgehead paid dividends, as the Canadians drove off several German counterattacks during the night of 21-22 May.[56]

At the break of dawn German guns unleashed a sustained bombardment against the new Canadian positions. Officers in the 2nd Brigade accepted the inevitable, withdrawing their men a few hundred yards to construct fresh barricades and escape total annihilation under relentless shellfire. A German counterattack force then formed up, only to be promptly destroyed by machine-gun and artillery fire.[57] According to 10th Battalion sources 'three distinct attacks were made by the enemy on the captured territory all of which were repulsed with heavy loss to the enemy.'[58] Notwithstanding the Canadians' successful defensive work, 22 May was an exhausting day that tested the troops' highest levels of endurance. As Private Sydney Cox recalled many years later, the supply of ammunition ran low, and there was no food or water available in the front trenches; thirsty men were compelled to drink the filthy muck from flooded shell craters.[59] The 10th Battalion launched no further attacks in front of Festubert, although it remained in the area for three more days before being relieved on 26 May. The K.5 operations and German counterattacks cost the battalion in excess of 250 casualties, including eighteen officers.[60]

On 22 May Alderson's Force reached the end of its short tenure. The 51st Highland Division was transferred to the Indian Corps, which had been operating on the Canadians' left flank. The 1st Canadian Division, meanwhile, was attached directly to Haig's First Army. In theory the new arrangement simplified Alderson's job, but the operational objectives did not change; Haig insisted that continued pressure be maintained along the Festubert Front.[61] For the Canadians this meant further attempts to capture the K.5 strongpoint. Lieutenant-Colonel Tuxford's 5th Battalion and elements of Lieutenant-Colonel Odlum's 7th Battalion were next in line to attack the fortress. After resting in bivouacs on 23 May, the troops were briefed for the operation, scheduled for early the next morning (fig. 9.8).

With full knowledge of the difficulties experienced by Guthrie's men during earlier attempts to reach K.5, Currie, Tuxford, and Odlum planned accordingly. At 02:45 the main battalion attack was preceded by a 'bombing' assault. The grenadiers, under the command of Lieutenant

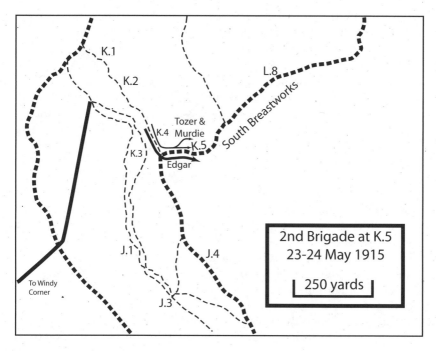

Figure 9.8

D. Tozer, raced up the communication trench leading to K.5, and on entering the German line, promptly attracted the attention of machine-gun crews. As Tozer's force created a diversion, a party of fifty men equipped with portable bridge-ladders broke left into the darkness under the command of Lieutenant Robert Murdie, a self-described Scottish-born 'gentleman' with pre-war Active Militia experience.[62] The bridges were thrown across a flooded ditch blocking access to the fortress. An infantry force of about 500 men under the command of Major Norman Edgar then followed up immediately behind Murdie, storming the strongpoint.[63] After an exceptionally violent man-to-man struggle, approximately 200 yards of German entrenchments surrounding K.5 were in Canadian hands.[64] The heart of the strongpoint, however, eluded capture.

Conflicting evidence makes it difficult to reconstruct the final moments of the K.5 attack, but it was probably the case that Canadian troops never actually occupied the main fort on the morning of 24 May.

According to Brigadier-General Arthur Currie's after-action report, Major Daniel Tenaille had informed him at 03:15 that the Germans had abandoned K.5. Tenaille, however, did not enter the strongpoint, but urged Currie to dispatch reinforcements immediately, possibly because a counterattack was expected. Currie sent forward a single company from the 7th Battalion at 04:45 and then erroneously informed divisional headquarters that Canadians occupied K.5.[65] In contrast with Currie's account, the 7th Battalion after-action report states that orders were received at 03:30 (a disparity of seventy-five minutes with Currie's version) to dispatch 'one company at the double' to reinforce the 5th Battalion. Lieutenant-Colonel Odlum complied, sending Major Alan Powley's A Company.[66] As late as at 05:20 – thirty-five minutes after K.5 was supposed to have fallen according to Currie's report – Powley's troops had yet to breach the fort. At some point that morning a few 5th Battalion troops did manage to enter K.5, only to withdraw soon after, when it appeared that German reinforcements might envelope the position.[67]

As a consequence of the 5th Battalion's high rate of officer casualties, Odlum assumed temporary command of both battalions at 07:00. His report does not indicate when or if K.5 was actually captured. In any event, a wall of friendly shrapnel fire saved his advanced troops from German counterattack.[68] Despite this small victory, a message from Odlum to Currie indicates that K.5, situated squarely in no man's land, remained unoccupied by the Canadians:

> Your [message] asking for artillery barrage has already been answered. Major Powley has just come down wounded in left wrist. As soon as he is dressed I will send him on to you to explain position.
>
> Officers of relieving units should be here early so as to see situation and have it explained to them before dark. Owing to the small number of officers left here available for duty and confusion of units relief will otherwise be difficult.
>
> I am sending in a lot of shovels and sending ammunition to Lord Strathcona's Horse.
>
> Apparently, from Major Powley's report, we do not hold K.5. It is not held by either party. Stretcher bearers and bombers are badly needed.
>
> (signed) V.W. Odlum[69]

Machine gunners and two troops of Lord Strathcona's Horse provided additional support that morning, but the LDSH regimental war diary provides no further information regarding the status of K.5.[70]

Odlum's message to Currie, based on Powley's report, is probably closest to the truth: the enemy no longer occupied the fortress, but neither did the Canadians.[71]

Although the Germans responded with concentrated artillery fire on the K.5 area, Tuxford's and Odlum's troops maintained their gains until relieved during the night of 24-25 May. By then the 7th Battalion had suffered approximately 180 casualties, including nine officers.[72] The cost for the 5th Battalion was also predictably high: forty-four men killed, 193 wounded, and twenty-five missing. Among the dead were five officers, including Major Daniel Tenaille – who was reportedly 'riddled' by an exploding shell – Captain James Randall Innes-Hopkins, and Lieutenant James Maxwell Currie. These three now lie together in Le Touret Cemetery.[73] The bodies of 31-year-old Lieutenant David Meikle and 38-year-old Captain Charles McGee, the latter an experienced soldier and veteran of the South African War, were never recovered.[74] Thirty-seven-year-old Captain Frederick Bagshaw, a lawyer who had served with an Active Militia cavalry regiment before the war, was one of the officers who lived through the ordeal.[75] The day after the attack, the battalion adjutant ordered Bagshaw to take a roll-call for the whole unit. For dozens of names there was no answer from the ranks; survivors broke down in tears as they described what had happened to this or that missing man. Although heavy, the losses were not as high as Bagshaw had initially feared. Quite a few of the missing men had actually been evacuated through British channels, and later turned up in hospital.[76]

Among the last Canadian attacks delivered at Festubert in May 1915 was that of the 3rd and 4th Battalions against German positions east of the Orchard, between M.10 and N.14 (fig. 9.9). In early May the 3rd Battalion, which had suffered severe casualties, was reorganized and retrained with positive results. The condition of the 4th Battalion was less clear, not only as a consequence of the heavy losses it had sustained in April, but also because Lieutenant-Colonel R.H. Labatt had replaced the late A.P. Birchall as commanding officer. Birchall had been a dynamic officer and a capable trainer of troops. While Labatt's pre-war Active Militia service extended back to the Northwest Rebellion of 1885, by 1915 he was 51 years old and in poor physical health, suffering from serious heart problems and unable to walk more than a few steps without losing his breath.[77] It is doubtful if Labatt's poor physical state inspired much confidence in his troops after the trauma the 4th Battalion had gone through at Second Ypres.

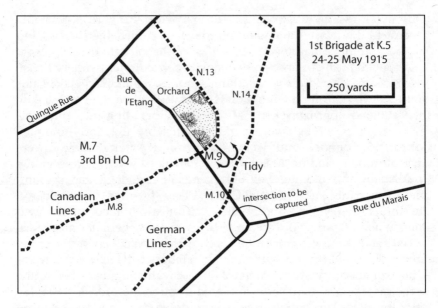

Figure 9.9

On 24 May Brigadier-General Mercer issued orders for the attack. Besides the German wire, the British and Canadian artillery were instructed to hit buildings and trenches along the Rue d'Ouvert, with specific targets assigned to particular batteries. Then, as the infantry attack commenced, the guns were to interdict German reinforcements by shooting at likely avenues of approach.[78] Following the bombardment, the 3rd Battalion was to capture a house at the intersection of Rue du Marais and Rue de l'Etang (M.10) and the fortifications at N.14. All German breastworks joining these points were also to be captured and reversed to face the enemy. Two integrated combat teams prepared to carry out the assault. With the assistance of engineers, grenadiers, and specially detailed 'bayonet' men, Captain Frank Tidy's C Company was to enter the German lines through a house at M.9 and work through towards the main trench between M.10 and N.14. Behind Tidy's troops, a second team under the command of a Lieutenant Rogers was to consolidate the positions. The 1st Field Company supplied the engineers for Tidy's and Rogers's assault teams; one party of twenty men joined Tidy's group, while a second party remained behind with Rogers's men. The grenadiers, under the command of

34-year-old Lieutenant W.D. Sprinks, a 4th Battalion officer, came from the brigade grenade company. In addition to the brief preliminary bombardment, the operation was supported by three trench mortars.[79] Lieutenant-Colonel Rennie, in command of the 3rd Battalion, asked the mortar crews to concentrate on the main trench directly behind the house at M.9, as well as the house at M.10.[80]

The 3rd Battalion assault plan contrasts sharply with the Great War stereotype of unsophisticated linear wave attacks. Instead, each of the combat teams was broken down into smaller groups of about two sections. Extra grenades, sandbags, and pioneer tools were spread throughout the force, so that materiel would be readily available during the consolidation phase. Compared with earlier attacks on the La Bassée Front, the objective of the 1st Brigade's assault was limited. The troops were to advance only a few hundred yards to capture a 600-yard stretch of trench. While the ground favoured the Germans, the Canadians took maximum advantage of every available asset. Brigadier-General Mercer personally arranged for artillery support with Lieutenant-Colonel Morrison's guns. Fearing heavy losses, the brigadier asked medical officers to prepare for rapid evacuation of casualties.[81]

All did not go according to plan. The attack was originally slated for 23:00, but the preliminary artillery fire started late, delaying the assault troops by thirty minutes. In the meantime, telephone links between the gunners and the infantry were severed, leaving Tidy isolated until 23:30. Fortunately, the guns succeeded in cutting the wire between M.9 and the German breastwork, allowing the first assault group to enter the enemy lines without difficulty. The troops were immediately able to turn left and head towards N.14, but fire from machine guns concealed in a heap of derelict farm machinery near M.10 precluded any progress in that direction. Tidy reported the location of the machine guns to the artillery batteries before withdrawing the entire assault party to avoid casualties from friendly fire. As might be expected, German guns responded with heavy counterbombardment, preventing any secondary attempts to reach the objectives.[82] Brigadier-General Mercer soundly concluded from Lieutenant-Colonel Rennie's after-action report that the 'enemy's position [is] much stronger than previously believed.'[83] This was reconfirmed later on 25 May when working parties in the Orchard suffered badly under German artillery and small-arms fire.[84] Casualties in the 3rd Battalion for 24–25 May amounted to at least ten men killed and more than forty wounded or missing; it could have been much worse had Tidy not conducted an orderly withdrawal.[85] The losses among Labatt's troops were also heavy, even though the 4th Battalion launched no attack of its own. As of late May, the battalion had lost nineteen men killed and more than a hundred wounded, virtually all by German artillery fire.[86]

Canadian operations at Festubert were supported by Allied guns until the 1st Division's artillery arrived on 23 May 1915. As the artillery brigades prepared to move into the La Bassée Front, shortages in personnel were made good with transfers from the divisional ammunition column.[87] These exchanges would not have been feasible without the artillery cross-training programs completed back in England. But if gunners could be relatively easily replaced, there was no similar formula for overcoming ammunition deficits.[88] DAC records underscore the scarcity of key ordnance. On 22 May there were 5,093 rounds of 18-pounder shrapnel on hand in the DAC dumps, but only 716 rounds of 18-pounder high explosive, sixty-six rounds of 4.5-inch shrapnel, and 396 rounds of 4.5-inch high explosive. By the morning of 25 May, the supply of 18-pounder shrapnel had been increased to 10,622 rounds, but the reserve of high explosive had dwindled to a mere thirty-six shells. Brigade stocks must be added to these totals, but it is obvious that artillery ammunition was in dangerously short supply.[89] Indeed, the aggregate supplies of most calibres dipped to annual low points across the BEF in May–June 1915.[90] Making matters worse, the flat terrain and high water table seriously complicated the construction of properly concealed gun emplacements on the La Bassée Front. On 24 May the batteries of the 1st CFA Brigade found themselves in 'very exposed positions,' as they registered the German wire prior to the 3rd Battalion's abortive infantry assault.[91]

Although common enough, interruptions to telephone communication during the operations of 18–25 May were fewer than at Ypres. Shorter average distances between headquarters and the forward breastworks may in part account for this, but the cable-laying techniques of the divisional signal company also played a role. Throughout the 1st Division's tenure on the La Bassée Front, working parties as large as 300 men buried hundreds of yards of telephone cable. Although the trenches were rather shallow because of the high water table, even one or two feet of earth protected the wires from the grinding menace of troop and vehicle traffic. A signal company diary entry from 23 May 1915 is typical of the week's activities: '300 men buried 250 yds in divisional area, 125 men buried 115 yards in right sector, 70 men 25 yards in left sector, 60 men 80 yds in left artillery group area.'[92] The use of intermediate telephone offices between the front-line battalion command posts and brigade headquarters helped to keep information moving. As Major Guthrie explained, 'I dodged and ducked my way down to the village, where in an old house we had our office, with orderly room clerk and telephone orderlies. It was a kind of half-way place between my headquarters in the front line and Brigade headquarters. The Adjutant stopped here and we kept our extra ammunition, etc, in a shed near by. It was a convenient place because if our wire got blown up between this point and the front line we could send orderlies with messages down from the front, and telephone from here to the Brigade.'[93] The procedure that Guthrie described had also been practised at Second Ypres, but it was probably more useful at Festubert, where the operational situation was much more stable, and officers did not have to contend with unpredictable changes in position.

The divisional engineers performed an eclectic range of duties alongside the infantry at Festubert, despite awkward administrative arrangements that complicated an already demanding program of work. Although Turner's 3rd Brigade initially rotated into the front lines under the command of the 7th Division (I Corps), the 3rd Field Company was placed under the administrative control of a separate corps. The distances separating Lieutenant-Colonel Charles Armstrong's engineer headquarters from the various field companies and supply depots caused additional frustration, especially since no motor vehicle was available for daily use.[94] As a consequence, junior officers exercised personal initiative in a decentralized command environment.[95] Although higher headquarters assigned tasks to the field companies on a regular basis, the manner in which jobs were carried out depended very much on the company officers' discretion.

The engineers' chores included manufacturing grenades and signal flags, excavation of saps and communication trenches, and building roads capable of sustaining heavy truck and armoured car traffic. In the confusion that resulted from frequent attacks and counterattacks near Festubert, headquarters depended on engineer reconnaissance surveys to gain a clearer picture of exactly who occupied what ground, and report on the general conditions of friendly and enemy fortifications.[96] In late May a sapper officer assessed the condition of old German positions with a view to improving communication trenches between Indian Village, Quinque Rue, and the Orchard, while the 2nd Field Company prepared detailed topographical plans of the K.5 area for use by divisional staff officers.

After the rush of attacks at Festubert, the engineers carried out technical training activities during the final week of May. When the field companies received new searchlights, Armstrong called on the First Army for instructors. Three days later a batch of Royal Engineers arrived to show the Canadians how the lights could be best employed.[97] Later in the month two men from each field company went to St Venant to receive training from a British chemist in the use of gas grenades.[98]

With such wide-ranging responsibilities, it was often engineer officers who first noticed general training deficiencies within the division. At Festubert the officer commanding the 2nd Field Company grew frustrated by unintentional interference with detonator wires leading into mine shafts. Apparently some soldiers had mistaken the cords for telephone cable and tampered with them during the laying of signal lines. The field company officer explained the situation to headquarters, requesting that all ranks receive basic instruction in the recognition of British and German signal wires and demolition cables.[99] It was a small detail, but small details mattered on the Western Front.

Engineering duties transcended infrastructure development and purely technical work. As the Canadian operations against K.5 or M.10–N.14 reveal, divisional engineers supplied special assault equipment, such as bridge-ladders, sending parties forward with the infantry to circumvent obstacles and consolidate gains. While the scale of operations at Festubert was small relative to the Canadian offensives of 1916–18, the model for inter-arm cooperation had been established.

The Canadian field ambulances were overwhelmed with casualties at Second Ypres. Although there were far fewer wounded men to evacuate and treat at Festubert, the general conditions were just as difficult as they had been back in April. Private Charles Lyttle, a druggist in civil life, joined the CEF in September 1914 with no prior military experience, serving with the 3rd Field Ambulance in 1915.[100] His diary entries from May 1915 describe the impossible conditions confronting stretcher bearers, as they attempted to bring wounded soldiers out of the forward areas:

(18 May) mud something fierce, never saw the likes before ... Enemy driven out of trenches which had cement floors, chairs, etc. ... British dug in 600 yards beyond ... couldn't get to wounded, no roads, dark, shells bursting ...

(19 May) Canadians advanced last night. Number lying out in mud and rain, cannot get to them ... had not got very far when [heard] the whistle of a J.J. [Jack Johnson] ... [101]

The experiences of medical personnel working at the battalion level reflect what Lyttle recorded in his pocket diary. As the 14th Battalion regimental history explains, 'the task of collecting the wounded at night, amid the complicated maze of trenches, mud, and watery ditches … was exhausting in the extreme.'[102] Despite these horrendous conditions, Lieutenant-Colonel Walter Langmuir Watt's 3rd Field Ambulance wasted no time when it arrived at the La Bassée Front with the 3rd Brigade on 18 May. A tent subdivision was opened near a schoolhouse, regimental aid posts were established near Indian Village, and an advanced dressing station was set up at Le Touret. But before the wounded could be treated at any of these locations, stretcher bearers had to collect them from the breastworks, no man's land, or newly captured positions. It was a deadly business. After the Orchard was secured on 20 May, a medical officer and eight stretcher bearers ventured among the smashed trees to collect the wounded. Four of the eight bearers were hit by German shellfire, and two of them later died. One was 29-year-old Charles Lyttle.[103] In his last diary entry, scribbled the day before he was killed, Lyttle remarked how lucky he had been to survive unscathed for so long.

Despite the best efforts of the medical personnel, many wounded men died in no man's land, or eventually fell into enemy hands because they could not be located or safely reached by stretcher bearers or other friendly troops. In one instance a Canadian infantry patrol operating near L.8 during the night of 26–27 May 1915 discovered three soldiers of the Cameron Highlanders, who had been wounded nine days earlier, on 17 May. All three were still alive, although only one was capable of speaking. He reported to his rescuers that a German patrol had approached on the night of 19–20 May. One of the German soldiers kicked him, but when no response was elicited, the 'body' was left for dead.[104] This man was lucky, not only because he managed to evade capture or summary execution, but also because the Canadians saved him from slow starvation or death from thirst. It is frightening to contemplate the last hours of life for the multitude of unknown soldiers who lay wounded, isolated, and undiscovered by friendly troops after a pitched battle.

Motor and horse-drawn ambulances carried the wounded away from front-line collecting points under cover of darkness as well as during the day. The 2nd Field Ambulance's daily evacuations between 21 and 26 May ranged from between twenty-five and 125 men.[105] The 3rd Field Ambulance admitted approximately 325 Canadian soldiers to hospital from 19 through 26 May, along with about fifty-five imperial troops and a single German prisoner.[106] According to the commanding officer of the 2nd Field Ambulance, the casualties evacuated from Festubert had 'very nasty wounds, the worst he had seen yet.' The officer blamed some of the traumatic injuries on 'dum dum bullets or bullets reversed in [their] cartridge[s]' and claimed that a German charger clip loaded with such ammunition was captured and shown to him. Neither the field ambulance nor the brigade diaries categorize injuries by type, but artillery wounds were especially common.

Some of the evacuees bore no physical injuries. About 200 Canadians were hospitalized with shell shock or neurasthenia in May and June 1915, but it is likely that many others went uncounted and untreated.[107] Compared with Second Ypres, there are fewer explicit references to such cases in the sources for Festubert, although Lieutenant-Colonel Odlum's 7th Battalion after-action report mentions that an officer suffered from 'nervous collapse' on 24 May.[108] Twenty-three-year-old Howard Curtis, a machine gunner in the 2nd Battalion, was not too proud to admit that the stress of front line service and the loss of a close pal were taking a toll. Curtis wrote to his mother shortly after the toughest fighting at Festubert: 'It is nerve shattering to be under shell fire ... no matter how strong a man's nerves are they are affected. I have seen many a poor fellow break under the strain. I am sticking it fairly well myself but I'm not as steady as I was a few months ago ... I miss Bert Carpenter. For the last month or so I was with him nearly every day. No. 1 Company is a lonesome place now without him.'[109] Unfortunately for Private Curtis and his fellows, there were more attacks to come before the 1st Canadian Division moved to a quieter sector.

Improvised military cemeteries appeared with the first hostilities of 1914, but by the middle of 1915, hundreds of burial plots had been established, many of which still exist as beautifully manicured Commonwealth War Graves Cemeteries. A few of the Canadians who died at Festubert are buried at Le Touret Cemetery, and several more at the Windy Corner Guards or Post Office Rifles Cemeteries. Further away from the battlefield, near Béthune, about 25 per cent of the graves at the Hinges Military Cemetery are Canadian. These men, from all corners of the 1st Division, were killed during the worst days at Festubert and buried near Alderson's divisional headquarters. Thanks in part to Lieutenant-Colonel Armstrong of the Canadian engineers, the burial ground survives today as a Commonwealth War Graves Cemetery. In early June 1915 Armstrong ordered his sappers to surround the Hinges burial ground with a white picket fence. A six-foot-wide gate was installed, with generous paths left between the rows of graves and additional space set aside for future burials.[110] Armstrong's fence is now long gone, yet the handiwork of Canadian engineers at Hinges shows how postwar commemorative practices originated with ordinary soldiers in the midst of the fighting.

There were additional operations around Festubert before the end of May, when the 1st Division moved further south to take up new positions between Givenchy and the La Bassée Canal, but the last attacks followed patterns agonizingly similar to those at K.5, the Orchard, and M.10–N.14. Among the Canadian commanders, Brigadier-General Arthur Currie expressed particular outrage with the orders he had received, before as well as after the K.5 battles.[111] According to Duguid's official history, the difficulties resulted from poor quality maps coupled with an operational scenario 'where confusion in topography was only rivalled by confusion in tactics and confusion of troops.'[112] In the later official history, Nicholson blamed setbacks on strong German defences, a shortage of guns, and the inability of Canadian battalions to assimilate reinforcements in the short time since Second Ypres.[113] At least in part, both interpretations are as valid as Currie's anger at having to send his troops into action with inadequate support, but other aspects of the May 1915 operations transcend tactical success or failure. For strategic reasons beyond their control the Canadian troops participated in attacks against very steep odds. Canadian officers minimized losses by exercising common sense; when an attack appeared likely to fail at the outset, it was simply called off, as in the case of Major Guthrie's initial attempt to capture K.5. And while most of the Festubert attacks fell short of hopes in terms of ground captured, the evidence shows that Canadian teams of infantry and engineers were capable of delivering agile combined assaults without much notice and often with a level of artillery support that was meagre even by the standards of 1915. Finally, the Canadian attacks did succeed in drawing German reinforcements into battle, away from the French offensives, and this was one of the original strategic imperatives for the La Bassée Front in May 1915. It is small consolation, but worse was to come in this war.

Arthur Currie was not the only Canadian to lose his temper in the immediate aftermath of Festubert. Sam Hughes, a long-time believer in the natural superiority of citizen soldiers over professionals, was already convinced that British regular commanders were unfit to lead his boys. On top of April's high losses, the blood-letting at Festubert confirmed the minister's long-standing prejudices in his own mind. At the end of May Hughes scathingly criticized Alderson's conduct at the Second Battle of Ypres and Festubert in a letter to Prime Minister Robert Borden. Lord Kitchener also received a copy, while Hughes took the liberty of reading excerpts at a press conference. Most damningly, he accused Alderson of cowardice at Second Ypres and outright negligence at Festubert.[114] Just about everyone, with the obvious exception of Hughes himself, realized that both charges were totally unfounded. Alderson, quite naturally, was deeply offended, and even Hughes soon realized that he had gone too far this time. During a trip overseas later that summer, the minister, under pressure from Borden, personally apologized to Alderson 'in as gracious a manner as the man is capable of.'[115] Alderson accepted the apology, only to be further vindicated by the cool treatment that Hughes received from British commanders as well as the Canadian rank and file during his overseas visit. On one occasion the troops gladly avoided the 'gloomy prospect' of a long address from Hughes when a German aircraft dropped a bomb nearby.[116] At other times, however, both Alderson and Hughes delivered speeches near the front lines without interruption. Both were cheered, but Alderson elicited the more enthusiastic response from the men. In contrast to Hughes's blustery bravado, the British commander's understated manner of plain dealing ensured the continued confidence of his soldiers, in spite of all that they had suffered over the past weeks. As Alderson wrote after Hughes's departure, 'all things considered I think I may say that I won all along the line.'[117]

Givenchy

As Hughes penned his accusatory letter to Borden in late May, the men of the 1st Canadien Division were occupied with more pressing concerns of their own. Along with the 7th and the 51st Highland Divisions, Alderson's Canadians were assigned to Lieutenant-General Rawlinson's IV Corps. Under Haig's First Army, Rawlinson's forces prepared to continue their costly offensive work, drawing German reserves away from the Tenth Army's front. The town of La Bassée, about three miles east of Festubert, remained the nominal territorial objective for the BEF. Now the Canadians were responsible for a zone between the canal and the village of Givenchy, just south of their previous frontage near Festubert. Although the 1st Division was destined to play a considerably smaller offensive role during the June attacks than it had in May, the outcome was hardly less devastating for the soldiers of the 1st Brigade, who participated directly.

The German forces in front of Givenchy consisted mainly of troops from the 134th Infantry Regiment, originally from the 89th Brigade of the 40th Division. In August 1914 the 40th Division, from Saxony, served in General Max Klemens von Hausen's Third Army, seeing action on the Marne near Vitry le François. Throughout 1915 and until August 1916 the division, posted near Ploegsteert Wood and Bois Grenier, regularly siphoned off reinforcements to other units as needed. Selected troops were dispatched to Neuve Chapelle in March, while the entire 133rd Regiment was permanently donated to the 24th Division at the same time, evidence that Allied offensive pressure was taking a toll on German strength. Elements of the 40th Division fought at Festubert in May. Continued Anglo-French operations compelled the division to send the 134th Regiment to Givenchy in June, where it was attached to the 14th Division.[118]

As the German infantry manned their defences, the tired battalions of the Canadian 1st Brigade retrained, enjoying a much-needed opportunity to recuperate in the lovely Béthune countryside. The 2nd and 3rd Battalions rested for a few days before resuming their usual route marches, company drills, and grenade practice.[119] The exhausted troops of the 4th Battalion arrived at Essars on the afternoon of 1 June and were allowed to relax for the day. During the following week a selection of training activities, including anti-gas instruction, was interspersed with rest, bathing, and short periods of leave in Béthune. On 7 June a gravely ill Lieutenant-Colonel Labatt was finally replaced by Major Malcolm Colquhoun.[120] A more suitable candidate for battalion command, Colquhoun had led B Company in the counterattack against Mauser Ridge, and was one of the few 4th Battalion officers to come through Second Ypres unscathed. Under their new commanding officer the men of the 'Mad Fourth' trained until ordered to the front lines.[121] The 2nd Battalion moved into the trenches on the 4th Battalion's left flank, while Lieutenant-Colonel Rennie's 3rd Battalion assumed brigade reserve positions further west. For the moment Lieutenant-Colonel Hill's 1st Battalion remained in divisional reserve.

While the other battalions of the 1st Brigade occupied the front lines, Hill and his company commanders inspected the forward and second-line trenches in preparation for the 1st Battalion's pending deployment (fig. 9.10). Hill's troops were charged with protecting the right flank of the neighbouring 21st Brigade (7th Division) as it advanced towards Chapelle St Roch in the upcoming attack of 15 June. On 11–12 June all

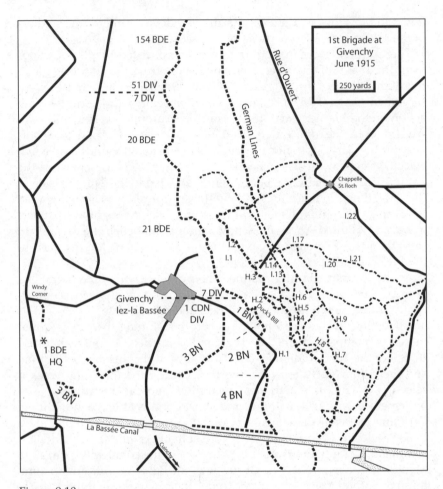

Figure 9.10

officers and non-comissioned officers of B, C, and D Companies toured the trenches. The next day Hill's troops exchanged their Ross rifles for British Lee-Enfields. Company training continued until 15 June when the battalion joined the rest of the brigade in the front lines.[122]

Brigadier-General Mercer received attack orders from Alderson on 12 June and proceeded to discuss the details with Hill.[123] The broad objective of the IV Corps offensive was to capture the line running north from the Givenchy–Chapelle St Roch road up to the Rue d'Ouvert. The 1st Brigade was to press forward on the right flank of the 7th and the 51st Highland Divisions on the evening of 15 June (fig. 9.10). The brigade's specific task was to advance past the line H.2–H.3 up to I.14–H.6, and finally beyond to the German communication trench running between I.17 and I.20. At this point the brigade needed to establish a protective flank for the 7th Division, with the exact location to be determined by the actual progress of the British troops.

Engineers, machine gunners, and grenadiers were integral to the plan of attack. 'Bombing' parties were instructed to turn right at a series of three phase lines (H.2, H.6, and I.20) and 'bomb down each line' to secure the flank. Machine-gun teams were also to be dropped off at the phase lines with orders to bring fire on German trenches to the south. Engineers, with the help of infantry working parties from another battalion, were detailed to consolidate each line as the assault troops moved forward. A separate engineering party, meanwhile, was to construct a communication trench from the original Canadian front line across no man's land, such that supplies and reinforcements could safely move forward during the consolidation phase, the moment of truth in any attack.

Like the May operations, the 15 June assault was based on a combined arms plan that accounted for contingencies within realistic limits. To provide headquarters with a timely sense of the attack's progress, Canadians carried blue marker flags fashioned by the divisional engineers, while the neighbouring 7th Division sported red-and-blue flags. In the meantime, Canadian signallers strung fresh telephone cable between Hill's headquarters and the artillery batteries.[124] Lines were laid in triplicate as an added precaution against breaks; an incredible fifty-eight miles of cable were required to connect headquarters with the batteries and forward observation officers.[125]

Guns from all three Canadian artillery brigades supported the June operations. Lieutenant-Colonel J.H. Mitchell's 3rd CFA Brigade focused on wire-cutting and destruction of the German parapets during the seven days leading up to the attack. That week's operation orders emphasized the extreme importance of this task: 'A slow steady rate of fire is to be maintained. 6 rounds per yard of front on each line of trenches should suffice, but the wire must be cut. Every effort must be made to combine economy of ammunition with efficiency.'[126] Despite shortages of ammunition, the wire-cutting continued right up to 15 June. Close contact was maintained with forward observation officers and infantry commanders to ensure that sufficiently broad paths were cleared. Once this was achieved, Mitchell's guns were detailed to fire on pre-registered boxes during the night to prevent enemy working parties from repairing the broken wire.[127]

While the Canadian 18-pounders concentrated on the German wire, heavier British and French artillery hammered away at enemy strongpoints and communication arteries, depriving the German infantry of sleep and fresh rations. The largest were the 6-, 8-, and 9.2-inch howitzers of No. 1 Group, Heavy Artillery Reserve, along with one brigade of French 155 mm guns. The 43rd Howitzer Group, consisting of the 43rd and the 118th Howitzer Brigades, operated under the control of the 1st Division. Orders from Brigadier-General Burstall's headquarters specified that the commanding officer of the 43rd Group must stay in close touch with the 1st Brigade, as well as with the 21st Brigade and the Canadian field batteries. Highly specific fire plans were drawn up to make the best use of limited supplies of high-explosive ammunition. Every shell counted. Burstall warned his subordinates at brigade level not to allow their forward observers or signallers to become overly tired prior to the attack; the guns would be firing close to friendly troops, and there was little margin for error.[128] As an added safety measure, no high-explosive shells were to be fired at the first line of German trenches within five minutes of zero hour. This may well have given the German infantry extra time to emerge from dugouts and man their parapets, but Canadian commanders did not dare risk hitting their own troops with gunfire. It was a difficult compromise.

Lieutenant-Colonel Maclaren's 2nd CFA Brigade was largely responsible for shelling the area in front of the 1st Brigade on the day of attack.[129] Beginning on 14 June three batteries hit the German second line between I.13 and H.4, opposite the 1st Battalion's frontage, while others bombarded an east–west sunken roadway (H.1–H.8) in the 2nd Battalion's area.[130] One of the guns in the 6th Battery was given a somewhat more unusual assignment: to offer direct support from a front-line emplacement. Special armoured 'Wardrop' shields arrived on 11 June to be fitted to the assault gun.[131] At least one other gun from the 1st CFA Brigade was similarly deployed in the forward trenches.[132]

Maclaren's guns opened fire at 15:00 on 14 June, remaining in action for much of the evening. By 20:00 forward observation officers estimated that three-quarters of the 2nd CFA Brigade's shells had found their targets. The German parapet near H.8 was badly smashed, and infantry officers in the 2nd Battalion reported that the gunfire on their frontage 'left nothing to be desired.'[133] In addition to the assigned tasks, the 6th Battery responded when information was received that enemy troops were attempting to infiltrate the 21st Brigade's lines.[134]

For once, the situation seemed favourable on the morning of the attack. The 2nd CFA Brigade learned from forward observers that the Germans had made no obvious repairs to their damaged defences in the vicinity of H.3. Likewise, the 4th Battalion reported that further south, near H.8, the enemy wire had neither been repaired nor replaced. Later in the morning the batteries were permitted to fire at targets of opportunity, an example of the devolution of authority to lower levels of command. The main pre-assault bombardment began at 17:30.

Having conferred with Brigadier-General Mercer back on 12 June, Lieutenant-Colonel Hill issued specific orders two days later. According to the plan, D Company was to lead the attack that evening under the command of Major George Smith, a Chatham-area militiaman.[135] Captain George Wilkinson's C Company was to follow in support, while A and B Companies would help to consolidate. Like Smith, Wilkinson had served with the Active Militia in southwestern Ontario before the war.[136]

Hill's plan left as little as possible to chance. The attack was to be preceded by a mine detonation at H.2 – just opposite the 'Duck's Bill' – but alternative arrangements were detailed should the mine fail to explode. Sections of grenadiers, plus bayonet men and working parties were to advance on Smith's flanks, establishing 'blocks' against German counterattacks along the trenches running through H.2 and H.6. Wilkinson was then to bring forward additional machine guns to discourage counterattacks during the consolidation phase. Signal flags, rockets, pioneer tools, and sandbags were issued so that each echelon could consolidate and communicate its progress to rear headquarters. Contrary to the popular impression, however, the assault troops were not overburdened with extraneous gear in this attack. As was the usual practice throughout the war, large packs were left in the rear. Only essential items were carried in small packs, along with water and ammunition on the soldiers' field equipment.[137]

The mine at H.2 detonated on time, but the plan did not survive contact with the enemy.[138] Tragically, about fifty Canadian infantrymen and almost half of the grenadiers in the right flanking party were killed or wounded in the explosion. The blast also killed the commander of the right-hand bombing party, while the reserve depot of grenades was lost on that flank. According to the divisional engineer war diary, the 176th Tunnelling Company, Royal Engineers, had warned an unnamed 1st Battalion major – probably Smith – to evacuate a clearly delineated danger zone near the mine. Lieutenant-Colonel Armstrong, in command of the Canadian engineers, relayed this information to Mercer's and Alderson's headquarters.[139] Mercer, however, recorded in his private diary that IV Corps Headquarters refused permission to evacuate the 1st Battalion troops a safe distance from the shaft.[140] Smith's men paid dearly, but the explosion also created havoc in the German first line, leaving few troops able to resist as D Company advanced through the dust and debris. Captain Wilkinson followed directly with the extra machine-gun teams. The infantry soon discovered that the preliminary bombardment had indeed smashed the German wire and parapet to bits.

Major Smith's depleted company was able to overrun H.2 in short order, but the troops ran into trouble near H.3, where the Germans were making a stand against the 21st Brigade. D Company bypassed this problem area, continuing forward to the enemy's second line. Twenty-nine-year-old Captain Fred Robinson's B Company moved up to consolidate in the wake of D Company, but Robinson and his second-in-command, Lieutenant Peter Pick, were almost immediately killed by machine-gun fire from H.3.[141] Lieutenant Tweedie Sims, a twelve-year veteran of the Royal Navy, took over, pressing on under heavy fire.[142] Within thirty minutes of the mine explosion, officers in the 2nd and 4th Battalions reported to Mercer that they could see the blue flags carried by Smith's troops. It was difficult, however, to keep constant track of the 1st Battalion's progress because smoke often obscured visibility across no man's land.[143]

As the infantry struggled forward under machine-gun fire from H.3, the grenadiers managed to clear the German trenches as far south as H.5 and as far north as I.13. The final reserve troops, from Captain Thomas Delamere's A Company, were ordered forward at 19:00, just before the Germans launched strong counterattacks from the direction of H.5 and I.14.[144] Although generously equipped with hand and rifle grenades and supported by automatic weapons fire from H.3, the Germans were rudely answered by Canadian machine gunners, under the command of the 48-year-old Lieutenant Frederick Campbell, the 1st Battalion machine-gun officer. Merciless hand-to-hand combat ensued, as Smith's men used up their last grenades against the counterattack. Under the weight of the German troops, the Canadians could do little but fall back to the original German front line. Lieutenant Campbell, a veteran of the South African War, died with his gun crews and was posthumously decorated with the Victoria Cross.

By this point in the operation, it was nearly impossible for the forward troops to communicate with battalion headquarters. Not until after 20:00 did a messenger reach Lieutenant-Colonel Hill with news that the 1st Battalion was holding the German front line. It was equally difficult for Hill to move fresh supplies of grenades and ammunition forward, as the Canadian front line was jammed with dead and wounded men, probably from the mine explosion. Brigadier-General Mercer was reluctant to order artillery support against H.3 for fear of hitting friendly troops. Engineers from the 1st Field Company attempted to dig a communication trench forward to H.2 from the Duck's Bill, but it was impossible to complete this work in time to be of any use to the infantry.

With few options, Mercer ordered Lieutenant-Colonel Rennie's 3rd Battalion to provide a full company of reinforcements. Rennie dispatched B Company under the command of a Major Osborne. Troops of C Company, meanwhile, attempted to rush additional grenades forward to the captured German lines.[145] The 3rd Battalion troops made little progress under heavy fire, and were unable to influence the situation, despite sustaining well over a hundred casualties, including five officers.[146]

Meanwhile, Major Smith decided that the situation in the German trenches was untenable, and ordered a general retirement to the Canadian front line. Already wounded, Smith was killed just as the withdrawal was completed. Mercer considered ordering the whole of the 3rd Battalion forward in a second attempt to capture H.3, but the idea was wisely postponed until the following afternoon, pending the outcome of attacks on other parts of the IV Corps front.

Efforts against H.3 were renewed the next day with an abortive assault by two platoons of the 3rd Battalion. The front Canadian trenches came under shellfire even before the platoons set out late that afternoon. According to the divisional war diary, enemy small-arms fire forced the men to ground immediately, with the action ending almost as soon as it began.[147] An eyewitness later recalled that 'very few of us ever got beyond our own wire.'[148] The incident represents yet another example of combat leaders exercising common sense on the spot, since it appears that the battalion commander committed the smallest possible number of men to what appeared to be a hopeless operation. The battalion war diary dismissed the attack as unfeasible because of the 7th Division's inability to make progress on the left: 'The advance was made as ordered, but owing to the 7th Div not being able to go forward on account of the heavy machine-gun and rifle fire, the 2 Coys of 3rd Bn were checked, and subsequently retired to the

British trench.'[149] The episode is not even mentioned separately from the events of 15 June in the 3rd Battalion's regimental history. As was the case with the 10th Battalion's initial attack against K.5 on 18 May, 3rd Battalion sources do not provide separate casualty lists for the 15 and 16 June operations, possibly with the intention of concealing low rates for 16 June in the 15 June figures. If the two platoons had in fact been fully committed on 16 June, a significant tally of losses would have been reported specifically for that day. In all probability, either Rennie or one of company commanders practised rational economy of force.

The 1st Brigade attacks at Givenchy failed not because of unsophisticated planning or poor training, but because it was not possible to provide adequate levels of support for the forward assault troops once they had entered the German lines. The first, and even the second German trenches could be captured, but holding them against counterattack was extremely difficult when enemy troops enjoyed the benefit of approaching the contested zone under cover of their own communication trenches, while Canadian reinforcements were forced to advance over a shattered and fire-swept no man's land. The cost for the 1st Battalion in this case was painfully high. All but one of the officers who participated directly in the attack were killed or injured; ten officers were dead, two missing, and eight wounded. All four company commanders had become casualties. Major Smith, Captain Robinson, and Lieutenant Pick of D and B Companies were dead. Captains Wilkinson and Delamere of C and A Companies were wounded. Lieutenant Cecil James, a British army veteran and militiaman, was killed in the mine blast at the head of a bombing party.[150] Lieutenant Gordon was wounded while leading the left party. By the end of the operation Wilkinson's company had lost so many officers that it was under the command of Sergeant-Major Charles Owen, who was later awarded the Distinguished Conduct Medal for his actions that day. Among the other ranks, fifty-eight were killed, eighty-two were missing, and more than 200 were wounded. It is uncertain exactly how many of these men were killed or injured in the mine explosion at zero hour, but Hill's battalion suffered nearly as many casualties on 15 June as during the entire Second Battle of Ypres. Today George Smith, Fred Robinson, Peter Pick, and Cecil James rest side by side in the Beauvry Communal Cemetery Extension, just outside of Béthune. About a hundred men from British, Indian, and Canadian units are buried there, most of them killed during the 1915 fighting.

With hindsight it is easy to criticize the Allied operations of May and June 1915, but decision makers were left with few options other than to persist against the odds if the broader objectives of the war were to be achieved. The tactical and operational difficulties at Festubert and Givenchy were largely the results of factors beyond the control of anyone in the 1st Canadian Division, IV Corps, or even the First Army for that matter. The strategic imperatives of the moment dictated that British forces attack a determined, well-equipped, and solidly entrenched enemy.

As at Second Ypres, the Canadians suffered from a crippling shortage of heavy artillery support at Festubert and Givenchy. Inexperienced reinforcements were spread throughout infantry battalions and artillery and engineer brigades. Despite these obvious disadvantages, the La Bassée offensives of May and June demonstrated that the division was capable of mounting limited set-piece operations with whatever resources were available. Infantry, grenadiers, and engineers worked together as combined arms teams in repeated attacks. Territorial objectives were rarely attained, but this was primarily a function of strong defensive fortifications and a determined enemy. In some cases where the cost of offensive action was too far out of proportion with potential gains, company and battalion commanders pulled their troops back. Overall, the limited scale of these attacks – most were of company size – suggests that commanders at the brigade and divisional levels sought to minimize losses as far as possible.

For the Canadians it was again time to dig. The dead who could be recovered from no man's land were buried in neat makeshift cemeteries. But the living were also relegated to an underground existence. In the front lines, the survivors carved fresh dugouts, tunnels, and support trenches out of the damp soil.[151] This flurry of defensive work was to continue after the 1st Division settled into new positions on the III Corps front between Ploegsteert and Messines that summer. In the heavy fighting of April, May, and June Alderson's soldiers had defended and attacked in pitched battles. For the rest of the year they were to engage in 'static' trench warfare on a 'quiet' front. Both terms are deceptive, for while the second half of 1915 was far less bloody for the Canadians than the first, they continued to engage the enemy under the siegelike conditions that prevailed across the Western Front in between major offensive actions.

10 Trench Warfare:
The Ploegsteert–Messines Front

In the official history of the Canadian Expeditionary Force, G.W.L. Nicholson remarked that a 'strange' tranquillity characterized the later months of 1915, coming as they did in the shadow of grinding offensives at Festubert and Givenchy.[1] In strictly relative terms, Nicholson was correct. On their new frontage between the towns of Ploegsteert and Messines, life for the Canadians was far less dangerous than it had been in the Ypres Salient or on the La Bassée Front.[2] But to pass over the second half of 1915 as little more than a quiet interlude between more notable offensives would be to ignore a rich dimension of the First World War experience on the Western Front: the character of static trench warfare in 'inactive' sectors of the front.

Studies of trench warfare have shown that opposing soldiers on quiet fronts often followed a 'live and let live' routine; direct confrontation and violence were avoided as long as both sides reciprocated.[3] In recent years popular writers and film-makers have revisited prominent, albeit isolated, examples of live and let live, mostly notably the so-called Christmas Truce of 1914–15.[4] Although the evidence for live and let live is compelling, the practice was by no means universal during the periods of operational inactivity that punctuated the heaviest fighting. In the summer and autumn of 1915 neither the Canadians nor their German adversaries displayed much interest in fraternization. On the contrary, with the knowledge that some of the German soldiers on the other side of no man's land were possibly veterans of the gas attack at Ypres, there was hardly any reason for the Canadians to participate in tacit cooperation. Despite shortages of artillery ammunition and support weapons, inventive soldiers found ways to continue the fight.

The men of the 1st Canadian Division predicated their day-to-day existence on two basic assumptions: first, that they might be asked to resume offensive activities at any moment, and second, that the enemy was capable of striking with little warning. The scattered trail of Canadian war graves hidden away in the shady cemeteries of Ploegsteert Wood reminds today's visitor that caution and respect for the enemy were well advised in 1915. In a damp, isolated clearing beyond reach of motor vehicles, the determined tourist will discover Ploegsteert Wood Military Cemetery. Greenish moss stains the grave markers, as if to erase the last vestiges of a forgotten battlefield. It is hard to imagine that more than ninety years ago 'Plugstreet' was as Canadian as any community across the Dominion. So much so that during the Great War the burial ground was known as Strand Canadian Cemetery, after the nearby Strand Trench that the 1st and 3rd Brigades manned in 1915. Today the cemetery contains 164 burials from throughout the war, twenty-eight of whom are Canadian soldiers killed between June and October 1915. Among them is 27-year-old Lance-Corporal William Allen. On 11 July this machine gunner from the 13th Battalion lost his life to a stray bullet in a communication trench at St Ives. Resting nearby is Private Joseph Breton, probably a victim of sniper fire. The 25-year-old iron worker from Alberta had been a militiaman before enlisting in the 51st Battalion in January 1915. He was transferred to the 4th Battalion in early August 1915. Three weeks later he was dead. Twenty-nine-year-old Private Ernest Buckley was born in England, but emigrated to Canada and enlisted in the CEF in January 1915. He was mortally wounded after joining the 1st Battalion as a reinforcement. Most battalions lost a few men to enemy action each month that summer. Daily 'wastage' increased as the pleasant weather turned to rainy autumn. The extra losses were victims of illness and exposure rather than German fire.

As was true of the earlier months of 1915, the 1st Canadian Division was fully integrated with the British Expeditionary Force at Ploegsteert–Messines. Beneath the sprawling metropolis of trenches, Royal Engineer tunnellers protected the infantry from German miners until Canadian mining sections could be reconstituted. Far above, in the open skies, Royal Flying Corps aircraft of No. 4 Squadron duelled with enemy airplanes as pilots on both sides searched for artillery targets. And on the ground, British trench mortar batteries were deployed in the Canadian lines, while the 118th Howitzer Brigade remained under Canadian

Figure 10.1. This 1919 photograph illustrates the ruins of Ploegsteert. Although the village was not completely destroyed, the damage suggests that 'quiet' sectors of the front were hardly immune to violence. (LAC, PA-004479)

command. It was increasingly typical for subunits to fall under the tactical command of a separate division, especially during reliefs. On one occasion a howitzer battery from the 17th British Division was temporarily attached to Alderson's command. On another, several field artillery brigades from the 12th Division operated under Canadian command while a new division moved into the area. Elements of the 3rd Brigade were attached to the 28th Division, 2nd Canadian Division, and 50th Division all within the span of five days.[5] Meanwhile, the batteries of the 3rd CFA Brigade were loaned to the 8th Division for the Loos offensive. Canadian personnel also served as instructors and advisers for newly arrived divisions.[6] With a constant flow of personnel and units between neighbouring brigades, divisions, and corps, the 1st Canadian Division was truly incorporated into the British Expeditionary Force.

In many respects the 1st Division was very different from what it had been in February 1915. Thousands of reinforcements had joined since Second Ypres, Festubert, and Givenchy, bringing the division into its second and third generations. There were also new formations on the scene. Elements of the Canadian Cavalry Brigade, under the command of Brigadier-General J.E.B. 'Jack' Seely, had arrived in time to see dismounted action at Festubert and then to serve alongside the 1st Division throughout the summer. Lieutenant-Colonel Raymond Brutinel's 1st Canadian Motor Machine-Gun Brigade crossed the English Channel in mid-June, playing instructional and combat roles in the months that followed. Brutinel was a colourful character who had served in the French army before immigrating to Canada in 1905. At the beginning of the war his interest in machine guns and motor vehicles captured the imagination of former Liberal cabinet minister Sir Clifford Sifton. The two men devised a plan to form a motorized machine-gun unit, and recruiting began in Ottawa in August 1914. Like the specialized elements within the 1st Canadian Division, the evidence suggests that the 1st Canadian Motor Machine-Gun Brigade's initial complement of officers and men possessed useful pre-war experience. About one-quarter had seen military service of some kind, but more importantly, as many as half of the men had worked as chauffeurs or mechanics, and about 30 per cent were skilled in other technical trades.[7]

Important changes in personnel accompanied the arrival of the 2nd Canadian Division and the formation of the Canadian Corps in mid-September 1915. With Alderson appointed to command the new corps, Arthur Currie was promoted to major-general to command the 1st Division. Richard Turner was also promoted and appointed to command the 2nd Division – against Alderson's wishes.[8] The two officers had quarrelled at Second Ypres, where Alderson seemed to have lost confidence in Turner over the withdrawal to the General Headquarters line. Brigadier-General Lipsett, formerly CO of the 8th Battalion, was the new commander of the 2nd Brigade, while the 3rd Brigade was now under Brigadier-General Leckie, recently CO of the 16th Battalion. Brigadier-General Mercer remained in command of the 1st Brigade until November, when he was appointed to command the 3rd Canadian Division.

These promotions were the first of a series witnessing the rise of the 1st Division's 1915 officer cadre to ever higher levels of responsibility in the Canadian Corps and beyond. Some would not survive the war. Malcolm Mercer was killed in a hurricane bombardment at Mount Sorrel in June 1916 and is buried between Ypres and Poperinghe, in the Lijssenthoek Military Cemetery. At 44 years of age, Major-General Louis Lipsett fell at the head of the 4th British Division in October 1918, just weeks before the war's end. Not all First World War generals died in bed.

Despite the high losses between April and June and the influx of new men, a sense of continuity can be traced through the latter part of 1915. Veteran troops displayed the same enthusiasm and skill that had characterized their service during earlier operations, sharing their hard-won knowledge with the reinforcements. All ranks were consistently busy with garrison duties and infrastructure work, but there was still time for training and schooling. Recognizing that practical instruction was especially important for fresh reinforcements, commanding officers sent the newcomers and newly promoted off to specialist schools and courses to study the latest techniques, weapons, and equipment. The front lines may have been static, but the war was in a constant state of flux, always with lessons to teach. As the Canadian reinforcements settled into their new battalions, the combat environment was changing as the BEF reorganized its defences on the Western Front.

A Modified Defensive Approach

In the last days of June 1915, elements of the 1st Canadian Division moved into the line between the Messines–Neuve Eglise road and the village of Ploegsteert, occupying a series of trenches numbered consecutively from 121 through 142 (fig. 10.2). Prior to the Canadians' arrival, this frontage had been defended by the recently formed 12th (Eastern) Division and the 48th (South Midland) Division. Major-General Robert 'Fanny' Fanshawe, the highly regarded commander of the 48th Division, had outlined the key vulnerabilities of the area in a memorandum to III Corps earlier that month; this information was later shared with Alderson's incoming headquarters. Fanshawe was concerned especially with the defence of the Messines–Neuve Eglise road where it crossed British lines. From this intersection one could see straight south all the way across the Douve River Valley, and as far west as Wulverghem. Should the Germans ever mount a successful advance along the road, Fanshawe feared that they could easily outflank British positions to the north. The Douve River would complicate a southward German flanking manoeuvre, but even still, enemy observation of the British rear areas below the Douve could prove disastrous for whoever defended the line between the river and Ploegsteert. Fanshawe recommended, among other steps, that the forward line be only lightly garrisoned, with reserves ready for action in strong dugouts to the rear – defence in depth.[9]

As Fanshawe reorganized his lines, GHQ issued directives reflecting the divisional commander's emphasis on secondary defences and

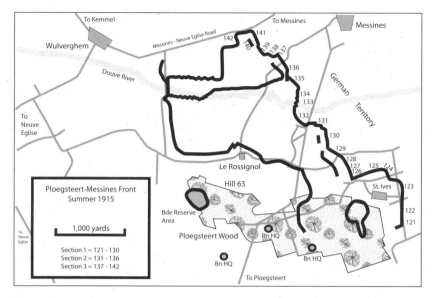

Figure 10.2

support trenches. This approach filtered down to the 1st Division through III Corps in early July and was reconfirmed later in the month when the division was reassigned to II Corps. According to Lieutenant-General William 'Putty' Pulteney's III Corps directives, new support trenches must be constructed immediately:

> The support trenches, together with good communications to and from them, should be considered to be a matter of the very first necessity, and all available labour should be concentrated on them, the only works of equal importance being
> (1) The upkeep of the front defence works.
> (2) The strengthening of certain of the more important supporting points, which should be made as strong as possible and have specially strengthened places for machine guns.
> The support trenches should be about seventy yards from the front line.[10]

Orders issued by II Corps later in July echoed Pulteney's approach, underlining the importance of mutually supportive localities situated anywhere from fifty to a hundred yards behind the front line.[11] All spare hands in the 1st Division set to work on the new defensive scheme. At any given moment this usually amounted to about 300 men per infantry brigade, plus the divisional engineers. In many instances the existing front-line defences were in poor condition, so the Canadian troops had their work cut out for them. To their chagrin, the men of the 1st Brigade discovered that communication trenches near St Ives were 'neglected' and 'practically impassable.' Within days the passageways were cleared, parapets raised, fresh wire strung, and dugouts excavated. New trenches were also dug and connected with existing positions, and the whole area was 'put into [a] fit state for occupation.'[12] The other brigades were no less ambitious. By early July Brigadier-General Arthur Currie's troops had dug or improved 450 yards of communication trench, 180 yards of shelter trench, 350 yards of subsidiary defences, and twelve dugouts.[13]

One week after arriving at Ploegsteert-Messines, the Canadians found themselves occupying 4,500 yards of trenches divided into three sections. The right was defended alternately by the 1st and 3rd Brigades. In the centre was the 2nd Brigade, while Seely's cavalry brigade defended the left section. Each brigadier was in direct contact with an artillery group responsible for his area. Facilitating this support, one forward observation officer was available for about every 250 to 300 yards of frontage. As well, an officer from the nearest artillery brigade was generally on duty at an associated infantry brigade headquarters from dusk until dawn.[14] At this stage the bulk of the trench garrison was still concentrated in the first-line trench, as work on the new second line was not yet complete. Troop density per yard of trench was a function of local terrain and the proximity of the enemy lines. In mid-July, for example, there were in excess of a hundred men in Trench 140 – a second-line position – but only sixty in Trench 141, a forward position. In Trench 142, a second-line trench next to the Messines–Neuve Eglise road, there were just twenty-five soldiers on garrison duty. There was an average of one machine gun for about every 215 yards of trench in the sector.

GHQ directives specified that the second-line positions need not consist of a continuous line of trenches. So long as visibility was good in all directions, it was sufficient to lay out a series of mutually supportive localities. Accordingly, the Canadian engineers set to building concrete redoubts capable of absorbing punishment and breaking up an attack that might succeed in penetrating the first line of trenches. The new positions were situated to defend Hill 63, the tallest local feature behind the

Canadian front.[15] By day the all-round defensive positions were occupied by just a few sentries, but a full garrison was posted to each redoubt during the night. As the trench system grew more sophisticated, divisional headquarters saw fit to name and number each trench, marking all with signboards. In the absence of such indicators it was easy to get lost in the expanding subterranean metropolis.

The arrangement of detached localities in the second line required flexibility and close liaison among neighbouring battalions and brigades. Alderson's Canadians displayed an aptitude for cooperation, both within and outside of their own division. During a rotation of the 3rd Brigade in Ploegsteert Wood, Canadian battalions coordinated their machine-gun defences with elements of the adjacent 35th Brigade (12th Division). When German troops were observed to be massing opposite the Ploegsteert trenches on 10 July, Brigadier-General Turner informed not only his own superiors, but also his counterparts in the 35th Brigade; careful lateral communication could mean the difference between withstanding a surprise attack or being overrun. It also avoided costly mistakes. In one instance, Canadian artillery batteries planned to register some targets in front of the neighbouring 50th Division. Prior to firing, Canadian headquarters enquired with the 50th Division, discovering that the selected points had recently been incorporated into the British lines. Sights were adjusted accordingly and friendly casualties avoided. In turn, Canadian battalion and brigade commanders were advised when British batteries planned to fire over the heads of Canadian troops.[16]

No defensive scheme was of much value without effective communication infrastructure. As the infantry and engineers built new trenches and redoubts, the divisional signallers worked to establish a flexible and reliable network. This included buried telephone cable and visual signalling arrangements among headquarters, as well the use of carrier pigeons. Rarely satisfied with the status quo, signal officers sought improvements. To this end experiments were conducted with different types of telephone cable to determine which were least prone to 'leakage' that might be picked up by eavesdroppers. To lessen the chances of breaks in telephone networks, the signal company employed infantry working parties to bury cable at depths of three feet. Throughout the summer of 1915, signallers from across the division were selected to attend special technical courses at the Second Army.[17]

It is tempting to interpret the emphasis on the second-line trenches and interlocking redoubts as an example of British forces mimicking

German defensive practices such as those encountered at Festubert. This was not completely true. From the outset of trench warfare British defensive doctrine was based on the principle of multilayered defence. In practice, this usually meant that forward trenches were backed up by intermediate subsidiary positions (such as Locality C at Ypres) and a more distant General Headquarters line. The revisions of June and July 1915 modified rather than transformed the general defensive lay-out. Efforts and resources were redirected from the GHQ line to a reinforced second line about a hundred yards behind the forward trenches. In some cases, a subsidiary line continued to be maintained behind the second line. Commanders based this arrangement on the understanding that significant numbers of German troops were being transferred to the Eastern Front, while the tally of BEF battalions on the Western Front increased. It seemed unnecessary to expend labour and scarce building materials on a distant GHQ line that was unlikely to be needed in the foreseeable future, since the German forces were not strong enough to mount a strategic offensive in the west. Instead, materials and manpower were devoted to the construction of more immediate second-line defences that might prove useful in the event that limited German attacks broke into the forward trenches, such as at Second Ypres. Because of their close proximity to the first line, soldiers manning the second-line fortifications could cope more easily with a breach without necessarily having to expose themselves through hasty counterattacks.[18] The directive made sense under the circumstances, and it is hardly surprising that intelligent commanders such as Fanny Fanshawe were already concentrating their defensive resources on key features such as the Messines–Neuve Eglise road even as the new orders were issued.

Learning, Training, and Schooling

The operational inactivity on the Ploegsteert–Messines Front presented an opportunity to train and digest the lessons from the first months of 1915. As had been the custom since the early days of the First World War, reports and bulletins on recent operations and a range of other subjects were circulated throughout the BEF. These included *Notes on Co-operation between Artillery and Aircraft, Description of German Defensive Organization, Notes from the Front*, and translations of captured German directives. In more practical terms, the possession of German trenches around Givenchy permitted British engineers to examine the design and layout of enemy fortifications. A Second Army report revealed that German defences were built to last. Observation loopholes featured steel shutters, as well as overhead cover, while dugouts were very strongly constructed with the liberal use of timber for reinforcement. Communication trenches were found to be narrow, but also especially deep, so there was little wonder that German troops were able to counterattack Allied footholds with such ease. So impressed were the British with the construction of the German trenches that they were surprised that any ground at all had been captured on the La Bassée front. Summed up, the Second Army analysis reinforced GHQ plans to hold the front line with smaller garrisons while concentrating reserves and grenadiers in a reinforced second line. The report also suggested that additional engineer personnel remain on hand in the front lines to design and maintain fortifications alongside the infantry garrison.[19]

It was fine for staff officers to make recommendations, but implementing these lessons on the ground was not always straightforward. Alderson agreed that as few men as possible should garrison the front-line trench, but only in zones where a properly constructed second line existed. As he noted in his response to the army-level report, completion of the second line and improvement of the first line depended not only on manpower, but also on the availability of scarce materials, mostly notably timber and corrugated steel.[20] Without adequate building supplies, dugouts were dangerous liabilities, likely to collapse even under light shelling. Alderson, moreover, rejected the idea of keeping large numbers of technical specialists from the engineer field companies in the front lines for indefinite periods. He was only willing to risk these experts at night, feeling that they were better employed as advisers to brigade headquarters and instructors to infantry battalions. Finally, the divisional commander noted that every Canadian infantryman was undergoing bombing training. As long as adequate supplies of grenades were within reach, all ranks could serve as grenadiers in the event that German assault troops penetrated the front trenches.[21]

Just as the Second Army report had been passed on to divisional commanders for comment and observation, a further dialogue developed at the brigade level. For the most part, the Canadian brigadiers underscored Alderson's arguments. Turner observed that it would be pointless to install small numbers of steel loophole assemblies in the front trenches since these would simply draw the attention of German snipers. He agreed with Alderson that engineer troops need not be exposed in the front lines for continuous periods: Their services were 'too valuable to be wasted in the trenches. We have found that small daily classes in wiring and other engineering work have given our men sufficient knowledge to carry out minor work (revetting, building up parapets) without being wholly dependent on Royal Engineer supervision.'[22] Turner was even more emphatic about the building material shortage and its impact on proper dugout construction: 'non bomb proof dugouts are worse than none – they are veritable death traps.' Like Alderson, Turner recognized the importance of grenades as infantry weapons, suggesting that grenade companies be provided with additional staff and resources. Brigadier-General Mercer's response accorded with Turner's and Alderson's. In addition, Mercer asked that optical equipment and telescopic rifle sights be issued to the infantry battalions on greater scales as sniping countermeasures.[23]

By the summer of 1915 the 1st Division was a veteran organization boasting a solid cadre of seasoned officers and men. Whereas the Canadians had depended on instruction from experienced British regiments when they had first arrived at the front, back in February, it was now the colonials' turn to share their expertise with fresh arrivals. Throughout the summer the division was visited by officers of the 2nd Canadian Division, then completing its organization and training at Shorncliffe. British units also called on the 1st Canadian Division for instructional purposes. In August the artillery headquarters of the 37th Division attached a group of officers and non-commissioned officers from its ammunition columns. The guests reportedly made steady progress with their training, while the 37th Divisional artillery commander visited gun emplacements and forward observation posts of the 2nd and 3rd CFA Brigades. Likewise, in September a group of twenty machine-gun officers from the 24th Division joined Canadian gun detachments, while troops of the 25th Division were dispersed throughout the 3rd Brigade at the platoon level for trench instruction.[24]

In addition to visits and lectures, 1st Division officers passed reports and advice along to their counterparts in the 2nd Division. In late July Lieutenant W.M. Everall, of the divisional cyclist company, prepared a set of notes on the employment of cyclists in combat areas, for the benefit of 2nd Division cyclists.[25] Every minor detail counted for Turner's division, since it was afforded no additional period of formal instruction after moving to France in September.[26] Indeed, Alderson worried that the 2nd Division possessed far less training and experience than had been true of the 1st Division back in March, possibly even less than 'any division that has yet gone in.'[27] New divisions did not always have time to learn the lessons of their predecessors.

Meanwhile, the officers and men of the 1st Canadian Division honed their skills at specialist schools at the brigade, division, and corps levels. While many original members of the division were already familiar with the topics covered in these courses, recent replacements benefited from the instruction. In early August two captains and three non-commissioned officers attended a II Corps machine-gun course at Wisques.[28] Within the division itself, Brutinel offered a series of seven-day courses on the Colt machine gun. Although these were administered by the Motor Machine-Gun Brigade, they incorporated practical experience gathered from battalion machine-gun officers throughout the division.[29] The basic premise was to teach course participants how to act as machine-gun instructors for their own units. Students learned about the gun mechanism, tactical employment of machine guns, theoretical principles of fire, and the selection of emplacements.

In late July six officers, six non-commissioned officers, and sixteen privates attended Brutinel's course. Among them were one subaltern, one lance-corporal, and four privates from the 16th Battalion. The officer, Lieutenant Frank Bressey, was an original member of the battalion commissioned from the ranks in early June, while Lance-Corporal Lancelot Warn was a reinforcement who had joined the battalion on 26 April. Of the four privates, Ernest Davies was a reinforcement with two years of pre-war service in the British army; for some reason, however, the course instructor judged Davies unfit to be a machine gunner. Private William Bruce was an original member of the battalion who had been wounded at Festubert. He received a good ranking in the course, and survived four years of service only to be struck down by disease in February 1918. Private Robert Clarke was a reinforcement who had joined the battalion on 16 April 1915. He achieved positive results in Brutinel's course and in 1916 received a commission in a British regiment. The fourth man from the 16th Battalion, Private James Notman, had arrived as a replacement in early May. He also received good marks in the course, but was killed in action in 1916.

The examples of Bressey, Warn, Davies, Bruce, Clarke, and Notman – some of them recent arrivals – suggest that commanding officers used courses and schools to improve the training of junior battalion members and to integrate them more fully into the life and work of the unit. Moreover, the future service careers of these soldiers raise questions about the process of learning and the dissemination of knowledge and doctrine throughout the Canadian forces. Two of the men were killed, and none of the survivors finished the war with the 16th Battalion.[30]

Skills and experience acquired in one unit could easily be transferred to another, and the character and combat capability of any unit were liable to improve or decline unpredictably as new generations of officers and men passed through.

By September 1915 increasing numbers of students participated in longer machine-gun courses. One such school was attended by sixty non-commissioned officers and men drawn from every battalion in the division.[31] In common with earlier trends among students of Brutinel's courses, most of these men had joined their battalions in France or Belgium as reinforcements at some point since the spring. This was true for all of the 4th Battalion men who attended, and in the case of the 16th Battalion, three out of four men were taken on strength after April 1915. Among the reinforcements in this class was a mixture of men who had joined the Canadian Expeditionary Force in September 1914, but were left back in England with reserve battalions, and those who enlisted with higher numbered battalions, such as the 30th or 43rd, and were then channelled into the 1st Division to fill vacancies. While the training of men in the former category likely would have been more complete than for men in the latter, it made sense for battalion commanders to send men from both groups on courses since each would have lacked the practical knowledge that the Second Ypres or La Bassée survivors had.

The earlier combat of 1915 proved that hand grenades had become key infantry weapons. Newspapers and illustrated weeklies of the period regularly featured illustrations of soldiers duelling with these sometimes odd-looking gadgets.[32] As Alderson noted in correspondence with the Second Army, the 1st Division's plan was to train all Canadian soldiers as grenadiers. To this end, grenade instruction occupied an increasing number of hours at the battalion and brigade levels.[33] As well, grenade courses at the corps level were attended by a broad range of personnel from the 1st Division. For example, nine officers and men completed a II Corps school in early September. Two of these Canadians were from Seely's cavalry regiments, four were from various infantry battalions, one from an infantry brigade headquarters, and two from a brigade grenade company. These students, representing a broad divisional cross-section, facilitated the dissemination of new skills within their home units.[34]

Anti-gas training was an obvious priority in the aftermath of the Second Battle of Ypres. A First Army bulletin issued in late May 1915 warned that enemy 'use of gas will in future be increased in volume and intensity.'[35] There were frequent, albeit unconfirmed reports of German gas shelling on the Ploegsteert–Messines Front throughout the summer. Canadian troops took extra precautions whenever winds blew from the east.[36] By early July the improvised protective pads issued during May and June had been supplemented throughout the BEF with the Hypo helmet, a chemically impregnated bag that covered the wearer's entire head.[37] Now that standardized protective gear was available, training memoranda on the latest precautions were circulated throughout the British forces. According to an army-level memorandum, troops should continue to carry the earlier mask-type pads at all times in case their Hypo helmets became damaged. In the front lines, decontamination sprayers were issued at the unit level to clean out trenches and dugouts in the event of a gas concentration.[38] An officer from the Second Army visited the 1st Division in early August to convene a 'live' gas demonstration employing several hundred troops in a mock-up trench system.[39] The event was attended by all available officers and non-commissioned officers from the entire division. According to 2nd Brigade accounts, the demonstration focused on the correct use of the new gas helmets.[40] This may seem like a very obvious lesson, but experience had already proven that explicitly detailed instruction was required if protective measures were to be effective. Needless British gas casualties had resulted back in May when soldiers removed their respirators at the wrong moment, inadvertently washed the chemicals out of their masks, or excessively saturated their masks with sodium thiosulphate, resulting in accidental suffocation.

Because hundreds of reinforcements had been taken on strength throughout the division since April and May 1915, it was important for battalions and brigades to keep up with routine individual and unit training. The regimen of the 4th Battalion for July to September can be taken as representative. During rotations through billets the troops performed daily physical training, bayonet drill, and route marches. Grenade practice, visual training, and marksmanship were also typical. It appears that most of these activities were organized at the company level. To keep the troops motivated and in good spirits, the battalion spent rest days at the divisional baths or playing sports.[41]

Trench Warfare

The second half of 1915 marked the first extended period of static warfare for Canadian troops. As far as ordinary infantrymen were concerned, trench service at Ploegsteert–Messines was a cyclical, mundane affair. Private Morris Wiseman joined the 7th Battalion as a reinforcement that summer. He later recalled the routine familiar to countless First World War soldiers: 'We stayed outside in [wooden] huts, for about four or five days and we did working parties. We'd dig trenches or carry up ammunition to the main trench, and then after that we took our turn to stay in the trenches. I think it was three or four days you had to be in the front line trench and then another lot would take your place … The first time we went in we just stayed in the trench and kept our eyes open. Then about sundown they'd call a stand-to. The sergeant would come along with a shot of rum for you.'[42]

The rotational system offered relief from the odd mixture of boredom and stress that accompanied trench duty. Particularly in wet or cool weather, the daily rum ration provided much-needed comfort. Even non-drinkers like Wiseman modified their convictions when dry summer turned to rainy autumn. All along the Western Front the exercise of 'standing-to' with weapons ready at the parapet was a regular routine at dawn and dusk. These were the hours when attacks were most expected.

The summer weather was pleasant enough on the Ploegsteert front, but the winter of 1915–16 proved as cold and damp as any in recent memory. That November it rained at least ten days out of thirty in the Canadian sector, a cruel reprise of Salisbury Plain the year before. Even without the heavy downpours, flooding was already a problem in the Flanders lowlands, where a year of artillery fire had smashed generations-old drainage systems and turned the battle zone into a morass. Engineers did their best to keep trenches dry, transforming all manner of battlefield junk into clever devices. Broken wagon wheels, for example, were converted into primitive paddle wheels. Fitted with a simple hand crank, these contraptions at least kept water from pooling in low spots.[43] Standing for hours in knee-deep water, especially during the colder months, resulted in high rates of trench foot, a condition that immobilized men for weeks or months. Soldiers on trench duty were ordered to remove their boots and puttees at lest once every twenty-four hours to get the blood flowing. Applying grease or oil to the bare feet and boot leather also helped.[44]

The damp and cold aggravated other illnesses, some of them easily transmitted among unwashed men living in close quarters under primitive sanitary conditions. In the 13th Battalion, a representative example, the troops had only one opportunity to visit the bath-houses and only one issue of fresh underclothing in November. Whether in the front lines, or back in the drafty billets, much time was spent out of doors. Although the usual daily casualties from sniper and artillery fire never ceased, evacuations because of sickness – nearly sixty all together that month – outstripped losses to enemy action. Soldiers were regularly diagnosed with any of a long list of ailments. At least sixteen different conditions plagued the battalion throughout November, including influenza, pleurisy, nephritis, bronchitis, peritonitis, and rheumatism, not to mention trench foot and back injuries caused by overexertion. There was also one recorded case of shell shock in the 13th Battalion, even though the men were not directly involved in any offensive activity.[45] The war on the Western Front was the first major conflict to see combat losses exceed losses resulting from disease, but this aggregate trend was often locally reversed in the trenches during the winter months.[46]

Sanitary conditions demanded daily attention in the front lines as well as billeting areas in nearby villages. The sudden appearance of tens of thousands of soldiers and horses in confined operational areas strained the resources of an agricultural region that had been lightly populated before the war. Safe disposal of excrement was a matter of first priority for medical officers and engineers. Of course, there were nowhere near enough latrines in the farming villages of Flanders and northern France to accommodate the troops. Open latrines and urine pits were filled in and relocated on a regular basis, but an unlucky artillery shell could easily churn up disused facilities with unpleasant results for anyone in the vicinity.[47]

Unwelcome company exacerbated the dangers of trench living. Soldiers shared their dugouts with rats and their uniforms with lice. Keeping the nasty critters out of one's clothing was an unending chore. Under ideal circumstances, uniforms were turned in periodically for steam cleaning, but within hours of returning to the front, a man was again infested with the irritating little beasts. Applying hot candle wax to the seams of shirts and pants offered a more immediate, if also temporary solution.[48] With high concentrations of unwashed bodies, excrement, rats, and decomposing corpses, trenches were smelly places to live. Again, recycled material offered a partial solution. Ashes from cooking braziers were mixed with the sawdust used as packing material in cases of rum jars. The resulting potpourri was sprinkled about the trenches and dugouts as a sort of primitive deodorizer.[49]

Notwithstanding the operational inactivity on the Ploegsteert–Messines Front and the myriad distractions of poor weather, sickness, and filth, an alert defensive posture was required of all. On more than one occasion warnings were issued when enemy behaviour suggested a pending assault. In early July intelligence sources reported that German forces were massing troops and supplies for a large-scale attack between Perenchies and Lille.[50] In other instances, the perceived threat was more local. In mid-July it appeared that enemy troops were gathering directly opposite the Canadian frontage. Heavy shelling against Neuve Eglise warned that an attack might be in the offing. Suspicions appeared well founded when the 9th and 11th CFA Batteries discovered that the Germans had removed segments of wire in front of their own line, creating passageways for assault troops to enter no man's land. Fearing an attack at any moment, Brigadier-General Turner suggested that his forces employ a ruse to throw the enemy off balance. After withdrawing all Canadian working parties from the area, Turner proposed to rake the German lines with indirect machine-gun fire, as if to suggest that the 3rd Brigade and neighbouring units were about to launch an assault of their own. It was hoped that this burst of activity would draw the German infantry out from their covered positions in a redoubt dubbed the 'Birdcage' to man the forward parapets, at which time the Canadian artillery would respond suddenly with high-explosive fire. As usual, divisional headquarters refused to expend precious high-explosive rounds, but Lieutenant-Colonel Mitchell's 3rd CFA Brigade was permitted to fire shrapnel in compliance with Turner's request.[51] During the night of 10-11 July the gunners of the 10th Battery fired about sixty rounds at the Birdcage. Evidence of German troop concentrations disappeared by the following morning.[52]

The Germans gave as good as they got, inflicting much damage on fortifications. A 2nd Brigade situation report reveals that German artillery was active against Hill 63, destroying a machine-gun redoubt after aircraft marked it with smoke. Later in the summer the 10th Battalion lost a machine gun when shellfire slammed into its concrete emplacement.[53] German machine guns regularly fired at rear echelon working parties during the night, often from extended ranges. Entering no man's land to complete tasks was always dangerous, but even rear areas were not immune to harassment; according to the 2nd Brigade, 'any movement behind our front line draws fire.'[54]

The accuracy of German small-arms and artillery fire was in no small part facilitated by the volume of air activity above the battlefield. German aircraft constantly marked targets with smoke or flares in view of their battery observers. Zeppelins were also deployed in the skies. It was believed that these slower moving craft were communicating with a tower in Lille using searchlight signals.[55] Meanwhile, observation aircraft and balloons of the Royal Flying Corps took to the skies to gather information. Private Frank Walker, a stretcher bearer from Prince Edward Island, was captivated by the daily displays of aerobatics: 'I was much fascinated, this afternoon, in watching the manoeuvres of one of our air-men. For an hour he has been patrolling the Line, changing his position and elevation continually to keep out of range of the German gunners, who are deliriously firing all about him. He managed his machine with the skill of a wizard. This spectacle is, of course, a daily occurrence here. But I cannot get over the wonder of it.'[56] The crash landing of a plane from No. 4 Squadron into a tree generated a flurry of excitement among the ground troops. The pilot was uninjured, and although the observer was wounded by splinters from anti-aircraft rounds, an eyewitness gladly reported that he casually smoked a pipe while being carried off to a field ambulance.[57]

Although British anti-aircraft units were operating in the vicinity, the Canadians lacked their own integral anti-aircraft artillery. As a temporary solution, divisional headquarters summoned the resources of Lieutenant-Colonel Raymond Brutinel's 1st Canadian Motor Machine-Gun Brigade.[58] After training in England, the brigade arrived in France in mid-June and moved into the front-line area around Le Rossignol later that month. In July mobile gun sections, each comprising six men and two guns, were deployed in the areas most commonly visited by German pilots. At this time the brigade's Colts were mounted in reverse on Mark IV tripods to achieve a greater degree of elevation against airborne targets.[59] The machine gunners found no targets during their first few days in the line, but finally a gun section engaged a German plane above Le Rossignol. The pilot turned about and headed east, ultimately crashing into German lines. Brutinel's men had made their first kill. In mid-August the concentrated fire of three gun teams (two guns per team) – each firing from a different location – brought down a second German plane.[60] To avoid incidents of friendly fire, anti-aircraft gunners were warned in advance if British aircraft were to be operating in the area, especially when new and unfamiliar types of machines were flown.

As the number of aircraft roaming the skies above the Western Front increased, aerial combat regularly occurred. In one instance, Canadian divisional headquarters reported that a British plane, possibly of No. 4 Squadron, engaged a German craft of 'the latest type' with machine-gun fire. The German's engine stalled, but at an altitude of a hundred feet the pilot managed to restart it successfully. It was too late; the plane was now within range of infantry weapons. Nearby British troops opened fire with their rifles, killing both the pilot and the observer. In another instance, a British plane took the worst of it from a German Albatros, crashing in the Canadian lines. Soldiers rushed to the scene and found a badly shot-up plane and wounded observer. The pilot, miraculously, was unharmed.[61]

Airmen claimed no monopoly on duelling. Although the daily volume of artillery fire on the Ploegsteert–Messines Front was small compared with previous months, gunners on both sides engaged in frequent contests that posed a constant menace to troops in the lines, not to mention the battered villages in the area. Target information came from a range of sources; forward observers attached to infantry units are obvious examples, but patrols and static observation posts also supplied fresh intelligence to the guns. Occasional German deserters and prisoners offered useful bits of information, most often concerning enemy routine and traffic patterns in rear areas. Finally, aerial observers in propellor-driven aircraft and balloons were able to see what was going on well behind the enemy's front line, assisting the batteries with target registration.[62]

Canadian batteries and British batteries under Canadian divisional command fired at targets of opportunity or fulfiled infantry requests for support if and when ammunition was available. During the morning of 6 July 1915, German heavy batteries registered targets near Trench 137, while other parts of the Canadian front were subjected to artillery and small-arms fire throughout that day.[63] When a forward observation officer with the 3rd Brigade asked for retaliatory shelling against German positions, the guns of the 3rd CFA Brigade responded with enough shells to prompt German troops to release SOS flares.[64] In contrast, the 2nd CFA Brigade was unable to help, since its remaining ammunition allowance on that particular day was limited to just two rounds. The chronic deficit of shells is painfully evident in tables of ammunition allotment for II Corps. For the week ending 25 August the artillery batteries of the 1st Division received just 1,100 rounds of 18-pounder shrapnel, 220 rounds of 4.5-inch shrapnel, and a meagre 125 rounds of 4.5-inch high explosive. These allotments barely fluctuated throughout the summer. High-explosive shells were always carefully rationed.[65]

In some instances, the guns responded to sightings of enemy working parties or general troop and vehicle noise coming from the direction of

Messines, as with the following episode reported by the 1st CFA Brigade: 'enemy linesmen seen crossing fields south easterly towards Lone Tree. Fired one round and got two of them … At 1:45 straggling party of about 30 men observed going south on same road. Fired two rounds and observed 5 men drop. Others scattered on the run.'[66] It was also typical for batteries on both sides to seek out and destroy specific targets. Enemy gunners attempted to flatten the church and other large buildings in Neuve Eglise throughout the summer. By mid-July German guns near Messines had smashed the church spire with 'coal boxes,' setting the building ablaze, and leaving only a gutted shell.[67] A Canadian soldier recorded the devastation in his diary: 'Of Neuve Eglise, a once lovely town, not a single house is standing whole. There is yet one inhabitant there, an old, old woman, who insists on sticking to her little cottage, despite the fact that buildings on both sides of her are in ruins … What misery has been thrown upon the closing years of this poor creature's life!'[68]

The Canadians struck back where it hurt most: against German field kitchens in Messines. A deserter had recently revealed to his Canadian captors that eighteen kitchens were brought into the town from Warneton at the same time every night. Once the kitchens were set up, as many as 500 troops gathered around to collect their meals, providing a very rich target. To foil German counterbattery fire, the CFA batteries and the 118th Howitzer Brigade were to shoot from emplacements where their muzzle flashes would be completely invisible. After an initial postponement, the shoot was rescheduled for the evening of 24 July, to be carried out in conjunction with guns of the neighbouring 28th Division. Firing began with a two-minute concentration followed by eight minutes of silence, and then a further sixty seconds of shooting. According to Burstall's artillery headquarters, the 'effect of the shoot (fall of shot) [was] apparently good – but impossible to judge the damage done.'[69] As a final precautionary measure, the timetables of British and Canadian kitchens were altered to save them from inevitable retaliatory fire. As it was, German batteries replied with a dozen howitzer shells near St Ives, plus additional shelling near some of the Canadian batteries. Several enemy shells reportedly fell short on the German trenches.[70]

Little effort was spared to avoid the ravages of German artillery fire. According to Brigadier-General Seely, dummy trench systems drew gunfire away from carefully camouflaged infantry positions and communication trenches. Infantry officers learned from their artillery counterparts how to make the decoys look most convincing. Seely was satisfied with the results: 'imagine my delight when I stood in the front line and saw the whole of the enemy shells dropping on the dummy trenches, dug-outs and strong points. Of course we could not deceive the Germans all the time, although we kept deceiving them at intervals.'[71] In common with Allied gunners, the German batteries were supplied with a finite number of shells. Every round that fell on the empty trenches saved Canadian lives and materiel.

Ammunition deficits limited the amount of daily artillery fire, but there were other ways to reach the enemy. Snipers were constantly 'busy' on both sides, trying to outdo each other with new techniques; on one occasion a German sniper was seen to be dressed completely in sandbags. These 'invisible' menaces, along with a range of other targets, were often answered with trench mortars in lieu of artillery fire.[72] Although less destructive than artillery, the mortars were useful when precision shooting was required against small targets at short ranges. When mortar rounds were in short supply, they were supplemented with improvised catapults capable of launching grenades across no man's land. During one such exchange, men of the 13th Battalion used 'Gamage' catapults to throw 'jam pots' into the Birdcage, along with mortar fire and a number of rifle grenades. This mixture of ordnance dissuaded a German working party from completing its chores, while damaging the enemy's parapet.[73]

The tactical challenges of siege warfare on the Western Front spawned an eclectic variety of 'inventions' during the summer of 1915. The 'smoke bag' was an improvised device used to cover the activities of friendly troops or simulate the presence of gas. This primitive smoke generator consisted of a dampened cloth bag stuffed with paraffin-soaked straw. Several slits were cut along the length of the sack. When the contents were ignited, heavy smoke was emitted.[74] That summer, Lieutenant-Colonel Brutinel unveiled a new machine-gun mount for representatives from each of the infantry brigades.[75] Brutinel's invention was one aspect of a larger effort to enhance the 1st Division's automatic firepower. Earlier that year, before the division deployed to France, Alderson had asked Brutinel to modify the tripod mounts of Vickers guns destined for Canadian use – sometimes innovation actually preceded combat experience.[76]

In August an improvised catapult known as the West bomb-thrower was demonstrated by its British inventor for members of the Canadian brigade grenade companies.[77] The following month Canadian officers attended a class on the recently developed Newton hand and rifle grenades at the Terdeghem Grenade School. Like the West bomb-thrower, the Newtons were named after their British inventor, in this case a captain who operated the Second Army grenade workshops at Hazebrouck. Newton's design used a standard .303 cartridge case as the detonator for a cast-iron body. His grenades were simple to manufacture, among the first reliable types to be issued in large numbers to the BEF.[78]

While the infantry held the line with their eclectic armoury of gadgetry and pilots vied for control of the skies, the war continued in earnest deep below the battlefield. During the night of 30 June 1915, German tunnellers exploded a mine in front of the 4th Battalion's positions at Trench 121. There was no damage to the Canadian line, but the following week sappers of the 174th Tunnelling Company, Royal Engineers, responded with their own detonation in the same vicinity. A party of thirty men from the 13th Battalion under the command of Captain Kenneth Perry and Sergeant Arnold Rushton – both pre-war militiamen – rushed forward in silence, occupying the fresh crater without firing a shot, despite a hail of trench mortar bombs, artillery, and small-arms fire from the Germans.[79] Captain Perry and his men were called on for a second operation during the night of 13–14 August, when two additional mines were exploded in front of Trench 121. The infantrymen and a band of grenadiers captured the crater under cover of rifle and machine-gun fire. Meanwhile, an engineer working party dug fresh trenches to connect the new positions. By morning the crater was consolidated and protected by wire, as snipers forced German working parties opposite Trench 121 to go to ground.[80]

Brigade mining sections were supposed to have been formed earlier in the year, but the initiative was interrupted by the German offensive at Ypres. In any event, there was little scope for mining activity on the water-logged Canadian front at Gravenstafel Ridge, so it is not surprising that the original directive was temporarily shelved. There is evidence, however, that Canadian infantry brigades engaged in their own defensive mining on the La Bassée Front as early as mid-June, well before any mining sections were officially reconstituted. In one instance, troops from the 1st Brigade detected the presence of a German mine immediately north of the La Bassée Canal. An unnamed 'mining expert' confirmed that the Germans were indeed working underground. With no time to lose waiting for the arrival of hard-pressed Royal Engineer companies, the infantrymen immediately began their own countermining operations under supervision of the expert.[81]

As underground operations intensified throughout July, the Royal Engineer mining companies attached to each British corps were no longer able to protect the entire front against German miners while also carrying out their own offensive activities. Consequently, the infantry brigades were instructed to reconstitute their own defensive mining sections, an arrangement permitting the engineer companies to engage more fully in offensive operations. In July the new brigade mining officers were selected based on their knowledge of mining techniques, while the sections were to be filled out with troops who had worked as miners in civil life. The mining sections were expected not simply to detect and report enemy mining activities, but to directly counteract any such attempts by blocking German tunnels with defensive galleries. Several weeks passed while personnel were selected and organized, but the sections were prepared to start work in early September under the supervision of the officer in command of the 171st Tunnelling Company.[82]

It was discovered in early August that German miners were working underground in front of Trench 121, a sector occupied by the 1st Battalion opposite the Birdcage. The Germans were allowed to continue uninterrupted, but after the sounds of digging stopped, engineers demolished the German galleries with explosive charges from a defensive shaft. In a grisly display, the surprise blast blew 'parts of dead Germans' and at least one complete German into the air. Canadian troops immediately returned to their forward trenches without further incident.[83] At the end of August, however, the Germans were back at work in their old galleries in front of Trench 121. Engineers responded with a 750-pound charge, followed by grenadiers of the 4th Battalion who rushed forward to occupy the 80-foot diameter crater under heavy rifle and machine-gun fire.[84] German snipers harassed the outpost throughout the rest of the day and night, but the Canadians were able to hold.[85] These miniature battles were real enough for the men involved, and no less savage than the larger affairs.

The Battle for No Man's Land

Sharp, nasty engagements like the crater battle at Trench 121 were typical of the ongoing struggle to control no man's land, the deadly zone separating opposing lines of trenches and redoubts. Good intelligence gathering was the first step to maintaining the initiative. Throughout the summer of 1915 the Canadians collected all manner of information on enemy activities, issuing regular reports to corps headquarters. No detail was too small for consideration. If sentries heard sounds of digging or underground tapping, engineers were called to determine if German miners were at work. When a German gun emplacement appeared overnight opposite Trench 133 and enemy spotter aircraft scanned the Canadian lines in the same area, corps headquarters were informed at once – such activities might have indicated a pending attack. Even the music of a German marching band emanating from Messines was duly noted, since it might herald the arrival of reinforcements in the area. The appearance of fresh earth in front of the German parapet was recorded, as the hue of the soil revealed how deeply the enemy had been digging. Such information, collected from a variety of sources, was routinely collated and circulated in the form of divisional intelligence summaries. These were typically divided into three or four sections: artillery, general notes on front-line activity, special reconnaissance, and reports from neighbouring divisions.

While senior commanders and staff officers were always interested in German activities, they were also keen to learn about enemy weapons and equipment. Spent German ordnance and parts thereof were carefully gathered up and sent to the rear for examination by artillery experts, although soldiers often kept a few bits for themselves as souvenirs. After Brigadier-General Seely's headquarters were shelled on 10 July, twenty or thirty German artillery fuzes and shell splinters of various sizes were collected and sent back to corps headquarters for analysis. Later in the month several fragments of unfamiliar dimensions and shape were discovered and carefully measured. It was suspected that these might be from gas shells, so the findings were of considerable importance.[86]

On the Ploegsteert Front Canadian battalions were not launching the daily attacks that had been commonplace at Festubert and Givenchy, but smaller parties of men regularly ventured into no man's land to gather intelligence, and more generally, to stake a claim on this hotly contested ground. The enemy pursued similar initiatives. During one such incursion in early July, soldiers of the 1st Brigade shot and killed a German soldier who had been lurking near Trench 123. The Canadians carried the body away with them, later removing the shoulder straps and buttons from the German's tunic for analysis. Reports on the man's regimental affiliation were inconclusive. By some accounts he belonged to the '25th Landwehr Regiment of the 4th Infantry Division,' but other sources, including Duguid's official history, mention the 25th Bavarian Regiment.[87] Later in July fresh troops seem to have arrived in the enemy trenches opposite the 1st Brigade's sector; the Germans suddenly grew more vocal, hoisting a large sign up above their lines boasting that Warsaw had fallen with 100,000 Russians captured.[88] A few days later a 3rd Battalion sentry observed three enemy soldiers moving about in tall wheat near a suspected German sniping post opposite Trench 129. Captain Frank Tidy, a veteran of Festubert, and three privates ventured into no man's land to take the men by surprise. Tidy drew his revolver, convincing two of the Germans to surrender at once; the third German fired at the Canadians but missed. Private Joe Bruno, a well-tattooed native of Brooklyn, New York, and former U.S. Navy sailor, responded with two lethal shots. The prisoners, Max Kufner and George Erhard, were taken back for interrogation and identified as members of the 25th Bavarian Regiment.[89]

In September 1915 it appeared that new troops of more light-hearted disposition had arrived on the German front. A Canadian officer reported on the behaviour of the new men:

> General attitude [of the enemy] noisy. During the night they did much singing, and several times during the day they shouted over to us in the Canadian vernacular. They appeared quite careless and whenever our snipers would ring their loophole plates, a miss was signalled by the waving of a shovel or rifle over their parapet ... We are inclined to believe that there has been a relief opposite our position and that they are new troops. The voices calling to us yesterday were quite boyish and the chorus sounded last night more like a boys choir than a soldiers chorus.[90]

The Germans may have been good singers, but they were still dangerous adversaries. According to the 4th Battalion, 'enemy more active ... 7 whiz-bangs fell into right of trench 121 and 8 sausages into trench 123. One of the latter remained on the ground 30 seconds before exploding. Enemy were very noisy and constantly shouted across to our trenches.'[91] About this time a German Landsturmmann from the 78th Landwehr Regiment of the 37th Landwehr Brigade – a veteran outfit of 1914 and Second Ypres – entered Trench 86, south of Ploegsteert Wood, and gave himself up to British troops of the 12th Division. It is not known if elements of the 37th Landwehr Brigade were also in the line opposite the Canadian trenches, but if so, there may have been old scores to settle from the April fighting. In any event, intelligence reports make clear that although boisterous at times, the Germans at Ploegsteert–Messines generally remained alert and combative.

Patrols sometimes avoided contact with the enemy in order to gather specific information. Under cover of darkness, Seely's dismounted cavalry troopers surveyed no man's land in search of hidden obstacles that might impede future operations, or to locate avenues of attack that would be of advantage to the enemy. In mid-July two officers of Lord Strathcona's Horse ventured into no man's land to investigate reports that the Germans were now using copper barbed wire; the interlopers soon discovered that the wire was in fact rusty steel.[92] Both sides excavated saps into no man's land, crowning them with listening posts. In July Germans pioneers aggressively pushed their saps forward to block Canadian patrols. The Canadians responded by extending their own posts ever deeper. Whoever rested also risked forfeiting local advantage.[93]

That summer it was increasingly typical for two or three men to assume a position, perhaps in a listening post, and remain there for an extended period to observe German fortifications and routine. This became official divisional policy later in July, when all brigades were ordered to establish semi-permanent observation teams to be equipped with specialized optical equipment. The observers usually set up their positions behind the second line, but occasionally ventured beyond the front trenches into no man's land. These dangerous forays provided target information for friendly artillery and other useful details regarding German trench routine.[94] Canadian infantry officers took all of this very seriously, preparing copious daily reports detailing every aspect of enemy routine in a given sector.[95] Attention to detail paid dividends. One morning a group of Germans was spotted working stealthily under cover of heavy mist. Artillery batteries were notified, and when the mist lifted later in the morning, they opened fire on the unsuspecting party, inflicting many casualties.[96]

From Patrolling to Raiding

The mythology of the Great War sometimes ascribes the invention of trench raiding to the Canadians.[97] It seems only natural that these colonial roughnecks, with a leavening of Aboriginal soldiers in their ranks, should have excelled at irregular frontier tactics.[98] In fact, other British Empire forces were already executing trench raids in 1914, months before the 1st Division arrived on the scene. In particular, Gurhka regiments from distant Nepal earned a reputation for surprise visits to the German trenches, where they are alleged to have dispatched enemy sentries with the kukri, a machetelike weapon with a heavy curved blade.[99] But even if Canadians did not invent trench raiding, they soon claimed it as their trademark. The summer's minor forays into no man's land escalated into larger operations – almost miniature attacks – later in 1915.

The availability of semi-dependable grenades encouraged infantry-men to mount ever more daring raids, sometimes with artillery support. In early September intelligence reports revealed the Germans to be con-centrating more troops than usual in the forward lines. Believing an attack to be imminent, Lieutenant George Bellamy, of the 5th Battalion, organized a 'bombing expedition' against a German barricade opposite Trench 128. During the day on 8 September Bellamy and a scout recon-noitred an approach to ensure that his bombing party would be able to safely reach the barricade under cover of darkness. As Bellamy and his three men crawled up to the enemy position later that night they could clearly make out a number of German voices. The raiders tossed all of their bombs over the parapet from a distance of twenty-five yards before beating a hasty retreat under a random hail of machine-gun fire. Rush-ing back across no man's land, Bellamy used a pocket flashlight to signal an officer of the 2nd CFA Battery. Within seconds, shells rained down on the German trench, now alive with commotion. A small victory had been won with no Canadian casualties. The audacious Bellamy, a ten-year pre-war Militia veteran with long service in South Africa, scored a second coup ten days later when he and another man crossed the Ger-man wire opposite Trench 131, locating a gap in the trench network that was otherwise invisible from Canadian lines.[100]

Bellamy's small enterprise was the seed of larger assaults before the year ended. During the night of 16–17 November the 5th and 7th Battal-ions struck German positions around La Petite Douve Farm, a fortified locality just north of the Douve River, along the Ploegsteert–Messines road. Although Nicholson's official history recounts the episode as one of the Canadians' first raids, the term never actually appeared in the opera-tion orders.[101] The plan in fact included features typically associated with a minor attack, including artillery, trench mortar, and machine-gun sup-port. In contrast with Bellamy's daring but modest four-man bombing expedition earlier that autumn, the Petite Douve operation involved between eighty and a hundred participants from the 7th Battalion, and about as many again from the 5th Battalion. Unlike larger attacks, how-ever, that at Petite Douve was not intended to capture ground. Instead, its purpose was to 'discover the enemy's strength' and 'gain information concerning his defences.'[102]

For the 7th Battalion, Petite Douve was a textbook operation. The troops were divided into scouts, grenadiers, wire teams, shovel men, bridge carriers, and riflemen. Captain Lionel Thomas, a pre-war Active Militia officer and original 1914 member of the battalion, was in overall command. Training began five to seven days before the raid, with each group rehearsing its allotted tasks while the battalion was posted in reserve.[103] On the night of the operation, the raiding party crossed 250 yards of no man's land, infiltrating the trenches of the 11th Reserve Brigade (117th Division) undetected. Even as the Canadians announced their presence with hand grenades, the response from the trench garrison was weak. By the time that German troops organized a counterattack, the interlopers had already killed about thirty men and whisked away a dozen prisoners. Captain Thomas's party suffered just two casualties, but the Germans almost certainly lost additional men when their belated counterattack was caught in the middle of Canadian and British artillery fire.[104]

The 117th Division was in admittedly poor shape that November, after losing more than a hundred officers and 5,200 men at Notre Dame de Lorette during the French summer offensive in Artois, followed by even greater casualties at Loos in September.[105] But even poorly motivated sentries did not guarantee a raid's success. At an early stage in the operation, and reminiscent of the La Bassée attacks, the 5th Battalion raiders got caught up in barbed wire concealed in a flooded ditch. The commotion drew German fire, to which the Canadians responded with hand grenades. Unable to surmount the obstacle, the 5th Battalion party withdrew, miraculously without injury.[106]

The level of gun support for the Petite Douve assault was considerable relative to the size of the raiding force. A Battery, Royal Canadian Horse Artillery, from Seely's cavalry force, was detailed to cut the German wire prior to the assault, but a line of trees blocked much of the target area from the gunners' view. In this case it was ultimately up to the infantry to cut through the barriers by hand.[107] In addition to the guns of the 25th Divisional artillery, the heavies of the 118th Howitzer Brigade smashed wire and trench parapets in the vicinity of Petite Douve Farm. As the Canadian raiders entered and exited the German trenches, the combined fire of 18-pounders, 60-pounders, and 6-inch howitzers wreaked havoc on the German communication trenches, probably just as reinforcements rushed forward.[108] It was the same technique that Bellamy had employed on a smaller scale at Trench 128.

The Loos Offensive

Towards the end of September 1915 the 1st Canadian Division received orders for its first major offensive since La Bassée. Encouraged by favourable force ratios, General Joffre was about to launch a renewed series of coordinated attacks in Artois and the Champagne. This time Joffre requested a BEF attack at Loos, on the left flank of French forces attempting to capture the Vimy Ridge in Artois. Field Marshal French questioned the feasability of Joffre's plans while General Haig, still in command of the First British Army, was deeply concerned with the difficult terrain around Loos and the now familiar shortage of munitions. Once again, however, coalition politics trumped operational considerations. Earlier in 1915 Lord Kitchener, secretary of state for war, had preferred to see British forces deployed on peripheral fronts until the BEF achieved closer parity with the French army. This view changed as Kitchener's liaison officer with the French war ministry, Lord Esher, convinced him that Britain must display unequivocal support for the French war effort on the Western Front, even if the available forces and munitions were not adequate to achieve decisive results. Although much of the contemporary evidence suggested otherwise, Lord Esher's French contacts made him believe that their people's morale was dangerously low and that if the BEF did not cooperate in an autumn offensive, France might be compelled to seek a separate peace with Germany at Belgium's expense. This danger, however remote, was totally irreconcilable with British strategic interests, so Kitchener decided it was best to placate Joffre for the sake of Allied solidarity. To this end Kitchener personally stressed the political importance of the operation during a visit with Haig on 20 September.[109] The attack may have served its political purpose, but the ultimate failure to secure meaningful territorial gains at Loos ultimately cost Sir John French his job, while the BEF lost 60,000 additional casualties before the year was through.[110]

With such great carnage in mind, Loos is popularly remembered as yet another unmitigated slaughter on the Western Front.[111] It was in fact a carefully planned operation within the limits that time and material resources permitted. Seeking to avoid heavy losses like those incurred at La Bassée, Field Marshal French limited the number of assault divisions to six, refusing to surrender control of reserve troops until the last possible moment. In hindsight this has been seen as unfortunate. While the attack did succeed in breaching the enemy line on 25 September, the reinforcements were not close enough at hand to exploit the advantage, a danger that Haig had recognized prior to the battle.[112] Despite this ironic outcome, it is difficult to criticize French for practising economy of force, since conservatism in this case may well have spared the 1st Canadian and other BEF divisions additional heavy losses in late 1915.[113]

While Haig's First Army attacked between Loos and the La Bassée Canal, elements of General Plumer's Second Army were charged with diversionary measures further north. The 1st Division's assignment was part of a deception plan designed to convince the enemy that an attack was pending on the Ploegsteert–Messines Front. At the same time, the 3rd and 14th Divisions were to launch an actual attack closer to Ypres, near Bellewaarde Lake. Each component of the 1st Division had a role to play in the ruse. The CFA brigades, in conjunction with No. 3 Group, Heavy Artillery Reserve, were to cut the German wire and smash the parapets. As the gunners hammered their targets, the infantry of the 2nd Brigade were to prepare assault lanes through their own wire and build dummy assembly trenches. If the wind was favourable, each of the three Canadian brigades would deploy smoke sacks to simulate a gas attack. Meanwhile, Brutinel's machine gunners were to saturate the enemy's road network and communication trenches with indirect fire. Each machine-gun battery was assigned specific target areas, with 20,000 rounds of ammunition per gun supplied for two nights of firing.[114] Besides deceiving the enemy, all of this activity functioned as a realistic divisional training exercise. Officers were able to observe the impact of the preparatory fire against the German trenches and guess at the adequacy of their attack preparations relative to the enemy's response.

While most of the the 1st Division prepared for the deception operations, the 3rd CFA Brigade was loaned to Major-General H. Hudson's 8th Division (III Corps), where the Canadian gunners supported subsidiary attacks near Bois Grenier on 25 September. Like the Canadian deception plan, Hudson's primary intention was to divert German resources away from the main thrust at Loos. However, if the 8th Division could secure useful tactical gains, so much the better.

Hudson's minor attack demonstrates the sophistication of British Empire forces in 1915, while underscoring the broader factors that hampered offensive operations then and later in the First World War. According to the 8th Division's plan, the 25th Brigade attacked along a 1,200-yard front early in the morning of 25 September. The British used no chlorine in this sector, but smoke was employed to cover the attack and convince the enemy that gas might in fact be in the air. The infantry of the 25th Brigade smashed through the forward German line, capturing 120 prisoners from the 16th Bavarian Reserve Regiment.[115] On the left flank of the attack, the 2nd Battalion of the Lincolnshire Regiment (2nd Lincolnshires) pushed forward, capturing much of the German support line. Further to the right, however, German machine-gun strong points held up the 2nd Battalion of the Royal Berkshire Regiment and the 2nd Battalion of the Rifle Brigade. In unison with enemy shelling, this automatic weapon fire prevented British reinforcements from crossing no man's land in strength, as German grenadiers gradually drove back the British right flank with strong counterattacks. On the left, however, the 2nd Lincolnshires brought forward a pair of mortars, halting the counterattacks at close range. On the morning of 26 September the Lincolnshires finally slipped away to an intermediate position that had been prepared under cover of darkness. The assault succeeded in gaining some local tactical advantage.[116]

The records of the 3rd CFA Brigade suggest that the 25th Brigade assault might have secured its complete objectives if additional ammunition and infantry reinforcements had been present. As it was, the artillery support was excellently coordinated throughout 25 September, thanks to the Canadian liaison officers and forward observers deployed up front with the British infantry. Shortly after 06:00 the 9th CFA Battery observer indicated that the forward infantry were running short of grenades under heavy pressure from German grenadiers. Such vital communication links remained open during much of the day. According to Lieutenant-Colonel Mitchell, 'during the whole action communications were kept up wonderfully well. The few interruptions which occurred were from shell fire in front trenches and close to front trenches. The wires were speedily repaired in all cases.'[117]

When necessary, the Canadian liaison officer with the 2nd Lincolnshires, Captain Elliot Greene, a pre-war artillery officer, called for support using map coordinates.[118] In addition to this direct support, the gunners also fired on communication trenches in attempts to interdict German counterattacks. Unfortunately, the German artillery was also blocking the British communication trenches, preventing friendly reinforcements from reaching the forward assault troops in the German lines. Canadian forward observers were quick to report if Canadian or British gunfire was falling too close to friendly infantry. Conversely, when circumstances permitted, the guns were asked to cover more of the enemy area by expanding their box barrages. With no man's land largely impassable to infantry reserves, the importance of artillery support increased as each hour passed, to the point that survival of the forward British infantry absolutely depended on it. The Canadian brigade ammunition column maintained a steady supply of ammunition throughout the action, but the absolute quantities available were frustratingly small. Although each of the batteries in Mitchell's brigade fired about 1,100 rounds during the attack, only one in ten was a high-explosive shell. The participants could only guess what might have been possible with greater resources.[119]

Further north, on the Ploegsteert–Messines Front, the 1st Division's deception plan was put in motion on 24 September. Canadian and British batteries opened fire with good effect against German wire and emplacements, but there was really not enough ammunition to support an infantry attack; the average expenditure per battery was only about 300 rounds. Battery and brigade commanders displayed great flexibility nevertheless, doing the best they could with what was at hand. Because retaliatory fire from German batteries was relatively light, ammunition was reallocated from counterbattery tasks to richer infantry targets. Some of the Canadian batteries changed their targets frequently to give the impression that more guns were firing than was actually the case.[120]

German defensive doctrine dictated that in the event of a suspected gas attack, all batteries within range should fire on the threatened sector without waiting for special orders.[121] In a few localities along the Canadian front it appears that the smoke bags did not fool the enemy, since the German gun batteries remained silent.[122] At many points, however, the Germans launched SOS rockets, immediately opening heavy small-arms and artillery fire as they discovered the mysterious clouds floating towards them at an altitude of about fifty feet. A 5th Battalion veteran later described the German response on his part of the front: 'our object was to divert the Germans in our area ... we put bridges over the wire [to suggest a pending infantry attack], we sopped wet bags of straw with oil and then in the morning we lit these and threw them over and we returned to the shell [shelter] trenches where we got a battering from the Germans. Throughout the Loos fight we carried on manoeuvres of that type. Holding the Germans in our position. That was quite an affair.'[123] Strong dugouts protected the Canadians from German retaliation. The second-line trenches and redoubts were serving their purpose.

Canadian infantry patrols remained in no man's land during the evening of 24 September to better observe the impact of artillery fire in misty and smoky conditions, but these troops had to be withdrawn before the machine-gun barrage could begin. Unfortunately, Brutinel's gunners encountered serious technical difficulties. All of the guns suffered stoppages on account of faulty ammunition, with five of the sixteen guns in action damaged beyond further use. Two gunners were injured as a result of these accidents.[124] Infantry action resumed during the following few days to keep the enemy guessing.

Lipsett's 2nd Brigade infantrymen maintained a steady level of transport activity behind the lines, while excavating new saps and attacking German working parties in no man's land.[125] This diversionary activity came at a price. The 5th Battalion suffered two men killed and twenty-five wounded on 25 September.[126] In contrast, the 10th Battalion lost only two men wounded, despite a heavy German counterbombardment on 24 September. According to the battalion's war diary, the new defensive works saved lives: 'Lack of casualties under heavy shelling by enemy due to efficacy of deep narrow safety trenches dug behind the front line trenches to which troops retired during enemy bombardment.'[127] The enemy's losses were hard to guess. Snipers and artillery spotters could report kills, but these were difficult to confirm. In at least one instance, Canadian gunners estimated local German loss rates by counting the number of new crosses in a burial ground that was visible from an observation position.[128]

Taking all reports into account, Major-General Arthur Currie concluded that the divisional ruse was successful. Statistical evidence supported his impression. During the first twenty-one days of September 1915 the average weekly number of shells bursting on the Canadian divisional frontage was approximately 830. In the final week of September, the total exceeded 1,200 rounds, an increase of 45 per cent.[129] The intensification of German artillery fire suggested that the enemy anticipated an assault at any moment. Throughout the deception operations, Canadian troops avoided injury by taking shelter in second-line redoubts and support trenches. Conversely, German soldiers manned their front lines in strength while suffering casualties from artillery and machine-gun fire, waiting for an attack that never came.

The 1st Canadian Division's experience on the Ploegsteert–Messines Front contrasted starkly with the sustained combat between April and June. Indeed, the 'tranquil' summer of 1915 is often passed over quickly in general studies of the First World War, but as this chapter has shown, the period offers a glimpse of Canadians at war during a momentary state of equilibrium. With the losses of Ypres and La Bassée replaced, the 1st Division reached its third generation by July 1915. Thankfully the Canadians were not pressed immediately back into combat yet again. Instead, the relative calm of the Ploegsteert–Messines Front afforded an opportunity to absorb the lessons of earlier fighting, acclimatize reinforcements, and develop new capabilities, such as brigade miners and observation teams. When troops were not training, they were building defensive works, digging mine galleries, or burning the lice out of their clothing. They also continued to fight the enemy, both in the ongoing struggle to dominate no man's land and as part of the larger Allied effort during the Loos offensive. As at Second Ypres and La Bassée, the Canadians lived, fought, and died on a shoestring. Improvisation helped offset the shortages of building materials, ammunition, and weapons to a degree. But as is so often the case in war, men simply had to make do.

Conclusion

The twilight of 1915 bordered on anticlimax for the 1st Canadian Division and the new Canadian Corps. Operational activity decelerated in the wake of the Loos offensive, leaving the Canadians to hold the line between Ploegsteert Wood and St Eloi. For the veterans of Salisbury Plain, the winter of 1915–16 was a nightmarish reprise of the previous year in England. Heavy rainfall melted the breastworks, transforming the front-line trenches into an undifferentiated web of flooded ditches. Days spent knee-deep in muck resulted in frequent cases of trench foot and flu, but the troops soldiered on. Many of them had already lived through much worse, and even more difficult days surely lay ahead.

Almost ninety years after the last shots were fired in 1918, the Western Front today is a landscape of cemeteries and monuments. Canada's most visited Great War site is Walter Allward's breath-taking memorial atop Hill 145 at Vimy Ridge, Canada's best-remembered battle. Although the Vimy Memorial was intended to serve as Canada's national monument on the Western Front, most of the visitors I have taken there on tours over the years associate Allward's creation with the April 1917 capture of Vimy Ridge by the Canadian Corps. Many Canadians see Vimy as the turning point for the Corps, the key moment in the transition from an amateur colonial force to the shock army of the British Empire. The massive twin limestone pylons reinforce this interpretation. Most of the muscular figures sculpted around the base of the monument gaze upward to the sky. They are victorious.

About thirty-five miles north of Vimy there is another Canadian monument along a path less travelled by tourists. The *Brooding Soldier*, designed by Frederick Chapman Clemesha, stands alone at Vancouver Corner. This is where the small village of Keerselaere once stood, although only older residents of the area remember the place. It was here that the westerners and Montrealers of the 7th and 13th Battalions fought for their lives in April 1915. Here the 1st Canadian Division was nearly destroyed in the first chlorine gas battle of the First World War. The *Brooding Soldier* is easily accessible along the main road between Ypres and Poelcapelle, but the site is not designed to accommodate anywhere near as many visitors as Vimy. Few large tour coaches ever stop here. Parks Canada tour guides are not on duty; one will find no interpretation centre, gift shop, or restrooms. The *Brooding Soldier* is a rather humble monument compared with the shining limestone pylons at Vimy. Quite unlike Allward's virile figures, the *Brooding Soldier* stares at the ground with downcast eyes. There is little evidence of victory here.

The contrast between the *Brooding Soldier* and the Vimy Memorial embodies Canadians' understanding of the First World War. Historians are trained to identify and explain processes of change. Canadians and their historians remember the war as a pivotal epic of accelerated maturation and development for the country, on and off the battlefield. On the Western Front, so the story goes, the Canadian Corps expanded in size and honed its art of attack to become a premier fighting formation in the British Expeditionary Force, indeed, a spearhead of the 1918 victory offensives. From a broader nationalistic perspective, the Great War is seen as a milestone in the Dominion of Canada's journey from colony to nation. The fighting of 1915 has played an important role in this narrative, but not really on its own terms. Valcartier, Salisbury Plain, Ypres, and Festubert have functioned as literal and figurative points of departure in the great transformation of the Canadian Corps and Canada itself. Events from the later months of 1915 have trailed off into obscurity. Rarely have the early war experiences been studied in their own context, at least not without the vested interest of constructing a 'useful' war narrative for today's Canada. Over the years the essence of the fighting and the fighting men of 1914–15 has been lost in grander, mythological epics of shock armies that conquered imposing ridges and forged nations in fire – enduring images that have helped later generations derive meaning from a conflict that claimed so many lives, only to be followed by another twenty years later.

This book explores the 1st Canadian Division's formative training and combat experiences. It recounts the Canadians' struggle to save Ypres from capture and themselves from annihilation. It shows the Dominion's soldiers at work in their first offensives, in the flat murder fields north of the La Bassée Canal. Finally, the book reconstructs the deadly routine of trench warfare near Ploegsteert and Messines, concluding with the 1st Division's participation in subsidiary operations during the ill-fated Loos offensive and a stubborn battle to control no man's land in a quiet sector.

The general conclusions we draw from the story depend greatly upon how the evidence is approached. If the goal is to show that the Canadian Corps developed and improved over time, then the events of 1914–15 can be framed to support the case. The 1st Division, after all, was trained under less than favourable circumstances in 1914, and by the standards of the later war years, was not especially well equipped or adequately supplied. Chronic shortages of artillery ammunition and heavy guns handicapped the division throughout the defensive and offensive operations of 1915. There was indeed much brooding during the first year of fighting.

But was the 1st Canadian Division a capable instrument of war at the beginning, given the material and logistical limitations of 1914–15? Was it effective given the circumstances of those years? If the war had ended in December 1915, say, would Canadians have concluded that their army's contribution had been worthwhile? That the division was effective becomes ever more apparent when one considers the odds stacked against the Canadians, who were fighting a modern war on a shoestring. Their weapons and equipment were far from ideal, but if more recent history is any indication, we seem not to have learned much from the First World War. In a matter of weeks more than 30,000 men and 7,000 horses were assembled and shipped overseas under the auspices of a minister of militia who was not recognized for his rational approach to problem solving. Some of the volunteers were highly educated and wealthy men, at least one was a Member of Parliament, and others could barely read or write their own names. They came not only from every corner of the Dominion of Canada, but throughout the Empire and the wider world. Indeed, more than a few of the contingent's most highly respected leaders were of foreign birth. Somehow this motley collection of individuals was welded into a combat division by the time it arrived in France. It is almost inconceivable that today's Canada could achieve a similar feat in the same amount of time.

Although Canada's Permanent Force numbered only a few thousand in 1914, a sizeable proportion of the first overseas contingent, perhaps as many as 40 to 50 per cent, were no strangers to the rigour and discipline of military service. Most of the pre-war soldiers had served in Canada's Active Militia, but others had spent years in the British army. Some of the older men had fought the Boers in South Africa, and at least a few had worn American or French uniforms at some point before 1914. Military experience was not always a blessing, as evinced by the first difficult encounters between a seasoned sergeant-major and the uninitiated citizen-soldiers placed under his charge. At the same time, anecdotal evidence suggests that practical experience counted for a great deal, probably averting more than a few minor disasters in otherwise chaotic operational situations where disasters were common enough.

Weather conditions on Salisbury Plain could hardly have been worse over the winter of 1914–15. Yet, the muddy training camp was part of a seasoning process for a generation of men who to begin with were less accustomed to modern creature comforts than we are today. Other interruptions to training ranged from drunkenness to conjugal visits to meningitis, but as a comprehensive analysis of evidence on a unit-by-unit basis has shown, Canadian troops trained for war according to a uniform series of directives. Each branch of service had its own sylla-bus to follow, in addition to a series of combined exercises based on pre-war doctrine as well as recent BEF combat experience. Training was not limited to elementary subjects, but also featured tactical exer-cises without troops and staff rides for junior and senior officers. The Salisbury experience can no longer be written off as inconsequential or unproductive. There is too much evidence to the contrary.

Training continued when the 1st Division landed in France in Febru-ary 1915, except that now the game was played for keeps. The Canadi-ans were fortunate to enter the line in a reasonably calm sector under the tutelage of seasoned British troops. The old hands of the 4th and 6th British Divisions were favourably impressed with the Dominion soldiers. In the open ground around Armentières, all ranks accumu-lated practical experience that could only be had on the battlefield. Some did not live long enough to apply it. Soldiers soon discovered what it meant to watch a pal bleed to death from a gunshot wound or be torn apart by artillery fire. Engineers worked with scant building materials to strengthen fortifications. Further to the rear, the gunners played a deadly game with their German counterparts, underscoring the importance of camouflage and concealment. The signallers braved shellfire and snipers to keep communication flowing within and beyond the division, while the service troops of the transport columns shuttled ammunition and supplies around the battle zone under the searching eyes of German artillerymen. From the very beginning the 1st Canadian Division was a living organism made up of many interconnected and interdependent parts.

A few weeks later the Canadians witnessed the BEF's first set-piece attack of the war, at Neuve Chapelle. After reconnoitring the strong German defences opposite the Canadian lines, the officers of the 1st Division were relieved that their troops had not been called on to attack in March 1915.

Given that much of the Canadians' training in England and France had been oriented towards offensive activities and siege warfare, it is ironic that the division's first protracted engagement was a fluid defensive battle. The Ypres Salient was already an active sector with a nasty reputation when the Canadians arrived there in April 1915, but few could have imagined what lay ahead. With its chlorine gas, violent artillery barrages, and massed German infantry attacks, the Second Battle of Ypres proved to be the ultimate challenge for the 1st Division.

Postwar mythology has ascribed Canadian performance in the battle to raw courage, frontier grit, and perhaps a deficit of good sense. No small amount of courage was needed to bear the horrors of gas warfare, but bravery or foolhardiness alone do not explain what happened to the 1st Division between 22 and 26 April 1915. Skill, experience, cohesion, leadership, and exhaustion were the true forces that shaped the battle, for better and for worse. Despite near encirclement at an early stage of the fighting, elements of the 3rd Brigade adjusted their defences in a bid to keep the Germans at bay, while battalions of the 1st and 2nd Brigades navigated shell-torn and refugee-choked roads to provide reinforcement. Courage was demanded, but hours of route marching and extended order drill made it all possible. As the infantry clashed with advancing German forces, the artillery and engineers moved about the battlefield to offer support. The gunners' first priority was to support the infantry, but they also had to defend their emplacements against direct attack from enemy troops. Circumstances could not have been more stressful.

Platoon and company officers played crucial roles throughout the battle, often making decisions without direct access to higher authority. The historical literature of the First World War makes much of the gradual devolution of authority on junior officers from year to year.[1] Second Ypres shows that personal initiative was a factor from the earliest months of the conflict. The actions of John Warden at Locality C or Edison Lynn on the General Headquarters line come to mind.

Commanders of battalions, brigades, and divisions faced even more ominous challenges, as they were responsible for troops spread over relatively wider areas. For the divisional commander distances were measured in miles, but even battalion commanders needed to think in thousands of yards. Officers such as Loomis, Tuxford, and Odlum found their companies and platoons distributed over broad areas, while communication with brigade headquarters was often tenuous.

From the outset of operations on 22 April 1915, Canadian brigadiers exercised command under extremely hazardous circumstances. The headquarters of the 2nd, 3rd, and eventually 1st Brigades were within range of enemy small-arms fire throughout the battle. It might even be argued that the brigade headquarters of Currie and Turner were too close to the action; proximity to the firing line tended to increase distractions while minimizing one's overall perspective of the operational situation at any given moment. Travelling the areas between brigade and battalion headquarters was always risky. In Turner's case, there were usually extra battalions with which to keep in touch. The brigadiers' problems were compounded by the arrival of reinforcements from a wide variety of British imperial formations. In many instances, it was simply not clear who should be accepting orders from whom. The brigades were beset with poor communication, resulting in the expenditure of much extra effort. Currie's long hike to Potijze is the best-remembered example, but Turner also spent considerable time moving about the area. While each brigadier was able to observe only a limited portion of the action, his decisions significantly affected all other parts of the front. In more than one instance the fog of war circumscribed effective decision making. So did fatigue and stress. This was true for Richard Turner as well as for Arthur Currie.

At the divisional level, Lieutenant-General Edwin Alderson has been criticized for keeping his headquarters in Brielen, far from the action.[2] It is difficult, though, to imagine how Alderson could have worked more effectively on the east side of the Yser. Had he relocated divisional headquarters closer to the battlefield, the situation may actually have worsened, since the divisional staff would have spent more of its time sheltering from German artillery fire and less of it running the battle. Wireless technology was still too primitive to be of widespread value in 1915. Although the telephone was simple and effective, time constraints and the shallow Flanders water table precluded the burial of a comprehensive cable network out of reach of shellfire. Commanders had to rely on runners and dispatch riders, neither of whom were guaranteed to reach their destinations in a timely fashion or at all. The lag often proved frustrating at both ends, but it is not obvious how anyone could have solved the problem in 1915.

Historians working during the late twentieth and early twenty-first centuries came of age in the shadow of the Second World War's 'populist' commanders. The best-remembered names – Montgomery, Patton, Rommel – were not necessarily the most proficient leaders, but their reputations were energetically promoted during the war years for public consumption. The command culture of 1914–18 was different. Officers of the First World War were relatively less sensitive to the realm of public relations, yet their careers have often been evaluated according to post-1945 standards. This may explain why Daniel Dancocks, writing on battalion-level command at Second Ypres, concluded that most of the Canadian officers of 1915 were 'competent, but not otherwise notable.'[3] It seems that the honest display of basic professional competence under harrowing combat conditions barely justifies a passing historical grade. A small minority of Great War officers became popular heroes, but this should not be construed as a requisite for effective command. After all, it was mostly ordinary men who fought the war.

The determination of most Canadian soldiers at Ypres was unimpeachable, but there were limits to what men could endure. Lord Moran, a veteran medical officer of the First World War, later wrote about the enigmatic nature of courage. According to his observations, most men possessed it, but few enjoyed an inexhaustible supply.[4] Hours of shelling, infantry attacks, and gassing took their toll, explaining in part why the 3rd Brigade largely ceased to exist as an organized force by the end of 24 April 1915. Historians have blamed Brigadier-General Richard Turner for mishandling his own troops, as well as his reserve forces. Under the crushing weight of the German attack, it is unlikely that any other commander would have fared much better. In common with gas casualties, the full impact of nervous breakdowns on the outcome of the Second Battle of Ypres is impossible to measure, since many cases were disguised within the broader divisional casualty figures, but the available evidence suggests that incidents of 'shell shock' were not uncommon. Few men were immune.

The exigencies of coalition warfare dictated that the 1st Canadian Division be committed to a series of nearly fruitless offensive operations along the La Basseé Canal less than three weeks after the gas battle at Second Ypres. Reinforcements and new equipment arrived quickly, but neither the Canadians nor their British counterparts possessed artillery or infantry reserves necessary to sustain a major breakthrough. With little time to plan, the setbacks at Festubert and Givenchy were almost forgone conclusions. Canadian commanders appear to have recognized this reality, limiting the scope of their efforts accordingly. The 'hidden transcript' of the operations suggests that token attacks were launched according to orders, but promptly discontinued when enemy resistance precluded further progress at anything but prohibitive cost.

Notwithstanding the unfavourable terrain and deep belts of German defences, the attacks at Festubert and Givenchy were minor set-piece battles in their own right. This is seen in the deliberate coordination among infantry, grenadiers, and engineers in the repeated assaults against K.5 and other notorious strongpoints. Imagination and improvisation could not offset the disadvantages of poor maps and woefully inadequate artillery support, but the tactics and techniques employed by the Canadian battalions testify to their skill.

The deployment at Ploegsteert–Messines finally afforded some breathing room for an exhausted 1st Division. In this static scenario the Canadians modified trenches and fortifications according to the most recent BEF standards while pursuing a policy of active defence in the form of patrols, small raids, intelligence gathering, mining, and artillery duelling. Strict limits on the ammunition supply prevented a truly aggressive firing program, but the batteries did what they could with available stocks. Throughout the summer of 1915, elements of the 1st Division cooperated effectively with each other, as well as with neighbouring divisions to make the best use of resources. This was evident during the Loos fighting, notably in the case of the 3rd CFA Brigade's operations with the 8th British Division.

Canadians and their historians tend to remember the First World War as a coming of age, a transition from colony to nation. Traditional military historical accounts of the 1st Division on Salisbury Plain and at Second Ypres complement this version of the war experience. Specifically, the notion that Canadian soldiers began the First World War as colonial amateurs and finished it as elite shock troops underscores broader arguments that Canada matured on the battlefields, that its nationhood was tempered in the crucible of combat. The learning curve paradigm is premised on the sense that the soldiers of 1914–15, while impossibly brave, were poorly trained and ineffectively commanded. As the story goes, the lessons of Second Ypres, the Somme, and Vimy shaped the Canadian Corps into the force that spearheaded the victory offensives of 1918.

Shoestring Soldiers offers a different appraisal of the early months of the Great War, suggesting that the first generations of Canadian soldiers to fight in Belgium and France possessed all the right training, skills, experience, and leadership, but lacked the tools to finish the job in 1915. Undeniably, the Canadian Corps of 1918 was larger, more complex, and much more generously equipped than that of late 1915, but its officers and men were not fundamentally more capable than their predecessors. In strictly military terms, the war was less transformative than we have come to remember. Perhaps it was also less transformative in a broader national sense, but the answer to that question transcends the scope of this book. Most certainly, however, historians need to reconsider the notion that Canadian forces ascended a neat slope of progress over time from 1914 to 1918 – from amateur recklessness to professional excellence. The foundations of the learning curve paradigm are increasingly uncertain. Fortunately for the Dominion of Canada and its wartime allies, the foundations of the 1st Canadian Division in 1914–15 were solid and true.

Appendices

Appendix A
1st Canadian Division Order of Battle, 1914–15*

Divisional Headquarters
(Lieut.-Gen. E.A.H. Alderson):

1st Canadian Infantry Brigade (Brig.-Gen. M.S. Mercer)	2nd Canadian Infantry Brigade (Brig.-Gen. A.W. Currie)	3rd Canadian Infantry Brigade (Brig.-Gen. R.E.W. Turner)
1st Battalion	5th Battalion	13th Battalion
2nd Battalion	7th Battalion	14th Battalion
3rd Battalion	8th Battalion	15th Battalion
4th Battalion	10th Battalion	16th Battalion

Divisional Artillery
(Brig.-Gen. H.E. Burstall):

1st Brigade, Canadian Field Artillery (Lieut.-Col. E.W.B. Morrison)	2nd Brigade, Canadian Field Artillery (Lieut.-Col. J.J. Creelman)	3rd Brigade, Canadian Field Artillery (Lieut.-Col. J.H. Mitchell)
1st Battery	5th Battery	9th Battery
2nd Battery	6th Battery	10th Battery
3rd Battery	7th Battery	11th Battery
4th Battery	8th Battery	12th Battery

Divisional Ammunition Column (Lieut.-Col. J.J. Penhale)

1st Heavy Battery (4 x 60-pounders) (Maj. F.C. Magee)

Canadian Cavalry Brigade (Brig.-Gen. J.E.B. Seely) –
(Did not join 1st Div in France until May 1915):
Royal Canadian Dragoons
Lord Strathcona's Horse
2nd King Edward's Horse
Royal Canadian Horse Artillery (A+B Bty)

Divisional Cyclist Company (Capt. R.S. Robinson)

---

*Order of battle is based on Duguid, *Official History*, 428–31.

1st Canadian Engineer Brigade (Lieut.-Col. C.J. Armstrong):
1st Field Company (Capt. W.W. Melville)
2nd Field Company (Capt. T.C. Irving)
3rd Field Company (Capt. J.P. Fell)

Divisional Signal Company (Maj. F.A. Lister)

Divisional Train, Canadian Army Service Corps (Lieut.-Col. W.A. Simson)

Canadian Army Medical Corps:
No. 1 Canadian Field Ambulance (Lieut.-Col. A.E. Ross)
No. 2 Canadian Field Ambulance (Lieut.-Col. D.W. MacPherson)
No. 3 Canadian Field Ambulance (Lieut.-Col. W.L. Watt)

Appendix B
5th Infantry Battalion Training Schedule, 6–14 November 1914
(total = 45 hours)

Date	Type of Training	Duration (hours)
6	Physical training	.5
	Company drill	2.5
7	Physical training	.5
	Musketry	2.5
8	Sunday	Nil
9	Physical training	.5
	Musketry and squad drill	2.5
	Musketry and extended order drill	2.5
10	Route march	3
	Squad drill & judging distance	2.5
11	Physical training	.5
	Bayonet training, extended order drill and squad drill	7
12	Physical training with weapons	.5
	Bayonet exercises and extended order drill	6
	Night route march	3.25
13	Rifle range	8.75
14	Squad drill and extended order drill	2

Source: 5th Bn war diary, 6–14 November 1914, RG 9, T-10708.

Appendix C
13th Infantry Battalion Training Schedule, 6–14 November 1914
(total = 36 hours)

Date	Type of Training	Duration (hours)
6	Route march	2.5
7	Company drill	3
	Relocation of battalion's tents	
8	Sunday	Nil
9	Physical training	.5
	Bayonet fighting	.5
	Platoon and extended order drill	1
	Company and extended order drill and company in attack	1
	Route march	2.5
10	Physical training and bayonet fighting	1
	Musketry, fire control and firing exercises	1
	Platoon drill	2.5
	Route march	
11	Physical training and bayonet fighting	.75
	Platoon extended order drill and musketry	2.5
	Route march	2.5
12	Physical training and bayonet fighting	.75
	Company extended order drill	2.5
	Platoon drill and musketry	2.5
13	Physical training and bayonet fighting	.75
	Platoon drill	1
	Musketry	1.5
	Platoon extended order and passing of orders [by voice]	1.5
	Musketry fire control	1
14	Physical training & bayonet fighting	.75
	Platoon extended order	1.5
	Musketry	1

Source: 13th Bn war diary, 6–14 November 1914, RG 9, T-10714.

Appendix D
Training Syllabus for Mounted Troops, 1914–15

Projected Timing	Type of Training
1st Phase (mid-November through end of December)	Cavalry – equitation, personal weapons handling, use of sword in charge, troop drill, dismounted action, outpost duties, map reading, night operations, patrols, reconnaissance, scouting, field engineering
	Cyclists – individual and platoon drill, route marches on bicycles, map reading, night operations, reconnaissance and detached duties, tactical problems, field engineering
2nd Phase (January)	Cavalry – as above, squadron drill, tactical exercises, mounted attacks, advance, rear, and flank guards, night operations, outposts
	Cyclists – as above, company drill, route marches, night marches, tactical exercises, advanced, flank, and rear guards, seizing positions in advance and to the flank of imaginary columns, outposts, night operations
3rd Phase (first two weeks of February)	Combined – simple exercises, combined attack and defence, combined outposts, cooperation with other arms where possible

Source: WD, 1st Cdn Div, November 1914, Appendix 8, RG 9, T-7182.

Appendix E
Training Syllabus for Artillery, 1914–15

Projected Timing	Type of Training
1st Phase (mid-November through mid-December)	Section and battery training: equitation, driving, laying, mounted drill, battery tactics, ammunition supply, field engineering, reconnaissance, communications, movements, march discipline, intercommunication, and orders
2nd Phase (mid-December through mid-January)	All of the above plus employment of artillery in war, cooperation with aircraft, and battery practice
3rd Phase (mid-January through mid-February)	Brigade training, divisional training, and training with other arms

Source: WD, 1st Cdn Div, November 1914, Appendix 8, RG 9, T-7182.

Appendix F
Training Syllabus for Engineers, 1914–15

Projected Timing	Type of Training
1st Phase (last two weeks of November)	Squad and section drill, physical training, marching order and care of equipment, company drill (extended order), night work, musketry (visual training and range finding)
2nd Phase (December through mid-January)	Field defences, redoubts, defence of localities, obstacles, camping arrangements, knotting and lashing, demolitions and explosives, blocks and tackles, reconnaissance
3rd Phase (mid-January through mid-February)	Bridging, riding, and fitting of harness, swimming of horses

Source: WD, 1st Cdn Div, November 1914, Appendix 8, RG 9, T-7182.

Appendix G
Training Syllabus for Signallers, 1914–15

Projected Timing	Type of Training
1st Phase (mid-November through mid-December)	Drill, musketry, riding, driving, care of motorcycles and bicycles, map reading, telephone and telegraph drill, visual signalling, dispatch riding
2nd Phase (mid-December through mid-January)	Drill, musketry, riding, driving, technical instruction for telephonists and telegraphists, visual training, permanent and moving stations
3rd Phase (mid-January through mid-February)	Field work of the signal company, cooperation with infantry and artillery training, review

Source: WD, 1st Cdn Div, November 1914, Appendix 8, RG 9, T-7182.

Appendix H
Training Syllabus for Infantry, 1914–15

Projected Timing	Type of Training
1st Phase (third week in November)	Physical training, musketry, squad drill, extended order, route marching, night work
2nd Phase (last week in November)	All of the above plus outposts
3rd Phase (first week in December)	All of the above plus entrenching
4th Phase (second week in December)	Company training (20 hours), battalion training (16 hours)
5th Phase (last two weeks of December and first three weeks of January)	Company training according to syllabus for regular British regiments
6th Phase (last week of January and first week of February)	Battalion training
7th Phase (second and third weeks of February)	Brigade training

Source: WD, 1st Cdn Div, November 1914, Appendix 8, RG 9, T-7182.

Appendix I
1st Canadian Casualty Statistics, April 1915 (not including sick)

Unit	Officers Killed	Officers WIA	OR KIA	OR WIA	Officers WIA & MIA	Officers MIA	OR WIA & MIA	OR Missing	Totals per Unit
Infantry									
1st Bde HQ	0	0	0	0	0	0	0	0	0
1st Bn[a]	2	9	54	304	0	0	0	35	404
2nd Bn	5	5	65	158	6	0	37	265	541
3rd Bn[b]	5	6	12	42	0	7	0	415	487
4th Bn[c]	3	14	52	333	1	0	0	48	451
2nd Bde HQ	0	3	0	0	0	0	0	0	3
5th Bn	1	8	19	160	0	1	0	42	231
7th Bn	6	5	63	128	2	4	0	372	580
8th Bn	1	12	51	176	1	5	27	143	416
10th Bn	9	12	195	217	0	2	0	20	455
3rd Bde HQ	0	1	0	0	0	0	0	0	1
13rd Bn[d]	3	5	66	157	2	1	27	206	467
14th Bn	3	9	26	113	1	0	29	84	265
15th Bn[e]	1	6	16	12	0	14	0	626	675
16th Bn	5	8	49	170	4	0	1	107	344
Artillery									
1st CFA[f]	1	?	5	50	?	?	?	?	56
2nd CFA[g]	?	1	?	64	?	?	?	?	65
3rd CFA	?	3	?	58	?	?	?	?	61
Engrs[h]	?	2	?	57	?	?	?	?	59
Cyclists	0	0	?	19	0	0	?	?	19
Transport	0	0	?	5	0	0	?	?	5
Signals	0	0	?	7	0	0	?	?	7

Note: This table is based on figures drawn from 1st Divisional records for the month of April, but a close examination of officer casualties indicates that these figures probably cover the specific period of 22–30 April. Total casualty figures reported in other secondary sources such as Dancocks, *Welcome to Flanders Fields*, 227, are slightly higher because they include losses during the first few days of May. Duguid, *Official History*, provides a casualty breakdown by date for the entire year of 1915 in Appendix 851, but he does not differentiate among killed, wounded, missing, or captured.

a. According to WD, 1st Bn, April 1915, Appendix 1, 'Narrative of Operations, 23-30 April,' virtually all of these casualties were suffered during the counterattack of 23 April.

b. According to Brigadier-General Mercer's diary, the 3rd Battalion reported that it had lost 400 men captured when 1st Brigade was reunited on 25 April (Mercer Diary, 25 April 1915). However, a subsequent head count revealed that approximately 250 of the 400 missing men had actually been captured. See RG 9, III C 5, vol. 4076, folder 5, file 2.

c. At midnight of 23-24 April, the diary of 1st Brigade reports that 4th Battalion's total effective strength was 250. See WD, 1st Cdn Bde, 24 April 1915.

d. These figures for other rank casualties conflict with those provided in Loomis's battle report, which indicates a grand total of 511 other ranks killed, wounded or missing (without providing a further breakdown), while the figures listed here add up to 456 killed, wounded or missing. There is no explanation for the discrepancy. See 'Action in Front of Ypres,' LAC, MG 27 IID23, vol. 3.

e. The casualty figures for the battalion are inconclusive. Seven officers were wounded while 14 were captured (one of the wounded officers, Captain Darling, later died). Sixteen other ranks were confirmed killed, and a dozen wounded, while 626 were listed as missing. It is uncertain how many of these were killed and how many were captured.

f. Based on a report from Morrison to Burstall, 2 May 1915, LAC, MG 30 E 6, file 17. Morrison states that his casualties up to 2 May consisted of 6 killed and 50 wounded. He does not break down the total for officers and other ranks, but does mention that at least one officer was killed and one wounded.

g. 2nd and 3rd CFA Bdes are based on total figures (killed, wounded, missing) for 22–30 April in Duguid, Appendix 851.

h. Engineers, Cyclist, Transport, and Signals figures are based on Duguid, Appendix 851.

Notes

Introduction

1 A.F. Duguid, 'Canadians in Battle, 1915–1918,' *Canadian Defence Quarterly* 13, no. 1 (1935), 12–27.
2 Bill Rawling, *Surviving Trench Warfare: Technology and the Canadian Corps, 1914–1918* (Toronto: University of Toronto Press, 1992), 7.
3 Desmond Morton, *When Your Number's Up: The Canadian Soldier in the First World War* (Toronto: Random House, 1993), viii-ix.
4 Ian Brown, 'Not Glamorous, but Effective: The Canadian Corps and the Set-piece Attack, 1917–1918,' *Journal of Military History* 58, no. 3, (1994), 421–44.
5 Shane Schreiber, *Shock Army of the British Empire: The Canadian Corps in the Last 100 Days of the Great War* (London: Praeger, 1997), 3.
6 Tim Cook, *No Place to Run: The Canadian Corps and Gas Warfare in the First World War* (Vancouver: UBC Press, 1999), 8–10.
7 Kenneth Radley, *We Lead, Others Follow: First Canadian Division, 1914–1918* (St Catharines, ON: Vanwell, 2006), 20–1.
8 On the logistical situation in 1915, see Ian Malcolm Brown, *British Logistics on the Western Front, 1914–1919* (Westport, Praeger, CT: 1998), 90–104.
9 H.R. Alley, 3rd Bn, (tape 1) 11, Library and Archives Canada (LAC), RG 41, B III 1, vol. 7; hereafter all the record groups (RGs) cited are from LAC.
10 Max Aitken, *Canada in Flanders* (Toronto: Hodder and Stoughton, 1916), 47.
11 *Canada in the Great World War*, vol. 2, *Days of Preparation* (Toronto: United Publishers of Canada, 1917–21), 283–4.
12 *Canada in the Great World War*, vol. 3, *Guarding the Channel Ports* (Toronto: United Publishers of Canada, 1919), 195.
13 A.F. Duguid, *Official History of the Canadian Forces in the Great War, August 1914 to September 1915.* General Series vol. 1 (Ottawa: J.O. Patenaude, 1938).

Tim Cook offers a comprehensive study of Duguid in *Clio's Warriors: Canadian Historians and the Writing of the World Wars* (Vancouver: UBC Press, 2006), 41–92.

14 Cook, *Clio's Warriors*, 84–5.

15 G.W.L. Nicholson, *Canadian Expeditionary Force, 1914–1919: The Official History of the Canadian Army in the First World War* (Ottawa: Queen's Printer, 1962), 35–8; hereafter cited as *CEF*.

16 Ibid., 92.

17 Ibid., 97–108; Duguid, *Official History*, 498.

18 George Cassar, *Beyond Courage: The Canadians at the Second Battle of Ypres* (Ottawa: Oberon, 1985); James McWilliams and R.J. Steel, *Gas! The Battle for Ypres, 1915* (St Catharines, ON: Vanwell, 1985); Daniel Dancocks, *Welcome to Flanders Fields: The First Canadian Battle of the Great War, Ypres, 1915* (Toronto: McClelland and Stewart, 1988).

19 Cook, *Clio's Warriors*, 225.

20 On later Canadian training developments, see Mark Osborne Humphries, 'The Myth of the Learning Curve: Tactics and Training in the 12th Canadian Infantry Brigade, 1916–1918,' *Canadian Military History* 14, no. 4 (2005), 15–30.

21 See Leonard Smith, *Between Mutiny and Obedience: The Case of the French Fifth Infantry Division during World War I* (Princeton, NJ: Princeton University Press, 1994), 16–17.

22 On Hughes's wartime activities refer to Ronald G. Haycock, *Sam Hughes: The Public Career of a Controversial Canadian, 1885–1916* (Waterloo, ON: Wilfrid Laurier University Press, 1986).

23 Ronald Haycock has comprehensively analysed wartime estimations of the Ross in his article, 'Early Canadian Weapons Acquisition: "That damned Ross rifle,"' *Canadian Defence Quarterly* 14, no. 3 (1985), 48–57. Also see Clive Law, ed., *A Question of Confidence* (Ottawa: Service Publications, 1999).

24 See Jeff Keshen, *Propaganda and Censorship during Canada's Great War* (Edmonton: University of Alberta Press, 1996), 153–9. For an alternative perspective on the nature of wartime propaganda, see Ian Hugh Maclean Miller, *Our Glory and Our Grief: Torontonians and the Great War* (Toronto: University of Toronto Press, 2002), 6–7.

25 Tim Cook, '"Literary Memorials": The Great War Regimental Histories, 1919–1939,' *Journal of the CHA* 13 (2002), 168.

26 Radley, *We Lead, Others Follow*.

27 For a broader assessment of battlefield study tours as analytical historical tools, refer to Michael Bechthold, '"One of the Greatest Moments of My Life": Lessons Learned on the Canadian Battle of Normandy Foundation Battlefield Tours,' *Defence Studies* 5, no. 1 (2006), 27–36.

1. Soldiering and Canadian Soldiers: The State of the Art at the Outbreak of War

1 Robert K. Massie, *Dreadnought: Britain, Germany, and the Coming of the Great War* (New York: Ballantine, 1991), 854.

2 For a detailed analysis of the outbreak of war, see Hew Strachan, *The First World War* (Oxford: Oxford University Press, 2001), 64–102.

3 See Miller, *Our Glory and Our Grief*, 10–13. For a comparative assessment of local Canadian reactions to the war, see Robert Rutherdale, *Hometown Horizons: Local Responses to Canada's Great War* (Vancouver: UBC Press, 2004).

4 On the changing defence relationship between Britain and Canada during the later part of the nineteenth century, refer to George F. Stanley, *Canada's Soldiers: The Military History of an Unmilitary People* (Toronto: Macmillan, 1974); Stephen Harris, *Canadian Brass: The Making of a Professional Army, 1860–1939* (Toronto: University of Toronto Press, 1988); and Barry Gough and Roger Sarty, 'Sailors and Soldiers: The Royal Navy, the Canadian Forces, and the Defence of Atlantic Canada, 1890–1918,' in Michael L. Hadley et al., eds., *A Nation's Navy: In Quest of Canadian Naval Identity* (Montreal: McGill-Queen's University Press, 1996), 112–30.

5 Not until 1940 was the 'Canadian Army' officially authorized. At this time, the PAM was redesignated the 'Active Force' and the NPAM became the 'Reserve Force'; after 1954 the Active Force became known as the 'Regular Force' and the Reserve Force was again simply referred to as the Militia. See David A. Morris, *The Canadian Militia from 1855: An Historical Summary* (Erin, ON: Boston Mills Press, 1983), 10.

6 Haycock, *Sam Hughes*, 166.

7 On mobilization plans, see Harris, *Canadian Brass*, 92–8; On Hughes's improvisational recruiting practices see Haycock, *Sam Hughes*, 198–224.

8 In this confused battle Canadian battalions of the 2nd Division struggled for control of a series of flooded mine craters. The ground was so badly torn up that commanders could scarcely position themselves on a map. See Tim Cook, 'The Blind Leading the Blind: The Battle of the St Eloi Craters,' *Canadian Military History* 5, no. 2 (1996), 32.

9 E.A.H. Alderson, *With the Mounted Infantry in the Mashonaland Field Force* (London: Methuen, 1898).

10 E.A.H. Alderson, *Pink and Scarlet, or Hunting as a School for Soldiering* (London: Heinemann, 1900).

11 Duguid, *Official History*, 119.

12 Ibid., 146.

13 Haycock, *Sam Hughes*, 211.

14 Edwin Alderson Correspondence, 15 Sept. 1915, National Archives and British Library, MSS 50088.

15 Carman Miller, *Painting the Map Red: Canada and the South African War, 1899–1902* (Montreal: Canadian War Museum and McGill-Queen's University Press, 1993), 231.

16 The data in this paragraph are from Duguid, *Official History*, 49–53. For a comprehensive social perspective of the CEF, see Morton, *When Your Number's Up*.

17 The author's preliminary research into the backgrounds of First World War volunteers from the Six Nations Reservation near Brantford, Ontario, reveals that at least 60 per cent had belonged to the Active Militia before the war.

18 On recruiting and race, see James W. St G. Walker, 'Race and Recruitment in World War I: Enlistment of Visible Minorities in the Canadian Expeditionary Force,' *Canadian Historical Review* 70, no. 1 (1989), 1–26; and Calvin W. Ruck, *The Black Battalion, 1916–1920: Canada's Best Kept Military Secret* (Halifax: Nimbus, 1987).

19 One hundred of the officers were members of the Permanent Force at the outbreak of war. Six were graduates of the Staff College at Camberley, 42 had completed the Military Staff Course, and over 100 had attended the Royal Military College at Kingston at some point. See Duguid, *Official History*, 52.

20 Kent Fedorowich, 'The Migration of British Ex-Servicemen to Canada and the Role of the Naval and Military Emigration League, 1899–1914,' *Histoire sociale/Social History* 25, no. 49 (1992), 75–99.

21 Ultimately more than 35,000 Americans put on Canadian uniforms during the First World War, accounting for nearly 6 per cent of the men who served in the CEF. See T.J. Harris, 'Yankees Who Fought for the Maple Leaf' (MA thesis, University of Nebraska, 1997), 59.

22 All calculations are based on nominal rolles found in LAC, MG 30, E 300, vol. 16, and the RG 150 service records of individuals in the sample groups; hereafter all manuscript groups (MGs) are from LAC, unless otherwise designated.

23 Desmond Morton's *Ministers and Generals: Politics and the Canadian Militia, 1896–1904* (Toronto: University of Toronto Press, 1970) surveys Canada's military forces during the later part of the nineteenth century.

24 Carman Miller, 'Sir Frederick William Borden and Military Reform, 1896–1911, *Canadian Historical Review* 50, no. 3 (1969), 265–84.

25 Gary Muir, 'Brantford Armoury Began Life as "Shed" in Alexandra Park,' *Brantford Expositor*, 9 Sept. 2000; Charles F. Winter, *Lieutenant-General The Hon. Sir Sam Hughes: Canada's War Minister, 1911–1916* (Toronto: Macmillan, 1931), 36–7.

26 Carman Miller, 'The Montreal Militia as a Social Institution before World War I,' *Urban History Review* 19, no. 1 (1990), 58–9; Frederick C. Curry, 'The Canadian Militia,' *Canadian Defence* 3, no. 4 (1911), 96–7.

27 Harris, *Canadian Brass*, 5–6.

28 Morton, *Ministers and Generals*, 60–1.

29 'Vancouver,' *Canadian Military Gazette*, 14 Feb. 1911, 5.

30 Brereton Greenhous, *Dragoon: The Centennial History of the Royal Canadian Dragoons, 1883–1983* (Ottawa: Guild of the Royal Canadian Dragoons, 1983), 142–3.

31 Andrew Iarocci, *Canadian Forces Base Petawawa: The First Century, 1905–2005* (Waterloo, ON: LCMSDS, 2005), 6–9.

32 Sessional Paper No. 35, Part II, 1903, 1904, Report of the General Officer Commanding (GOC).

33 James Wood, 'The Sense of Duty: Canadian Ideas of the Citizen Soldier, 1896–1917' (PhD diss., Wilfrid Laurier University, 2007).

34 Morton, *When Your Number's Up*, 3. During the immediate pre-war years there were about 3,500 men in the Permanent Force. For a force breakdown, refer to William Hamilton Merritt, 'The Canadian Militia,' *Canadian Field* 3, no. 3 (1911), 59–62.

35 *Infantry Drill: Field and Brigade Movements and Infantry in Attack* (Ottawa: Government Printing Bureau [GPB], 1899), 4. The manual included special instructions for the 1899 militia camp season.

36 W.T. Barnard, *The Queen's Own Rifles of Canada, 1860–1960: One Hundred Years of Canada* (Don Mills, ON: Ontario Publishing Co., 1960), 68–9.

37 'Manoeuvres in Eleventh Military District,' *Canadian Military Gazette*, 13 Aug. 1912, 8.

38 For detailed assessments of the various GOCs who served during this period, see Morton, *Ministers and Generals*.

39 Ivor Herbert, *Military Organization* (1892), 5–6.

40 Stewart H. Bull, *The Queen's York Rangers: An Historic Regiment* (Erin, ON: Boston Mills Press, 1984), 148.

41 Sessional Paper No. 35, Part II, 1900, Rep GOC, 24; Chas Flick, 'Semi-Ready Training,' *Canadian Defence* 3, no. 11 (1912), 323–4.

42 Sessional Paper No. 35, Part II, 1902, Rep GOC, 36.

43 On Hamiltons's tour, see Haycock, *Sam Hughes*, 165–70.

44 'General Ian Hamilton's Report to Government,' *Canadian Defence* 5, no. 4 (1913), 60–2.

45 The Canadian contingent included more battalions than required for a single division. Surplus units were cut from the order of battle and left behind in England to constitute administrative echelons and depot establishments where future recruits and reinforcements could be housed and trained.

46 David Love, *A Call to Arms: The Organization and Administration of Canada's Military in World War One* (Winnipeg: Bunker to Bunker Books, 1999), 78.

47 J.A. Currie, editorial, *Canadian Military Gazette*, 25 Aug. 1914, 12.

48 H.M. Urquhart, *Arthur Currie: The Biography of a Great Canadian* (Toronto: J.M. Dent, 1950); Daniel Dancocks, *Sir Arthur Currie: A Biography* (Toronto: Methuen, 1985); A.M.J. Hyatt, *General Sir Arthur Currie: A Military Biography* (Toronto: University of Toronto Press, 1987).

49 For a survey of Turner's career, see Thomas P. Leppard, '"The Dashing Subaltern": Sir Richard Turner in Retrospect', *Canadian Military History* 6, no. 2 (1997), 21–8.

50 See Gordon MacKinnon, 'The Junction's Forgotten General: Malcolm Smith Mercer,' *The Leader and Recorder, West Toronto Junction*, fall 2002. I am indebted to Mr MacKinnon for pointing out that Mercer's diary survives in the Queen's Own Rifles archives in Toronto.

51 Barnard, *Queen's Own*, 82; also see 'The Soo Troubles,' *Canadian Military Gazette*, 20 Oct. 1903, 6.

52 See Brevet-Major Hereward Wake, *The Four-Company Battalion in Battle* (London: J.J. Keliher, 1914), 3–4.

53 With the formation of the Machine-Gun Corps in Oct. 1915, the machine-gun sections were removed from battalion control and reorganized into machine-gun companies at the brigade level.

54 Dancocks, *Welcome to Flanders Fields*, 22–3.

55 Radley, *We Lead, Others Follow*, 40.

56 RG 150, Box 9853–30; unless otherwise noted, all subsequent personnel file citations from RG 150 refer to Accession 1992–93/166.

57 RG 150, Box 985–12; Daniel Dancocks, *Gallant Canadians: The Story of the Tenth Canadian Infantry Battalion, 1914–1919* (Calgary: Penguin, 1990), 218.

58 RG 150, Box 5508–20.

59 Dancocks, *Welcome to Flanders Fields*, 23.

60 RG 150, Box 5736–3.

61 Ibid., Box 22–3322.

62 Currie editorial, 25 Aug.

63 Nicholson, *CEF*, 39–40.

64 J.E.B. Seely, *Adventure* (London: Heinemann, 1930), 217.

65 *Field Service Regulations, Part I, Operations, 1909/1914* (London: General Staff, War Office [WO], 10 Nov. 1914), 15.

66 David Herrmann, *The Arming of Europe and the Making of the First World War* (Princeton, NJ: Princeton University Press, 1996), 17–19.

67 Shelford Bidwell and Dominick Graham, *Fire-Power: British Army Weapons and Theories of War, 1904–1945* (London: Allen and Unwin, 1985), 8–9.

68 *Field Service Regulations,* part 1, 15.
69 On artillery ammunition supply in 1915, refer to J.E. Edmonds, *History of the Great War, Military Operations, France and Belgium, 1915,* vol. 1 (Macmillan: London, 1927), 55–8.
70 Radley, *We Lead,* 61.
71 RG 150, Box 6403–49.
72 See *The Canadian Who's Who,* vol. 4, *1948* (Toronto: Trans Canada, 1948); RG 150, Box 2131–43.
73 RG 150, Box 6256–17.
74 *Field Service Regulations,* Part I, 222–5.
75 RG 150, Box 225–10; South Africa Medal Role, RG 9, 11–A-5, vol. 14, C-1863.
76 RG 150, Box 4716–24.
77 Ibid., Box 5670–37.
78 *Field Service Regulations,* part 1, 228.
79 John S. Moir (ed.), *History of the Royal Canadian Corps of Signals, 1903–1961* (Ottawa, 1962), 9; hereafter *Signal Corps.*
80 Love, *Call to Arms,* 215–16.
81 *Field Service Pocket Book, 1914* (London: General Staff, WO, 1914), 120–1.
82 RG 150, Box 8933–3.
83 For a general discussion of British military thought, see Bidwell and Graham, *Fire-Power,* 38–58. Norman Dixon is highly critical of British command, see his book, *On the Psychology of Military Incompetence* (London: Future, 1985), 80–5.
84 Paddy Griffith, *Battle Tactics of the Western Front: The British Army's Art of Attack, 1916–1918* (New Haven, CT: Yale University Press, 1994), 179–83.
85 *Training and Manoeuvre Regulations, 1913* (London: General Staff, WO, 17 Nov. 1913), 10–11.
86 B.C. Battye, *Some Notes on the Minor Tactics of Trench Warfare, 1914* (Ottawa: Government Printing Bureau, 1916). Battye was the well-known inventor of the famous Battye bomb, an early British grenade.
87 See, e.g., 2nd Cdn Bde to 1st Cdn Div, 18 Nov. 1914, MG 30, E 75, vol. 2. In this correspondence Brigadier-General Arthur Currie noted a shortage of infantry training manuals.
88 *Training and Manoeuvre Regulations,* 10–11.
89 A.P. Birchall, *Rapid Training of a Company for War* (London: Gale and Polden, 1915), 140–2.
90 Birchall, *Rapid Training,* 144–8.
91 Ibid., 29–31.
92 Ibid., 2, 34.
93 Ibid., 8–9.

94 *Manual of Physical Training, 1908* (London, 1908; amended 1 Dec. 1914), 7–8.
95 Birchall, *Rapid Training*, 14.
96 *Musketry Regulations*, Part I, *1909/1914* (London: General Staff, WO, 26 Sept. 1914), 249.
97 *Rifle and Musketry Exercises for the Ross Rifle* (Ottawa: GPB, 1914).
98 *Infantry Training, 1914* (London: General Staff, WO, 10 Aug. 1914), 2; Birchall, 11.
99 *Field Service Regulations*, Part I, 136–7.
100 *Infantry Training*, 82. In *The Four-Company Battalion in Battle*, 7, Wake states that 'fire to support movement … is the gist of the attack.' John A. English and Bruce I. Gudmundsson offer a comprehensive summary of the 'open order revolution' (1854–1914) in their book, *On Infantry, a rev. ed.* (Westport, CT: Praeger, 1994), 1–15.
101 *Infantry Training*, 148–62.
102 *Notes on Training*, Southern Command, 12 Aug. 1914, RG 9, vol. 4044, folder 4, file 10. The Great War was not really the first 'trench' war. Armies have constructed defensive earthworks for millennia, but more recently, the American Civil War witnessed extensive trench building. On nineteenth-century field fortification, see Edward Hagerman, *The American Civil War and the Origins of Modern Warfare* (Bloomington: Indiana University Press, 1992).
103 *Manual of Field Engineering, 1911* (London: General Staff, WO, 28 Jan. 1911/ reprinted 1914), 24–7.
104 *Infantry Training*, 116–19.
105 *Protection and Outposts: What to Do and How to Do It* (Aldershot, UK: Gale and Polden, 1915), 48–59.
106 Narrative of Operations, Fort Garry Horse, 9 Oct. 1918, RG 9, vol. 4956, T-10772–10773.
107 War Diary (WD), 1st Cdn Div, Dec. 1914, Appendix (App) 11, RG 9, T-7182.
108 *Field Artillery Training, 1914* (London: General Staff, WO, 9 April 1914), 8–13, 16–17, 373–7, 409–10.
109 *Manual of Field Engineering*, iii-vii, 10–14, 24, 44, 52–63.
110 See John Laffin, *The Western Front Illustrated, 1914–1918* (London: Grange, 1997), 23; *Illustrated London News*, 14 Nov. 1914, 674–5.
111 On pre-war military culture, see Mark Moss, *Manliness and Militarism: Educating Young Boys in Ontario for War* (Don Mills, ON: Oxford University Press, 2001).

2. Training for War: The Salisbury Plain Camps

1 WD, 1st Cdn Bde, 14 Oct. 1914, RG 9, T-10665; all of the primary sources in this chapter refer to 1914, unless otherwise stated.

2 WD, 2nd Bn, Oct., RG 9, T-10705.

3 WD, 4th Bn, 24 Oct., RG 9, T-10707.

4 See Rawling, *Surviving Trench Warfare*, 20–3.

5 H.M. Urquhart, *The History of the 16th Battalion (Canadian Scottish), Canadian Expeditionary Force in the Great War, 1914–1919* (Toronto: Macmillian, 1932), 31; hereafter cited as *16th Battalion*.

6 W.F. Graham, 2nd Bn, (tape 1) 6, RG 41, B III 1, vol. 7.

7 Harold R. Peat, *Private Peat* (Indianapolis: Bobbs-Merrill, 1917), 51.

8 George Herbert Rae Gibson, *Maple Leaves in Flanders Fields* (Toronto: William Briggs, 1916), 41.

9 A.M. McLennan, 16th Bn, (tape 1) 8, RG 41, B III 1, vol. 9.

10 Mercer Diary, 30 Oct., 11 Nov., QOR Museum.

11 Crerar Diary, 22 Oct., MG 30, E 157, vol. 15.

12 Tim Cook, 'Wet Canteens and Worrying Mothers: Alcohol, Soldiers and Temperance Groups in the Great War,' *Histoire sociale/Social History*, 35, no. 70, (2002), 311–30.

13 Barbara M. Wilson, '"There Is No Alternative": The Diary of Harry H. Coombs, 9th Battalion, CEF, August 1914–January 1915,' *Canadian Military History* 14, no. 3 (2005), 39–56.

14 Crerar Diary, 8 Nov.

15 Tim Cook, '"More a Medicine than a Beverage": "Demon Rum" and the Canadian Trench Soldier of the First World War,' *Canadian Military History* 9, no. 1 (2000), 7–22.

16 1st Contingent Horses, RG 9, III C 11, vol. 4580, folder 5, file 3.

17 Duguid, *Official History*, 130–1.

18 1st Cdn Div, Nov., App 2, 10, 12.

19 On Roberts's final inspection of Canadian troops, see 'Lord Roberts to the Canadian Troops,' *Canadian News Souvenir Edition* (1914), 25.

20 WD, 1st Cdn Div, Nov.

21 Ibid., App 3.

22 WD, Cyclist Coy, 6–14 Nov., RG 9, T-10773.

23 WD, 1st CFA Bde, 6–14 Nov., RG 9, T-10784.

24 Creelman Diary, 10 Nov., MG 30, E 8, vol. 1, file 1; WD: 2nd CFA Bde, 6–14 Nov., RG 9, T-10784–5; 3rd CFA Bde, 6–14 Nov., RG 9, T-10786–7.

25 John Swettenham, *McNaughton*, vol. 1, *1887–1939* (Toronto: Ryerson Press, 1968), 34–5. According to Swettenham, the postwar versions, which were eventually published as *The Eighteen Pounder in Close Support of Infantry*, differed only marginally from the original 1914 lectures.

26 WD, DAC, 1–14 Nov., RG 9, T-10806.

27 WD, 1st Bde Cdn Engineers, 1–15 Nov., RG 9, T-10824.

28 WD, Div Train, 1–11 Nov., RG 9, T-10903.
29 WD: 1st Bn, 5–14 Nov., RG 9, T-10704; 2nd Bn, 6–14 Nov., and 4th Bn, 2–15 Nov., T-10707.
30 WD, 5th Bn, 6–14 Nov., RG 9, T-10708.
31 8th Bn to 2nd Cdn Bde, 11 Nov., and 2nd Cdn Bde to 1st Cdn Div, 12 Nov., MG 30, E 75, vol. 2.
32 WD: 13th Bn, 6–14 Nov., RG 9, T-10714; 14th Bn, 6–15. Nov. 1914, RG 9, T-10716; 15th Bn, 6–14 Nov., RG 9, T-10717.
33 WD, 1st Cdn Div, Dec., App 5; Jan. 1915, App 4.
34 Captain R.S. Robinson to Mrs Robinson, 17 March 1915, New Liskeard Speakers Collection, Canadian Letters and Images Project, Malaspina University College.
35 WD, Cyclist Coy, 15–30 Nov., Dec.
36 WD, 1st CFA Bde, 10 Dec.
37 WD, DAC, 11 Dec.
38 G.W.L. Nicholson, *The Gunners of Canada: The History of the Royal Regiment of Canadian Artillery*, vol. 1, *1534–1919* (Toronto: McClelland and Stewart, 1967), 204.
39 Creelman Diary, 18 Nov.
40 Crerar Diary, 21 Nov.
41 Procedures for unlimbering the guns and getting them into action under covered positions received much emphasis at the time. See Crerar Diary, 2 Dec.
42 WD: 1st CFA Bde, 12–30 Nov., 3rd CFA Bde, 27 Nov.
43 WD, 7th Bn, 27 Nov.
44 Crerar Diary, 19 Dec.
45 WD, 2nd CFA Bde, 17–24 Nov.
46 Creelman Diary, 10 Dec.
47 WD: 2nd CFA Bde, 17 Nov., 21–8 Dec.; 3rd CFA Bde, 10, 15–17 Nov.
48 WD: 1st CFA Bde, 29 Dec. (see also the 2nd and 3rd CFA Bde diaries for 29 Dec.); DAC, 29 Dec. On wireless capability, see Bill Rawling, 'Communications in the Canadian Corps, 1915–1918: Wartime Technological Progress Revisited,' *Canadian Military History* 3, no. 2 (1994), 6–21.
49 Dunlop Diary, 29 Dec., MG 30, E 439, vol. 1.
50 WD, DAC, 23–5 Nov., 1–2 Dec.
51 Ibid., 16 Nov., 3–15 Dec., 5 Feb. 1915.
52 Ibid., 22 Dec.
53 WD, 1st Bde Cdn Engineers, 15–17 Nov., 1 Dec.
54 Ibid., 7–31 Jan. 1915.
55 Moir, *Signal Corps*. 10.
56 Charles Maitland Sprague to Jim, 19 Dec. 1915, MG 30, E 523.

57 Telegraph operators were seconded from the engineers. See Moir, *Signal Corps*, 8–10.
58 'Syllabus of Training Being Carried Out by Signallers of the 8th Battalion,' 1914, MG 30, E 75, vol. 2. Also see Signal Company Daily Orders, Nov.-Dec., RG 9, III C 5, vol. 4438.
59 WD, Div Train, 14–30 Nov.
60 Ibid., 5–10 Dec., 19–21 Jan. 1915.
61 WD, 1st Cdn Bde, 'Brigade Training / Brigade in attack of position,' App I, Jan. 1915.
62 WD, 3rd Bn, 6 Jan. 1915, RG 9, T-10706
63 WD, 1st Cdn Div, Nov., App 13.
64 Private Frank Betts to Mrs Betts, 25 Dec., Brant County Archives.
65 George Patrick, 2nd Bn, (tape 1) 9, RG 41, B III 1, vol. 7.
66 WD, 2nd Cdn Bde, 14–30 Nov., Dec. 1914, Jan. 1915, RG 9, T-10668.
67 WD, 5th Bn, 20–7 Nov.
68 Odlum Diary, 8 Dec., MG 30, E 300, vol. 16, file 5.
69 WD, 8th Bn, 17–19 Nov., RG 9, T-10710–11.
70 Ibid., 24–26 Nov., 2–3 Dec.
71 Ibid., 10 Dec.
72 Alldritt Diary, 8 Jan. 1915, MG 30, E 1. Dancocks cited the diary in *Welcome to Flanders Fields*, but omitted any portions indicative of useful training.
73 Alldritt Diary, 11, 13–20, 19–31 Jan. 1915.
74 WD, 5th Bn, Dec., 15–19 Jan. 1915.
75 WD, 3rd Cdn Bde, 18–23 Dec., 13 Jan. 1915, RG 9, T-10671.
76 Sinclair Diary, 28 Jan. 1915, MG 30, E 432, vol. 1, file 2.
77 A brigade field day is mentioned on 25 Jan. 1915; see WD, 13th Bn; R.C. Fetherstonhaugh, *The 13th Battalion Royal Highlanders of Canada, 1914–1919* (Toronto: Warwick and Rutter, 1925), 23; hereafter cited as *13th Battalion*.
78 WD, 14th Bn, Dec. Radley observes that the 14th Battalion was plagued with discipline problems later in the war; see his *We Lead, Others Follow*, 81.
79 R.C. Fetherstonhaugh, *The Royal Montreal Regiment, 14th Battalion, CEF, 1914–1925* (Montreal: Gazette Printing, 1927), 21; hereafter cited as *14th Battalion*.
80 WD, 15th Bn, 14 Jan. 1915.
81 J.A. Currie, *'The Red Watch': With the First Canadian Division in Flanders* (Toronto: McClelland, Goodchild, and Stewart, 1916), 86.
82 Urquhart, *16th Battalion*, 30.
83 Proceedings of a Board of Officers, 19 Dec., MG 30, E 84.
84 Machine Gun Section Syllabus, 5 Dec., MG 30, E 75, vol. 2.
85 See Programme of Training Machine Gun Section, 8th Bn, 7–12 Dec., MG 30, E 75, vol. 2.

86 2nd Cdn Bde Order, 28 Jan. 1915, MG 30, E 75, vol. 2.

87 WD, 1st Cdn Div, Dec., App 11.

88 *Training and Manoeuvre Regulations*, 23, 25.

89 Ibid., 44

90 WD, 1st Cdn Div, Nov. 1914, App 4, Operation Order No. 1; and Creelman Diary, 17 Nov.

91 WD, 1st CFA Bde, 13 Nov.

92 WD: 5th Bn, 3–4, 15–22 Dec.; 7th Bn, 22 Dec.; 8th Bn, 2–3 Dec.; 10th Bn, 22 Dec.; 3rd Cdn Bde, 10 Dec.

93 WD: 10th Bn, 30 Nov.; 7th Bn, 10, 17 Dec. 1914; 8th Bn, 13 Jan. 1915.

94 On the development of schools in the BEF, see Radley, *We Lead, Others Follow*, 253.

95 Siegfried Sassoon, *Memoirs of an Infantry Officer* (London: Faber and Faber, 1966), 11–12.

96 Griffith, *British Tactics*, 186–91.

97 For examples of such assessments, refer to Dennis Winter, *Death's Men: Soldiers of the Great War* (London: Penguin, 1988), 39–43; Tim Travers, *How the War Was Won: Command and Technology in the British Army on the Western Front, 1917–1918* (London: Routledge, 1992), 176; and Tim Travers, *The Killing Ground: The British Army, the Western Front and the Emergence of Modern Warfare, 1900–1918* (London: Allen and Unwin, 1987), 190.

98 WD, 1st Cdn Div, Dec., App 2. Brutinel's brigade did not join the division on the Western Front until June 1915. See Duguid, *Official History*, 524–6.

99 WD, 2nd Cdn Bde, 16–18 Dec.

100 WD, 1st Cdn Div, Jan. 1915, App 5.

101 Duguid, *Official History*, 135.

3. Across the Channel: Apprenticing for War

1 Both British divisions consisted primarily of pre-war regular troops. Since arriving on the Western Front in August 1914 the 4th Division had been commanded by Major-General Thomas D'Oyly Snow, Major-General Henry Rawlinson, and Major-General Henry Wilson. The division fought at the battles of Le Cateau, the Marne, and First Messines. Major-General J. Keir's 6th Division arrived on the Western Front in September 1914, seeing early action on the Aisne River heights.

2 WD, 1st Cdn Div, Feb. 1915, App 3, 4; all of the primary sources in this chapter refer to 1915, unless otherwise stated.

3 Ibid., App 3, Course of Instruction: Artillery.

4 WD, 1 East Yorkshire Regt, 18 Feb., Public Records Office (PRO), WO/95/1618.

5 WD, 1st Cdn Div, Feb., App 3, Course of Instruction: Infantry.

6 WD, Cyclist Coy, 16–28 Feb.

7 WD, Signal Coy, 16–28 Feb.

8 WD, 1st Bde Cdn Engineers, 22–8 Feb.

9 WD, Div Train, 17–28 Feb.

10 WD, 3rd CFA Bde, 22 Feb.

11 WD, 1st CFA Bde, 20–7 Feb.

12 WD, 2nd CFA Bde, 22 Feb.

13 Ibid., 25 Feb.

14 WD, 3rd CFA Bde, 25–6 Feb.

15 WD, DAC, 17–28 Feb.

16 Dunlop Diary, 26 Feb.

17 *Back to Blighty*, George Bell Fonds, MG 30, E 113, file 1.

18 WD, 2nd Bn, 18 Feb.

19 WD: 3rd Bn, 17–22 Feb.; 4th Bn, 17–22 Feb.; 1st Bn, 17–22 Feb.

20 WD, 1/16th London Regiment, 20–1 Feb., PRO, WO/95/1616.

21 WD: 5th Bn, 22–7 Feb.; 7th Bn, 22–5 Feb.; 8th Bn, 26 Feb.

22 Alldritt Diary, 24 Feb.

23 WD, 10th Bn, 22–7 Feb.

24 '3 Years and 8 Months in a German Prison,' George Drillie Scott Fonds, MG 30, E 28.

25 WD, 13th Bn, 23–4 Feb.

26 Fetherstonhaugh, *13th Battalion*, 35.

27 Ibid.; Lieutenant Ian Sinclair to James P. Walker, 3 March, MG 30, E 432, vol. 1, file 17.

28 WD: 14th Bn, 23–8 Feb.; 15th Cdn Bn, 24 Feb.; 16th Cdn Bn, 28 Feb.

29 WD, 1/16th London Regt, 24–6 Feb.

30 T.V. Scudamore, *A Short History of the 7th Battalion CEF* (Vancouver: Anderson and Odlum, 1930); hereafter cited as *7th Battalion*.

31 Currie, 'Red Watch,' 130.

32 Crerar Diary, 27 Feb.

33 Robinson to Mrs Robinson, 17 March.

34 WD, Cyclist Coy, 1–9 March.

35 A.B. Tucker, *The Battle Glory of Canada* (London: Cassell, 1915), 59–60.

36 WD: 1st CFA Bde, 12 March; 2nd CFA Bde, 9–10, 23 March.

37 Tim Cook has recently explored the rumour phenomenon in 'Black-Hearted Traitors, Leaning Virgins, Crucified Martyrs and Cannibalistic Deserters: The Role of Rumours in the Life of the Great War Canadian Soldier,' a

paper delivered at the 18th Military History Colloquium, Wilfrid Laurier University, Waterloo, ON, May 2007.

38 WD, 1st Bde Cdn Engineers, 3–8 March.

39 WD, Signal Coy, 1–9 March; also see Daily Orders, Feb., RG 9, III C 5, vol. 4438.

40 WD, 2nd CFA Bde, 1–9 March.

41 WD, 3rd CFA Bde, 2–9 March and 'Firing Report, 3rd Cdn Artillery Brigade, to 6:00 pm, 3, 8 March 1915,' RG 9, T-10786–7.

42 WD, 1st Cdn Heavy Battery, 1–9 March, RG 9, T-10805.

43 WD, DAC, 1–11 March.

44 WD, Div Train, 4–8 March.

45 *Back to Blighty.*

46 WD: 1st Bn, 1–9 March; 3rd Bn, 5–9 March; 2nd Bn, 1–9 March; 4th Bn, 5–9 March.

47 WD: 7th Bn, 2–8 March; 5th Bn, 5–8 March; 8th Bn, 1–5 March.

48 Alldritt Diary, 2 March.

49 WD, 10th Bn, 5–10 March.

50 WD, 14th Bn, 3 March.

51 Ibid., 4–6 March; WD, 15th Cdn Bn, 5–9 March.

52 WD, 15th Bn, 7 March.

53 WD: 16th Bn, 4–6 March; 13th Cdn Bn, 6–9 March 1915.

54 Currie, *'Red Watch,'* 127–9.

55 Nicholson, *CEF,* 49–50.

56 WD, 2 York and Lancaster Regt, Feb., PRO, WO/95/1610.

57 Robin Prior and Trevor Wilson, *Command on the Western Front: The Military Career of Sir Henry Rawlinson, 1914–18* (Oxford: Blackwell, 1992), 20–73.

58 1st Cdn Div Artillery to 1st, 2nd, 3rd CFA Brigades and Heavy Battery, 'Instructions for Artillery ... ' 9 March, RG 9, T-10786–7.

59 WD, 1st CFA Bde, 10–12 March.

60 Crerar Diary, 12 March.

61 WD: 1st CFA Bde, 17 March to 1 April; 2nd CFA Bde, 10–11, 17 March.

62 WD, 1st Cdn Heavy Battery, 28 March.

63 WD: 2nd CFA Bde, 18 March; 3rd CFA Bde, 11 March.

64 WD, 2nd CFA Bde, 31 March.

65 WD, 1st Bn, 10 March.

66 *Back to Blighty.*

67 WD: 1st Bn, 10–13 March; 2nd Cdn Bn, 10–13 March; 3rd Bn, 13–17 March; 4th Bn, 13–17 March.

68 WD, 16th Bn, 12–13 March; Urquhart, *16th Battalion,* 49–50.

69 Ibid., 47.

70 WD, 15th Bn, 21–4 March; Kim Beattie, *48th Highlanders of Canada, 1891–1928* (Toronto: Southam Press, 1932), 45; Currie, *'Red Watch,'* 143.

71 WD, 1st Cdn Div AA & QMG, 'Instructions for Brigade Grenade Companies,' March, RG 9, T-1921.

72 WD, 1st Bde Cdn Engineers, 1 April.

73 A.J. Kerry and W.A. McDill, *The History of the Corps of Royal Canadian Engineers*, vol. 1, *1749–1939* (Ottawa: Military Engineers Association of Ottawa, 1962), 87.

74 *Back to Blighty.*

75 WD, 1st Cdn Div AA & QMG, 'Instructions for Brigade Grenade Companies,' App 3; 7th Battalion Daily Orders, 1 April, MG 30, E 300, vol. 16, file 35.

76 Michael Boire, 'The Underground War: Military Mining Operations in Support of the Attack on Vimy Ridge, 9 April 1917,' *Canadian Military History* 1, no. 2 (1992), 15–24.

77 WD, 1st Cdn Div AA & QMG, 'G.641, establishing of mining sections,' App 4, April.

78 WD, Signal Coy, 2 April.

79 WD, 1st Bde Cdn Engineers, 29 March to 2 April.

80 WD, Div Train, 30 March and 6 April.

81 WD, 1st Cdn Div Artillery, 27–31 March, RG 9, T-10775.

82 WD: 1st CFA Bde, 30 March; 2nd CFA Bde, 27–31 March; 3rd CFA Bde, 27–30 March.

83 WD, 1st Cdn Heavy Battery, 28 March.

84 WD, DAC, 28 March to 1 April.

85 Tucker, *Battle Glory*, 70.

86 WD, 14th Bn, 1 April; Tucker, *Battle Glory*, 68–9.

87 WD, 1st Bn, 21 March to 5 April.

88 Tucker, *Battle Glory*, 72.

89 WD, 16th Bn, 3 April.

90 WD: 4th Bn, 30 March; 2nd Bn, 31 March.

91 E.N. Copping, 5th Bn, 7, RG 41, B III 1, vol. 8.

92 RG 9, III C 5, vol. 4364, folder 2, file 16.

93 W.W. Murray, *The History of the 2nd Canadian Battalion (Eastern Ontario Regiment), Canadian Expeditionary Force in the Great War, 1914–1919* (Ottawa: Mortimer, 1947), 31.

94 Tucker, *Battle Glory*, 73.

4. Ypres: The Salient and the Armies

1 Dominiek Dendooven, *Ypres as Holy Ground: Menin Gate and Last Post* (Koksijde: De Klaproos, 2003), 113–17.

2 'Row Over Fate of First World War Trench Unearthed on Belgian Motorway Route,' *Guardian Unlimited*, 11 Nov. 2003.

3 Lyn Macdonald, *1915: The Death of Innocence* (New York: Henry Holt, 1993), 188.
4 These references come from an exhibit on the early history of Ypres at the Passchendaele Memorial Museum at Zonnebeke Chateau.
5 *The Western Front, 1914* (Ottawa: Army Historical Section, General Staff, 1957), 144.
6 J.E. Edmonds, *History of the Great War, Military Operations, France and Belgium, 1914*, vol. 2 (London: Macmillan, 1929), 466–9.
7 See Dendooven, *Ypres*, for a discussion of the postwar memorial controversy.
8 *Eye-Witness Accounts of the Great War, Guide to Quotations* (Ieper, Belgium: Flanders Fields Museum, Cloth Hall, Market Square), 6.
9 Smith-Dorrien to General Sir William Robertson, Chief of the General Staff; the complete letter of 27 April is reproduced in Edmonds, *Military Operations, 1915*, vol. 1, App 29, 400–1. Smith-Dorrien's proposal was probably only a convenient pretext for Field Marshal Sir John French to dismiss him. The two men did not get along well. French deeply resented Smith-Dorrien's unsanctioned decision to make a daring stand with II Corps against the First German Army at Le Cateau back in August 1914.
10 This oversimplification has often been repeated; in *When Your Number's Up*, 45, Morton states that Smith-Dorrien wanted to abandon the 'whole' Ypres salient. It was not until June 1915 that Joffre suggested abandoning Ypres in order to free up British forces for duty in other zones of the Western Front. Field Marshal French refused, on the grounds that such a course would also shorten the line for German forces and do irreparable harm to British and Belgian morale. See Edmonds, *Military Operations, 1915*, vol. 2, 85.
11 Edmonds, *Military Operations, 1915*, vol. 1, 271.
12 Although the Allied press frequently exaggerated or misreported details of German atrocities in Belgium, the horror was very real for civilians under German occupation. In 1914 the Germans killed more than 4,400 Belgian and 700 French civilians, among them were many women, children, elderly people. See John Horne and Alan Kramer, *German Atrocities, 1914: A History of Denial* (New Haven, CT: Yale University Press, 2001), 74–5.
13 William Lockhard Campbell to his mother, 21 April 1915, New Liskeard Speakers Collection. All of the primary sources in this chapter refer to 1915, unless otherwise stated.
14 MG 30, E 100, vol. 50.
15 Engineers devised all sorts of inventions to combat the law of gravity. See 'Trench Devices,' Second Army, G.640, Feb., RG 9, III C 5, vol. 4365, folder 4, file 18.
16 Circular Memorandum, 12 April, RG 9, III C 5, vol. 4367, folder 9, file 2.

17 WD, 3rd CFA Bde, Brigade Order No. 14, April.
18 Scudamore, *7th Battalion.*
19 Fetherstonhaugh, *13th Battalion*, 41.
20 *Les Armées Françaises dans la Grande Guerre*, vol. 2, part 3, ch. 15, and Annexe 1397: Ordre géneral no. 1, 16 April.
21 Nicholson, *CEF*, 57; WD, 1st Cdn Div, April, App 4.
22 Edmonds, *Military Operations, 1915*, vol. 1, 161–2.
23 WD, 1st Bde Cdn Engineers, 'Report on Condition of Trenches,' 21 April.
24 WD, 5th Bn, 19–22 April; 'Tactical Situation of 5th Canadian Battalion,' 22 April, RG 9, T-10708.
25 WD, 1st Bde Cdn Engineers, 'Rep on Condition of Trenches.'
26 WD, 8th Bn, 19–20 April.
27 WD, 1st Bde Cdn Engineers, 19–20 April.
28 WD, 15th Bn, 20–1 April; Beattie, *48th Highlanders*, 54–6.
29 Lieutenant Ian Sinclair to Gus, 16 May, MG 30, E 432, vol. 1, file 18.
30 WD, 13th Bn, 16–21 April; Fetherstonhaugh, *13th Battalion*, 43; Sinclair to Gus, 16 May.
31 WD, 2nd CFA Bde, April, App III.
32 Ibid., Special Brigade Order, 15 April, App XIV.
33 V Corps to 1st Cdn Div, 15 April, RG 9, T-7182.
34 Bidwell and Graham, *Fire-Power*, 96–7. The monthly British output of 18-pounder shells reached 128,000 by February.
35 Creelman to Burstall, 16 June 1916, MG 30, E 6, vol. 3, file 17.
36 Burstall Diary, 22 April, MG 30, E 6, vol. 3, file 18.
37 WD, 2nd CFA Bde, 16–18 April.
38 Creelman Diary, 2 May.
39 WD, 1st Bde Cdn Engineers, 21 April. On the chronic shortage of timber on the Western Front, see Murray Maclean, *Farming and Forestry on the Western Front, 1915–1919* (Ipswich, UK: Old Pond Publishing, 2004), 96–7.
40 WD, 1st Cdn Bde, 21 April.
41 Erich von Falkenhayn, *The German General Staff and its Decisions, 1914–1916* (New York: Dodd, Mead, 1920), 58–61.
42 *Der Weltkrieg 1914 bis 1918: Sommer und Herbst 1915*, 8 vols. Prepared for the Germany War Ministry (Berlin: Mittler und Sohn, 1932), 1. The pagination cited here and for all future references to this volume of *Der Weltkrieg* refers to my own translations of relevant passages regarding 1915, and not to the original German version of the text. As *Shoestring Soldiers* goes to press, Mark Osborne Humphries, of Wilfrid Laurier University, and John Maker, of the University of Ottawa, are editing a selected English translation of *Der Weltkrieg*. An Excerpt, 'The First Use of Poison Gas at Ypres, 1915:

A Translation from the German Official History,' appears in *Canadian Military History*, 16, no. 3 (2007), 57–73.

43 Falkenhayn, *German General Staff*, 94; *Der Weltkrieg*, 6.
44 Donald Richter, *British Gas Warfare in World War I* (Lawrence: University of Kansas Press, 1992), 7.
45 Ibid., 7–8.
46 Stéphane Audoin-Rouzeau and Annette Becker, *14–18: Understanding the Great War* (New York: Hill and Wang, 2000), 155–6.
47 Rolf-Dieter Müller, 'Total War as a Result of New Weapons? The Use of Chemical Agents in World War I,' in Roger Chickering and Stig Förster, ed., *Great War, Total War: Combat and Mobilization on the Western Front, 1914–1918* (Cambridge: Cambridge University Press, 2000), 95–111.
48 See Cook, *No Place to Run*; and Edward M. Spiers, 'Chemical Warfare in the First World War,' in Brian Bond, ed., *'Look to Your Front': Studies in the First World War by the British Commission for Military History* (Staplehurst: Spellmount, 1999), 163–78.
49 *Der Weltkrieg, Karte 2, Der Kampf an der Yser und im Ypernbogen*.
50 Ibid., 7.
51 Hermann Cron, *The Imperial German Army, 1914–1918: Organisation, Structure, Orders of Battle* (Solihull: Helion, 2002), 109.
52 Falkenhayn, *German General Staff*, 58–61.
53 Estimates of typical German ammunition expenditure can be found in 'Expenditure of Ammunition on the Western Front,' General Staff, 28 Oct. 1915, RG 9, III C 5, vol. 4364, folder 1, file 11.
54 *Handbook of the German Army in War, January 1917* (Menston: EP Publishing, 1973), 11.
55 Ibid., 26–9.
56 Statistical information pertaining to the Reserve Corps is from the American Expeditionary Forces, Intelligence Section of the General Staff, *Histories of the Two Hundred and Fifty-One Divisions of the German Army which Participated in the War (1914–1918)*, originally published by the United States War Department in 1920 and reprinted by the London Stamp Exchange in 1989.
57 Lutz Knieling and Arnold Bölsche, *Reserve Infanterie-Regiment 234: Ein Querschnitt durch Deutschlands Schicksalsringen* (Zeulenroda: Sporn, 1931), 120–1.

5. 22 April 1915: Green Clouds

1 Duguid, 'Canadians in Battle,' 12–27.
2 MG 30, E 75, vol. 1, file 3.
3 *Back to Blighty.*

4 WD, 1st Cdn Div, 'Report on Operations [Rep Ops] of 1st Canadian Division from 22 April to 4 May 1915,' April 1915. All primary sources in this chapter refer to 1915, unless otherwise stated.

5 2nd Cdn Bde to 1st Cdn Div, 15:05, 16 April, RG 9, reel unknown.

6 WD, V Corps, 'Summary of Operations [Summ Ops] from April 7th to 13th,' App V, RG 9, T-11134.

7 Ibid., 15–21 April.

8 Ibid., 'Summ Ops from April 14th to 20th,' App VIII.

9 See McWilliams and Steel, *Gas!*, 11–20; Dancocks, *Welcome to Flanders Fields*, 108–11.

10 WD, 28th Div, General Staff (GS), 'Report on interrogation of German prisoner,' 14 April, RG 9, T-11134/11139.

11 Ibid., 'Copy of translation of précis of results of interrogation of Julius Rapsahl,' 15 April.

12 WD, V Corps, 'Summ Ops 14–20 April,' App VIII.

13 *Illustrated London News*, 3 April, 444.

14 W.H. Curtis to Mrs Curtis, 16 April, MG 30, E 505.

15 WD: 10th Bn, 15–19 April; 14th Cdn Bn, 16–24 April; 16th Bn, 17–20 April; 7th Bn, 15–16 April.

16 WD, 1st Cdn Div, 'Rep Ops 22 April–4 May.'

17 Alderson Correspondence, 6 May.

18 'Account of the Charge of the Canadian Scottish,' MG 27, II D 23, vol. 3.

19 WD, Div Train, 22 April.

20 WD, Cyclist Coy, 22 April.

21 WD, 2nd Cdn Bde, '2nd Canadian Infantry Brigade: Narrative of Events, 22–27 April 1915,' April.

22 Ibid., '7th Canadian Battalion: Narrative of Events, 22–27 April 1915,' April.

23 L.C. Scott, 7th Bn, (tape 1) 8, RG 41, B III 1, vol. 8.

24 WD, 2nd Cdn Bde, '2nd Cdn Inf Bde: Narrative 22–27 April.'

25 Ibid.

26 WD, 7th Cdn Bn, 'Report of Narrative of Events, Ypres, 22–26 April 1915, A Company, 7th Battalion' April; Hart-McHarg to A and D Companies, 20:30, 22 April, RG 9, T-10709.

27 WD, 2nd Cdn Bde, '7th Cdn Bn: Narrative 22–27 April.' This was not the first time that the 7th Battalion was exposed to chemical agents. The battalion's positions were hit with 'ammonia' shells on 19 April, which according to Scudamore's history, 'made the men cry, but did not seem to do any other damage.'

28 Fetherstonhaugh, *13th Battalion*, 43–5.

29 RG 150, Box 2676–50, 7372–21.

30 'Action in Front of Ypres … ' MG 27, II D 23, vol. 3; Fetherstonhaugh, *13th Battalion*, 45.
31 Philip Jensen to Frank and Arthur Jensen, from 2nd Southern General Hospital, Bristol, 1 May, Black Watch Archive.
32 Ian Sinclair to Mrs Sinclair, 28 April, MG 30, E 432, vol. file 17.
33 'Action in Front of Ypres.' The message is reproduced in Duguid, *Official History*, App 348.
34 Ibid., App 351.
35 Ibid., App 347.
36 Cassar, *Beyond Courage*, 77.
37 Dancocks, *Welcome to Flanders Fields*, 117–18. The messages in question are reproduced in Duguid, *Official History*, App 347–57.
38 Fetherstonhaugh, *14th Battalion*, 38–9; RG 150, Box 1113–78.
39 'Action in Front of Ypres.'
40 Odlum to Hart-McHarg, 24:30, 23 April 1915, RG 9, T-10709.
41 WD, 2nd Cdn Bde, '7th Cdn Bn: Narrative 22–27 April.'
42 WD, 2nd Cdn Bde, '2nd Cdn Inf Bde: Narrative 22–27 April.'
43 Duguid, *Official History*, App 345, 349.
44 RG 150, Box 5179–5.
45 'What a Herald Man Experienced at the Second Battle of Ypres,' *Montreal Herald*, 22 April 1921, 14.
46 10th Battery to 3rd CFA Brigade, April, RG 9, T-10786–7.
47 Beattie, *48th Highlanders*, 64.
48 'Report of Capt. G.M. Alexander,' MG 30, E 46. vol. 1, file 4.
49 10th Bty to 3rd CFA Bde, April.
50 9th Bty to 3rd CFA Bde, April, RG 9, T-10786–7.
51 12th Bty to 3rd CFA Bde, April, RG 9, T-10786–7.
52 RG 150, Box 6951–48.
53 DAC to 3rd CFA Bde, April, RG 9, T-10786–7.
54 Hanson to Burstall, 16 May, MG 30, E 6, vol. 3, file 17.
55 Burstall Diary, 22 April.
56 2nd CFA Bde to 1st Cdn Div Artillery, Firing Report, 23 April, MG 30, E 8, vol. 1, file 2; Knieling and Bölsche, *Reserve Infanterie*, 130–1.
57 Knieling and Bölsche, *Reserve Infanterie*, 130–1.
58 WD, 118th Howitzer Bde, 22 April, RG 9, T-11131.
59 118th Howitzer Bde to 1st Cdn Div Artillery, 28 April, MG 30, E 6, vol. 3, file 17.
60 WD, 1st Cdn Div, 'Rep Ops 22 April – 4 May.'
61 Fetherstonhaugh, *14th Battalion*, 40–1.
62 Ibid., 41–2.

63 Murray, *2nd Cdn Battalions*, 34–6; and WD, 2nd Bn, 22–3 April.
64 WD, 2nd Cdn Bde, 'Counterattack by 10th and 16th Battalions,' April.
65 Edmonds elaborates on these defensive tactics in *Military Operations, 1915,* vol. 1, 210–11.
66 RG 150, Box 7482–61.
67 WD, 2nd Cdn Bde, 'Counterattack.'
68 WD, 10th Bn, 22 April.
69 Knieling and Bölsche, *Reserve Infanterie*, 132.
70 WD: 16th Bn, 22 April; 10th Bn, 24:01, 23 April.
71 WD, 2nd Cdn Bde, 'Counterattack.'
72 Dancocks, *Gallant Canadians*, 39.
73 WD, 10th Bn, 23 April; Urquhart, *16th Battalion*, 59.
74 Urquhart, *16th Battalion*, 60.
75 WD, 16th Bn, 22 April; 'Diary of Operations, 3rd Canadian Infantry Brigade, 22 April to 5 May 1915,' MG 27, II D 23, vol. 3.
76 Murray, *2nd Cdn Battalion*, 38–44.
77 RG 150, Box 647–16.
78 WD, 2nd Cdn Bde, 'Detailed Rep Ops of 2nd Cdn Bn, 22–6 April 1915'; Murray, *2nd Cdn Battalion*, 43–4.
79 WD, 2nd Cdn Bde, 'Counterattack.'
80 Urquhart, *16th Battalion*, 61.
81 B.C. Lunn, 16th Bn (tape 2), 10, RG 41, B III 1, vol. 9.
82 WD, 2nd Cdn Bde, 'Counterattack.'
83 WD, 10th Bn, 22 April.
84 9th Bty to 3rd CFA Bde, April.
85 3rd CFA Bde, H9 Report, April, RG 9, T-10786–7.
86 12th Bty to 3rd CFA Bde, April.
87 For a discussion of officer-man relations in the BEF, see Gary Sheffield, *Leadership in the Trenches: Officer-Man Relations, Morale and Discipline in the British Army in the Era of the First World War* (Houndmills: Macmillan, 2000).
88 WD, 1st Cdn Div, 'Rep Ops 22 April–4 May.'
89 Leckie to Joe Edwards, May, MG 30, E 84.

6. 23 April 1915: Holding Back the Tide

1 Fetherstonhaugh, *13th Battalion*, 46.
2 RG 150, Box 1232–31.
3 WD, 13th Cdn Bn, 22 April 1915. All primary sources in this chapter refer to 1915, unless otherwise stated.
4 Duguid, *Official History*, 266.

5 Dancocks, *Welcome to Flanders Fields*, 138. Alderson's private correspondence reveals that he considered Turner unfit for divisional command. No mention, either positive or negative, is made of Mercer. Alderson correspondence, 21 Aug.

6 WD, 85th Bde, 'Narratives of Buffs / Col. Geddes' force,' 22–4 April, RG 9, T-11349.

7 F.W. Hill, 'History of the Canadian Forces in the Great War: A Review,' *Canadian Defence Quarterly* 16, no. 2 (1939), 211–14.

8 WD, 2nd Cdn Bde, '2nd Cdn Inf Bde: Narrative 22–27 April,' and '7th Cdn Bn: Narrative 22–27 April.' Fetherstonhaugh, *13th Battalion*, 46–7.

9 WD, 1st Cdn Div, 'Rep Ops 22 April–4 May.'

10 Fetherstonhaugh, *13th Battalion*, 48.

11 'Action in Front of Ypres.'

12 Fetherstonhaugh, *13th Battalion*, 48–9.

13 Philip Jensen to Frank and Arthur Jensen, 1 May.

14 RG 150, Box 6033–52.

15 William Johnson to his wife, 3 May, MG 30, E 321.

16 Odlum to Roberts, 7 Oct., MG 30, E 300, vol. 16, file 20.

17 RG 150, Box 7421–2.

18 WD, 2nd Cdn Bde, '7th Cdn Bn: Narrative 22–27 April'

19 WD, 3rd Cdn Field (Fd) Ambulance, 23 April, RG 9, T-10914.

20 WD, 16th Bn, 23 April.

21 3rd Fd Coy to 1st Bde Cdn Engineers, 11:30, 23 April, and 'Narrative of Work Performed by 3rd Field Company,' RG 9, III C 5, vol. 4367, folder 9, file 5.

22 WD, 2nd CFA Bde, 20 April.

23 2nd CFA Bde to 1st Cdn Div Artillery, Sit Rep, 23 April, MG 30, E 8, vol. 1, file 2.

24 2nd CFA Bde to 1st Cdn Div Artillery, Firing Rep, 23 April.

25 10th Bn to 3rd Cdn Bde, 16:10, 23 April, RG 9, T-10711–12; emphasis in original.

26 10th Cdn Bn to 3rd Cdn Bde, 17:25, 17:35, 23 April.

27 WD, 85th Bde, 'Narratives of 3 Middlesex / Col. Geddes' force,' 23 April.

28 WD, 4th Bn, 22–3 April.

29 Duguid to Ralston, 26 May 1934, RG 24, vol. 1904, file DHS 5–7–4.

30 WD, 1st Cdn Bn, 'Sketch Shewing Attack of April 23rd 1915 made jointly by 1st Cdn Bn (Lieut-Col Hill) and 4th Cdn Bn (Lieut-Col Birchall),' 23 April.

31 F. Douglas Reville, *History of the County of Brant* (Brantford, ON: Hurley Printing Company, 1920), 457.

32 Bennett to Young, 27 April 1920, MG 30, E 46, vol. 1, file 4.

33 An eyewitness account from Private Albert Adams of B Company gives a start time of 06:30. Adams's letter is reprinted in Reville, *Brant*, 455–6.

34 WD, 1st Bn, App B, 'Detailed Narration of Operations, 23 April.'

35 1st Bn to 1st Cdn Bde, 07:00, 23 April, RG 9, vol. 4866, T-10665.

36 4th Bn to 1st Cdn Bde, ??:00, 23 April. As of 07:20 Mercer was in telephone communication with both battalion headquarters. The lines remained open for the rest of the day.

37 1st Bn to 1st Cdn Bde, 07:45, 23 April.

38 1st Cdn Bde to 1st Cdn Div, 07:20, 8:20, 23 April.

39 WD, 85th Bde, 'Narratives … Geddes' force,' 23 April.

40 1st Cdn Bde to 1st Bn and 4th Bn, 08:30, 23 April.

41 4th Bn to 1st Cdn Bde, 10:50, 23 April.

42 1st Bn to 1st Cdn Bde, 10:30, 23 April.

43 1st Cdn Bde to 1st Bn and 4th Bn, 11:07, 23 April.

44 1st Cdn Bde to 1st Cdn Div, 11:25, 23 April.

45 1st Cdn Div to French HQ, 11:35, 23 April.

46 4th Bn to 1st Cdn Bde, 12:15, 23 April.

47 1st Cdn Div to 1st Cdn Bde, 12:35 and 13:20, 23 April.

48 WD, 28th Div, 'Narrative of Events 3rd Middlesex with Colonel Geddes' Detachments, 22 to 24th April,' RG 9, T-11134/11139, and Private Frank Betts to Mrs Betts, 28 April, Brant County Archives.

49 Nicholson, *CEF*, 68–70; WD, 13th Bde, 23 April, RG 9, T-11134; WD, 28th Div, 'Narrative … Geddes' Detachments.'

50 WD, 4th Bn, 23 April. It is possible that some of the missing men later found their way back to the battalion.

51 WD, 85th Bde, 'Narratives … Geddes' force,' 23 April.

52 WD, 1st Cdn Bde, 23 April, and Mercer Diary, 23 April.

53 See Wakeling's letter in Reville, *Brant*, 453.

54 Morrison to Burstall, 24 April, MG 30, E 6, vol. 3, file 18.

55 Burstall Diary, Sketch Map, 22 April, MG 30, E 6, vol. 3, file 18.

56 10th Bty to 3rd CFA Bde, April.

57 118th Howitzer Bde to 1st Cdn Div Artillery, 28 April, MG 30, E 6, vol. 3, file 17.

58 1st Cdn Bde to 1st CFA Bde, 06:20, 23 April.

59 10th Battery to 3rd CFA Bde, April.

60 Burstall Diary, 23 April.

61 9th Bty to 3rd CFA Bde, April.

62 12th Bty to 3rd CFA Bde, April.

63 Duguid, *Official History*, 267–70.

64 Reville, *Brant*, 455–6. It appears that 1st Bn troops employed similar tactics. See *Back to Blighty*.

65 Birchall, *Rapid Training*, 45.
66 Reprinted in Reville, *Brant*, 457.
67 *Der Weltkrieg*, 10–12; Nicholson, *CEF*, 70.
68 Loomis to Turner, FM 000201, 23 April, MG 30, E 46, vol. 1, file 5.
69 S.H. Radford, 1st Bn, 6–7, RG 41, B III 1, vol. 7.

7. 24 April 1915: The Breaking Point

1 Snow had been crushed under his own horse during the Battle of the Marne. See J.M. Bourne, *Who's Who in World War One* (London: Routledge, 2001), 270.
2 Creelman Diary, 29 April 1915. All primary sources in this chapter refer to 1915, unless otherwise indicated.
3 J.A. Currie to Turner, 24 April, MG 30, E 46, vol. 1, file 5, FM 000185, 000231, 000239.
4 *Illustrated London News*, 8 May, 583.
5 Nicholson, *CEF*, 71–2; AEF, *251 German Army Divisions*, 507, 515.
6 WD, 2nd Cdn Bde, '8th Battalion Narrative of Events …,' RG 9, T-10668.
7 Ibid.
8 J.A. Currie to 3rd Cdn Bde, 6 May, MG 27, II D 23, vol. 3.
9 Beattie, *48th Highlanders*, 70–1.
10 RG 150, Box 5962–8; RG 9, II A 5, vol. 13, C-1863.
11 'Report of No. 3 Company, 15th Bn,' April, MG 30, E 46, vol. 1, file 4.
12 Dancocks, *Welcome to Flanders Fields*, 182; Nicholson, *CEF*, 72.
13 10th Bty to 3rd CFA Bde, April.
14 WD, 3rd CFA Bde, 24 April.
15 9th Bty to 3rd CFA Bde, April.
16 12th Bty to 3rd CFA Bde, April.
17 WD, 8th Cdn Bn, April sketch map, RG 9, T-10710–11.
18 WD, 2nd Cdn Bde, '8th Bn Narrative.'
19 Osborne Report, April, RG 9, III C 5, folder 3, file 8.
20 WD, 14th Bn, 'Particulars and Summary of Operations,' April; Fetherstonhaugh, *14th Battalion*, 39–40.
21 'Action in Front of Ypres.'
22 C.B. Pitblado to Mrs Pitblado, from Bruderhaus, Paderborn, Westfalen, 5 May, Black Watch Archive; Fetherstonhaugh, *13th Battalion*, 50–1.
23 'Narrative of Brigadier-General G.S. Tuxford,' 10 March 1916.
24 WD, 5th Bn, App A, 'Tactical situation 5th Cdn Bn,' April.
25 'Narrative … Tuxford.'
26 WD, 2nd Cdn Bde, '8th Bn Narrative.'
27 Ibid.

28 Alldritt Diary, 24 April.
29 Dancocks, *Welcome to Flanders Fields*, 216.
30 WD, 2nd Cdn Bde, '8th Bn Narrative.'
31 The other three companies of 7th Battalion (B, C, and D) were at Keerselaere under the command of Major Odlum.
32 WD, 7th Cdn Bn, 'Report of Narrative of Events, Ypres, 22–26 April 1915, A Company, 7th Battalion.' After being seriously wounded on 24 April, Warden returned to Canada where he was promoted to the rank of lieutenant-colonel and authorized to raise the 102nd Battalion. Warden's men knew him as 'Honest John,' a sobriquet that lends credence to his eyewitness testimony. See Leonard McLeod Gould, '102nd Infantry Battalion, CEF,' www .donlowconcrete.com/102.
33 WD, 2nd Cdn Bde, '2nd Cdn Inf Bde: Narrative, 22–27 April.'
34 Hyatt, *Currie*, 38.
35 Alldritt Diary, 24 April.
36 WD, 7th Cdn Bn, 'Narrative … Ypres.'
37 'Diary Ops, 3rd Cdn Inf Bde, 22 April to 5 May.'
38 Dancocks, *Welcome to Flanders Fields*, 164–5.
39 Duguid, *Official History*, App 529.
40 8th Bn to 10th Bn, 24 April, RG 9, T-10711–12.
41 WD, 2nd Cdn Bde, 'Counterattack.'
42 WD, 7th Cdn Bn, 'Narrative … Ypres.'
43 WD, 2nd Cdn Bde, 'Counterattack.'
44 Thompson Report, 3rd Cdn Bde, 1915, RG 9, MG 27, II D 23, vol. 3, file 3–9.
45 Thorn to Odlum, 1 July, MG 30, E 300, vol. 16, file 26.
46 Scudamore, *7th Battalion.*
47 WD, 2nd Cdn Bde, '7th Cdn Bn: Narrative 22–27 April.'
48 Thorn to Odlum, 1 July.
49 N. Rice, 7th Bn, (tape 1) 3, RG 41, B III 1, vol. 8.
50 WD, 2nd Cdn Bde, '7th Cdn Bn: Narrative 22–27 April.'
51 *Der Weltkrieg*, 12.
52 Bellew's tenacity was rewarded with the Victoria Cross. See Arthur Bishop, 'Canada and the Victoria Cross: The Class of 1915,' *Legion Magazine*, (July/Aug. 2004), 34–7; 7th Cdn Bn to 2nd Cdn Bde, 9 May, MG 30, E 300, vol. 16, file 21.
53 234th Infantry Regiment to 101st Infantry Brigade, 28 May, in Knieling and Bölsche, *Reserve Infanterie.*
54 Byng-Hall to Odlum, 1 June, MG 30, E 300, vol. 16, file 24.
55 '3 Years and 8 Months in a German Prison,' a postwar account left by R. Carew Hunt, the stretcher bearer, confirms that he did indeed have a bottle of iodine shot out of his own hand. MG 30, E 300, vol. 24.

56 Byng-Hall to Odlum, 1 June, MG 30, E 300, vol. 16, file 24.
57 See J.C. Thorn, *Three Years a Prisoner in Germany* (Vancouver: Cowan and Brookhouse, 1919).
58 Duguid, *Official History*, App 565.
59 Photostat (2), 2nd Cdn Bde to 85th Bde, 24 April, MG 30, E 75, vol. 1.
60 Duguid, *Official History*, App 565a. Currie also assured 85th Brigade, on his right, that 5th Battalion would remain in contact with its left flank; see App 565b in Duguid, ibid.
61 Photostat (7) from Lipsett, 24 April, MG 30, E 75, vol. 1.
62 WD, 2nd Cdn Bde, '8th Bn Narrative.'
63 Photostat (4) Currie to Lipsett, 24 April, MG 30, E 75, vol. 1.
64 WD, 2nd Cdn Bde, '2nd Cdn Inf Bde: Narrative 22–27 April'; Duguid, *Official History*, App 566.
65 WD, 2nd Cdn Bde, 'Counterattack.'
66 Duguid, *Official History*, App 580.
67 Ibid., 586.
68 Ibid., 590.
69 The 150th Brigade remained at the GHQ line. WD, 28th Div, 'Report by York & Durham Infantry Brigade, 24–25 April 1915,' RG 9, T-11134/11139.
70 Thompson Report.
71 'Action in Front of Ypres.'
72 WD, 14th Bn, 'Particulars and Summary of Operations,' April; 14th Bn Report 'Covering Ypres Operation,' 6 May, MG 27, IID23, vol. 3.
73 'Account of the Charge of the Canadian Scottish'; Murray, *2nd Canadian Battalion* 49–50.
74 Murray, *2nd Canadian Battalion*, 51.
75 WD, 2nd Cdn Bn, 'Detailed Report on Operations of 2nd Cdn Bn, 22–26 April 1915.'
76 *A Brief History of the 3rd Canadian Battalion*, 3; WD, 3rd Bn, 24 April.
77 WD, 2nd Cdn Bde, '2nd Cdn Inf Bde: Narrative 22–27 April 1915.'
78 'Statement of Major E.F. Lynn, MC … ' MG 30, E 75, vol. 2.
79 Ibid.
80 Straggling was not limited to 1st Division troops in 1915; similar complaints were to resurface throughout the war. Operation orders from Oct. 1916 emphasize that wounded were to be evacuated only by designated stretcher bearers, while enemy prisoners were to be marched away in large groups, under officer supervision. See Operation Order, 4th Cdn Bn, 7 Oct. 1916, 'Wounded, Prisoners,' RG 9, T-10707.
81 'Statement of Major E.F. Lynn.'
82 Lynn to Irving, 11 May, RG 9, III C 5, vol. 4367, folder 9, file 7.

83 WD, 2nd Cdn Bde, '2nd Cdn Inf Bde: Narrative 22–7 April.'
84 Irving to Armstrong, 12 May, and Curry to Irving, 12 May, RG 9, III C 5, vol. 4367, folder 9, file 7.
85 WD, 2nd Cdn Bde, '7th Cdn Bn: Narrative 22–27 April.'
86 Kemmis-Betty to 1st Cdn Div, cited by Currie in WD, 2nd Cdn Bde, '2nd Cdn Inf Bde: Narrative 22–7 April.'
87 WD, 84th Bde, 24 April, RG 9, T-11349.
88 WD, 2nd Cdn Bde, '8th Bn Narrative.'
89 WD, 2nd CFA Bde, 24 April. The remaining batteries had been evacuated behind the GHQ line earlier that afternoon. With a shortage of ammunition, there was little alternative.
90 Hanson to Burstall, 16 May, RG 9, MG 30, E 6, file 17.
91 Urquhart, *Currie*, 92.
92 WD, 82nd Infantry Bde, 1st Royal Irish Regiment, 24 April, RG 9, T-11349.
93 WD, 150th Infantry Bde, 24 April, RG 9, T-11350.
94 WD, 5th Bn, App A, 'Tactical situation 5th Cdn Bn.'
95 1st Cdn Div Artillery to 2nd CFA Bde, 24 April, MG 30, E 8, vol. 1.
96 2nd CFA Bde to 1st Cdn Div Artillery, 24 April.
97 McLeod to Burstall, 16 May, RG 9, MG 30, E 6, file 17.
98 WD, DAC, 23–4 April.
99 Creelman Diary, 2 May.
100 'Narrative of Work Performed by 1st Field Company,' April, RG 9, III C 5, vol. 4367, folder 9, file 5.
101 'Reconnaissance of line beyond Yser canal,' 24 April; 'Report on work GHQ line,' 24–5 April, RG 9, T-10824.
102 'Narrative of Work … 2nd Field Company.'
103 'Narrative of Work … 3rd Field Company.'
104 Timothy H.E. Travers, 'Allies in Conflict: The British and Canadian Official Historians and the Real Story of Second Ypres,' *Journal of Contemporary History* 24, no. 2 (1989), 301–25; also see Travers, 'Currie and 1st Canadian Division at Second Ypres, April 1915: Controversy, Criticism and Official History' *Canadian Military History* 5, no. 2 (1996), 7–15.
105 Elizabeth Greenhalgh, of the Australian Defence Force Academy, has shown how historians have unfairly projected General Philippe Pétain's 'defeatism' from 1940 backward onto his reaction to the German counteroffensive of March 1918, thereby elevating Field Marshal Douglas Haig's reputation while further damaging Pétain's. See her 'Myth and Memory: Sir Douglas Haig and the Imposition of Allied Unified Command in March 1918,' *Journal of Military History* 68, no. 3 (2004), 771–820.

106 On Turner see Leppard, 'The Dashing Subaltern,' and Cook, 'The Blind Leading the Blind.'
107 Duguid, *Official History*, App 587.
108 In his battle report to V Corps, dated 28 May, Snow failed even to mention Currie's visit. MG 30, E 46, vol. 1, file 4.
109 Duguid, *Official History*, App 600.
110 Ibid., App 601.
111 Ibid., App 612.
112 Edmonds reviews the strengths of the GHQ positions in *Military Operations, 1915,* vol. I, 161–2.
113 Ibid., Sketch 19, 24 May.
114 Sinclair Diary, n.d., MG 30, E 432, vol. 1, file 2.
115 'Ypres, 1915, Creelman,' n.d., MG 30, E 8, vol. 1, file 2.
116 WD, 2nd Cdn Bde, 'Counterattack.' See also Tim Cook, "My Whole Heart and Soul Is in This War': The Letters and War Service of Sergeant G.L. Ormsby,' *Canadian Military History* 15, no. 1 (2006), 52.
117 Currie, '*Red Watch*,' 241–3, and House of Commons, 1049–50, 22 Feb. 1916, MG 30, E 46, vol. 12. It is clear from Warden's testimony that many soldiers withdrew between 05:00 and 06:00, but Osborne's D Company report verifies Currie's claim that part of the battalion remained in position until 09:00.
118 Currie Reports, RG 9, III C 3, vol. 4077, folder 3, file 7.
119 Alderson Correspondence, 20 Sep. Alderson was probably writing to E.T.H. Hutton regarding the court martial. Although he does not mention J.A. Currie by name, Alderson makes clear reference to the 'worst' battalion commander from 1st Division who 'practically' abandoned his men at Ypres.

8. 25–26 April 1915: The Canadian Denouement

1 *Der Weltkrieg*, 14–15.
2 Duguid, *Official History*, 335; Nicholson, *CEF*, 80.
3 Copies were distributed to the British 10th, 13th and 150th Brigades, the 1st, 2nd, and 3rd Canadian Brigades, the Canadian Divisional Artillery, 27th Division, and V Corps.
4 Operation Order No. 10, 24 April, MG 27, II D 23, vol. 3. All primary sources in this chapter refer to 1915, unless otherwise indicated.
5 The 10th Brigade comprised the 1st Royal Warwickshire Regiment, the 2nd Seaforth Highlanders, the 1st Royal Irish Fusiliers, the 2nd Royal Dublin Fusiliers, and the 1/7th Argyll and Sutherland Highlanders. All

were pre-war regular regiments, except for the Argylls, who came from the Territorial Force.

6 Edmonds, *Military Operations, 1915,* vol. 1, 240–3; John Dixon, *Magnificent but Not War: The Battle of Ypres, 1915* (Barnsley: Leo Cooper, 2003), 103–13.

7 Thompson Report.

8 Dixon, *Magnificent,* 109–11.

9 *Der Weltkrieg,* 14.

10 WD, 1st Cdn Bde, 24–5 April.

11 WD, 2nd Cdn Bde, '2nd Cdn Inf Bde: Narrative, 22–27 April.'

12 Lester Stevens, 8th Bn, 10–11, RG 41, B III 1, vol. 8.

13 WD, 2nd Cdn Bde, '8th Narrative.'

14 WD, 151st Infantry Bde, 25 April, RG 9, T-11350.

15 WD, 5th Bn, 25 April, and 'Tactical situation 5th Canadian Battalion,' 25 April.

16 'Narrative … Tuxford.'

17 An account by Tuxford's adjutant, Captain Edward Hilliam, states that the withdrawal order was not received until 16:00. See 'Tactical situation 5th Cdn Bn,' 25 April.

18 'Narrative … . Tuxford.'

19 WD, 2nd Cdn Bde, '8th Bn Narrative.' The timing of Northwood's order suggests that 8th Bn elements remained in the original front line almost as long as Tuxford's companies.

20 'Narrative … Tuxford.'

21 WD, 2nd Cdn Bde, '8th Bn Narrative.'

22 A.H. Fisher, 8th Bn, (tape 1) 15–16, RG 41, B III 1, vol 8.

23 WD, 2nd Cdn Bde, '7th Cdn Bn: Narrative 22–27 April.' For a detailed account of 10th Bn's experience that morning, see Dancocks, *Gallant Canadians,* 41–2.

24 The most recent study of the battle from the British perspective is equally critical of Arthur Currie's leadership on 25 April. See Dixon, *Magnificent,* 117.

25 WD, 85th Infantry Bde, 25 April, RG 9, T-11349.

26 1st Cdn Div to 1st Cdn Bde, 01:50, 25 April, RG 9, T-10665.

27 1st Cdn Bde to Hull, 07:45, 25 April, and 1st Cdn Bde to 2nd Cdn Bde and Hull, 09:45, 25 April.

28 Mercer Diary, 25 April.

29 'Action in Front of Ypres.'

30 Fetherstonhaugh, *13th Battalion,* 51–2.

31 Fetherstonhaugh, *14th Battalion,* 45.

32 Beattie, *48th Highlanders,* 78–9.

33 Duguid, *Official History,* 635; App 677.

34 'Reconnaissance of line beyond Yser canal,' 24 April; 'Report on work GHQ line,' 24–5 April; Message to 1st Fd Coy, 25–6 April, RG 9, T-10824.

35 1st Cdn Div Engineers to 1st Fd Coy, 07:55 and 08:15, 25 April.

36 'Narrative of Work … 1st Fd Company.'

37 'Narrative of Work … 2nd Fd Company.'

38 WD, ADMS, 24–5 April, RG 9, T-10910.

39 WD, Cyclist Coy, 25–6 April.

40 WD, 2nd CFA Bde, April, App XV.

41 WD, 2nd CFA Bde, 25 April.

42 Burstall Diary, 25.

43 9th Bty to 3rd CFA Bde, April.

44 WD, 3rd CFA Bde, 25 April.

45 12th Bty to 3rd CFA Bde, April.

46 Ibid.

47 Dunlop Diary, 25 April.

48 WD, DAC, 25 April.

49 Rawling, *Surviving Trench Warfare*, 35; RG 24, vol. 1866, file 9.

50 Except where otherwise indicated, these statistics are based on information in the April war diary of the 1st Canadian Division. Minor adjustments can made since some men may have died of wounds after 30 April, while others presumed missing later turned up, or were determined to have been killed or died of wounds while in captivity. Where possible, corrections have been footnoted directly on the table.

51 Field Message Book, 26 Feb. to 15 Nov., MG 30, E 300, vol. 15.

52 It will be recalled from Captain Irving's engineering report that the 5th Bn enjoyed no defensive advantages in Section 1 compared with the other battalions in Sections 2, 3, and 4.

53 Currie, '*Red Watch*,' 271.

54 Desmond Morton, *Silent Battle: Canadian Prisoners of War in Germany, 1914–1919* (Toronto: Lester, 1992), 26–7.

55 RG 9, III C 5, vol. 4076, folder 5, file 2.

56 On the reporting of gas casualties, see Cook, *No Place to Run*.

57 234th Infantry Regiment to 101st Infantry Brigade, 28 May, in Knieling and Bölsche, *Reserve Infanterie*.

58 For a recent study in the Canadian context, see Mark Osborne Humphries, 'The Treatment of Evacuated War Neuroses Casualties in the Canadian Expeditionary Force, 1914–19,' (Master's thesis, Wilfrid Laurier University, 2005).

59 'B.C. Battalion Did Its Duty, Says Maj. Odlum,' *Advertiser*, 23 June, MG 30, E 300, vol. 16, file 23; Mrs Cooper to Odlum, 17 July, MG 30, E 300, vol. 16, file 26.

60 Ian Sinclair to Mrs Sinclair, 28 April, MG 30, E 432, vol, file 17.

61 RG 150, Box 4508–33.

62 Creelman Diary, 9 May.

63 RG 150, Box 4030–23; N. Frey and E.N. Olson, 'Cardiac Hypertrophy: The Good, The Bad and the Ugly,' *Annual Review of Physiology* 65 (2003), 45–79.

64 Creelman Diary, 2 May.

65 Ibid., 13 May 1915.

66 RG 150, Box 2131–43.

67 In Jan. 1917 Creelman was awarded the Distinguished Service Order and mentioned in despatches before he returned to Canada the following month.

68 WD, 1st Cdn Div Admin, April, RG 9, T-1921.

69 John Baynes, *Morale: A Study of Men and Courage, The Second Scottish Rifles at the Battle of Neuve Chapelle, 1915* (New York: Praeger, 1967), 3–14.

70 Sheffield, *Leadership in the Trenches*, 103–9.

71 Refer to Smith, *Between Mutiny and Obedience*, 16–17.

72 WD, 1st Cdn Div, AA & QMG, App 10, 5 May.

73 Fetherstonhaugh, *13th Battalion*, 52. This early infusion explains why the battalion received only 61 men with the draft arriving on 5 May.

74 WD, 5th Bn, 1–11 May.

75 Ian Sinclair to Mr Sinclair, 8 May.

76 WD, 4th Bn, 29 April to 6 May.

77 WD, 7th Bn, 1–16 May.

78 WD, 14th Bn, 7 May.

79 Ibid., 5–10 May.

80 WD, 1st Cdn Div AA & QMG, April, App 12.

81 Ibid., App 9, 1 May.

82 Even before the battle had ended, the masks were already illustrated and carefully explained in newspapers. See the *Illustrated London News*, 8 May, 590.

83 WD, 1st Cdn Div AA & QMG, 'Precautions against Asphyxiating Gases,' 2 May.

84 *Back to Blighty.*

85 On respirator development, see Cook, *No Place to Run*, 39–45.

86 *Vancouver World*, 22 April 1916, 1.

87 Smith-Dorrien to Alderson, 6 May, MG 30, E 300, vol. 6.

88 WD, 14th Bn, 11 May.

89 'Canadians' "Glorious Gallantry" Says French,' *Expositor*, 23 April 1916.

90 MG 30, E 300, vol. 16.

91 Betts Papers, Brant County Archives.

92 'St Julien Day Stirred City,' *Toronto Globe*, 23 April 1918.

9. On the Offensive: The La Bassée Front, May–June 1915

1 I am indebted to Richard Holt, a doctoral candidate at the University of Western Ontario, for these estimates, drawn from his research on Canada's wartime reinforcement system.

2 *Back to Blighty.*

3 On the training of the 2nd Division, see David Campbell, 'The Divisional Experience in the CEF: A Social and Operational History of the 2nd Canadian Division, 1915–1918,' (PhD diss., University of Calgary, 2003).

4 Duguid, *Official History,* 498.

5 Smith, *Between Mutiny and Obedience,* 16–17.

6 William James Philpott, *Anglo-French Relations and Strategy on the Western Front, 1914–18* (New York: St Martin's Press, 1996), 5–12.

7 George Cassar, *The Tragedy of Sir John French* (Newark: University of Delaware Press, 1985), 227.

8 A. Kearsey, *1915 Campaign in France: The Battles of Aubers Ridge, Festubert and Loss, Considered in relation to Field Service Regulations* (Uckfield: Naval and Military Press Reprint, 1929), 11–12.

9 Robert Blake (ed.), *Private Papers of Douglas Haig, 1914–1919* (London: Eyre and Spottswoode, 1952), 93; Haig's emphasis.

10 J.E. Edmonds, *Military Operations, France and Belgium, 1915,* vol. 2, 40–1.

11 Paul Guinn, *British Strategy and Politics, 1914 to 1918* (Oxford: Clarendon Press, 1965), 88–9.

12 John Terraine, *Douglas Haig: The Educated Soldier* (London: Hutchinson, 1963), 125–6.

13 WD, DAC, 23 May 1915. All primary sources in this chapter refer to 1915, unless otherwise indicated.

14 Andrew Motion (ed.), *First World War Poems* (London: Faber and Faber, 2003), 41–2.

15 W.H. Curtis to Mrs Curtis, 2 June, MG 30, E 505.

16 Kearsey, *1915,* 11.

17 From the diary of 8th Westphalian Infantry Regiment 'Herzog Ferdinand von Braunschweig' (57th Regiment), translated by Christopher and Ute Wilde Linnell. The 'apple orchard' referred to in this passage is probably synonymous with the Canadian Orchard situated near M.9 and N.13 on British maps.

18 AEF, *251 German Army Divisions,* 55–7.

19 Kearsey, *1915,* 32–3.

20 WD, 16th Bn, 18 May.

21 Fetherstonhaugh, *14th Battalion,* 55–6; Urquhart, *16th Battalion,* 76–7, 140–1.

22 WD, 1st Cdn Div, AA & QMG, 19 May.

23 Gary Sheffield and John Bourne (eds.), *Douglas Haig: War Diaries and Letters, 1914–1918* (London: Weidenfeld and Nicolson, 2005), 125–6; Haig's emphasis.

24 '8th Bn Narrative.'

25 WD, 1st Cdn Div, GS, 20 May, RG 9, T-7183–4.

26 The houses are marked on Figure 9.6 as P.13 through P.16.

27 Operation Order No. 15, 20 May, RG 9, T-7183–4.

28 According to Duguid, the original order was rescinded because 2nd Division, which was then in the process of being relieved by 51st Highland Division, did not receive word to attack the assigned cluster of houses in a timely fashion. A hasty discussion between Haig and Alderson resulted in the new plan. It is less than obvious how this compromise eased the challenge for Canadian troops. See Duguid, *Official History*, 472.

29 Operation Order No. 16, 20 May, RG 9, T-10668.

30 RG 150, Box 3895–20. As a 20–year-old student Guthrie had served briefly in 1902 with the 4th Canadian Mounted Rifles in South Africa. See RG 38, A1a, vol. 41, T-2071.

31 WD, 10th Bn, 20 May.

32 Currie's after-action report for 2nd Brigade lists 18 officers and 260 other ranks killed, wounded, or missing for the period 19–24 May, but it is unknown how many were suffered on 20 May. See 'Narrative of Events, Festubert Action, 2nd Infantry Brigade,' May, RG 9, T-7183–4.

33 10th Bn Narrative of Events, 19–23 May, RG 9, T-10668.

34 P.A. Guthrie, *Festubert* (Montreal: Montreal Daily Star, 1916), 9–12.

35 5th Bn Narrative of Events, 19–27 May, RG 9, T-10668.

36 The body of 38–year-old Alexander Mackay was not recovered; he is commemorated among the missing war dead on the Vimy Monument. See Commonwealth War Graves Commission, Casualty Details, MacKay, Alexander Henry. Mackay joined the CEF in Dec. 1914 and had served four years in the Saskatchewan Light Horse before the war. RG 150, Box 6919–1.

37 WD, 7th Bn, 20 May 1915; 8th Bn, 20 May.

38 On the theory of 'hidden' and 'official transcripts' see Smith, *Between Mutiny and Obedience*, 11–19. Ordinary soldiers constructed the hidden transcript of a battle or other event in their private conversations, letters, and diaries. The official transcript, presented in formal military reports and press releases, often omitted or modified the undesirable, embarrassing, or otherwise inconvenient truths that characterized the hidden transcript.

39 On Guthrie's experience at Second Ypres, see Dancocks, *Gallant Canadians*, 38; All of the Currie biographies underscore the general's extreme distaste for the Festubert attacks.

40 In his biography of Currie, Dancocks noted that the 10th Bn was 'slaughtered' in this first attack, yet cited no source nor any precise figures; however, in his history of the 10th Bn, published three years later, Dancocks stated simply that 'casualties were not recorded.' See Dancocks, *Sir Arthur Currie*, 56, and *Gallant Canadians*, 90.

41 Robert B. Ross, *The Fifty-First in France* (London: Hodder and Stoughton, 1918), 94–5.

42 Unless otherwise noted, the details of the attack are based on Beattie's *48th Highlanders*, 85–9.

43 '8th Bn Narrative.'

44 WD, 8th Bn, 20 May.

45 WD, 15th Bn, 20 May; RG 150, Box 6459–40. Muir is commemorated on the Vimy Memorial.

46 WD, 16th Bn, 19–20 May.

47 Major Peck had joined the battalion less than one month earlier as a reinforcement after the worst of the fighting at Ypres. He was destined to command the battalion and win the Victoria Cross later in the war.

48 RG 150, box 6375–32.

49 Urquhart, *16th Battalion*, 80.

50 A.M. McLennan, 16th Bn, (tape 2) 8, RG 41, B III 1, vol. 9.

51 RG 150, Box 7693–14.

52 Guthrie, *Festubert*, 15.

53 '10th Bn Narrative of Events,' 19–23 May.

54 '5th Bn Narrative of Events,' 19–27 May.

55 Guthrie, *Festubert*, 13.

56 'Narrative of Events, Festubert Action, 2nd Infantry Brigade,' May 1915.

57 Ibid.

58 '10th Bn Narrative.'

59 Dancocks, *Gallant Canadians*, 50.

60 WD, 10th Cdn Bn, 22–6 May.

61 Duguid, *Official History*, 479–81.

62 RG 150, Box 6497–50.

63 The Indian Corps supplied three 1.5-inch mortars along with their crews and ammunition. A light mountain gun was also brought forward to provide direct fire support. See Operation Order No. 17, 23 May, RG 9, T-10814.

64 Guthrie, *Festubert*, 13.

65 'Narrative … Festubert Action, 2nd Inf Bde.'

66 Before the war Alan Powley served in the Active Militia with the 88th Regiment. He joined the 30th Battalion in Nov. 1914 before reassignment to the 7th Bn, probably in early May. Powley ultimately attained the rank of lieutenant-colonel, in command of the 143rd Bn in 1916. RG 150, Box 7950–35.

67 E.N. Copping, 5th Bn, (tape 2) 3–4, RG 41, B III 1, vol. 8.
68 7th Bn Ops, 19–24 May, RG 9, T-10668. The following field messages are also relevant: BC 66, 07:30, 24 May 1915; Gibson to Odlum, 10:45, 24 May; BC 68, 13:45, 24 May, RG 9, T-10709.
69 BC 72, Odlum to Currie, 10:35, 24 May, RG 9, T-10709.
70 WD, Lord Strathcona's Horse, 24–5 May, RG 9, T-10772. The regiment was part of Seely's Detachment, which included dismounted elements of the Canadian Cavalry Brigade.
71 An engineer field message from 26 May reinforces this conclusion; see Armstrong to 2nd Field Coy, RG 9, T-10824.
72 WD, 7th Bn, 24 May.
73 On the circumstances of Tenaille's death, see J.H. Bowyer, 5th Bn, (tape 1) 4, RG 41, B III 1, vol. 8.
74 '5th Bn Narrative'; WD, 5th Cdn Bn, 23–5 May 1915.
75 RG 150, Box 338–30.
76 F.B. Bagshaw, 5th Bn, 12–13, RG 41, B III 1, vol. 8.
77 RG 150, box 5270–62.
78 Operation Order No. 18, 24 May, RG 9, T-10775.
79 These were the same mortars that had participated in the 2nd Bde attack against K.5 on the morning of 24 May. See Operation Order No. 18, 24 May, RG 9, T-10814.
80 Operation Order No. 7, 24 May; Operation Orders by Lieutenant-Colonel Rennie, RG 9, T-10706.
81 Mercer Diary, 24 May.
82 3rd Bn Ops, 04:00, 25 May, RG 9, T-10706.
83 3rd Cdn Bde to 1st Cdn Div, 25 May, RG 9, T-10666.
84 Mercer Diary, 25 May.
85 List of Casualties, 3rd Cdn Bn, 17 May to 7 June, RG 9, T-10706.
86 WD, 4th Bn, 28 May; W.L. Gibson, *Records of the Fourth Canadian Infantry Battalion in the Great War, 1914–1918* (Toronto: Maclean Publishing, 1924).
87 For example, 22 gunners and two drivers were transferred from the DAC to the 3rd CFA Bde on 21 May.
88 It appears that this was particularly troublesome for the heavier calibres; Burstall received orders that 4.5- and 6-inch high-explosive rounds were not to be fired 'except in cases of necessity.' WD, 1st Cdn Div Artillery, 27 May.
89 WD, DAC, 21–6 May.
90 Brown, *British Logistics*, 93–5.
91 WD, 1st CFA Bde, 23–4 May.
92 WD, Signal Coy, 23 May.
93 Guthrie, *Festubert*, 13.
94 1st Cdn Div to Armstrong, 18 May, RG 9, T-10824.

95 Armstrong to 3rd Field Coy, 20:00, 18 May.

96 See divisional engineer field messages, 18–31 May, RG 9, T-10824.

97 Armstrong to First Army, 13:00, 22 May, and Armstrong to 2nd Field Coy, RE, 12:00, 24 May. Searchlights were used for anti-aircraft defence. See William F. Tompkins, 'Searchlight Air Defense Operations,' *General Electric Review* 22, no. 9 (1919), 663–7.

98 1st Cdn Div to 1st, 2nd, 3rd Fd Coys, 25 May, RG 9, T-10824.

99 2nd Fd Coy to Armstrong, 28 May.

100 RG 150, Box 5823–20.

101 Charles Lyttle Diary, 18–19 May.

102 Fetherstonhaugh, *14th Battalion*, 57.

103 Operations, No. 3 Cdn Fd Ambulance, 18–31 May, RG 9, T-10914.

104 Patrol Report, 1st Bn, 27 May, RG 9, T-7184.

105 WD, 2nd Cdn Fd Ambulance, 21–6 May, RG 9, T-10913–10914.

106 Admissions to Hospital, No. 3 Cdn Fd Ambulance, May, RG 9, T-10914.

107 Neurasthenia, Shell Shock and Hysteria Admissions, RG 9, Vol. 1844, GAQ 11.11.E.

108 7th Bn Ops, 19–24 May.

109 W.H. Curtis to Mrs Curtis, 2 June, MG 30, E 505. Corporal Herbert Carpenter, 20 years old, was killed by a shell while asleep in his dugout on 23 May. He is buried at Windy Corner Guards Cemetery.

110 FM, Armstrong to 2nd Fd Coy, 6 June, RG 9, T-10824.

111 Urquhart, *Currie*, 106–7; Hyatt, *Currie*, 46.

112 Duguid, *Official History*, 464.

113 Nicholson, *CEF*, 103–4.

114 Haycock, *Sam Hughes*, 268–70.

115 Alderson to Hutton, 21 Aug.; Haycock, *Sam Hughes*, 273.

116 Seely, *Adventure*, 227.

117 Alderson to Hutton, 21 Aug.

118 AEF, *251 German Army Divisions*, 443.

119 WD: 2nd Bn, 1–10 June; 3rd Bn, 1–10 June.

120 Labatt had originally commanded the battalion from its creation up until late Jan. 1915 when he fell ill and was replaced by Birchall.

121 WD, 4th Bn, 1–10 June.

122 WD, 1st Bn, 11–15 June.

123 See Operation Order No. 24, 1st Cdn Div, 12 June, RG 9, T-10665–6.

124 WD, Signal Coy, 12 June.

125 WD, 1st Cdn Div Artillery, 11 June.

126 Operation Order No. 24, 3rd CFA Bde, 12 June, RG 9, T-10786–7.

127 Operation Order No. 25, 3rd CFA Bde, 13 June, RG 9, T-10786–7.

128 Operation Order No. 6, 1st Cdn Div Artillery, 13 June, RG 9, T-10784–5.
129 Creelman, the brigade's original commander, had suffered a breakdown during Second Ypres, but would return to his post in Sept. 1915. His replacement, 36–year-old Charles Maclaren, had initially served with the 2nd CFA Battery.
130 Operation Order No. 3, 2nd CFA Bde, 13 June, RG 9, T-10784–5.
131 WD, 2nd CFA Bde, 11–15 June. A second armoured gun – from the 5th Battery – was also supposed to go forward, but was cancelled at the last minute.
132 WD, 1st CFA Bde, 15 June.
133 These are the words of the 2nd CFA diarist; the 2nd Bn diary entry for 14 June simply states; 'very heavy bombardment by our artillery preparatory to the attack.' WD, 2nd Bn.
134 WD, 2nd CFA Bde, 14 June.
135 RG 150, Box 9047–44.
136 Ibid., Box 10368–30.
137 Operation Order No. 5, 14 June, RG 9, T-10704.
138 Unless otherwise noted, the following account is based on Hill's Narrative of Operations, 15 June, RG 9, T-10704.
139 WD, 1st Bde Cdn Engineers, 15 June.
140 Mercer Diary, 15 June.
141 Peter Pick was born in Wellington County, Ontario. In peacetime he was a foreman in a woodworking factory, as well as a 14–year Active Militia veteran. RG 150, Box 7811–67.
142 RG 150, Box 8937–19.
143 WD, 1st Cdn Bde, 15 June.
144 Delamere was a 17–year militia veteran and had served in the South African War with the 2nd Canadian Mounted Rifles. RG 150, Box 2414–55.
145 WD, 3rd Bn, 15 June.
146 *A Brief History of the 3rd Canadian Battalion*, 5.
147 WD, 1st Cdn Div, 16 June.
148 H.R. Alley, 3rd Bn, (tape 1), 12, RG 41, B III 1, 12.
149 WD, 3rd Bn, 16 May.
150 RG 150, Box 4770–10.
151 1st Cdn Div Progress Report, 24 June, RG 9, T-7184.

10. Trench Warfare: The Ploegsteert–Messines Front

1 Nicholson, *CEF*, 108.
2 On the Ploegsteert–Messines front the 1st Div was initially under the command of III Corps, before moving to II Corps later in the summer. When

the 2nd Cdn Div arrived in France in Sept., the two dominion divisions were united under a Canadian Corps command.

3 See Tony Ashworth, *Trench Warfare, 1914–1918: The Live and Let Live System* (New York: Holmes and Meier, 1980).

4 Stanley Weintraub's book, *Silent Night: The Story of the World War I Christmas Truce* (New York: Plume, 2002), makes use of extensive eyewitness accounts to reconstruct the fraternization of Dec. 1914. In 2006 French film director Christian Carrion released *Joyeux Noel*, a less than convincing portrayal of the truce within one localized sector of the front.

5 WD, 3rd Cdn Bde, 21–9 Sept. 1915. All primary sources used in this chapter refer to 1915, unless otherwise indicated.

6 WD, 3rd CFA Bde, Sept.

7 Cameron Pulsifer, 'Canada's First Armoured Unit: Raymond Brutinel and the Canadian Motor Machine Gun Brigades of the First World War,' *Canadian Military History* 10, no. 1 (2001), 44–57.

8 Alderson Correspondence, 21 Aug.

9 Fanshawe to III Corps on Defence of Messines road, 10 June, App 1, [WD, 1st Cdn Div], July, RG 9, T-7184–7185. Appendices listed in succeeding notes refer to WD, 1st Cdn Div, for whichever month is specified.

10 App 1, III Corps to 1st Cdn Div, 1 July.

11 App 23, II Corps to 1st Cdn Div, 23 July.

12 App 2, 1st Cdn Bde to 1st Cdn Div, 2 July.

13 App 2, 2nd Cdn Bde to 1st Cdn Div, 2 July.

14 App 4, 'Defence Scheme, Ploegsteert, trenches 130–122,' 4 July.

15 App 4, Brutinel to 1st Cdn Div, 4 July; App 2, 'Romer report,' 2 July.

16 App 13, 50th Div to 1st Cdn Div, 13 July; App. 16, No. 3 Group HAR to 1st Cdn Div, 17 Aug.

17 WD, Signal Coy, July-Aug.

18 GS to 12th, 27th, and 48th Divisions, 14 June, App 3, July 1915.

19 App 5, July, 'Report on the German Trenches Captured 16 June, Second British Army.'

20 On timber shortages, see Maclean, *Farming and Forestry*, 96–7.

21 App 9, Alderson to III Corps, 8 July.

22 App 9, Turner to 1st Cdn Div, 8 July.

23 App 9, Mercer to 1st Cdn Div, 7 July.

24 App 13, 1st Cdn Div to 1st Cdn Div Arty, 14 Aug.; App 22, 1st Cdn Div to II Corps, 23 Aug.; App 11, 1st Cdn Div to all Cdn Bdes, 11 Sept.; App 12, 24th Div to 1st Div, 12 Sept.; App 28; 1st Cdn Div to all Cdn Bdes, 28 Sept. Also see WD, 1st Cdn Div Artillery, 16 Aug. The 24th, 25th, and 37th Divisions were New Army formations that arrived in France during the summer and autumn of 1915.

25 App 24, MacBrien to 1st Cdn Div Mounted Troops, 10 July.

26 Nicholson, *CEF,* 113–14; Campbell, 'Social and Operational History of the 2nd Cdn Div.'

27 Alderson Correspondence, 20 Sept.

28 App 2, 1st Cdn Div to II Corps, 2 Aug.

29 App 16, 1st Cdn Div to all Cdn Bdes, 16 July; WD, 1st Cdn MMG Bde, July 1915, App W, RG 9, T-10818–10819.

30 Warn was later commissioned as a lieutenant in the 30th Bn, while Bressey finished the war as corps staff officer. See Urquhart, *16th Battalion*, 447, 825.

31 App 9, 1st Cdn Div to 1st Cdn MMG Bde, 9 Sept.

32 *Expositor,* 9 April.

33 App 24, Lawrence to 1st Cdn Mounted Bde, 22 July.

34 App 7, 1st Cdn Div to II Corps, 7 Sept.

35 DG No 280/2, First Army, 27 May, MG 30, E 300, vol. 16.

36 App 9, 2nd Cdn Bde to 1st Cdn Div, 9 July; App 14, 1st Cdn Div to III Corps, 14 July; App 26, 1st Cdn Div to all Cdn Bdes, 27 Aug.

37 Cook, *No Place to Run,* 41.

38 'Memorandum on the use of Respirators, Smoke Helmets and other devices against Poisonous Gases,' First Army, 4 June, MG 30, E 300, vol. 16.

39 App 7, 1st Cdn Div to 2nd, 3rd Cdn Bdes, 8 Aug.

40 WD, 2nd Cdn Bde, 10 Aug.

41 WD, 4th Bn, July–Sept.

42 M. Wiseman, 7th Bn, 4–5, RG 41, B III 1, vol. 8.

43 'Trench Devices,' Second Army, 1915, RG 9, vol. 4365, folder 4, file 5.

44 *Memorandum on the Treatment of Injuries in War Based on Experience of the Present Campaign* (London: Harrison and Sons, 1915), 112–14.

45 WD, 13th Bn, Nov.

46 John Keegan, *A History of Warfare* (Vintage: Toronto, 1994), 361.

47 'Billeting Troops,' MG 30, E 300, vol. 16, file 11.

48 Ibid.

49 'Trench Devices,' Second Army.

50 App 9, III Corps to 1st Cdn Div, 9 July.

51 App 11, 3rd CFA Bde to 1st Cdn Div Arty, 11 July.

52 WD, 1st Cdn Div Artillery, 11 July.

53 WD, 10th Bn, 24 Sept.

54 App 9, 2nd Cdn Bde Weekly Sit Rep, 9 July.

55 App 25, II Corps to 1st Cdn Div, 25 July.

56 Mary F. Gaudet (ed.), *From a Stretcher Handle: The World War I Journal and Poems of Pte. Frank Walker* (Charlottetown: Institute of Island Studies, 2000), 75.

57 App 11, Unknown to 1st Cdn Div, 11 July; WD, 5th Bn, 11 July.

58 Infantry brigade machine-gun officers may have received anti-aircraft instruction. See App 9, Alderson to II Corps, 10 Aug.

59 WD, 1st Cdn MMG Bde, July 1915, App G, H, I, M, S.

60 WD, 1st Cdn MMG Bde, 31 July, 18 Aug.

61 App 13, 1st Cdn Div to all Cdn Bdes, 13 Sept.; WD, 8th Cdn Bn, 25 Sept., RG 9, T-10710–11.

62 WD: 1st CFA Bde, 4 July; 2nd CFA Bde, 25 July.

63 WD, 2nd CFA Bde, 6 July.

64 App 6, 3rd Cdn Bde to 1st Cdn Div, 6 July.

65 App 9, 'Allotment of Ammunition for Week ending 15 August,' Aug.

66 App 5, 'Div Intel Summary No. 46,' Sept.

67 WD: 1st Cdn Div Artillery, 15 July; KEH, 13 July, RG 9, T-10773.

68 Gaudet, *From a Stretcher Handle*, 77.

69 WD, 1st Cdn Div Artillery, 24 July.

70 App 20, 'Movement of German field cookers,' 18 July; App 4, 1st Cdn Div Arty to 1st Cdn Div, 24 July.

71 Seely, *Adventure*, 225.

72 App 19, 1st Cdn Div Arty to 14th TM Bty, 20 Aug.

73 WD, 13th Bn, 20 July. On the origins of the Gamage catapult, refer to Anthony Saunders, *Weapons of the Trench War, 1914–1918* (Stroud: Sutton, 2000), 52–3. In a Sept. 1915 diary entry, Douglas Haig referred to the Gamage as a useful device for making a 'flank curtain of fire by dropping bombs from very close to our trenches up to the Enemy's lines.' See Sheffield and Bourne, *Haig*, 147.

74 App 17, 'Instructions for Using Smoke Bags,' 23 Sept.

75 App 9, 1st Cdn Div to 1st Cdn MMG Bde, 10 July.

76 Yves Tremblay, 'Brutinel: A Unique Kind of Leadership,' in Bernd Horn and Stephen Harris, ed., *Warrior Chiefs: Perspectives on Senior Canadian Military Leaders* (Toronto: Dundurn, 2001), 62.

77 WD, 1st Cdn Bde, 4 Aug.

78 App 2, Second Army to II Corps, 1 Sept. E.R. Pratt, 'The Origin of a Fuse,' 1965. Available at www.fylde.demon.co.uk.

79 App 9, 13th Bn to 3rd Cdn Bde, 9 July; Fetherstonhaugh, *13th Battalion*, 65–6.

80 WD, 13th Bn, 9, 13–14 July.

81 App 16, 1st Cdn Div to IV Corps, 16 June. The individual in question may have been a pre-war miner who happened to be serving in 1st Bde.

82 App 10, 1st Cdn Div to all Cdn Bdes, 10 Sept.

83 WD: 1st Bn, 11 Aug.; 1st Cdn Bde, 11 Aug., RG 9, T-10665–6. See also, App 11, Report on Defensive Mine,' 11 Aug.

84 App 29, Aug., 'Report on Mine Fired in Front of Trench 121,' 2 Sept.

85 WD, 4th Bn, 31 Aug.

86 App 16, 1st Cdn Div to II Corps, 16 July.

87 App 6, 'Report on Exploits and Enterprises,' 6 July; App 2, 1st Cdn Div to III Corps, 2 July. See also WD, 1st Cdn Bde, 1 July; Duguid, *Official History*, 531.

88 App 25, 1st Cdn Bde to 1st Cdn Div, 25 July.

89 WD, 3rd Bn, 27 July. The problem with all of the evidence is that neither the 25th Bavarian Regiment nor the 25th Landwehr Regiment appear to have existed anywhere in the German order of battle for mid-1915, so it is likely that whoever interpreted the insignia or acted as translator made some mistake.

90 App 13, 'Div Intel Summary No. 54,' Sept.

91 WD, 4th Bn, 22 Sept.

92 App 20, 'LSH Summary of Ops,' 20 July.

93 App 10, 'Work Proposed to Be Done,' 7 July; App 3, 'Exploits and Enterprises,' 13 July.

94 App 19, 1st Cdn Div to all Cdn Bdes, 20 July.

95 WD, 1st Bn, Aug., App A.

96 App 1, 'Div Intel Summary No. 42,' App 3, 'Div Intel Summary No. 44,' Sept.

97 See Frederick P. Todd, 'The Knife and Club in Trench Warfare, 1914–1918,' *Journal of the American History Foundation* 2, no. 3 (1938), 140; Captain F. Haws Elliott, *Trench Fighting* (Boston, 1917), 49.

98 More than a few Aboriginal soldiers serving in the Canadian forces lived up to their reputations as highly skilled warriors. Corporal Francis Pegahmagabow, an Ojibway, joined the 1st Bn in 1914 and was decorated with the Military Medal three times before the war ended. See Fred Gaffen, *Forgotten Soldiers* (Penticton, BC: Theytus Books, 1985), 28.

99 'The Gurkhas Surprise the Germans,' *Illustrated London News*, 7 Nov. 1914.

100 RG 150, Box 627–4; App 10, 'Report re Bombing Party,' 10 Sept, App 20, 'Div Intel Summary No. 61,' Sept.

101 Nicholson, *CEF*, 122–5; 7th Bn Operation Order No. 59, 15 Nov., RG 9, T-10709.

102 7th Bn Operation Order No. 59.

103 WD: 7th Bn, 9 Nov.; 5th Bn, 11 Nov.

104 WD, 7th Bn, 16 Nov.

105 AEF, *251 German Army Divisions*, 610. The battle experience of this particular division illustrates the impact of attrition on German forces during the first year of war.

106 Nicholson, *CEF*, 124.

107 WD, RCHA, 16 Nov., RG 9, T-10798.

108 WD, 118th Howitzer Bde, 16 Nov.

109 Sheffield and Bourne, *Haig*, 150.

110 Rhodri Williams, 'Lord Kitchener and the Battle of Loos: French Politics and British Strategy in the Summer of 1915,' in Lawrence Freedman et al. eds, *War, Strategy and International Politics: Essays in Honour of Sir Michael Howard* (Oxford: Clarendon Press, 1992), 117–32.

111 For a popular account, see Geoffrey Regan, *The Book of Military Blunders* (Santa Barbara, CA: ABC-Clio, 1991), 119–20.
112 On 19 Sept. Haig wrote: 'the reserves are not to reach the area south of Lillers till 24th. This is too late!' See Sheffield and Bourne, *Haig*, 149.
113 Philpott, *Anglo-French Relations*, 104–5.
114 App 23, Operation Order No. 38 and Operation Order No. 1, 1st Cdn MMG Bde, 23 Sept.; WD, 1st Cdn MMG Bde, Sept. 1915, App 29a.
115 This regiment belonged to the 6th Bavarian Reserve Division, which had suffered heavily in the fighting at First Ypres. AEF, *251 German Army Divisions*, 139.
116 Edmonds, *Military Operations, 1915*, vol. 2, 262–3.
117 WD, 3rd CFA Bde, 'Report on Operations about Bois Grenier,' 27 Sept.
118 RG 150, Box 3773–18.
119 WD, 3rd CFA Bde, 'Report … Bois Grenier.'
120 App 25, 'Report on Operations,' 1st Cdn Div Artillery, 24–5 Sept.
121 Sixth German Army, Ia No. 17969, 7 July, MG 30, E 300, vol. 16.
122 1st Cdn Div to Cdn Corps, 25 Sept.; App 25, Canadian Cavalry Brigade, Report, Sept.
123 R. Wilson, 5th Bn, (tape 1) 3–4, RG 41, B III 1, vol. 8.
124 WD, 1st Cdn MMG Bde, Sept., App 26a.
125 App 26, Situation on 2nd Cdn Bde Front, 26 Sept.; App 27, 2nd Cdn Bde to 1st Cdn Div, 27 Sept.
126 WD, 5th Bn, 25 Sept.
127 WD, 10th Bn, 24 Sept.
128 App 27, 'Div Intel Summary No. 67,' Sept. 1915.
129 App 26, 1st Cdn Div to Cdn Corps, 26 Sept.; App 30, 'Approximate Number of Enemy's Shells Directed on Our Front,' Sept.

Conclusion

1 See Peter Simkins, 'Somme Reprise: Reflections on the Fighting for Albert and Bapaume, August 1918,' in Brian Bond, ed., *'Look to Your Front': Studies in the First World War* by the British Commission for Military History (Staplehurst: Spellmount, 1999), 147–62. The devolution of leadership was clearly appreciated before the war when British battalions were reorganized on the four-company basis. See Wake, 3–4, 15.
2 Dancocks, *Welcome to Flanders Fields*, 243.
3 Ibid., 242.
4 See Lord Moran, *The Anatomy of Courage* (London: Constable, 1945).

Bibliography

Archival Sources

Black Watch Collection, Montreal
  Jensen Letters

Brant County Museum and Archives, Brantford, ON
  Betts Letters

Canadian Letters and Images Project, Malaspina University College
  New Liskeard Speakers Collection
  R.S. Robinson Letters

Commonwealth War Graves Commission
  Online Casualty Details

Library and Archives of Canada
  E.A.H. Alderson Fonds, MG 30, E 92
  W.A. Alldritt Fonds, MG 30, E 1
  George Bell Fonds, MG 30, E 113
  Henry Edward Burstall Fonds, MG 30, E 6
  Canadian Broadcasting Corporation, Records, RG 41
  John Jennings Creelman Fonds, MG 30, E 8
  Arthur William Currie Fonds, MG 30, E 100
  W.H. Curtis Fonds, MG 30, E 505
  Department of Militia and Defence, Records, RG 9 (CEF war diaries from RG 9
    are posted at www.collectionscanada.ca/02/020152_e.html)
  Department of National Defence, Records, RG 24

Department of Veterans' Affairs, Records, RG 38
A.F. Duguid Fonds, MG 30, E 12
Edward Hilliam Fonds, MG 30, E 239
Garnet Burke Hughes Fonds, MG 27, IID23
William Johnson Fonds, MG 30, E 321
Robert Gilmour Edward Leckie Fonds, MG 30, E 84
Ministry of Overseas Military Forces of Canada, Records, RG 150
F.W. Newberry Diary, MG 30, E 525
Victor Odlum Fonds, MG 30, E 300
George Drillie Scott Fonds, MG 30, E 28
Ian MacIntosh Roe Sinclair Fonds, MG 30, MG 30, E 432
Sprague Family Fonds, MG 30, E 523
R.E.W. Turner Fonds, MG 30, E 46
Hugh MacIntyre Urquhart Fonds, MG 30, E 75

National Archives and British Library, United Kingdom
War Diaries, First World War, WO 95
Edwin Alderson Correspondence, MSS 50088

Private Collections
Charles Lyttle Diary, 3rd Field Ambulance
8th Westphalian Infantry Regiment, War Diary

Queen's Own Rifles Collection
M.S. Mercer Diary

Military Manuals and Pamphlets

Battye, Major B.C., Royal Engineers, *Some Notes on the Minor Tactics of Trench Warfare, 1914*. Ottawa: Government Printing Bureau, 1916.
Birchall, Captain A.P. *Rapid Training of a Company for War*. London: Gale and Polden, 1915.
General Staff, War Office. *Field Artillery Training, 1914*. London: author, 9 April 1914.
– *Field Service Pocket Book, 1914*. London: author, 1914.
– *Field Service Regulations, Part 1, Operations, 1909/1914*. London: author, 10 November 1914.
– *Field Service Regulations, Part 2, Organization and Administration, 1909/1914*. London: author, 1914.
– *Infantry Training, 1914*. London: author, 10 August 1914.

– *Manual of Field Engineering, 1911*. London: His Majesty's Stationary Office, 28 January 1911; reprinted 1914.
– *Manual of Physical Training, 1908*. London: author, 1908; amended 1 December 1914.
– *Musketry Regulations, Part I, 1909/1914*. London: author, 26 September 1914.
– *Training and Manoeuvre Regulations, 1913*. London: author, 17 November 1913.
– *Training Manual – Signalling, 1907/1911*. London: author, 1 May 1911.
Handbook of the German Army in War, January 1917. Menston: EP Publishing, 1973.
Herbert, Ivor. *Military Organization*. N.p., 1892.
Infantry Drill: Field and Brigade Movements and Infantry in Attack. Ottawa: Government Printing Bureau, 1899.
Langlois, General H. *Lessons from Two Recent Wars*. London: Mackie and Company, 1909.
Memorandum on the Treatment of Injuries in War Based on Experience of the Present Campaign. London: Harrison and Sons, 1915.
Protection and Outposts: What to Do and How to Do It. Aldershot: Gale and Polden, 1915.
Rifle and Musketry Exercises for the Ross Rifle. Ottawa: Government Printing Bureau, 1914.
Wake, Brevet-Major Hereward. *The Four-Company Battalion in Battle*. London: J.J. Keliher, 1914.

Other Sources

Aitken, Max. *Canada in Flanders*. Toronto: Hodder and Stoughton, 1916.
Alderson, E.A.H. *Pink and Scarlet, Or Hunting as a School for Soldiering*. London: William Heinemann, 1900.
– *With the Mounted Infantry in the Mashonaland Field Force*. London: Methuen 1898.
American Expeditionary Forces, Intelligence Section of the General Staff, Chaumont. *Histories of the Two Hundred and Fifty-One Divisions of the German Army which Participated in the War (1914–1918)*. London: Stamp Exchange, 1989.
Les Armées Françaises dans la Grande Guerre. Vol. 2, Pt. 3. Paris: Imprimerie Nationale, 1931.
Army Historical Section, General Staff. *The Western Front, 1914*. Ottawa: author, 1957.
Ashworth, Tony. *Trench Warfare, 1914–1918: The Live and Let Live System*. New York: Holmes and Meier, 1980.
Audoin-Rouzeau, Stéphane, and Annette Becker. *14–18: Understanding the Great War*. New York: Hill and Wang, 2000.

Balck, Colonol. *Tactics*. Vol. 1. *Introduction and Formal Tactics of Infantry*. London: Hugh Rees, 1911.

Barnard, W.T. *The Queen's Own Rifles of Canada, 1860–1960: One Hundred Years of Canada*. Don Mills, ON: Ontario Publishing, 1960.

Baynes, John. *Morale: A Study of Men and Courage. The Second Scottish Rifles at the Battle of Neuve Chapelle, 1915*. New York: Praeger, 1967.

Beahen, William. 'A Citizens' Army: The Growth and Development of the Canadian Militia, 1904 to 1914.' PhD diss., University of Ottawa, 1981.

Beattie, Kim. *48th Highlanders of Canada, 1891–1928*. Toronto: Southam Press, 1932.

Bechthold, Michael. '"One of the Greatest Moments of My Life": Lessons Learned on the Canadian Battle of Normandy Foundation Battlefield Tours.' *Defence Studies* 5, no. 1 (2006), 27–36.

Beckett, Ian F.W. *The Great War, 1914–1918*. Harlow, UK: Pearson, 2001.

Bell, F. McKelvey. *The First Canadians in France: The Chronicles of a Military Hospital in the War Zone*. Toronto: McClelland, Goodchild and Stewart, 1917.

Berton, Pierre. *Vimy*. Toronto: McClelland and Stewart, 1986.

Bethune, Brian. 'It Haunts Us Still.' *Maclean's*, 8 November 2004, 46–8.

Bidwell, Shelford, and Dominick Graham. *Fire-Power: British Army Weapons and Theories of War, 1904–1945*. London: Allen & Unwin, 1985.

Bishop, Arthur. 'Canada and the Victoria Cross: The Class of 1915.' *Legion Magazine*, July/August 2004, 34–7.

Blake, Robert, ed. *Private Papers of Douglas Haig, 1914–1919*. London: Eyre and Spottswoode, 1952.

Bloch, I.S. *Modern Weapons and Modern War*. London: Grant Richards, 1900.

Boire, Michael. 'The Underground War: Military Mining Operations in Support of the Attack on Vimy Ridge, 9 April 1917.' *Canadian Military History* 1, no, 2 (1992), 15–24.

Bourne, J.M. *Who's Who in World War One*. London: Routledge, 2001.

A Brief History of the 3rd Battalion, C.E.F. (Toronto Regiment). Toronto, 1934.

Brown, Ian. 'Not Glamorous, but Effective: The Canadian Corps and the Set-piece Attack, 1917–1918.' *Journal of Military History* 58, no. 3 (1994), 421–44.

Brown, Ian Malcolm. *British Logistics on the Western Front, 1914–1919*. Westport, CT: Praeger, 1998.

Brown, Malcolm. *The Imperial War Museum Book of the Somme*. London: Sidgwick and Jackson, 1996.

Brown, R.C. *Robert Laird Borden, A Biography*. Vol. 2. *1914–1937*. Toronto: Macmillan, 1980.

Browne, Thaddeus A. *The White Plague and Other Poems*. Toronto: William Briggs, 1909.

Bull, Stewart H. *The Queen's York Rangers: An Historic Regiment*. Erin, ON: Boston Mills Press, 1984.

Campbell, David. 'The Divisional Experience in the CEF: A Social and Operational History of the 2nd Canadian Division, 1915–1918.' PhD diss., University of Calgary, 2003.

– 'Schooling for War: Canadian Infantry Training, 1914–1917.' In *Perspectives on War: Essays on Security, Society and the State*, ed. Chris Bullock and Jillian Dowding, 15–30. Calgary: University of Calgary Press, 2001.

Canada in the Great World War. 6 vols. Toronto: United Publishers of Canada, 1917–21.

Canadian Field Comforts Commission. *With the First Canadian Contingent*. Toronto: Hodder and Stoughton, 1915.

Canadian Who's Who. Vol. 4. *1948*. Toronto: Trans Canada, 1948.

Cassar, George. *Beyond Courage: The Canadians at the Second Battle of Ypres*. Ottawa: Oberon, 1985.

– *The Tragedy of Sir John French*. Newark: University of Delaware Press, 1985.

Cook, Tim. 'The Blind Leading the Blind: The Battle of the St. Eloi Craters.' *Canadian Military History* 5, no. 2 (1996), 24–36.

– *Clio's Warriors: Canadian Historians and the Writing of the World Wars*. Vancouver: UBC Press, 2006.

– '"Literary Memorials": The Great War Regimental Histories, 1919–1939.' *Journal of the Canadian Historical Association* 13 (2002), 167–90.

– '"More a Medicine than a Beverage": "Demon Rum" and the Canadian Trench Soldier of the First World War.' *Canadian Military History* 9, no. 1 (2000), 7–22.

– '"My Whole Heart and Soul Is in This War"': The Letters and War Service of Sergeant G.L. Ormsby.' *Canadian Military History* 15, no. 1 (2006), 51–63.

– *No Place to Run: The Canadian Corps and Gas Warfare in the First World War*. Vancouver: UBC Press, 1999.

– 'Wet Canteens and Worrying Mothers: Alcohol, Soldiers and Temperance Groups in the Great War.' *Histoire social/Social History* 35, no. 70 (2002), 311–30.

Coombs, R.E.B., ed. *The Battles of Ypres, 1914–1918*. London: Imperial War Museum, 1972.

Cron, Hermann. *The Imperial German Army, 1914–1918: Organisation, Structure, Orders of Battle*. Solihull: Helion, 2002.

Currie, J.A. *'The Red Watch': With the First Canadian Division in Flanders*. Toronto: McClelland, Goodchild and Stewart, 1916.

Curry, Frederick C. 'The Canadian Militia.' *Canadian Defence* 3, no. 4 (1911), 96–7.

Dancocks, Daniel. *Gallant Canadians: The Story of the Tenth Canadian Infantry Battalion, 1914–1919*. Calgary: Penguin, 1990.

- *Sir Arthur Currie: A Biography.* Toronto: Methuen, 1985.
- *Welcome to Flanders Fields: The First Canadian Battle of the Great War, Ypres, 1915.* Toronto: McClelland and Stewart, 1988.
Dendooven, Dominiek. *Ypres as Holy Ground: Menin Gate and Last Post.* Koksijde: De Klaproos, 2003.
Dixon, John. *Magnificent but Not War: The Battle of Ypres, 1915.* Barnsley: Leo Cooper, 2003.
Dixon, Norman. *On the Psychology of Military Incompetence.* London: Future, 1985.
Duguid, A.F. 'Canadians in Battle, 1915–1918.' *Canadian Defence Quarterly* 13, no. 1 (1935), 12–27.
- *Official History of the Canadian Forces in the Great War, August 1914 to September 1915, Chronology, Appendices and Maps.* Ottawa: J.O. Patenaude, 1938.
Du Picq, Ardant. *Battle Studies: Ancient and Modern Battle.* New York: Macmillan, 1921.
Echevarria, Antulio J. *After Clausewitz: German Military Thinkers before the Great War.* Lawrence: University of Kansas Press, 2000.
Edmonds, J.E. *History of the Great War, Military Operations, France and Belgium, 1914.* Vol. 1. London: Macmillan, 1925.
- *History of the Great War, Military Operations, France and Belgium, 1914.* Vol. 2. London: Macmillan, 1927.
- *History of the Great War, Military Operations, France and Belgium, 1915.* Vol. 3. London: Macmillan, 1928.
Elliott, F. Haws. *Trench Fighting.* Boston, 1917.
Ellis, John. *The Social History of the Machine Gun.* Baltimore: Johns Hopkins University Press, 1975.
English, John. "Lessons from the Great War.' *Canadian Military Journal* 4, no. 2 (2003), 55–61.
English, John A., and Bruce I. Gudmundsson. *On Infantry.* Rev. ed. Westport, CT: Praeger, 1994.
Eye-Witness Accounts of the Great War, Guide to Quotations. Ieper, Belgium: Flanders Fields Museum, Cloth Hall, Market Square, n.d.
Falkenhayn, Erich von. *The German General Staff and Its Decisions, 1914–1916.* New York: Dodd, Mead, 1920.
Fedorowich, Kent. 'The Migration of British Ex-Servicemen to Canada and the Role of the Naval and Military Emigration League, 1899–1914.' *Histoire Social/Social History* 25, no. 49 (1992), 75–99.
Fetherstonhaugh, R.C. *The Royal Montreal Regiment, 14th Battalion, CEF, 1914–1925.* Montreal: Gazette Printing, 1927.
- *The 13th Battalion Royal Highlanders of Canada, 1914–1919.* Toronto: Warwick & Rutter, 1925.

Fletcher, David. *The British Tanks, 1915–1919*. Ramsbury: Crowood Press, 2001.

Flick, Chas. 'Semi-Ready Training.' *Canadian Defence* 3, no. 11 (1912), 323–4.

Frey N., and E.N. Olson, 'Cardiac Hypertrophy: the Good, the Bad and the Ugly,' *Annual Review of Physiology* 65 (2003), 45–79.

Gaffen, Fred. *Forgotten Soldiers*. Penticton, BC: Theytus Books, 1985.

Gaudet, Mary F., ed. *From a Stretcher Handle: The World War I Journal and Poems of Pte. Frank Walker*. Charlottetown: Institute of Island Studies, 2000.

Gibson, George Herbert Rae. *Maple Leaves in Flanders Fields*. Toronto: William Briggs, 1916.

Gibson, W.L. *Records of the Fourth Canadian Infantry Battalion in the Great War, 1914–1918*. Toronto: Maclean Publishing, 1924.

Godefroy, Andrew. 'Portrait of a Battalion Commander: Lieutenant-Colonel George Stuart Tuxford at the Second Battle of Ypres, April 1915.' *Canadian Military Journal* 5, no. 2 (2004), 55–61.

Gough, Barry, and Roger Sarty. 'Sailors and Soldiers: The Royal Navy, the Canadian Forces, and the Defence of Atlantic Canada, 1890–1918.' In *A Nation's Navy: In Quest of Canadian Naval Identity*, ed. Michael L. Hadley et al., 112–30. Montreal: McGill-Queen's University Press, 1996.

Greenhalgh, Elizabeth. 'Myth and Memory: Sir Douglas Haig and the Imposition of Allied Unified Command in March 1918.' *Journal of Military History* 68, no. 3 (2004), 771–820.

Greenhous, Brereton. *Dragoon: The Centennial History of the Royal Canadian Dragoons, 1883–1983*. Ottawa: Guild of the Royal Canadian Dragoons, 1983.

Griffith, Paddy. *British Tactics of the Western Front: The British Army's Art of Attack, 1916–1918*. New Haven, CT: Yale University Press, 1994.

Guinn, Paul. *British Strategy and Politics, 1914 to 1918*. Oxford: Clarendon Press, 1965.

Gustavson, Wesley. 'Missing the Boat? Colonel A.F. Duguid and the Canadian Official History of World War I.' MA thesis, University of Calgary, 1999.

Guthrie, P.A. *Festubert*. Montreal: Montreal Daily Star, 1916.

Hagerman, Edward. *The American Civil War and the Origins of Modern Warfare*. Bloomington: Indiana University Press, 1992.

Harris, Stephen. *Canadian Brass: The Making of a Professional Army, 1860–1939*. Toronto: University of Toronto Press, 1988.

Harris, T.J. 'Yankees Who Fought for the Maple Leaf.' MA thesis, University of Nebraska, 1997.

Haycock, Ronald. 'Early Canadian Weapons Acquisition: "That Damned Ross Rifle."' *Canadian Defence Quarterly* 114, no. 3 (1985), 48–57.

– *Sam Hughes: The Public Career of a Controversial Canadian, 1885–1916*. Waterloo, ON: Wilfrid Laurier University Press, 1986.

Herrmann, David. *The Arming of Europe and the Making of the First World War.* Princeton, NJ: Princeton University Press, 1996.

Hill, F.W. 'History of the Canadian Forces in the Great War: A Review.' *Canadian Defence Quarterly* 16, no. 2 (1939), 211–14.

Horne, John, and Alan Kramer. *German Atrocities, 1914: A History of Denial.* New Haven, CT: Yale University Press, 2001.

Humphries, Mark Osborne. 'The Myth of the Learning Curve: Tactics and Training in the 12th Canadian Infantry Brigade, 1916–1918.' *Canadian Military History* 14, no. 4 (2005), 15–30.

– 'The Treatment of War Neuroses Casualties in the Canadian Expeditionary Force, 1914–19.' MA thesis, Wilfrid Laurier University, 2005.

– 'What Bloody Good Are We? A Case Study in the Mobilization and Training of the 38th Canadian Infantry Battalion, 1915-1916.' Undergraduate thesis, Wilfrid Laurier University, 2004.

Humphries, Mark Osborne, and John Maker. 'The First Use of Poison Gas at Ypres, 1915: A Translation from the German Official History.' *Canadian Military History* 16, no. 3 (2007), 57–73.

Hyatt, A.M.J. *General Sir Arthur Currie: A Military Biography.* Toronto: University of Toronto Press, 1987.

Iarocci, Andrew. *Canadian Forces Base Petawawa: The First Century, 1905–2005.* Waterloo, ON: Laurier Centre for Military, Strategic, and Disarmament Studies, 2005.

Jenkins, Dan Richard. 'Winning Trench Warfare: Battlefield Intelligence in the Canadian Corps, 1914–1918.' PhD diss., Carleton University, 1999.

Kearsey, A. *1915 Campaign in France: The Battles of Aubers Ridge, Festubert and Loos, Considered in Relation to Field Service Regulations.* Uckfield: Naval & Military Press Reprint, 1929.

Keech, Graham. *St. Julien.* Barnsley: Leo Cooper, 2001.

Keegan, John. *A History of Warfare.* Vintage: Toronto, 1994.

Kerry, A.J., and W.A. McDill. *The History of the Corps of Royal Canadian Engineers.* Vol. 1. *1749–1939.* Ottawa: Military Engineers of Canada, 1962.

Keshen, Jeff. *Propaganda and Censorship during Canada's Great War.* Edmonton: University of Alberta Press, 1996.

Knieling, Lutz, and Arnold Bölsche. *Reserve Infanterie-Regiment 234: Ein Querschnitt durch Deutschlands Schicksalsringen.* Zeulenroda: Sporn, 1931.

Laffin, John. *The Western Front Illustrated, 1914–1918.* London: Grange, 1997.

Law, Clive, ed. *A Question of Confidence.* Ottawa: Service Publications, 1999.

Layman, R.D. *The Cuxhaven Raid: The World's First Carrier Air Strike.* London: Conway Maritime Press, 1985.

Leppard, Thomas P. '"The Dashing Subaltern': Sir Richard Turner in Retrospect.' *Canadian Military History* 6, no. 2 (1997), 21–8.

Liddle, Peter. *The 1916 Battle of the Somme: A Reappraisal*. London: Leo Cooper, 1992.

Love, David. *A Call to Arms: The Organization and Administration of Canada's Military in World War One*. Winnipeg: Bunker to Bunker Books, 1999.

Macdonald, Lyn. *1915: The Death of Innocence*. New York: Henry Holt, 1993.

MacKinnon, Gordon. 'The Junction's Forgotten General: Malcolm Smith Mercer.' *Leader and Recorder, West Toronto Junction* (Fall 2002).

Maclean, Murray. *Farming and Forestry on the Western Front, 1915–1919*. Ipswich, UK: Old Pond Publishing, 2004.

Maroney, Paul J. 'Recruiting the Canadian Expeditionary Force in Ontario, 1914-1917.' MA thesis, Queen's University, 1992.

Martyn, Robert. 'Canadian Military Intelligence and the Revolution in Military Affairs, 1914–1918.' Third Annual Society for Military and Strategic Studies Conference, Calgary, February 2001.

Massie, Robert K. *Dreadnought: Britain, Germany, and the Coming of the Great War*. New York: Ballantine, 1991.

McCulloch, Ian. '"The Fighting Seventh": The Evolution & Devolution of Tactical Command and Control in a Canadian Infantry Brigade of the Great War.' MA thesis, Royal Military College, 1997.

McLeod Gould, Leonard. *102nd Infantry Battalion, CEF*. Available at www .donlowconcrete.com/102.

McWilliams, James, and R.J. Steel, *Amiens: Dawn of Victory*. Toronto: Dundurn, 2001.

– *Gas! The Battle for Ypres, 1915*. St Catharines, ON: Vanwell, 1985.

Merritt, William Hamilton. 'The Canadian Militia.' *Canadian Field* 3, no. 3 (1911), 59–62.

Miller, Carman. 'The Montreal Militia as a Social Institution before World War I.' *Urban History Review* 19, no. 1 (1990), 57–65.

– *Painting the Map Red: Canada and the South African War, 1899–1902*. Montreal: Canadian War Museum and McGill-Queen's University Press, 1993.

– 'Sir Frederick William Borden and Military Reform, 1896–1911.' *Canadian Historical Review* 50, no. 3 (1969), 265–84.

Miller, Ian Hugh Maclean. *Our Glory and Our Grief: Torontonians and the Great War*. Toronto: University of Toronto Press, 2002.

Mitchell, Gary A. 'The Appraisal of Canadian Military Personnel Files of the First World War.' MA thesis, University of British Columbia, 1985.

Moir, John S., ed. *History of the Royal Canadian Corps of Signals, 1903–1961*. Ottawa: RCCS, 1962.

Moran, Lord. *The Anatomy of Courage*. London: Constable, 1945.

Morris, David A. *The Canadian Militia from 1855: An Historical Summary*. Erin, ON: Boston Mills Press, 1983.

Morton, Desmond. *Ministers and Generals: Politics and the Canadian Militia, 1896–1904.* Toronto: University of Toronto Press, 1970.

– *Silent Battle: Canadian Prisoners of War in Germany, 1914–1919.* Toronto: Lester, 1992.

– *When Your Number's Up: The Canadian Soldier in the First World War.* Toronto: Random House, 1993.

Morton, Desmond, and J.L Granatstein. *Marching to Armageddon: Canadians and the Great War, 1914–1919.* Toronto: Lester and Orpen Dennys, 1992.

Moss, Mark. *Manliness and Militarism: Educating Young Boys in Ontario for War.* Don Mills, ON: Oxford University Press, 2001.

Motion, Andrew, ed. *First World War Poems.* London: Faber and Faber, 2003.

Müller, Rolf-Dieter. 'Total War as a Result of New Weapons? The Use of Chemical Agents in World War I.' In (eds), *Great War, Total War: Combat and Mobilization on the Western Front, 1914–1918,* ed. Roger Chickering and Stig Förster, 95–111. Cambridge: Cambridge University Press, 2000.

Murray, W.W. *The History of the 2nd Canadian Battalion (Eastern Ontario Regiment) Canadian Expeditionary Force in the Great War, 1914–1919.* Ottawa: Mortimer, 1947.

Nicholson, G.W.L. *Canadian Expeditionary Force, 1914–1919: The Official History of the Canadian Army in the First World War.* Ottawa: Queen's Printer, 1962.

– *The Gunners of Canada: The History of the Royal Regiment of Canadian Artillery.* Vol. 1. *1534–1919.* Toronto: McClelland and Stewart, 1967.

Peat, Harold R. *Private Peat.* Indianapolis: Bobbs-Merrill, 1917.

Pedley, James. *Only This: A War Retrospect, 1917–1918.* Ottawa: CEF Books, 1999.

Philpott, William James. *Anglo-French Relations and Strategy on the Western Front, 1914–18.* New York: St Martin's Press, 1996.

Pitt, Barrie. *1918: The Last Act.* London: Cassell, 1962.

Prior, Robin and Trevor Wilson, *Command on the Western Front: The Military Career of Sir Henry Rawlinson, 1914–18.* Oxford: Blackwell, 1992.

Pulsifer, Cameron. 'Canada's First Armoured Unit: Raymond Brutinel and the Canadian Motor Machine Gun Brigades of the First World War.' *Canadian Military History* 10, no. 1 (2001), 44–57.

Radley, Kenneth. 'First Canadian Division, CEF, 1914–1918: Ducimus (We Lead).' PhD diss., Carleton University, 2000.

– *We Lead, Others Follow: First Canadian Division, 1914–1918.* St Catharines, ON: Vanwell, 2006.

Rawling, Bill. 'Communications in the Canadian Corps, 1915–1918: Wartime Technological Progress Revisited.' *Canadian Military History* 3, no. 2 (1994), 6–21.

– *Surviving Trench Warfare: Technology and the Canadian Corps, 1914–1918.*
Toronto: University of Toronto Press, 1992.

Regan, Geoffrey. *The Book of Military Blunders.* Santa Barbara, CA: ABC-Clio, 1991.

Reville, F. Douglas. *History of the County of Brant.* Brantford. ON: Hurley Printing Co., 1920.

Richter, Donald. *British Gas Warfare in World War I.* Lawrence: University of Kansas Press, 1992.

Ross, Robert B. *The Fifty-First in France.* London: Hodder and Stoughton, 1918.

Ruck, Calvin W. *The Black Battalion, 1916–1920: Canada's Best Kept Military Secret.* Halifax: Nimbus, 1987.

Rutherdale, Robert. *Hometown Horizons: Local Responses to Canada's Great War.* Vancouver: UBC Press, 2004.

Sassoon, Siegfried. *Memoirs of an Infantry Officer.* London: Faber and Faber, 1966.

Saunders, Anthony. *Weapons of the Trench War, 1914–1918.* Stroud: Sutton, 2000.

Schreiber, Shane. *Shock Army of the British Empire: The Canadian Corps in the Last 100 Days of the Great War.* London: Praeger, 1997.

Scott, Frederick George. *The Great War As I Saw It.* Ottawa: CEF Books, 2000.

– *In the Battle Silences: Poems Written at the Front.* Toronto: Musson, 1917.

Scudamore, T.V. *A Short History of the 7th Battalion CEF.* Vancouver: Anderson and Odlum, 1930.

Seely, J.E.B. *Adventure.* London: William Heinemann, 1930.

Sheffield, Gary. *Leadership in the Trenches: Officer-Man Relations, Morale and Discipline in the British Army in the Era of the First World War.* Houndmills, UK: Macmillan, 2000.

Sheffield, Gary, and John Bourne, eds. *Douglas Haig: War Diaries and Letters, 1914–1918.* London: Weidenfeld and Nicolson, 2005.

Simkins, Peter. *Kitchener's Army: The Raising of the New Armies, 1914–1916.* Manchester: Manchester University Press, 1988.

– 'Somme Reprise: Reflections on the Fighting for Albert and Bapaume, August 1918.' In *'Look to Your Front': Studies in the First World War by the British Commission for Military History,* ed. Brian Bond, 147–62. Staplehurst, UK: Spellmount, 1999.

Smith, Leonard. *Between Mutiny and Obedience: The Case of the French Fifth Infantry Division during World War I.* Princeton, NJ: Princeton University Press, 1994.

Spiers, Edward M. 'Chemical Warfare in the First World War.' In *'Look to Your Front': Studies in the First World War by the British Commission for Military History,* ed. Brian Bond, 163–78. Staplehurst, UK: Spellmount, 1999.

Stanley, George F. *Canada's Soldiers: The Military History of an Unmilitary People.* Toronto: Macmillan, 1974.

Steel, Arthur W. 'Wireless Telegraphy and the Canadian Corps in France.'
    Canadian Defence Quarterly (July 1929), 443–61.
Strachan, Hew. *The First World War*. Oxford: Oxford University Press, 2001.
Swettenham, John. *McNaughton*. Vol. 1. *1887–1939*. Toronto: Ryerson Press, 1968.
Terraine, John. *Douglas Haig: The Educated Soldier*. London: Hutchinson, 1963.
Thorn, J.C. *Three Years a Prisoner in Germany*. Vancouver: Cowan and Brook-
    house, 1919.
Todd, Frederick P. 'The Knife and Club in Trench Warfare, 1914–1918.' *Journal
    of the American Military History Foundation* 2, no. 3 (1938), 139–53.
Tompkins, William F. 'Searchlight Air Defense Operations.' *General Electric
    Review* 22, no. 9 (1919), 663–67.
Travers, Tim. 'Currie and 1st Canadian Division at Second Ypres, April 1915:
    Controversy, Criticism and Official History.' *Canadian Military History* 5,
    no. 2 (1996), 7–15.
– *How the War Was Won: Command and Technology in the British Army on the
    Western Front, 1917–1918*. London: Routledge, 1992.
– *The Killing Ground: The British Army, the Western Front and the Emergence of
    Modern Warfare, 1900–1918*. London: Allen and Unwin, 1987.
Travers, Timothy H.E. 'Allies in Conflict: The British and Canadian Official
    Historians and the Real Story of Second Ypres.' *Journal of Contemporary His-
    tory* 24, no. 2 (1989), 301–25.
Tremblay, Yves. 'Brutinel: A Unique Kind of Leadership.' In *Warrior Chiefs:
    Perspectives on Senior Canadian Military Leaders*, ed. Bernd Horn and Stephen
    Harris, 57–70. Toronto: Dundurn, 2001.
Tucker, A.B. *The Battle Glory of Canada*. London: Cassell, 1915.
Urquhart, H.M. *Arthur Currie: The Biography of a Great Canadian*. Toronto: J.M.
    Dent, 1950.
– *The History of the 16th Battalion (Canadian Scottish) Canadian Expeditionary
    Force in the Great War, 1914–1919*. Toronto: Macjmillan, 1932.
Vance, Jonathan. *Death So Noble: Memory, Meaning, and the First World War*.
    Vancouver: UBC Press, 1997.
Walker, James W. St. G. 'Race and Recruitment in World War I: Enlistment of
    Visible Minorities in the Canadian Expeditionary Force.' *Canadian Historical
    Review* 70, no. 1 (1989), 1–26.
Weintraub, Stanley. *Silent Night: The Story of the World War I Christmas Truce*.
    New York: Plume, 2002.
Williams, Rhodri. 'Lord Kitchener and the Battle of Loos: French Politics and
    British Strategy in the Summer of 1915.' In *War, Strategy and International
    Politics: Essays in Honour of Sir Michael Howard*, ed. Lawrence Freedman,
    et al., 117–32. Oxford: Clarendon Press, 1992.

Wilson, Barbara. '"There Is No Alternative"': The Diary of Harry H. Coombs, 9th Battalion, CEF, August 1914-January 1915.' *Canadian Military History* 14, no. 3 (2005), 39–56.

Winter, Charles F. *Lieutenant-General The Hon. Sir Sam Hughes: Canada's War Minister, 1911–1916*. Toronto: Macmillan, 1931.

Winter, Dennis. *Death's Men: Soldiers of the Great War*. London: Penguin, 1988.

Der Weltkrieg 1914 bis 1918: Sommer und Herbst 1915. Vol. 8. *Im Auftrage des Reichskriegsministeriums*. Berlin: Mittler und Sohn, 1932.

Wood, Herbert Fairlie. *Vimy!* Toronto: Macmillan, 1967.

Wood, James. 'The Sense of Duty: Canadian Ideas of the Citizen Soldier, 1896–1917.' PhD diss., Wilfrid Laurier University, 2007.

Index